A BASIC COURSE IN IRAQI ARABIC with Audio MP3 Files

Wallace M. Erwin

Georgetown University Press
Washington, D.C.

Georgetown University Press, Washington, D.C.

Printed in Canada

10 9 8 7 6 5 4 3 2 1 2004

This book is printed on acid-free paper meeting
the requirements of the American National Standard
for Permanence in Paper for Printed Library Materials.

The research reported herein was performed pursuant to a contract with the United States Office of Education, Department of Health, Education, and Welfare.

Library of Congress Cataloging-in-Publication Data

Erwin, Wallace M.
A basic course in Iraqi Arabic : with audio MP3 files / Wallace M. Erwin.
p. cm. — (Georgetown classics in Arabic language and linguistics)
Originally published: Washington, D.C. : Georgetown University Press, 1969, in series: The Richard Slade Harrell Arabic series ; no. 11.
Includes index.
ISBN 1-58901-011-6 (pbk. : alk. paper)
1. Arabic language—Dialects—Iraq. 2. Arabic language—Grammar.
I. Title. II. Series.

PJ6823.E685 2004
492.7'7'09567—dc22

2003049539

Georgetown Classics in Arabic Language and Linguistics

Karin C. Ryding and Margaret Nydell, series editors

For some time, Georgetown University Press has been interested in making available seminal publications in Arabic language and linguistics that have gone out of print. Some of the most meticulous and creative scholarship of the last century was devoted to the analysis of Arabic language and to producing detailed reference works and textbooks of the highest quality. Although some of the material is dated in terms of theoretical approaches, the content and methodology of the books considered for the reprint series is still valid and, in some cases, unsurpassed.

With global awareness now refocused on the Arab world, and with renewed interest in Arab culture, society and political life, it is essential to provide easy access to classic reference materials, such as dictionaries and reference grammars, and to language teaching materials. The components of this series have been chosen for their quality of research and scholarship, and have been updated with new bibliographies and introductions to provide readers with resources for further study.

Georgetown University Press hereby hopes to serve the growing national and international need for reference works on Arabic language and culture, as well as provide access to quality textbooks and audiovisual resources for teaching Arabic language in its written and spoken forms.

Books in the Georgetown Classics in Arabic Language and Linguistics series

Arabic Language Handbook
Mary Catherine Bateson

A Basic Course in Iraqi Arabic with Audio MP3 Files
Wallace M. Erwin

A Basic Course in Moroccan Arabic
Richard S. Harrell with Mohammed Abu-Talib and William S. Carroll

A Dictionary of Iraqi Arabic: English–Arabic, Arabic–English
B. E. Clarity, Karl Stowasser, Ronald G. Wolfe, D. R. Woodhead, and Wayne Beene, Editors

A Short Reference Grammar of Iraqi Arabic
Wallace M. Erwin

A Short Reference Grammar of Moroccan Arabic with Audio CD
Richard S. Harrell

Contents

Contents of the Audio MP3 Files

A CD-ROM containing MP3 files accompanies *A Basic Course in Iraqi Arabic*. MP3 files can be played back on computers with a CD-ROM drive and free software that plays MP3 files (Winamp and iTunes are two), on MP3-compatible portable CD players, and on MP3-compatible CD/DVD players. The files can also be copied onto portable MP3 players and onto MP3-enabled handheld devices.

These MP3 files were remastered from the original audiocassettes, and the sound quality reflects the technology of the originals.

Unit	Exercise	Filename	Time	Page
1	Instructions for units 1–10	0001	0:52	—
	Drill 1	0101	1:52	6
	Drill 2	0102	3:06	7
	Drill 3	0103	4:03	7
	Drill 4	0104	1:16	8
	Drill 5	0105	1:25	8
	Drill 6	0106	3:30	8
	Drill 7	0107	1:17	8
	Drill 8	0108	1:25	9
	Drill 9	0109	3:22	9
	Drill 10	0110	2:12	10
	Drill 11	0111	3:40	10
	Drill 12	0112	5:57	10
	Drill 13	0113	2:00	11
	Drill 14	0114	3:29	11
	Drill 15	0115	5:12	12
	Drill 16	0116	3:59	13
	Drill 17	0117	1:41	13
	Drill 18	0118	1:17	13
	Drill 19	0119	2:07	14
2	Drill 1	0201	1:51	15
	Drill 2	0202	2:01	15
	Drill 3	0203	0:52	15
	Drill 4	0204	0:56	16
	Drill 5	0205	0:59	16
	Drill 6	0206	2:37	16
	Drill 7	0207	1:24	16
	Drill 8	0208	1:33	17
	Drill 9	0209	1:48	17
	Drill 10	0210	2:16	18
	Drill 11	0211	0:50	18
	Drill 12	0212	1:01	18
	Drill 13	0213	2:06	19
	Drill 14	0214	2:04	20

Unit	Exercise	Filename	Time	Page
	Drill 15	0215	1:36	20–21
	Drill 16	0216	0:50	21
	Drill 17	0217	2:46	21
3	Drill 1	0301	1:10	22
	Drill 2	0302	2:56	22
	Drill 3	0303	1:25	23
	Drill 4	0304	0:55	23
	Drill 5	0305	1:08	23
	Drill 6	0306	1:06	23
	Drill 7	0307	1:05	24
	Drill 8	0308	2:40	25
	Drill 9	0309	3:18	25
	Drill 10	0310	1:39	25
	Drill 11	0311	0:55	26
	Drill 12	0312	1:27	27
	Drill 13	0313	0:52	27
	Drill 14	0314	1:45	27
	Drill 15	0315	0:25	28
	Drill 16	0316	3:31	28
	Drill 17	0317	2:49	30
	Drill 18	0318	3:01	30
	Drill 19	0319	1:27	30
4	Drill 1	0401	1:36	31
	Drill 2	0402	0:34	31
	Drill 3	0403	2:57	31
	Drill 4	0404	1:39	32
	Drill 5	0405	2:11	33
	Drill 6	0406	2:51	33
	Drill 7	0407	2:10	34
	Drill 8	0408	0:52	34
	Drill 9	0409	1:48	36
	Drill 10	0410	0:40	37
	Drill 11	0411	1:03	37
	Drill 12	0412	2:11	37
	Drill 13	0413	1:50	38
	Drill 14	0414	1:25	38
	Drill 15	0415	1:29	39
	Drill 16	0416	1:16	39
	Drill 17	0417	1:35	39
	Drill 18	0418	1:39	40
5	Drill 1	0501	0:54	41
	Drill 2	0502	1:29	42

Unit	Exercise	Filename	Time	Page
	Drill 6	0806	2:34	63
	Drill 7	0807	0:43	64
	Drill 8	0808	3:05	64
9	Drill 1	0901	1:18	65
	Drill 2	0902	2:37	66
	Drill 3	0903	2:40	67
	Drill 4	0904	2:23	67
	Drill 5	0905	2:57	68
	Drill 6	0906	2:55	68
	Drill 7	0907	1:24	68
	Drill 8	0908	1:52	69
	Drill 9	0909	2:35	70
	Drill 10	0910	1:28	70
	Drill 11	0911	1:25	70
	Drill 12	0912	1:58	70
	Drill 13	0913	3:03	71
	Drill 14	0914	2:41	71
	Drill 15	0915	2:43	71
	Drill 16	0916	2:40	71
	Drill 17	0917	1:49	72
10	—	1000	4:55	—
11	Instructions for Units 11–40	1100	0:36	—
	Dialogue	1100a	1:13	79
	Dialogue: A form of address	1100b	4:16	82
	Dialogue at normal speed	1100c	0:33	82
	Instructions for remainder of unit	1100d	0:22	—
	Drill 1	1101	1:13	85
	Drill 2	1102	1:04	85
	Drill 3	1103	1:17	85
	Drill 4	1104	1:07	86
	Drill 5	1105	1:15	86
	Drill 6	1106	1:09	86
	Drill 7	1107	1:17	86
	Drill 8	1108	1:26	86
	Drill 9	1109	1:28	87
	Drill 10	1110	2:29	87
12	Dialogue	1200a	5:31	87
	Dialogue at normal speed	1200b	0:33	87
	Drill 1	1201	3:32	93
	Drill 2	1202	1:42	94
	Drill 3	1203	2:14	94
	Drill 4	1204	1:47	94

Unit	Exercise	Filename	Time	Page
	Drill 5	1205	2:00	95
	Drill 6	1206	2:37	95
	Drill 7	1207	1:54	95
	Drill 8	1208	2:02	96
	Drill 9	1209	2:16	96
	Drill 10	1210	1:50	96
	Drill 11	1211	3:00	97
	Drill 12	1212	3:55	97
13	Dialogue	1300a	5:46	98
	Dialogue at normal speed	1300b	4:27	98
	Drill 2	1302	2:19	104
	Drill 3	1303	2:29	104–5
	Drill 4	1304	2:45	105
	Drill 5	1305	3:01	105
	Drill 6	1306	4:01	106
	Drill 7	1307	4:11	106
	Drill 8	1308	3:07	107
	Drill 9	1309	3:27	107
	Drill 10	1310	3:57	107
	Drill 11	1311	4:02	108
	Drill 12	1312	4:09	108
14	Dialogue	1400a	6:24	109
	Dialogue at normal speed	1400b	0:37	109
	Drill 1	1401	6:59	119
	Drill 2	1402	3:28	120
	Drill 3	1403	3:19	120
	Drill 4	1404	3:32	121
	Drill 5	1405	2:47	121
	Drill 6	1406	3:26	121
	Drill 7	1407	1:50	122
	Drill 8	1408	2:03	122
	Drill 9	1409	2:15	122
	Drill 10	1410	2:29	122
	Drill 11	1411	2:18	123
	Drill 12	1412	2:27	123
15	Narrative	1500a	6:32	124
	Dialogue at normal speed	1500b	0:32	124
	Drill 1	1501	2:50	135
	Drill 2	1502	2:08	135
	Drill 3	1503	2:19	135
	Drill 4	1504	2:37	136
	Drill 5	1505	8:55	136

Arabic Research at Georgetown University

In the thirty-five years since the original publication of Wallace M. Erwin's *A Basic Course in Iraqi Arabic*, the world of research in Arabic theoretical linguistics has expanded but the production of professional quality textbooks in colloquial Arabic has remained limited. Despite the passage of years, the Richard Slade Harrell Arabic Series has consistently been in demand from Georgetown University Press because of the quality of research that went into its composition, the solid theoretical foundations for its methodology, and the comprehensive coverage of regional Arabic speech communities.

The Arabic Department at Georgetown University (now Department of Arabic Language, Literature and Linguistics) recognizes the need to sustain the tradition of research and publication in Arabic dialects and has continued dialectology field research and textbook production, most notably with Margaret (Omar) Nydell's Syrian Arabic Video Course, a three-year research project funded by the Center for the Advancement of Language Learning from 1991 to 1994.

Currently, Dr. Nydell is leading a four-year dialectology research project aimed at producing "conversion" courses to assist learners of Modern Standard Arabic in converting their knowledge and skills of written Arabic to proficiency in selected Arabic dialects. This project is part of a proposal prepared by the National Capital Language Resource Center under the directorship of Dr. James E. Alatis and Dr. Anna Chamot. The first Arabic dialect tackled under this research project was Iraqi, and the Iraqi conversion short course was field tested successfully in the summer of 2003. In developing the materials for the conversion course, the most authoritative English sources of information were the two seminal texts produced by Wallace Erwin and published by Georgetown University Press in the 1960s, and which the Press is reissuing this year, *A Basic Course in Iraqi Arabic* and *A Short Reference Grammar of Iraqi Arabic*.

We pay tribute to the tradition initiated and led by Richard Harrell, the founder of this series and of the original Arabic Research Program at Georgetown University. Harrell's scholarship and creative energy set a standard in the field and yielded an unprecedented and as yet unsurpassed series of, as he put it, "practical tools for the increasing number of Americans whose lives bring them into contact with the Arab world."

For more information about the Department of Arabic Language, Literature and Linguistics at Georgetown University, its course offerings, its degree programs, and its research agenda, see www.georgetown.edu/departments/arabic.

Karin C. Ryding
Sultan Qaboos bin Said Professor of Arabic

The History of the Arabic Research Program School of Languages and Linguistics Georgetown University

The Arabic Research Program was established in June of 1960 as a contract between Georgetown University and the United States Office of Education under the provisions of the Language Development Program of the National Defense Education Act.

The first two years of the research program, 1960–62 (contract number SAE-8706), were devoted to the production of six books, a reference grammar, and a conversational English–Arabic dictionary in the cultivated spoken forms of Moroccan, Syrian, and Iraqi Arabic. The second two years of the research program, 1962–64 (contract number OE-2-14-029), have been devoted to the further production of Arabic–English dictionaries in each of the three varieties of Arabic mentioned above, as well as comprehensive basic courses in the Moroccan and Iraqi varieties.

The eleven books of this series, of which the present volume is one, are designed to serve as practical tools for the increasing number of Americans whose lives bring them into contact with the Arab world. The dictionaries, the reference grammars, and the basic courses are oriented toward the educated American who is a layman in linguistic matters. Although it is hoped that the scientific linguist and the specialist in Arabic dialectology will find these books both of interest and of use, matters of purely scientific and theoretical importance have not been directly treated as such, and specialized scientific terminology has been avoided as much as possible.

As is usual, the authors or editors of the individual books bear final scholarly responsibility for the contents, but there has been a large amount of informal cooperation in our work. Criticism, consultation, and discussion have gone on constantly among the senior professional members of the staff. The contribution of more junior research assistants, both Arab and American, is also not to be underestimated. Their painstaking assembling and ordering of raw data, often in manners requiring considerable creative intelligence, has been the necessary prerequisite for further progress.

In most cases the books prepared by the Arabic Research Program are the first of ther kind in English, and in some cases the first in any language. The preparation of them has been a rewarding experience. It is hoped that the public use of them will be equally so. The undersigned, on behalf of the entire staff, would like to ask the same indulgence of the reader as Samuel Johnson requested in his first English dictionary: To remember that although much has been left out, much has been included.

Richard S. Harrell
Professor of Linguistics
Georgetown University
Director,
Arabic Research Program

Before his death in late 1964, Dr. Harrell had done the major part of the work of general editor for the last five books of the Arabic Series, and to him is due the credit for all that may be found of value in that work. It remained for me only to make some minor editing decisions, and to see these books through the process of proofreading and printing; for any errors or inadequacies in the final editing, the responsibility is mine alone.

Wallace M. Erwin
Associate Professor of
Linguistics and Arabic
Georgetown University

Foreword to the Georgetown Classics Edition

A Basic Course in Iraqi Arabic, published in 1969, is still the definitive study of the language. Dr. Wallace Erwin wrote this introductory course along with a reference grammar, accompanied by dictionaries of the dialect, and it stands as a major contribution to Arabic dialectology.

This basic course is written for beginners with no previous knowledge of Arabic. It is very comprehensive.

There are not many books that deal with Iraqi as a whole. In the 1950s some Iraqi materials were produced by oil companies and at the Jesuit college in Baghdad, but Iraqi has been less studied than most dialects. The Defense Language Institute (DLI) in Monterey, California, has developed much training material in the dialect that is military-oriented but very useful. Other titles include *Introduzione ai Dialetti Arabi* by Oliver Duran (Milan: Centro Studi Camito-Semitici, 1995); and *From MSA to the Iraqi Dialect* by Margaret Nydell (Arlington, VA: DLS Press, 1991).

The subjects discussed in this book include communal dialects, the use of auxiliary particles, the "analytical genitive" word /maal/, verb morphology, and broken plurals. In the past thirty years there have been monographs, articles, and dissertations dealing with certain features of Iraqi, and these are readily available to specialists. However, far more research is needed, and perhaps the current political prominence of Iraq will lead to this result.

It is gratifying to have this important and timely book once again in print and widely available.

Margaret Nydell

This basic course is a prime example of the audiolingual method of teaching. Although now considered outdated by some, the audiolingual method produced some of the finest Arabic dialect textbooks, the Georgetown University series being the best example. That the text is still popular and usable in the classroom points to the soundness and thoroughness of its design and production. The dialogues, examples, drills and, especially, the grammar explanations are models of clarity and appropriateness.

Wallace Erwin's contributions to Arabic linguistics and language teaching during the 1960s, 1970s, and 1980s formed a body of impeccable scholarship that was foundational to the field of teaching Arabic as a foreign language, and to Arabic descriptive structural linguistics. In addition to his two volumes on Iraqi Arabic (*A Short Reference Grammar of Iraqi Arabic* and *A Basic Course in Iraqi Arabic*), he was one of the founding authors of the original audiolingual-based Elementary Modern Standard Arabic series published by the University of Michigan in 1968, and which had a profound impact on the field of Arabic language teaching—generations of Arabists have an indelible memory of the "big orange book."

As a scholar, teacher, and administrator, Wallace Erwin embodied the highest professional standards. As chairman of the Arabic Department at Georgetown University from 1964 to 1981, Erwin pioneered the development of the Arabic curriculum and teaching methodology at Georgetown to the point where it led most other American universities in size, quality, and effectiveness at the undergraduate and graduate levels. He served on the executive board of the American Association of Teachers of Arabic and was elected its president in 1972.

Fortunately, I was able to have Wallace Erwin as a professor of Arabic linguistics (Classical Arabic Structure and Arabic Dialectology) and as the mentor of my dissertation, but the most lasting impression made on me by Dr. Erwin was the result of being his teaching assistant for two years in basic and intermediate Arabic. His methodology consisted of a style of gifted, energetic, demanding, systematic, and yet deeply humanistic elements that made lasting impressions on his students and on this apprentice teacher. He was able to combine an aura of control and authority with an artful use of humor and easy-goingness. He was, quite simply, the best.

Now that Wally is retired and enjoying himself, we hope that seeing these books reissued will give him cause to celebrate and know how much his contributions have been appreciated.

Karin C. Ryding
Sultan Qaboos bin Said Professor of Arabic

Acknowledgments

This book is a product of the cooperation and assistance of many people, and here, while affirming my sole responsibility for the final form of the book, I would like to express my thanks to all those who assisted in its preparation. To Majid Damah, who wrote the dialogues and served as a competent and cheerful source of linguistic information, goes my particular appreciation. I am also very grateful to Riyadh Al-Any, who kindly read the entire manuscript and made a number of helpful corrections and suggestions. Thanks are due as well to Faisal Al-Khalaf, Wayne Beene, Husain Mustafa, Ronald Wolfe, and Daniel Woodhead, all of whom gave useful aid and advice on many occasions; to Elen Byrnes, who generously undertook the laborious task of typing slips for the glossaries; and to R. J. McCarthy, S.J., and Faraj Raffouli, to whose book *Spoken Arabic of Baghdad: Part One* (Beirut: Librairie Orientale, 1964) I referred for information on several points of vocabulary and usage. I would like to express my gratitude also to the authors of the National Defense Education Act and its efficient and understanding administrators in the Office of Education of the Department of Health, Education, and Welfare, for the contract which made this book possible, and to the dean and the associate dean of the School of Languages and Linguistics, Georgetown University, for the facilities and the extra time necessary for the completion of the work. And, as always, I am deeply grateful to my wife, whose constant encouragement has sustained my efforts from the beginning to the end of this undertaking.

Introduction

This book is designed to be used in an oral-aural approach to language-teaching, which involves the memorization of short dialogues, and extensive oral drilling as an aid toward mastering the major grammatical structures. It is arranged in 40 units, the first ten of which deal with phonology, and the remaining 30 with grammar. The kind of Arabic presented here is that spoken by educated Muslims in the city of Baghdad, and the term "Iraqi" or "Iraqi Arabic" as used throughout the book should be understood to mean specifically Muslim Baghdad Arabic. This variety of Arabic can generally be understood throughout Iraq and, with varying degrees of difficulty, in most parts of the Arab world. A full description of the phonology, morphology, and syntax of this dialect may be found in my book *A Short Reference Grammar of Iraqi Arabic* (Washington: Georgetown University Press, 1963); the analysis presented in that work forms the basis of the grammatical explanations in this textbook. For dictionaries of the same dialect, the reader is referred to *A Dictionary of Iraqi Arabic: English–Arabic,* edited by B. E. Clarity, Karl Stowasser, and Ronald G. Wolfe (Washington: Georgetown University Press, 1964), and *A Dictionary of Iraqi Arabic: Arabic–English,* edited by D. R. Woodhead and Wayne Beene (Washington: Georgetown University Press, 1967). Another extensive presentation of Baghdad Arabic may be found in *Spoken Arabic of Baghdad: Part One* by R. J. McCarthy, S.J., and Faraj Raffouli (Beirut: Librairie Orientale, 1964), which includes grammatical explanations, exercises, and vocabularies, and in *Spoken Arabic of Baghdad: Part Two (A)* by the same authors (Beirut: Librairie Orientale, 1965), which contains conversations, narratives, plays, songs, and proverbs.

Units 1 to 10 of this texbook present a description of the phonological system of Iraqi Arabic, with rather detailed explanations and drills designed to help the student learn to pronounce the vowels and difficult consonants in acceptable fashion. It is probably more satisfactory in the long run to cover these ten units thoroughly before proceeding to the dialogues and grammar drills beginning in Unit 11, but some teachers may wish to supplement the purely phonological work of the first ten units by presenting (orally) simple phrases of greeting, classroom expressions, and the like; these should however be carefully chosen at each stage to include only those sounds which have been covered by that time.

Each of the untis from 11 to 40 consists of three main parts: (A) a short dialogue or narrative, with a list of new vocabulary items, (B) grammatical explanations, and (C) drills; in addition there are, where appropriate, brief cultural notes on features touched upon in the dialogues. Following is a discussion of each of the three main parts, with suggestions on their use:

A. *Dialogues.* These are short conversations, involving two or more people, and dealing generally with matters of everyday living in Baghdad. Every fifth unit has, in place of a dialogue, a narrative, which is usually a third-person account of the events of the preceding four dialogues. A loose thread of connection runs through the dialogues and narratives, in that for the most part they concern the affairs of two or three specific families (all quite fictitious, of course), and eventually touch on the engagement, marriage, and honeymoon of a young man and woman of two of the families. Thus the dialogues may serve to present an introduction—though a slight and superficial one—to some aspects of the culture in question. They will also serve to introduce, in an appropriate context, the words and phrases which will ultimately form the core of the student's most frequently required vocabulary. Their primary and most important purpose, however, is to serve as a framework for the presentation of the basic grammatical structures of the language, the mastery of which is an essetial step toward fluency. For the most satisfactory results in proceeding toward this goal, each dialogue or narrative should be thoroughly memorized by the students, in such a way that they can unhesitatingly repeat the entire dialogue, or take the role of any speaker, at normal conversational speed and without any pauses for trying to recall what comes next. One way in which this kind of memorization can be achieved in the classroom is as follows:

Step 1. Books open. Teacher says first sentence of dialogue or narrative aloud, at normal speed. (If sentence is too long, teacher takes shorter segments at a time, but saying each segment at normal speed, and putting them all together at the end.) Students note general meaning of sentence by glancing at the English translation, and repeat aloud in chorus. Teacher repeats the same sentence; students repeat aloud in chorus. Teacher repeats, pointing at individual students in random order; each one repeats after teacher; if necessary, teacher makes brief corrections in pronunciation or intonation. Teacher continues process through all sentences of dialogue. As last step, teacher says each sentence once, students repeating aloud in chorus, straight through dialogue.

Step 2. Books closed. Teacher says first sentence (or shorter segment), always at normal speed; students repeat in chorus. Teacher says next sentence; students repeat. Teacher says first two sentences; students repeat after each. Teacher says third sentence; students repeat. Teacher says first three sentences; students repeat after each. Teacher continues this buildup until entire dialogue has been covered.

Step 3. Books closed. Teacher takes first speaker's role, and says first sentence. Students take second speaker's role and respond with second sentence in chorus, teacher prompting when necessary. Teacher proceeds thus through entire dialogue; then does the same with roles reversed.

Step 4. Books closed. Teacher enacts dialogue with each individual student, taking now one role and now the other, often enough to ensure that each student plays every role at least once, preferably several times.

Step 5. Books closed. Teacher points at a student, who says the first sentence. Teacher points at another student, who says the second sentence, and so on through the dialogue several times. Pointing should be in random order, and fast enough to ensure normal tempo throughout.

Step 6. Books closed. Teacher chooses two students (or whatever number of speakers the dialogue involves), who enact the entire dialogue. Teacher should insist on normal speed, and lifelike intonation and gesture. Teacher then chooses other students, and these enact dialogue in similar fashion. This continues until all students have enacted each role one or more times.

If tapes are available, a new dialogue can be briefly introduced toward the end of a class session, along the line of Step 1 above, and the students given the outside assignment of memorizing the dialogue by listening to the tapes. Then, at the following class session, less time can be spent on memorizing and more on realistic enactment and on drills.

B. *Grammar.* The grammatical explanations, especially those in the earlier units, are given in considerable detail, and are meant to be read by the students as homework. Valuable classroom time can be spent far more efficiently and profitably on dialogue work, as suggested in the preceding paragraph, and on drills.

C. *Drills.* In memorizing and enacting a given dialogue or narrative, the students actually use a number of new and important grammatical structures; after reading the grammatical explanations, they have an intellectual grasp of the forms and uses of those structures. The purpose of the drills is to transform their intellectual understanding of the structures into actual skill in using and understanding them. The development of this kind of skill requires a good deal of repetitive, mechanical exercise, not unlike that required in the development of skill in say tennis, or piano-playing. In language-learning, skill in the mechanics of the language—an ability to handle its grammatical structures without continually having to think about them—frees the speaker's conscioius mind for the vital business of thinking about the content of what he says and hears. The drills help the student toward this goal by providing controlled practice in manipulating grammatical structures, for example in repeating a sentence over and over but changing one word each time, in changing a series of sentences from affirmative to negative or from present to past, or in answering questions in a prescribed format. The most frequently occurring drill types in Units 11 to 40 are described below. ALL DRILLS ARE DESIGNED AS ORAL WORK AND SHOULD BE DONE WITH BOOKS CLOSED.

1. *Substitution drill.* In this type of drill, successive students repeat a given sentence, each changing one word at the teacher's cue. Example:

In the following sentence, replace the underlined word with the item given.

štireena <u>xariiṭa</u> bis-suug.	We bought a <u>map</u> at the market.
gḷaaṣ	glass
saaƐa	watch
qalam	pencil
(etc.)	(etc.)

Procedure: Teacher says the basic sentence, making sure the students understand the meaning, what they are supposed to do, which word they are to replace, and so on. Students repeat several times in chorus after the teacher. Teacher points to a student, and gives the first cue word, *gḷaaṣ*. That student then repeats the sentence, replacing the word *xariiṭa* with *gḷaaṣ*. Teacher points to another student, giving the next cue word, *saaƐa*; that student repeats the sentence, replacing *gḷaaṣ* with *saaƐa*. Teacher continues until all students have had several turns, going through the list of words as often as necessary. Drills of this type are useful in two ways:

First, they provide a framework for introducing and practicing new or review vocabulary in a suitable context; and, second, they impress upon the student the general structure of the particular sentence-type illustrated, or of other structural features within the sentence, while his mind is consciously focussed on the changing cue words.

2. *Substitution drill with other changes.* This type is like the simple substitution drill shown above, with one additional feature: When a new word is substituted, some other word in the sentence may have to be changed to agree in some way with the new word. Example:

In the following sentence, replace the underlined word with the item given, and make any other necessary changes.

štireena xariiṭa jdiida bis-suug.	We bought a new map at the market.
gḷaaṣ	glass
saaɛa	watch
qalam	pencil
(*etc.*)	(etc.)

Procedure: As in 1. above, except that when the first student repeats the sentence, replacing *xariiṭa* with *gḷaaṣ,* he must also change the adjective *jdiida* to its masculine form *jidiid,* to agree with the masculine noun *gḷaaṣ*. The next student, who replaces *gḷaaṣ* with *saaɛa*, must also change the adjective back to its feminine form *jdiida,* to agree with the feminine noun *saaɛa*, and so on.

3. *Transformation drills.* These consist of a series of sentences, all with some common feature, such as a verb in the imperfect tense. Each student repeats a sentence, but makes a certain change in that feature, such as changing the verb to perfect tense. Example:

In the following sentences, change the verb forms from imperfect to perfect tense.

nišrab gahwa saaɛa ɛašra.	We drink coffee at ten o'clock.
naakul simač kull yoom.	We eat fish every day.
(*etc.*)	(etc.)

Procedure: Teacher explains what kind of change is required, and gives an example. Teacher says the first sentence, *nišrab gahwa saaɛa ɛašra.* Students repeat in chorus. Teacher points to a student, who repeats the sentence, changing the verb to the perfect tense: *širabna gahwa saaɛa ɛašra.* Teacher follows same procedure with the next sentence, and so on, going through the whole set of sentences as often as may be necessary to give each student several turns.

As it stands, this textbook can be covered easily in one academic year at the usual pace of three or four class hours per week, or in less time at a more intensive pace. Teachers who wish to expand the material for use over longer periods of time may do so by holding review sessions after every five units, by devising additional dialogues and drills, and by introducing, in the appropriate places, additional vocabulary items of a type suited to the particular needs of their own students.

UNIT 1

A. Consonants *p b k g f v θ ð s z š ž č j m n w y*

There are more consonant sounds in Iraqi than in English. As you will see later, some of these sounds are quite unlike anything in English, and therefore require considerable practice on the part of the English-speaking learner. Others are in some respects like certain English sounds, but are still different enough to deserve special attention. About half of them, however, are so much like English sounds that they present little or no difficulty, and it is these relatively familiar sounds that we take up in this section. The following table shows the symbols which will be used to represent the sounds in question, with an English word or two to illustrate each one.

Voiceless			**Voiced**		
p	as in	*p*ay	*b*	as in	*b*ay
k	" "	*k*ale	*g*	" "	*g*ale
f	" "	*f*eel	(*v*	" "	*v*eal)
θ	" "	*th*ick, e*th*er	*ð*	" "	*th*is, ei*th*er
s	" "	*s*eal	*z*	" "	*z*eal
š	" "	*sh*ake, fi*ss*ion	(*ž*	" "	vi*s*ion)
č	" "	*ch*oke	*j*	" "	*j*oke
			m	" "	*m*ail
			n	" "	*n*ail
			w	" "	*w*ell
			y	" "	*y*ell

The two consonant sounds *v* and *z,* shown in parentheses above, are very rare in Iraqi. They occur only in a few words borrowed from other languages, and under certain circumstances as variants of *f* and of *š* or *j* respectively. Iraqi words illustrating the other consonants in the table will be given in later sections of this unit.

Voice. In Iraqi, as in English, some consonant sounds are **voiceless** and some are **voiced.** A voiceless consonant is one which is produced without any accompanying vibration of the vocal cords, for example the *s* sound at the beginning of the English word *seal.* A voiced consonant is one which is accompanied by vibration of the vocal cords, for example the *z* sound at the beginning of *zeal.* To hear clearly the distinction between voicelessness and voicing, plug your ears with your thumbs and make a prolonged *sssss* sound and then a prolonged *zzzzz* sound. In the former you will hear only a friction noise, produced in the front part of the mouth. In the latter you will hear the same friction noise, but together with it you will also hear a strong buzzing tone, which is produced by rapid vocal cord vibration: this is voicing. The consonants in the table above are arranged according to the feature of voice, voiceless consonants on the left and voiced on the right. In both Iraqi and English, and in many other languages as well, there are consonants which can be grouped together in pairs, each pair consisting of two consonants produced in the same way—this is, by the same movements or positions of the lips, tongue, and other elements of the speech mechanism—except that one is voiceless and the other is voiced. In the table, such voiceless-voiced pairs are shown on the same horizontal line, for example *p* and *b*, *s* and *z*, and *č* and *j*. There are also sounds in both languages which are not members of such pairs; these may be voiceless with no voiced counterpart, or voiced with no voiceless counterpart. In Iraqi, as the table indicates, the voiced consonants *m*, *n*, *w*, and *y* have no voiceless counterparts; and since *v* and *ž* are so rare, the voiceless consonants *f* and *š* may be said for all practical purposes to have no voiced counterparts.

Point of articulation. In addition to the matter of voice, consonants can be described according to their **point of articulation,** the place along the vocal tract at which the sound is produced. By this criterion, the consonants in the table above fall into the following groups. Those produced by the action of the two lips are **bilabial:** *p*, *b*, *m*, and *w*; those produced by the lower lip and the upper teeth are **labiodental:** *f* and *v*; consonants in both these groups may be called simply **labial.** Those produced by the tongue tip protruding slightly between the teeth are **interdental:** *θ* and *δ*. Those produced by the tongue tip approaching or touching the back of the upper teeth or the gum area just behind them are **dental:** *s*, *z*, and *n*. Those produced by the front of the tongue approaching or touching the palate are **palatal:** *š*, *ž*, *č*, *j*, and *y*. (The **front** of the tongue is the forward part of the upper surface; the **palate** is the hard part of the roof of the mouth behind the gum ridge.) Those produced by the back of the tongue approaching or touching the velum are **velar:** *k* and *g*. (The **velum** is the soft rear part of the roof of the mouth, behind the palate.)

Manner of articulation. A third way in which consonants can be described is according to their **manner of articulation.** This term refers to the question whether, in the production of a given sound, the breathstream is momentarily cut off altogether or only impeded, and, in the latter case, in what way. By this criterion, the consonants in the table above fall into the following groups. Those in which the breathstream is momentarily cut off altogether, by a complete closure somewhere along the vocal tract, are **stops:**

p, b, k, and *g*. Those in which there is an obstruction or narrowing—but not a complete closure—at some point along the vocal tract, so that although the breathstream continues to pass through, it produces an audible friction noise in passing, are **spirants**: *f, v, θ, δ, s, z, š,* and *ž*. Those consisting of two stages, an initial stage in which there is a complete closure as in a stop, and a final stage in which the closure is opened slightly so that the breathstream is released and passes through with friction noise as in a spirant, are **affricates**: *č* and *j*. Those in which there is a complete closure at some point in the mouth but the breathstream continues to pass out through the nose are **nasals**: *m* and *n*. Finally, those which do not fit into consonant classifications such as those just given—and indeed are vowel-like rather than consonant-like in quality—but nevertheless function as consonants in a given language, are **semivowels**: *w* and *y*.

Each of the Iraqi consonants in the table above can thus be distinguished from all the others by a phrase consisting of three terms, one referring to voice, one to point of articulation, and one to manner of articulation. For example, *p* is a voiceless bilabial stop, *δ* is a voiced interdental spirant, and *č* is a voiceless palatal affricate. This three-dimensional classification can be shown in the form of a chart (see page 4). This is of course not a complete chart of all Iraqi consonants, but only of the eighteen thus far discussed. A complete chart is given in a later unit.

B. Vowels: General comments

The Iraqi vowel system is composed of five long vowels, four short vowels, and a number of vowel-semivowel combinations called diphthongs. In this unit we take up only the long vowels, leaving the short vowels and the diphthongs for later units. First, however, there are two comments to be made about Iraqi vowels in general.

Vowel length. For four of the Iraqi long vowels there are corresponding short vowels; for example there is a long vowel *aa* and a corresponding short vowel *a*. A long vowel differs from the corresponding short vowel, first of all, in duration; that is, in the actual length of time during which the sound continues. A long vowel lasts anywhere from half again to twice as long as a short vowel. Absolute duration is not significant: a slow speaker's short vowels may be as long as a fast speaker's long vowels; but in a given stretch of speech every speaker maintains a fairly constant relative distinction of length between the two types. In English, a vowel may be physically long or short in duration, usually depending on what consonant follows it; for example, in the speech of most people the vowel in *has* is measurably longer than the vowel in *hat*. But—and this is the important thing—in English such a dif-

	BILABIAL	LABIODENTAL	INTERDENTAL	DENTAL	PALATAL	VELAR
STOPS Voiceless	*p*					*k*
Voiced	*b*					*g*
SPIRANTS Voiceless		*f*	*θ*	*s*	*š*	
Voiced		*v*	*δ*	*z*	*ž*	
AFFRICATES Voiceless					*č*	
Voiced					*j*	
NASALS Voiced	*m*			*n*		
SEMIVOWELS Voiced	*w*				*y*	

ference in vowel length alone does not ever make the difference between one word and another: there is no difference in meaning between *hat* with a short vowel and *hat* with the vowel prolonged. In Iraqi, on the other hand, it often happens that two otherwise identical words of quite different meanings are distinguished only by the fact that one has a long vowel and the other a short; thus the long-short distinction is a basic and important feature of the Iraqi sound system. In addition to the matter of duration, a long vowel may differ from the corresponding short vowel in quality; that is, in the way it sounds. Details about this will be given as part of the individual vowel descriptions below.

Vowel range. All the Iraqi vowels, long or short, have wider ranges of variation than English vowels. This statement can best be explained by an example. In English, the vowels of the words *pet, pat,* and *pot* are three different vowels: they sound quite different to our ears precisely because, in English, the difference between any two of them is enough to make the difference between one word and another, and we are accustomed from childhood to hearing and reproducing this difference. In Iraqi there is a vowel *a,* which in some words sounds (to English-speakers) like the vowel of *pet,* in others like that of *pat,* and in still others like that of *pot.* These different-sounding qualities, however, are determined entirely by the **environment** of the *a* in a word; that is, next to certain consonants it sounds more like the vowel of *pet,* next to others more like that of *pat,* and so on. The differences, in other words, are automatic: they are not subject to conscious choice by the Iraqi-speaker, but are determined for him by the environment; and they never serve to distinguish two otherwise identical words as the corresponding differences do in English. Thus we say that the one Iraqi vowel *a* has a range of variation covering the qualities heard in several different English vowels, and the same is true to a greater or lesser degree of the other Iraqi vowels as well.

Having made these general comments, we can now proceed to a description of the individual vowels. As you will see, the words given to illustrate the vowels also illustrate the consonants discussed in Section A above.

C. Long vowel *aa*

This vowel has qualities ranging roughly from that of the vowel in *has* to that of the vowel in *calm.* Listen to the Iraqi examples given below. If you hear variations in the quality of the vowel from one word to another, remember that these variations are automatically determined by the environment—the neighboring consonant sounds—and that they are merely different aspects of the same vowel. Actually, in these particular examples you may not hear much variation in the vowel quality, because the particular consonants occurring in these words all happen to have somewhat the same effect on the vowel *aa.* In later examples the variation will be more noticeable. In any case, both here and later, listen carefully and imitate what you hear as closely as you can, vowel variation and all. In time the variation will become as automatic for you as it is for Iraqis.

Note:

1. Do NOT try to memorize the English meanings of the examples given below and throughout Units 1 to 10. Many of them are common and useful words, and you will learn these in the proper place as you proceed through the course. Others have been chosen only to illustrate certain

sounds, and some of these you may never need to learn. English meanings are given as a matter of interest, but in these units your primary concern is to become accustomed to the sounds of Iraqi, so that later you may devote your full attention to matters of grammar and vocabulary. So, to repeat, do NOT waste your time trying to memorize meanings now.

2. Capital letters in some of the English translations, such as the M in the last two items on the left below, refer to certain grammatical features indicated by the Iraqi word but not by the English. They will be explained later on; until then they can be ignored.
3. The vertical arrow means that the examples are to be read downward, first all those in the left column, then all those in the right.

Drill 1. Long vowel *aa*. Listen and repeat.

↓ *jaa*	'he came'	*šaaf*	'he saw'
maa	'not'	*faas*	'hatchet'
yaa	'which?'	*naas*	'people'
baab	'door'	*naaš*	'he reached'
jaab	'he brought'	*naam*	'he slept'
δaab	'it M melted'	*gaas*	'he touched'
δaak	'that M'	*čaan*	'he was'

The next drill illustrates the difference between the Iraqi vowel *aa* and the English vowel sounds which most closely resemble it. The point is that, although these English vowels are more like *aa* in quality than are other English vowels, they are not exactly like *aa*. Your task, therefore, is first to become aware of the differences, and then to develop the automatic habit of making the *aa* like an *aa* and not exactly like one of your usual English vowels. Remember also in doing these drills that *aa* is a long vowel, and thus will differ from the English vowels not only in quality but also in duration.

Note:

1. In some of the examples below, the English word has the same consonant sounds as the contrasting Iraqi word; in others one consonant may be different. This is not important, as we are concerned here with the contrast in vowel sounds only.
2. The horizontal arrow in each set of columns means that within that set the examples are to be read across, first the word on the left, then the word on the right, and so on down the column.

Drill 2. Contrast between English vowels and long vowel *aa*. Listen and repeat.

Bab	→	*baab*	gas	→	*gaas*
Bob		*baab*	gloss		*gaas*
jab		*jaab*	gnash		*naaš*
job		*jaab*	gosh		*naaš*
sack		*δaak*	cam		*naam*
sock		*δaak*	calm		*naam*
gaff		*šaaf*	Chan		*čaan*
doff		*šaaf*	John		*čaan*

In the final drill of this section you are asked to concentrate solely on the Iraqi words again. Notice both length and quality of the vowel, and imitate very precisely what you hear.

Note: Some of the examples below are single words, and some are groups of words separated by a short dash. The dash means that the group is to be read with only a very brief break between words, and that you are to repeat the whole group as a unit.

Drill 3. Long vowel *aa*. Listen and repeat.

↓ *jaa*	*δaak*	*jaa - maa*	*jaa - maa - yaa*
jaab	*čaan*	*baab - jaab*	*maa - yaa - jaa*
naam	*naas*	*faas - naas*	*baab - jaab - δaab*
yaa	*baab*	*gaas - faas*	*naas - gaas - faas*
δaab	*naaš*	*yaa - jaa*	*naaš - naas - jaab*
faas	*šaaf*	*šaaf - naaš*	*čaan - δaab - δaak*
maa	*gaas*	*δaab - naam*	*šaaf - naam - čaan*

D. Long vowel *ii*

This vowel has qualities ranging around that of the vowel in the English word *bees*. In the production of this English vowel, however, the tongue moves a little upward at the end, thus changing the quality of the vowel slightly; while in the production of the Iraqi *ii*, the tongue is tenser and remains in the same position throughout, thus giving to the vowel a more uniform quality than in English. The drills which follow are similar to those of the preceding section. As you go through them, remember to notice both the length and the quality of the vowel.

Drill 4. Long vowel *ii*. Listen and repeat.

↓ *bii*	'in him'	*δiič*	'that F'
šii	'thing'	*šiiš*	'rod, bar'
biik	'in you M'	*piip*	'keg, barrel'
jiib	'bring M'	*giis*	'touch M'
δiib	'wolf'	*čiis*	'bag, sack'

Drill 5. Contrast between English vowels and long vowel *ii*.

bee	→	*bii*	leash	→	*šiiš*
she		*šii*	peep		*piip*
beak		*biik*	geese		*giis*
teach		*δiič*	peace		*čiis*

Drill 6. Long vowel *ii*. Listen and repeat.

↓ *bii*	*giis*	*bii - šii*	*biik - δiič - δiib*
δiič	*δiib*	*bii - biik*	*δiib - jiib - čiis*
jiib	*šii*	*giis - čiis*	*šiiš - čiis - biik*
piip	*biik*	*jiib - δiib*	*bii - giis - šii*
čiis	*šiiš*	*piip - jiib*	*δiič - piip - šiiš*

E. Long vowel *uu*

This vowel has qualities ranging around that of the vowel in the English word *booze*. In the production of this English vowel, however, the lips move, just at the end, to a more rounded position, thus changing the quality of the vowel slightly; while in the production of the Iraqi *uu*, the lips are in fully rounded position throughout, both the tongue and the lips are tenser, and the whole vowel has a more uniform quality than in English. As you work through the drills below, remember to notice both the length and the quality of the vowel.

Drill 7. Long vowel *uu*. Listen and repeat.

↓ *muu*	'not'	*šuuf*	'look M'
buub	'doors'	*kuub*	'cup'
buuz	'snout'	*kuun*	'be M'
θuum	'garlic'	*muus*	'razor blade'
suug	'market'	*guum*	'get up M'

Drill 8. Contrast between English vowels and long vowel *uu*. Listen and repeat.

moo	→	*muu*	goof	→	*šuuf*
boob		*buub*	rube		*kuub*
booze		*buuz*	coon		*kuun*
doom		*θuum*	moose		*muus*

Drill 9. Long vowel *uu*. Listen and repeat.

↓ *θuum*	*suug*	*muu - muus*	*buub - kuub - suug*
muus	*buub*	*guum - θuum*	*šuuf - muus - θuum*
guum	*kuun*	*buub - buuz*	*buuz - muu - guum*
muu	*šuuf*	*kuub - kuun*	*kuun - kuub - buub*
buuz	*kuub*	*suug - šuuf*	*muu - muus - kuun*

F. Long vowel *oo*

This is not very much like any English vowel. If you will say the English word *hose* aloud several times very slowly, you will notice that during the course of the vowel sound your lips move from a somewhat rounded to a more rounded position and the back of your tongue moves slightly upward. These movements cause the vowel to change quality toward the end, becoming more like the vowel of *ooze*. Now if you can prolong the first part of the vowel in *hose,* keeping your lips and tongue in the same position and thus not allowing the vowel to glide off into the vowel of *ooze,* you will be approximating the Iraqi *oo*. It is a long vowel, but it has the same quality throughout—no off-glide as in English. Another way to approach the problem of learning to produce the Iraqi *oo,* which for some English-speakers may work better than starting from the vowel of *hose* as above, is this: Say the English word *caw* and note the sound of the vowel. Now say it again, but this time round your lips more, keep your lower jaw up so that your upper and lower teeth are only very slightly apart, and try to keep lips and tongue fairly tense and in the same position throughout. This should result in a reasonably good Iraqi *oo*. As you work through the drills, remember to notice both the length and the quality of the vowel, and if necessary repeat the exercises suggested above until you can produce the sound at will.

Drill 10. Long vowel *oo*. Listen and repeat.

↓ *boog*	'theft'	*foog*	'above'
boos	'kissing'	*koom*	'pile'
θoob	'shirt'	*mooj*	'waves'
jooz	'walnuts'	*mooz*	'bananas'
δook	'those'	*noom*	'sleep'
zooj	'pair'	*yoom*	'day'
šoof	'seeing'	*gooz*	'bow' (for arrows)
šook	'thorns'	*čook*	'choke' (on a car)

Drill 11. Contrast between English vowels and long vowel *oo*. Listen and repeat.

vogue	→	*boog*	vogue	→	*foog*
dog		*boog*	fog		*foog*
dose		*boos*	comb		*koom*
boss		*boos*	Mose		*mooz*
robe		*θoob*	maws		*mooz*
daub		*θoob*	Nome		*noom*
Joe's		*jooz*	goes		*gooz*
jaws		*jooz*	gauze		*gooz*
loaf		*šoof*	choke		*čook*
cough		*šoof*	chalk		*čook*

Drill 12. Long vowel *oo*. Listen and repeat.

↓ *koom*	*gooz*	*yoom - koom*	*jooz - gooz - mooz*
yoom	*šoof*	*δook - šook*	*δook - šook - čook*
δook	*boog*	*gooz - jooz*	*noom - koom - yoom*
θoob	*noom*	*mooj - zooj*	*foog - mooj - boog*
mooj	*šook*	*šoof - šook*	*zooj - mooj - θoob*
čook	*zooj*	*noom - yoom*	*šoof - gooz - jooz*
boos	*jooz*	*boog - foog*	*δook - boos - šook*
mooz	*foog*	*gooz - mooz*	*θoob - yoom - čook*

G. Long vowel *ee*

This vowel too is not exactly like anything in English. It has two major variants, depending mainly on what consonant it follows. The first is a long vowel sound with the same quality throughout. Say the English word *phase* several times aloud, very slowly, and notice that during the course of the vowel sound the front of your tongue moves upward. This movement causes a change in the quality of the vowel, so that at the end it becomes more like the vowel of *ease.* Now if you can prolong the first element of the vowel in *phase,* holding your tongue (and jaw) in the same fixed position throughout, and thus not allowing the vowel to glide off into the vowel of *ease,* you will be approximating the first variant of *ee.* Remember that it is a long vowel sound, but has the same quality throughout—no off-glide as in English. The second major variant of *ee,* on the other hand, does not have the same quality throughout. It begins like a short version of the vowel of English *eat,* and this changes quickly to the vowel of *fez.* The duration of the whole sequence is about the same as for any Iraqi long vowel. For most speakers of Iraqi, the first of these two variants occurs after the consonants *k* and *g* (and certain others which we will take up later), and the second variant after all others. However, you may notice some differences from speaker to speaker. The best plan is to imitate the pronunciation of your own teacher as closely as you can.

Drill 13. Long vowel *ee.* Listen and repeat.

↓ *beeš*	'how much?'	*keek*	'cake'
been	'between'	*meez*	'table'
jeeb	'pocket'	*ween*	'where?'
zeen	'good M'	*peek*	'a drink'
seef	'sword'	*geej*	'gauge'
šeeb	'old age'	*gees*	'touching'
keef	'mood, feeling'	*čeef*	'as, because'

Drill 14. Contrast between English vowels and long vowel *ee.* Listen and repeat.

bane	→	*been*	wane	→	*ween*
Ben		*been*	wen		*ween*
Gabe		*jeeb*	take		*peek*
Jeb		*jeeb*	peck		*peek*
Zane		*zeen*	gauge		*geej*
Zen		*zeen*	hedge		*geej*
cake		*keek*	face		*gees*
neck		*keek*	guess		*gees*
maze		*meez*	chafe		*čeef*
fez		*meez*	Jeff		*čeef*

Drill 15. Long vowel *ee.* Listen and repeat.

↓ *zeen*	*been*	*seef - keef*	*zeen - been - ween*
peek	*jeeb*	*zeen - been*	*seef - čeef - keef*
beeš	*meez*	*jeeb - šeeb*	*keek - gees - geej*
keef	*seef*	*peek - keek*	*beeš - jeeb - keek*
čeef	*keek*	*gees - geej*	*šeeb - peek - gees*
šeeb	*gees*	*meez - ween*	*meez - been - geej*
geej	*ween*	*beeš - čeef*	*zeen - beeš - keef*

H. Long vowels: Summary

Vowels can be described and classified in terms of four variables: (1) **length;** (2) **tongue height**—whether a given part of the tongue is relatively **high** (raised toward the roof of the mouth), or in a **mid** position, or **low;** (3) **tongue advancement**—which part of the tongue (**front, central,** or **back**) is in high, mid, or low position; and (4) **lip-rounding**—whether the lips are **rounded** or **unrounded.** Thus, for example, *ii* can be described as a long high front unrounded vowel. This means that (1) it is relatively long in duration, as compared to the short vowels; (2) that the tongue is in a relatively high position, almost touching the roof of the mouth; (3) that the front part of the tongue is in this high position; and (4) that the lips are not rounded. Similarly, *ee* can be described as a long mid front unrounded vowel; *uu* as a long high back rounded vowel; *oo* as a long mid back rounded vowel; and *aa* as a long low central unrounded vowel. These facts about the five long vowels of Iraqi can be shown in the form of a chart, as follows:

	FRONT Unrounded	CENTRAL Unrounded	BACK Rounded
HIGH	*ii*		*uu*
MID	*ee*		*oo*
LOW		*aa*	

In the case of *aa,* although we label it "central" for the sake of convenience, you will recall from Section C that it has a fairly wide range of qualities: not only a central quality, as in *calm,* but also a more front quality, as in *has,* and in some environments even a more back quality, as in *cause* (but with unrounded lips). In any event, it is always distinguished from the other long vowels by being low rather than mid or high.

The following drills will illustrate contrasts among the five long vowels. You may find the distinction between *ii* and *ee* and between *uu* and *oo* a little harder to hear and reproduce than the others, and the last two drills below are devoted to these cases.

Drill 16. Long vowel contrasts. Listen and repeat.

↓ *jiib - jeeb*	*šaaf - šuuf*
giis - gaas	*naam - noom*
biik - buub	*buuz - biik*
ðiič - ðook	*muus - meez*
gees - giis	*buub - baab*
jeeb - jaab	*šuuf - šoof*
been - buuz	*boos - biik*
meez - mooz	*gooz - geej*
jaab - jiib	*ðook - ðaak*
gaas - gees	*koom - kuun*

Drill 17. Contrast between long vowels *ii* and *ee*. Listen and repeat.

↓ *bii - beeš*	*šeeb - šiiš*
šii - šeeb	*gees - giis*
biik - been	*čeef - čiis*
jiib - jeeb	*peek - piip*

Drill 18. Contrast between long vowels *uu* and *oo*. Listen and repeat.

↓ *muu - mooz*	*koom - kuun*
θuum - θoob	*mooj - muus*
šuuf - šoof	*gooz - guum*

I. Automatic stress (1)

Stress is the relative loudness of one syllable over others in a word. In English, for example, stress falls on the first syllable of *apple* and *animal,* and on the second syllable of *appeal* and *enamel*. With certain overall limitations, stress in English is unpredictable—that is, there is nothing in the syllable structure of a word or in the consonant-vowel arrangement in a word which automatically determines where the stress will fall. To take three random examples, it falls on the first syllable of *interlude,* on the second syllable of *interpret,* and on the third syllable of *interfere*. Sometimes it is the only feature which distinguishes one word from another, as in the noun *pérmit* and the verb *permít*. In Iraqi, on the other hand, stress usually is predictable, in the sense that if you know what the consonants and vowels of a word are, you can tell where the stress will fall. (There are exceptions, which will be noted as they arise.) The ways of making this kind of prediction can be summarized in a fairly simple statement called the **automatic stress rule,** which we will develop in subsequent units. Here we are concerned with only one aspect of the rule, as follows:

> If the last syllable of a word contains a long vowel, that syllable has the stress.

This statement holds true regardless of the number of syllables in the word and regardless of the presence or absence of other long vowels in preceding syllables. Thus, if you know that the word *jaamuus* 'buffalo' has a long vowel in the last syllable, you can automatically assume that the stress is on the last syllable. The drill below presents a number of two-syllable words, all with a long vowel in the last syllable, and thus all with stress on the last syllable. As you go through the drill, notice for each word that the vowel in the first syllable, though unstressed, is still a long vowel, and be on your guard against the tendency to shorten it or change its quality.

Drill 19. Automatic stress. Listen and repeat.

↓ *jaaboo*	'they brought him'	*jaamuus*	'buffalo'
šaafoo	'they saw him'	*zeeniin*	'good, well P'
šuufii	'look at F him'	*kaabuus*	'nightmare'
šuufuu	'look at P him'	*miizaan*	'scales' (for weight)
naašoo	'they reached him'	*naamuus*	'honor'
gaasoo	'they touched him'	*niisaan*	'April'
giisii	'touch F him'	*niišaan*	'aim'
giisuu	'touch P him'	*čaakuuč*	'hammer'

UNIT 2

A. Short vowel *a*

As we mentioned in 1 B, this vowel has a fairly wide range of qualities, depending on what consonants precede or follow it. In the examples below, the quality ranges generally around that of the vowel in English *pat,* in some cases toward that of *pet* or *pot* (the latter as said by most Americans other than New Englanders). Later, when we take up other consonants, you will notice that *a* may have other slightly different qualities as well. Remember, as you go through the drills below, that *a* is a short vowel, and guard against any tendency to drawl it out or prolong it.

Note: The examples given from here on will include some words written with a double consonant letter at the end. This is a spelling convention only. As far as pronunciation of the consonant is concerned, there is no difference at all between a single and a double consonant letter at the end of a word. The reason for writing a double consonant in some cases will be explained later.

Drill 1. Short vowel *a*. Listen and repeat.

↓ *baθθ*	'it M transmitted'	*fazz*	'he was startled'
baδδ	'he surpassed'	*fann*	'art'
jazz	'he sheared'	*fačč*	'jaw'
jass	'he felt'	*naθθ*	'it M sprinkled'
δabb	'he threw away'	*wazz*	'geese'
šakk	'doubt'	*wann*	'he moaned'
šagg	'he tore'	*čakk*	'check'

Drill 2. Contrast between English vowels and *a*. Listen and repeat.

bath	→	*baθθ*	fez	→	*fazz*
jazz		*jazz*	fan		*fann*
mass		*jass*	fetch		*fačč*
dab		*δabb*	was		*wazz*
shack		*šakk*	wan		*wann*
shag		*šagg*	check		*čakk*

Drill 3. Contrast between long vowel *aa* and short vowel *a*. Listen and repeat.

baab	→	*δabb*		*faas*	→	*jass*
δaak		*čaan*	*šakk*			*fann*

Drill 4. Short vowel *a* in unstressed syllables. (Even when unstressed, *a* retains the same qualities described above: it does not become an "uh" sound as in the first syllable of English *malign, collide, support.*) Listen and repeat.

↓ *jabaan*	'coward'	*zawaaj*	'marriage'
jafaaf	'drought'	*maziij*	'mixture'
dawaam	'working hours'	*nasiij*	'textiles'

Drill 5. Contrast between long vowel *aa* and short vowel *a* in unstressed syllables. Listen and repeat.

jaamuus	→	*jabaan*	*naamuus*	→	*nasiij*
kaabuus		*jafaaf*	*čaakuuč*		*maziij*

Drill 6. Short vowel *a.* (In listening to these examples, notice particularly that the vowel has the same length (that is, short) wherever it occurs. You may find that you have a tendency to hold it a little longer in repeating the words in the second column and the words after the dash in the third, because, in English, vowels are automatically a little longer before voiced consonants than before voiceless. This is not true in Iraqi, however, so imitate carefully what you hear.) Listen and repeat.

↓ *fačč*	*δabb*	*baθθ - baδδ*
baθθ	*wazz*	*jass - jazz*
čakk	*baδδ*	*šakk - šagg*
jass	*šagg*	*fačč - fann*
naθθ	*fann*	*čakk - wann*
šakk	*jazz*	*jass - fazz*

B. Automatic stress (2)

In 1 I we began to discuss the position of stress in Iraqi words, and noted as one aspect of the automatic stress rule that if the last syllable of a word contains a long vowel, that syllable has the stress, as in *naamuus* 'honor' or *zawaaj* 'marriage.' Now we can proceed one step further and note the following:

> In a two-syllable word, if the last syllable ends in a short vowel, the preceding syllable has the stress.

Thus words like those in the drill below, which end in a short *a,* all have stress on the next-to-last syllable (that is, on the first syllable). In going through this drill, note that the final *a* in these Iraqi words, though unstressed, still has the same qualities as it does when stressed. When you repeat the words, do not allow the final *a* to become an "uh" sound as in English *sofa* or *Edna*.

Drill 7. Automatic stress. Listen and repeat.

jaaba	'he brought him'	*suuga*	'drive M him'
gaasa	'he touched him'	*boosa*	'kiss'
jiiba	'bring M him'	*mooza*	'banana'
biina	'in us'	*jeeba*	'his pocket'
muusa	'his razor blade'	*zeena*	'good F'

C. Short vowel *i*

This vowel, like others, has a certain range of qualities, depending on the consonants it precedes and follows, and also on its position in the word. At the end of a word it has a quality like that of the long vowel *ii*, but it is shorter in duration.

Drill 8. Short vowel *i* in final position. Listen and repeat.

↓ *baači*	'having cried M'	*jiibi*	'bring F'
θaani	'second M'	*giisi*	'touch F'
naasi	'having forgotten M'	*šuufi*	'look F'
bači	'crying'	*muusi*	'my razor blade'
sagi	'irrigation'	*θoobi*	'my shirt'
nabi	'prophet'	*jeebi*	'my pocket'

When *i* is not in final position, its qualities range from the short version of *ii* just described to the vowel sound in English *fit*. In the examples given in the following drill it is more like the vowel of *fit*.

Drill 9. Short vowel *i* in non-final position. Listen and repeat.

↓ *δibb*	'throw away M'	*bina*	'he built'
simm	'poison'	*bača*	'he cried'
sinn	'tooth'	*sima*	'sky'
šimm	'smell M'	*fina*	'he destroyed'
fišš	'deflate M'	*nisa*	'he forgot'
mišš	'dust off M'	*niša*	'starch'
min	'from'	*čima*	'truffles'

Later, when we take up other consonants, you will notice that *i* may have some other slightly different qualities as well.

D. Short vowel *u*

This vowel, like *i,* has a range of qualities, depending on the consonants it precedes and follows, and also on its position in the word. At the end of a word it has a quality like that of the long vowel *uu,* but it is shorter in duration.

Drill 10. Short vowel *u* in final position. Listen and repeat.

↓ *saawu*	'level P'	*buusu*	'kiss P'
šaafu	'cure P'	*buugu*	'steal P'
naamu	'sleep P'	*šuufu*	'look P'
jiibu	'bring P'	*kuunu*	'be P'
giisu	'touch P'	*guumu*	'get up P'

When *u* is not in final position, its qualities range from the short version of *uu,* as described above, to a vowel sound like that in English *foot,* but with the lips more rounded. In the examples given in the following drill it is more like the latter.

Drill 11. Short vowel *u* in non-final position. Listen and repeat.

↓ *šugg*	'tear M'	*kuff*	'hem M'
fukk	'open M'	*wučč*	'face'
kušš	'shoo away M'	*čukk*	'jab M'

Drill 12. Contrast between an English vowel and *u.* Listen and repeat.

sugar	→	*šugg*	hoof	→	*kuff*
book		*fukk*	butch		*wučč*
push		*kušš*	hook		*čukk*

Later, when we take up other consonants, you will notice that *u* may have some other slightly different qualities as well.

E. Medial consonant clusters

A **consonant cluster** is a series of two or more consonant sounds not separated by any vowel, for example the *st* in the English words *steps, pester,* and *rest.* Depending on its position within the word, a cluster is classified as **initial, medial,** or **final,** as illustrated respectively by the three examples just given. In Iraqi, clusters of three or more consonants are very rare in any position, and final clusters of even two consonants are also somewhat rare. Initial clusters of two consonants, however, are quite common; these will be discussed in a later unit. Medial clusters of two consonants are extremely common; in fact, most of the theoretically possible two-consonant combinations actually do occur. The examples given below illustrate only a few of these.

Drill 13. Medial consonant clusters. Listen and repeat.

saakna	'living F'	*jibnaa*	'we brought him'
čaaδba	'having lied F'	*šifnaa*	'we saw him'
θanya	'fold'	*yinsuu*	'they forget him'
šakwa	'complaint'	*samnaan*	'having grown fat M'
nafsi	'myself'	*miskiin*	'poor, unlucky M'
čiswa	'bathing trunks'	*majnuun*	'crazy M'
niksib	'we earn'	*masmuum*	'poisoned M'
yikšif	'he reveals'	*mamnuun*	'grateful M'

F. Medial double consonants

A **double consonant** may be thought of as a special kind of two-consonant cluster in which the two are identical. In English, double consonants within a simple (i.e., non-compound) word are quite rare. (Double consonant *letters* are of course used in the spelling of many words, but we are here talking about *sounds.*) One example, for most speakers, is the double *n* sound in the word *unknown;* another may be the double *l* sound in *coolly,* as opposed to the single *l* sound in coolie. Double consonant sounds occur more commonly, in English, in phrases or compound words when the first element ends with, and the second begins with, the same consonant, for example *top post, hot time, coat-tail, book-case, sub-base, home-maker, pen-knife.* In Iraqi, on the other hand, both single and double consonant sounds occur very commonly within simple words. In speaking or hearing Iraqi, it is just as important to distinguish between a single and double consonant as it is in English to distinguish between, say, a *p* and a *b,* since the difference between the two may alone make the difference between one word and another, or between a real word and a form which will not be understood at all. In terms of articulation, the difference between a single and a double consonant is a matter of relative duration, very much like the difference between a short and a long vowel. In fact, double consonants are sometimes called "long consonants". In the case of spirants and nasals (1 A), a double consonant is produced in the same way as the corresponding single consonant, except that it is slightly prolonged, or held—for approximately two beats of time instead of one. Some examples are given below.

Drill 14. Medial double spirant and nasal consonants. Listen and repeat.

↓ *kaffa*	'it M sufficed'	*wazza*	'goose'
kuffi	'hem F'	*bazzuun*	'cat M'
baθθa	'it M transmitted it M'	*naššа*	'he starched'
jiθθa	'corpse'	*kaššaaf*	'boy scout'
čaδδab	'he told lies'	*samma*	'he named'
čaδδaab	'liar M'	*yamma*	'beside him'
bassam	'he smiled'	*minna*	'from him'
jassa	'he felt it M'	*fannaan*	'artist M'

In the case of double stops, it is the moment of complete closure which is slightly prolonged—the moment during which the breathstream is completely cut off and no sound at all is heard. Thus in the production of a double stop there are three stages: first, the closure is made; second, it is held for an additional beat instead of being released immediately as in a single stop; and third, it is released. An example is the sequence *b b* in English *sub-base*. In the case of double affricates, the first stage is a complete closure like that of a stop, the second stage is a moment during which that closure is held, and the third stage is the spirant-like release typical of affricates in general. For the two Iraqi affricates *č* and *j*, this means that a double *čč* sounds very much like the sequence *t ch* in English *hat check*, and the double *jj* like the sequence *d j* in English *bed jacket*. Here are some examples.

Drill 15. Medial double stop and affricate consonants. Listen and repeat.

↓ *δibba*	'throw M it M away'	*fačča*	'his jaw'
yabbas	'he dried'	*sičča*	'rail'
makka	'Mecca'	*siččiin*	'knife'
čukka	'jab M him'	*fajja*	'he split it M'
šagga	'he tore it M'	*najjam*	'he soared'
naggas	'he dirtied'	*sajjaan*	'jailer'

In all the examples thus far given, the double consonant is preceded by a short vowel. There are also words in which a double consonant is preceded by a long vowel. In practicing these, try to keep from shortening either the vowel or the consonant.

Drill 16. Medial double consonants preceded by a long vowel. Listen and repeat.

↓ *baaθθa*	'having transmitted F'	*δaabba*	'having thrown away F'
baaδδa	'outstanding F'	*saamma*	'poisonous F'
jaaffa	'dry F'	*šaagga*	'having torn F'

The last drill provides practice in distinguishing between single and double consonants.

Drill 17. Contrast between medial single and double consonants. Listen and repeat.

šifa	'he got well'	→	*šiffa*	'lip'
jiθaθ	'corpses'		*jiθθa*	'corpse'
jaδib	'attracting'		*čaδδib*	'tell lies M'
masa	'evening'		*massa*	'he spent the evening'
mazig	'tearing'		*mazzig*	'tear up M'
maši	'walking'		*mašši*	'make go M'
šamis	'sun'		*šammis*	'put in the sun M'
bina	'he built'		*činna*	'we were'
sabab	'cause'		*sabbab*	'he caused'
δaki	'clever M'		*šakki*	'allow to complain M'
saguf	'ceiling'		*sagguf*	'put a roof on M'
bači	'crying'		*bačči*	'make cry M'
sijan	'he jailed'		*fijja*	'small rug'

UNIT 3

A. Consonant *t*

The Iraqi *t* is a **voiceless dental stop.** It is similar to the English *t* sound in *take,* but there is one difference between the two. Say the word *take* aloud several times, and you will notice that to produce the *t* sound the tip of the tongue touches the roof of the mouth somewhere on the gum-ridge, behind the upper teeth. For the Iraqi *t*, on the other hand, the tip of the tongue touches farther forward, at the point where the upper teeth emerge from the gum, so that the tongue-tip actually touches both the gum and the back of the upper teeth at the same time. This may not seem like a great difference, but it is an important one, because if you make an Iraqi *t* just like your normal English one, it is likely to be mistaken for another kind of Iraqi *t* sound which will be taken up later, and you will find that you have said a word you did not mean at all.

Drill 1. Contrast between English and Iraqi initial and final *t*. Listen and repeat.

tab →	*taab*	'he repented'	bat →	*baat*	'he spent the night'
teen	*tiin*	'figs'	bait	*beet*	'house'
tome	*toom*	'twins'	moat	*moot*	'death'

Drill 2. Initial and final *t*. Listen and repeat.

↓ *taabuut*	'coffin'	*faat*	'he passed'
tanak	'tin'	*beet*	'house'
tamaam	'exact M'	*jeet*	'I came'
tammuuz	'July'	*zeet*	'oil'
tiin	'figs'	*moot*	'death'
tikit	'ticket'	*muut*	'die M'
timman	'rice'	*naamat*	'she slept'
tinsa	'you M forget'	*nisat*	'she forgot'
tiktib	'you M write'	*šifit*	'I saw'
toom	'twins'	*δabbeet*	'I threw away'
tuunis	'Tunis'	*sammeet*	'I named'

In normal-speed American English, the *t* sound in certain environments is a **flap** rather than a stop. This flap *t* is made by a very rapid flick of the tongue-tip against the gum-ridge. It commonly occurs, for example, when the *t* is between two vowel sounds of which the second has weak stress, as in *attic, city, matter,* and *catapult.* (Contrast the (first) *t* sound in those words with that in *tick, satirical, material,* and *catastrophe.*) In Iraqi, on the other hand, the *t* never has this flap quality, but is invariably a voiceless dental stop as described at the beginning of this section. Thus, when speaking Iraqi, you will have to guard against the English-speech habit of automatically using the flap *t* in certain positions, for if you use it in Iraqi it will be mistaken for a totally different sound which we will take up later. The following drill provides practice.

Drill 3. Medial *t* between vowels. Listen and repeat.

↓ *beeta*	'his house'	*mitan*	'it M grew thick'
jeeti	'you F came'	*nitaj*	'it M resulted'
maatat	'she died'	*titin*	'tobacco'
šita	'winter'	*čitif*	'shoulder'
kitab	'he write'	*kutub*	'books'

The following drill illustrates the double *tt*. When practicing this, remember that the tongue-tip touches the back of the upper teeth, as for the single *t*, and that this closure is held for a brief moment longer before release.

Drill 4. Double *tt*. Listen and repeat.

↓ *jatti*	'she came'	*fattat*	'he crumbled'
sitta	'six'	*fattaan*	'tattletale'
šattam	'he cursed'	*sittiin*	'sixty'

B. Consonant *d*

The Iraqi *d* is a **voiced dental stop.** It is produced in the same way as the Iraqi *t*, except that it is voiced. It differs from English *d* as in *date* in the same way as Iraqi *t* differs from English *t*: for the Iraqi *d* the tongue-tip touches the back of the upper teeth.

Drill 5. Initial and final *d*. Listen and repeat.

↓ *diin*	'religion'	*faad*	'it M benefitted'
deen	'debt'	*sadd*	'dam'
damm	'blood'	*sidd*	'close M'
dijaaj	'chicken'	*majiid*	(man's name)

In Section A above we noted that for speakers of American English the consonant *t* in certain environments is a flap rather than a stop. The same is true of *d*. Note the flap *d* in these words: *lady, caddie, pedestal;* and contrast it with the stop *d* in these: *deep, cadet, pedestrian.* In Iraqi, however, the *d* never has the flap quality; it is always a voiced dental stop as described above. The following drill provides practice.

Drill 6. Medial *d* between vowels. Listen and repeat.

↓ *badu*	'Bedouins'	*naadi*	'club'
bida	'he began'	*duuda*	'worm'
nadif	'carding'	*sooda*	'black F'
sudus	'one-sixth'	*saadis*	'sixth'

Drill 7. Double *dd.* Listen and repeat.

↓ *yadda*	'handle'	*saddeet*	'I closed'
mudda	'a while'	*šaddeet*	'I fastened'
saddad	'he paid off'	*faddaan*	(measure of land)
jiddan	'very'	*giddaam*	'in front of'

C. Consonant *l*

This Iraqi consonant is a **voiced dental lateral.** A lateral is a sound in which the breathstream is blocked at the center of the oral passage, usually by the tongue, but continues to pass through along the sides. The Iraqi *l* has a quite different sound from the normal American English *l.* Say the English word *mill* aloud several times very slowly, and you will notice that the *l* has what is sometimes called a "dark" or "heavy" quality: the first part of the word is like the first part of *miss,* but the *l* seems to be preceded by a kind of "uh" sound, so that the last part of the word is like the last part of *mull*—something like "mih-ull". This effect is caused by the gradual movement of the tongue, as the word progresses, from its position for the vowel to its position for the *l.* Say the word again, and this time prolong the *l* at the end as long as you can, and notice the position of your tongue. The front part is touching the roof of the mouth on the ridge behind the upper teeth, while the air passes through along the sides, but the back part of the tongue—and this may be harder to feel at first—is raised slightly higher than the middle part, so that the tongue surface has a somewhat concave shape. Iraqi too has one kind of *l* sound which is made in this way and sounds approximately the same; it is one of a number of consonants called emphatics, and will be taken up in a later unit. The kind of *l* we are now concerned with—the plain *l*—is not very common in American English. For some speakers it occurs at the beginning of some words such as *leaf,* especially when followed by the vowel sound of that word. For some speakers, also, it occurs in the word *million.* Say this word, and try to cut it off just before you come to the *y* sound in the second syllable. If the kind of *l* you hear there sounds different from the kind you usually make in the word *mill,* then the former is probably fairly close to the Iraqi (plain) *l.* For this Iraqi sound, the front part of the tongue touches the forward part of the gum ridge just behind, and sometimes touching, the upper teeth, and the air passes through along the sides of the tongue; but the central and back parts of the tongue form a fairly regular slope, without the concave shape mentioned above. The first drill below illustrates the difference between the usual heavy English *l* and the Iraqi plain *l.* The difference will probably be easiest to hear at the end of a word, as in the first examples below, but the difference is there in other positions as well. In repeating the Iraqi words, try to make each *l* different from the *l* in the corresponding English word, and of course also notice and imitate differences in other consonants and in the vowels.

Drill 8. Contrast between English and Iraqi *l*. Listen and repeat.

tell	→	*tall*	'hill'	laugh	→	*laff*	'he wrapped'
shell		*šall*	'he paralysed'	lamb		*laam*	'he blamed'
sill		*sill*	'tuberculosis'	loan		*loon*	'color'
moll		*maal*	'he leaned'	Molly		*maali*	'mine'
feel		*fiil*	'elephant'	belly		*bali*	'yes'
ghoul		*guul*	'say M'	fill 'im		*filim*	'film'
tail		*teel*	'wire'	Phyllis		*filis*	'penny'
knoll		*nool*	'loom'	skillet		*gilit*	'I said'

Some additional examples of Iraqi *l* are provided in the following drills.

Note: The examples given from here on will include some forms written with a hyphen. As far as pronunciation is concerned, these forms can be regarded as single words, the same as if written all together. The reason for the hyphen will be explained later.

Drill 9. Consonant *l*. Listen and repeat.

↓ *laabis*	'wearing M'	*badla*	'suit, dress'
laazim	'necessary M'	*jiib-li*	'bring M to me'
liilu	'pearls'	*balwa*	'trouble'
leeš	'why?'	*čilma*	'word'
leela	'night'	*šaal*	'he picked up'
looz	'almonds'	*gaal*	'he said'
lamm	'he collected'	*miil*	'mile'
libas	'he put on'	*guul*	'say M'
lizag	'he pasted'	*δeel*	'tail'
malik	'king'	*δool*	'these'
walad	'boy'	*daliil*	'guide'
šiilu	'pick up P'	*faaluul*	'warts'

Drill 10. Double *ll*. Listen and repeat.

↓ *falla*	'excellent'	*kallaf*	'it M cost'
kalla	'sugar-loaf'	*sallim*	'greet M'
gal-la	'he told him'	*čallib*	'hang M'
gul-li	'tell M me'	*sallaat*	'baskets'
θallaj	'he froze'	*čillaab*	'hook'
dallal	'he pampered'	*bil-leel*	'at night'

D. Diphthongs *aaw* and *aw*

A diphthong is a sequence of two or more vowel (or vowel-like) sounds in the same syllable. Diphthongs in English, for example, include the vowel sequences of *bout, bite,* and *joint.* In Iraqi, all diphthongs consist of two elements: (1) a long or short vowel, and (2) a semivowel *w* or *y.* A semivowel, as we noted in 1 A, is a sound which functions like a consonant in the language but has a phonetic quality very much like some vowel. (The meaning of the phrase "functions like a consonant" will become clearer to you later on, but we can give one illustration here: both *w* and *y,* like any other consonant, can occur doubled between vowels, as in *jawwa* 'under' and *jayya* 'coming'.) The phonetic quality of *w* is close to that of the vowel *uu,* but shorter in duration—something like the vowel of English *boot;* and the phonetic quality of *y* is close to that of the vowel *ii,* but shorter in duration—something like the vowel of English *feet.* Thus all Iraqi diphthongs begin with some vowel sound, and end with a quick smooth glide into a sound like the vowel of English *boot* (*w*) or into a sound like the vowel of English *feet* (*y*). In this unit we take up two of the most common.

The diphthong *aaw* consists of the long vowel *aa* followed smoothly by a glide into a vowel sound like that of English *boot.* The whole sequence is somewhat like the vowel sequence in the English word *rouse* or *cows;* but in practicing it you should remember three things: first, that the *aa* element is closer in quality to the vowel of *calm* than to the vowel of *has;* that the *aa* element is a long vowel and should be held for the appropriate length of time; and that the *w* element at the end is produced with somewhat tenser and more rounded lips than the corresponding glide in English. Here are some examples.

Drill 11. Diphthong *aaw.* Listen and repeat.

↓ *faaw*	'Faw' (Iraqi town)	*jaawbat*	'she answered'
waaw	(an Arabic letter)	*daawmat*	'she continued'
kaawli	'gypsy'	*naawšat*	'she handed'

The diphthong *aw* consists of the short vowel *a* followed by the same glide as above. It is similar to the vowel sequence in English *bout,* but is uttered in a more clipped fashion, without any drawling, and the *w* element at the end is produced with tenser and more rounded lips. Examples follow.

Note: In the examples below, and elsewhere in this book, you will notice that the diphthong *aw* is written "aw" in some words and "aww" in others. The reason for this will be explained later; for now you need only note that both spellings represent the same pronunciation.

Drill 12. Diphthong *aw*. Listen and repeat.

↓ *jaww*	'weather'	*kawkab*	'planet'
mawja	'wave' (radio)	*mawjuud*	'present M'
mawwta	'beat M him up'	*mawsim*	'season'
šawwfat	'she showed'	*nisaw*	'they forgot'
nawwmat	'she put to bed'	*šaafaw*	'they saw'

It is important to make a clear distinction of length between *aaw* and *aw*. The following drill will illustrate.

Drill 13. Contrast between *aaw* and *aw*. Listen and repeat.

faaw	→	*jaww*
kaawli		*kawkab*
jaawbat		*šawwfat*
naawšat		*nawwmat*

E. Medial double *ww*

Like any other consonant (see 2 F), *w* may occur double in the middle of a word between two vowels, as for example in *sawwa* 'he made'. When the preceding vowel is *a*, as in this word, it and the first *w* together form the diphthong *aw*, as described in the preceding section; thus the first syllable of *sawwa* rhymes with the first syllable of *mawja* or *kawkab*. The second *w* begins the next syllable, and sounds like English *w* in *wait* or *well*. Here are some examples.

Drill 14. Medial double *ww* preceded by *a*. Listen and repeat.

↓ *jawwa*	'under'	*lawwin*	'color M'
sawwa	'he made'	*kawwum*	'pile up M'
bawwab	'he classified'	*sawwuu*	'make P him'
δawwab	'he dissolved'	*sawwoo*	'they made him'
sawwi	'make M'	*sawweet*	'I made'
sawwu	'make P'	*bawwaag*	'thief'

When the preceding vowel is *u*, it and the first *w* together form the sequence *uw*, which sounds very much like the long vowel *uu*. The second *w* begins the next syllable and, as above, sounds like English *w* in *wait* or *well*.

Drill 15. Medial double *ww* preceded by *u*. Listen and repeat.

↓ *juwwa*	'flower-bed'
nuwwaab	'delegates'

Drill 16. Contrast between single *w* and double *ww*. Listen and repeat.

šawi	'roasting'	→	*šawwi*	'roast M'
čawi	'burning'		*čawwi*	'burn M'
dawaam	'working hours'		*sawwaa*	'he made him'
zawaaj	'marriage'		*bawwaag*	'thief'
duwa	'medicine'		*juwwa*	'flower-bed'

F. Syllable structure; automatic stress (3)

In preceding units we have noted that stress falls automatically on the last syllable of a word if that syllable contains a long vowel (1 I), and on the first syllable of a two-syllable word ending in a short vowel (2 B). We are now ready to make a more comprehensive statement about automatic stress, covering these cases and others as well. In order to do this, however, we must first make some general comments on Iraqi syllable structure. Three matters are important: the number of syllables in a word, the point of division between one syllable and the next, and the distinction between long and short syllables.

There are as many syllables in an Iraqi word as there are vowels, both long and short vowels counting as one each. Thus we can tell that there is one syllable in *beet* 'house' and *dazz* 'he sent', two in *beeta* 'his house' and *dazzat* 'she sent', three in *siinama* 'movies' and *dazzatni* 'she sent me', and so on. The question of stress, of course, arises only in words of two or more syllables, so we will not consider one-syllable words further in this section.

The first syllable of an Iraqi word may begin with one consonant or two, but every syllable other than the first always begins with one consonant only. Thus, whenever there are two consonants or a double consonant in the middle of a word, the point of syllable division is between the two. Some examples are given below, with syllable division marked by hyphens. (Note: For reasons to be explained later, some words in this book are spelled with a sequence consisting of a double consonant *letter* followed by a single consonant letter, for example *zzn* in *dazzni* 'he sent me' and *wwf* in *šawwfat* 'she showed'. In such cases the double consonant letter always represents a single consonant *sound,* and of course the following consonant letter represents another single consonant sound; therefore the point of syllable division, as in any word, is between the two consonant sounds, as indicated in 4 and 7 below. On the other hand, when a double consonant letter is followed by a vowel, it always represents a double consonant sound, and the point of syllable division is between the two consonant elements, as in 2, 5, and 8 below.)

1. *čaa-kuuč* 'hammer'
2. *duk-kaan* 'shop'
3. *waz-na* (a weight)
4. *dazz-ni* 'he sent me'
5. *daz-zat* 'she sent'
6. *maw-sim* 'season'
7. *šaww-fat* 'she showed'
8. *jaw-wa* 'under'
9. *šaa-yif* 'having seen M'
10. *šaa-yif-ni* 'having seen M me'
11. *mak-ta-ba* 'library'
12. *mak-ta-bat-na* 'our library'
13. *ni-sa* 'he forgot'
14. *kitab* 'he wrote'
15. *bi-naw* 'they built'
16. *ta-na-ka* 'can'

We define a **long syllable** as any syllable which contains (1) a long vowel, or (2) a short vowel followed immediately in the same word (not necessarily in the same syllable) by two consonants or a double consonant. A **short syllable** is one containing a short vowel followed immediately in the same word by a single consonant or by none. Thus, in the examples given above, the long syllables are: both syllables of 1 and 2, the first syllable of 3 through 9, the first and second syllables of 10, the first syllable of 11, and the first and third syllables of 12. The other syllables, including all those of 13 through 16, are short.

With the foregoing comments on syllable structure in mind, we can proceed to the formulation of a statement by means of which we can predict the position of stress in the great majority of Iraqi words. (There are a few exceptions, which will be noted as they arise.) The statement, known as the ***automatic stress rule,*** is as follows:

> Stress may fall only on one of the last three syllables of a word.
> If there are long syllables among the last three, stress falls on the long syllable nearest the end of the word.
> If there are no long syllables among the last three, stress falls on the next-to-last syllable in two-syllable words and on the third-from-last syllable in all others.

To illustrate how this rule is applied, we list the above examples again, this time without showing syllable division, but indicating the position of stress by an acute accent mark placed over the vowel of the stressed syllable.

1. *čaakúuč*
2. *dukkáan*
3. *wázna*
4. *dázzni*
5. *dázzat*
6. *máwsim*
7. *šáwwfat*
8. *jáwwa*
9. *šáayif*
10. *šaayífni*
11. *máktaba*
12. *maktabátna*
13. *nísa*
14. *kítab*
15. *bínaw*
16. *tánaka*

Notice particularly in 9 and 10 above, and again in 11 and 12, how the position of stress automatically shifts from one syllable to another when elements are added to or removed from a word.

Following are some drills on stress. In these drills, and from now on, the position of stress will not be marked except in those few cases where it deviates from the automatic stress rule. Your goal is to become so accustomed to the stress patterns of the language, as described in the rule, that you automatically stress the proper syllable as a matter of unconscious habit, just as the Iraqis do themselves.

Drill 17. Automatic stress on last syllable. Listen and repeat.

↓ *binoo*	'they built it M'	*niswaan*	'women'
ligaa	'he found him'	*mamnuun*	'grateful M'
dawaam	'working hours'	*δabboo*	'they threw it M away'
zawaaj	'marriage'	*minnaa*	'from here'
šaafoo	'they saw him'	*čaδδaab*	'liar M'
šuufii	'look at F him'	*sammeet*	'I named'
zeeniin	'good, well P'	*sanawaat*	'years'
moozaat	'bananas'	*stilamnaa*	'we received it M'
tinsii	'you F forget him'	*makaatiib*	'letters'
yibnuu	'they build it M'	*sammeenaa*	'we named him'

Drill 18. Automatic stress on next-to-last syllable. Listen and repeat.

↓ *liga*	'he found'	*zawaaja*	'his marriage'
sana	'year'	*makiina*	'machine'
ligat	'she found'	*šaafooni*	'they saw me'
sabab	'cause'	*foogaani*	'upper M'
jiiba	'bring M him'	*difanta*	'I buried him'
beeta	'his house'	*jaawabta*	'I answered him'
nafsi	'myself'	*naawušni*	'hand M to me'
damma	'his blood'	*jaddadna*	'we renewed'
niktib	'we write'	*wannasna*	'we amused'
wannas	'he amused'	*maktabatna*	'our library'
yaakul	'he eats'	*makiinatna*	'our machine'

Drill 19. Automatic stress on third-from-last syllable. Listen and repeat.

↓ *siinama*	'movies'	*mujaadala*	'debate'
neešana	'aiming'	*mujaazafa*	'adventure'
tanaka	'can'	*mujaamala*	'courtesy'
θakana	'barracks'	*mudaawala*	'conference'
sanawi	'yearly M'	*mumaθθila*	'actress'

UNIT 4

A. Consonant *h*

The Iraqi *h,* like the English *h* sound, is a **voiceless glottal spirant:** the vocal cords are held open, and the breathstream passes through the space between them (the **glottis**) with a little friction noise, not much more than in ordinary breathing. For a speaker of English there is nothing difficult about the sound of the Iraqi *h,* as it is quite similar to the English *h* sound in *hope* or *ahead.* The only difficulty lies in its **distribution,** meaning the various positions in which it occurs in a word. In English, the *h* sound occurs only before a vowel (and, for some speakers, a semi-vowel) ; whereas in Iraqi, the *h* may occur not only before a vowel but also before another consonant or at the end of a word. Speakers of English, therefore, will find a certain amount of practice necessary in order to become accustomed to producing the *h* in all these positions. The first drill below illustrates *h* before a vowel, as in English.

Drill 1. Consonant *h* before a vowel. Listen and repeat.

↓ *haaδa*	'this M'	*jaahil*	'child M'
hadaf	'target'	*dihin*	'grease'
hawa	'air'	*nisaaha*	'he forgot her'
hiič	'thus, so'	*šaafhum*	'he saw them'
hooš	'cattle'	*minha*	'from her'
hoosa	'riot'	*mafhuum*	'understood M'

Like any Iraqi consonant, *h* can occur doubled. For this, simply keep the breath moving out for a fraction longer than for the single *h.*

Drill 2. Double *hh.* Listen and repeat.

↓ *dahhan*	'he greased'	*sahhal*	'he simplified'
δahhab	'he gilded'	*fahham*	'he explained'

Drill 3. Contrast between single *h* and double *hh.* Listen and repeat.

dihin	'grease'	→	*dahhin*	'grease M'
δahab	'gold'		*δahhab*	'he gilded'
sahil	'easy M'		*sahhil*	'simplify M'
fahim	'understanding'		*fahhim*	'explain M'

The following drill illustrates *h* before another consonant and at the end of a word. In repeating these examples, make sure that for each *h* you produce a slight but audible puff of breath.

Drill 4. Consonant *h* before a consonant and final. Listen and repeat.

↓ *dahša*	'surprise'	*taah*	'he strayed'
zahdi	(kind of date)	*šaah*	'king' (chess)
sahla	'easy F'	*šibah*	'he resembled'
gahwa	'coffee'	*šibih*	'resemblance'
zahgaan	'fed up M'	*šabiih*	'similar'
lahjaat	'dialects'	*naziih*	'honest'

B. Consonant *r*

The first and most important thing to be said about the Iraqi sound which we symbolize *r* is that it is *not at all* like the American English sound represented by the same letter. Say the following words aloud several times and notice what your tongue and lips do to produce the normal American English *r* sound:

↓ rat	carry
run	hurry
rob	sorry

The front part of the tongue retracts and the tip curls slightly up and back; at no point does the tip touch the roof of the mouth. At the same time, the lips move to a slightly rounded position, a movement of which you may not be aware but which you can observe in a mirror. The sound thus produced is quite unlike the Iraqi *r*, or for that matter any Iraqi sound.

Now say the following words aloud several times and notice what your tongue does to produce the second consonant sound in each word. Don't say them in a slow, artificial way, syllable by syllable, but say each word as a whole, at normal speed.

caddie
buddy
body

In words like these most speakers of American English make a flap sound; that is, the tip of the tongue flicks up and very briefly touches the gum ridge behind the upper teeth (see also 3 A and B). The result is a different sound from that of English *d* at the beginning of a word. Contrast the *d* sounds in each of the following pairs:

a dam	→	Adam
a duck		paddock
a dish		radish

The flap *d* is also quite different from the American English *r* sound in the same position. Contrast the following pairs:

carry	→	caddie
hurry		buddy
sorry		body
harem		Adam
barrack		paddock
garish		radish

The Iraqi sound which we symbolize *r* is very similar to the American English *d* sound in such words as those in the right-hand column above. It is classified as a **voiced dental flap,** and is produced by a very brief flick of the tongue-tip against the gum just behind the upper teeth. Whereas the flap variety of English *d* occurs only between two vowel sounds of which the second has weak stress, the Iraqi *r* is always a flap no matter what its position in a word. The following drills illustrate *r* in various positions.

Drill 5. Medial *r* between two vowels. Listen and repeat.

↓ *baarid*	'cold M'	*bariid*	'mail'
daari	'take care of M'	*kariim*	'generous M'
tirak	'he left'	*giriib*	'close M'
diras	'he studied'	*kaaruuk*	'cradle'
juru	'puppy'	*jariida*	'newspaper'
biira	'beer'	*jariima*	'crime'
jigaara	'cigarette'	*dirasna*	'we studied'
kuura	'hive'	*jiiraan*	'neighbor'

Drill 6. Medial *r* preceded or followed by another consonant. Listen and repeat.

↓ *kabraan*	'grown up M'	*tartiib*	'arrangement'
sitra	'jacket'	*warda*	'flower'
matruus	'filled M'	*sirdaab*	'basement'
madrasa	'school'	*markaz*	'police station'
tadriib	'training'	*warga*	'leaf'
sakraan	'drunk M'	*surgi*	'bolt'
safra	'trip'	*darbuuna*	'alley'
kisrat	'she broke'	*darzan*	'dozen'
jizra	'carrot'	*čarčaf*	'cover'
samra	'brunette F'	*tarjam*	'he translated'
tamriin	'drill'	*barmiil*	'barrel'

Although in general *r* is classified as a voiced sound, you may sometimes hear a voiceless variety when it occurs in certain positions, for example before a voiceless consonant, or at the end of a word as in the examples on the right below.

Drill 7. Initial and final *r*. Listen and repeat.

↓ *raas*	'head'	*biir*	'well'
rasim	'picture'	*door*	'turn, move'
ramiš	'eyelash'	*zaar*	'he visited'
rabu	'asthma'	*seer*	'belt'
risam	'he drew'	*šakar*	'sugar'
rijil	'leg'	*safiir*	'ambassador'
raššaaš	'nozzle'	*diinaar*	'dinar' (Iraqi money)
rijjaal	'man'	*kaafuur*	'camphor'

Like other Iraqi consonants, *r* also commonly occurs double. A double *rr* is more than just two flaps: it is a **trill**; that is, a series of very rapid flaps made by the tip of the tongue vibrating against the gum ridge just behind the upper teeth. This kind of trill does not occur as a speech-sound in English, but small boys may sometimes be heard producing it in imitation of the sound of airplane engines and the like. It is common as the double *rr* of Spanish or Italian.

Drill 8. Double *rr*. Listen and repeat.

↓ *jarrad*	'he deprived'	*karras*	'he devoted'
δarri	'atomic'	*warrad*	'it M bloomed'
darras	'he taught'	*sirri*	'secret M'

C. Consonant ˀ

The sound represented by the symbol ˀ is called a **glottal stop.** In English the glottal stop is not used as a distinctive speech-sound, but all English-speakers nevertheless frequently produce it. It occurs, for example, in the exclamation commonly used when something wrong has just been noticed: "Uh-oh!" If you say this aloud a few times you will hear a slight break—a split second of silence—between the *uh* and the *oh*. This break is the glottal stop. As English-speakers, we tend to think of this feature, if at all, in a negative way, calling it a "break" or a "second of silence", precisely because in English it is not used as a distinctive sound like other stops, say *t* or *k*, and consequently we are not attuned to it or even aware of it. Consider by way of contrast a word like *bucko,* in which the same two vowel sounds are separated by another kind of "break"—but this break happens to be a *k* sound, which is very much a distinctive speech-sound in English, and which we therefore think of not negatively, as a momentary cessation of sound, but positively, as a sound in its own right.

In Iraqi, the glottal stop *ˀ* is a positive speech-sound, just as much as *p, t* and *k.* All these four consonants are stops (see 1 A); that is, in all of them the breathstream is completely cut off for a brief moment and then released. The difference is the point at which this blocking takes place. For a *p,* the air is blocked momentarily when the two lips come together; for a *t,* when the tip of the tongue touches a point behind the upper teeth; for a *k,* when the back part of the tongue touches a point on the velum. For a glottal stop, the air is blocked when the two vocal cords come together, making a complete closure in the **glottis** (the space in the larynx between the two cords). Like the other three stops mentioned above, the glottal stop is voiceless; but unlike them it has no voiced counterpart, since the vocal cords cannot be completely closed and vibrating at the same time.

As we said before, when speaking English we produce glottal stops more often than we realize. For example, besides the exclamation *uh-oh!* mentioned above, we regularly make a glottal stop in two familiar utterances meaning 'no': *unh-unh,* which consists of two nasalized vowel sounds separated by a glottal stop, and *mm-mm* (said with closed lips), which consists of two brief *m*-sounds separated by a glottal stop. Nevertheless we are not aware of the glottal stop in the same sense as we are aware of other speech sounds, and therefore we need a good deal of practice in order to learn to produce it consciously, at will, in various positions in a word. Here are two exercises which may prove helpful to you in learning to gain conscious control of the sound. First, say "ah", as you would for the doctor, then say a series of eight or ten repeated "ah's": *ah-ah-ah-ah-ah-ah-ah-ah.* Make sure that you are not making just one long-drawn-out "aaahhh", but that each individual "ah" is clearly cut off from the next, and don't make each individual one too long. While saying the series, concentrate on what is happening *between* the "ah's", because that is the glottal stop: between each pair of "ah's" your vocal cords come together and draw apart again, thus for a fraction of a second completely cutting off the passage of air through the glottis. If we were to write the same sequence of sounds in Iraqi symbols, it would be *ˀaaˀaaˀaaˀaaˀaaˀaaˀaaˀaa.* Now, instead of saying the series of "ah's" aloud as before, *whisper* it. Again, make sure that the air does not slide through steadily or raggedly, but that it is cut off abruptly and completely after each "ah". Plug your ears with your fingers and listen carefully. You should now hear, between the "ah's", a tiny popping or clicking sound from down in your larynx—that is the glottal stop. Now, keeping your ears plugged, and still whispering, make the individual "ah's" shorter and shorter—don't try to go too fast—until there is practically nothing left of the vowel sounds at all but only the click of the vocal cords opening and closing. Try the same exercise with different vowels: *ʔiiʔiiʔii* . . ., *ʔuuʔuuʔuu* . . ., *ʔooʔooʔoo* . . ., *ʔeeʔeeʔee* . . . . Try listening for the glottal stop without plugging your ears. Try the exercise in a normal voice throughout, without whispering.

A second exercise, which gets to the same goal from a different direction, is the following. Take a medium breath and hold it, keeping your mouth open and your tongue relaxed. At this point your vocal cords are completely closed, holding the air in. Now allow a small puff of air to escape, and cut it off again sharply. You do this, though you may not be aware of it, by opening the vocal cords briefly and closing them again. Pause, let another small puff escape, cut it off, pause, another puff, and so on. Take another breath when necessary. Practice varying the length of the puffs, making some shorter and some longer, as an aid in gaining conscious control of the vocal cord mechanism. Now make each puff shorter and shorter, and finally as short as you possibly can. The result, each time, should be an extremely rapid opening and closing of the vocal cords, and you can probably hear the little click that this makes. Listen with ears plugged, and then with ears unplugged. Practice varying the length of the interval between the clicks.

The Iraqi glottal stop, like other consonant sounds, can occur not only between two vowels but also in various other positions in a word. Given below are drills and comments on all these possibilities.

Drill 9. Medial *ʔ* between two vowels. Listen and repeat.

↓	*siʔal*	'he asked'	*masaaʔil*	'problems'
	riʔas	'he headed'	*kahrabaaʔi*	'electric M'
	yiʔas	'he despaired'	*suʔaal*	'question'
	saaʔil	'having asked M'	*laʔiim*	'mean M'
	haaʔil	'huge M'	*muʔaamara*	'conspiracy'
	daaʔira	'office'	*muʔallif*	'author'

Like any Iraqi consonant, the glottal stop can occur doubled. As in the case of other stops, such as *p, t,* or *k,* doubling a *ʔ* simply means holding the closure a fraction of a second longer than for the single sound. The double *ʔʔ* is not as common as other double stops, however. Here are the most important examples.

Drill 10. Double *ˀˀ*. Listen and repeat.

↓ *raˀˀas*	'he named as head'	*yaˀˀas*	'he discouraged'
saˀˀaal	'inquisitive M'	*yitlaˀˀam*	'he is mean'

The next drill gives examples of *ˀ* at the end of a word. (Some words of this type also have variant forms without the final *ˀ*, but here we are concerned with the forms which have it. In any case you should learn to hear when it occurs and when it does not, and be able to produce it yourself at will.)

Drill 11. Final *ˀ*. Listen and repeat.

↓ *suuˀ*	'evil'	*jariiˀ*	'daring M'
binaaˀ	'construction'	*laajiˀ*	'refugee M'
liwaaˀ	(administrative division)	*naašiˀ*	'resulting M'
bariiˀ	'innocent M'	*haadiˀ*	'calm M'

The glottal stop very commonly occurs immediately preceding or following another consonant in a cluster. Here are examples.

Drill 12. Medial *ˀ* preceding or following another consonant. Listen and repeat.

↓ *taˀjiil*	'postponement'	*masˀuul*	'responsible M'
taˀsiis	'foundation'	*mitˀakkid*	'certain M'
taˀliif	'composition'	*mitˀallim*	'pained M'
taˀmiim	'nationalization'	*mitˀassif*	'sorry M'
raˀsan	'directly'	*masˀala*	'problem'
siˀlat	'she asked'	*jurˀa*	'boldness'
yiˀsaw	'they despaired'	*yisˀal*	'he asks'

The matter of the glottal stop at the beginning of an Iraqi word deserves some comment. In English, words which we think of as beginning with a vowel actually quite often begin with a glottal stop, although we are not usually aware of it. This is most frequently the case when the word is the first, or the only, word in the utterance. Try the following, one at a time: *ox, each, ache, open, all, ouch.* Whisper each one with your ears plugged, and listen for the click of the glottal stop just before each initial vowel. Probably you will hear it in some instances and not in others. In Iraqi, as it happens, the physical facts are quite similar, but they are regarded from the opposite point of view. That is, words which Iraqi-speakers think of as beginning with a glottal stop sometimes actually begin without it, although the speakers are not usually aware of this fact. To put it another way, English-speakers tend not to hear an initial glottal stop even when it is physically there, while Iraqi-speakers tend to hear it even when it is physically not there. In neither language is there a distinction between a word which begins with a glottal stop and an otherwise identical word which begins without it, but the total consonant system of each language leads us to state that in English the words in question begin with a vowel, and that in Iraqi the words in question begin with a glottal stop. Here are examples.

Drill 13. Initial ʔ. Listen and repeat.

↓ *ʔaab*	'August'	*ʔakbar*	'bigger'
ʔaala	'tool'	*ʔaswad*	'black M'
ʔaani	'I'	*ʔii*	'yes'
ʔaadmi	'man'	*ʔiid*	'hand'
ʔab	'father'	*ʔibin*	'son'
ʔaw	'or'	*ʔuuti*	'iron' (for pressing)
ʔakil	'food'	*ʔoozin*	'I weigh'

D. Diphthongs *aay* and *ay*

The diphthong *aay* is a sequence consisting of the long vowel *aa* followed smoothly by a glide into a vowel sound like that of English *feet.* The whole sequence is somewhat like the vowel sequence in the most common American pronunciation of such words as *rise* and *size;* but in practicing it you should remember that the *aa* element is closer in quality to the vowel of *calm* than to any other, that the *aa* element is a long vowel and should be held for the appropriate length of time, and that the *y* element at the end, though short in duration, is more like the vowel of *feet* than that of *fit.*

Drill 14. Diphthong *aay.* Listen and repeat.

↓ *jaay*	'coming M'	*binaayta*	'his building'
naay	'flute'	*daayta*	'his wetnurse'
haay	'this F'	*raayta*	'his banner
yaay	'spring'	*daaynatni*	'she lent me'
čaay	'tea'	*yitbaaynuun*	'they contrast'

The diphthong *ay* is a sequence consisting of the short vowel *a* followed by the same glide as above. In some words it sounds somewhat like the vowel sequence in English *bite* or *fight,* in others more like that of *bait* or *fate,* and in still others like something in between. In any case, in the Iraqi sequence the first element is short—it is important to distinguish this diphthong from *aay* above—and the second element, though short in duration, is more like the vowel of *feet* than that of *fit*.

Note: In the examples below, and elsewhere in this book, you will notice that the diphthong *ay* is written "ay" in some words and "ayy" in others. The reason for this will be explained later; for now you need only note that both spellings represent the same pronunciation.

Drill 15. Diphthong *ay*. Listen and repeat.

↓ *ˀay*	'which?'	*layyna*	'lenient F'
rayy	'irrigation'	*mayyta*	'dead F'
zayy	'costume'	*nayymat*	'she put to bed'
fayy	'shade'	*zayynuuhum*	'shave P them'
jayyta	'his coming'	*yitrayyguun*	'they have breakfast'

Drill 16. Contrast between *aay* and *ay*. Listen and repeat.

jaay	→	*jayyta*
haay		*fayy*
čaay		*zayy*
binaayta		*nayymat*
daayta		*mayyta*
raayta		*rayy*

E. Medial double *yy*

Like any other consonant (see 2 F), *y* may occur double in the middle of a word between two vowels, as for example in *bayyan* 'he appeared'. When the preceding vowel is *a*, as in this word, it and the first *y* together form the diphthong *ay*, as described in the preceding section; thus the first syllable of *bayyan* rhymes with *ˀay* or the first syllable of *mayyta*. The second *y* begins the next syllable, and sounds like English *y* in *yes* or *yell*.

Drill 17. Medial double *yy* preceded by *a*. Listen and repeat.

↓ *bayyan*	'he appeared'	*layyin*	'lenient M'
zayyaf	'he counterfeited'	*mayyit*	'dead M'
zayyan	'he shaved'	*dayyaan*	'lender M'
mayyaz	'he distinguished'	*tayyaar*	'current'
zayyin	'shave M'	*sayyaara*	'car'

When the preceding vowel is *i,* as in the examples below, it and the first *y* together form the sequence *iy,* which sounds somewhat like the long vowel *ii,* but is a little shorter. The second *y* begins the next syllable and, as above, sounds like English *y* in *yes* or *yell.*

Drill 18. Medial double *yy* preceded by *i.* Listen and repeat.

↓ *biyya*	'in me'	*jinsiyya*	'nationality'
miyya	'hundred'	*šahiyya*	'appetite'
niyya	'intention'	*kammiyya*	'quantity'
hiyya	'she'	*kulliyya*	'college'
wiyya	'with'	*baladiyya*	'municipality'

UNIT 5

A. Emphatic consonants: General comments

In the Iraqi phonological system there are several pairs of consonants of which the two members are articulated in basically the same way, except that one member lacks, and the other member has, a feature called **emphasis.** The one without emphasis is called a **plain** consonant and the other an **emphatic** consonant. (The words "emphasis" and "emphatic" as used here in the description of consonant sounds are technical terms, to be understood in the special sense explained below. They should not be taken to imply any particular loudness or forcefulness in the pronunciation of the consonants concerned.)

Four such pairs are *l* and *ḷ, t* and *ṭ, s* and *ṣ,* and *δ* and *δ̣*. (In our transcription system, as you see, a plain consonant and its emphatic counterpart are distinguished by a dot under the latter.) The four plain members *l t s δ* have already been described; the point to notice about them now is that they are all produced by the action of the tip—or at least the front part—of the tongue. This leaves the central and back parts free to assume various positions, and it is the action of these parts of the tongue which makes the important difference between the plain consonants and their emphatic counterparts. For the plain consonants, while the front part of the tongue is forming the basic articulation of the sound in the front of the mouth, the central and back parts of the tongue are relatively relaxed, and form a fairly even slope running down from front to back. For the emphatics, on the other hand, while the front part of the tongue is forming approximately the same basic articulation in the front of the mouth as for the plain consonants, the central part is somewhat depressed, and the back part raised a little higher than that, the whole surface forming a slightly concave shape like a shallow bowl. This may sound like a very complicated set of tongue gymnastics, but in fact it is exactly what we do in English in producing a final *l* sound as in the words ***bell*** or ***hill***. As you will recall from 3 C, it is the sound of the Iraqi *plain l* which is different from the English *l* sound and which therefore requires some practice. You should find the sound of the Iraqi emphatic *ḷ* much easier. The plain *s* and *δ*, on the other hand, are quite like the corresponding English sounds, and it is the emphatic *ṣ* and *δ̣* which are different. In the case of *t* and *ṭ*, both are somewhat different from the English *t* sound; see 3 A for the former.

When you first hear the contrast between a plain and an emphatic consonant, your reaction will probably be to say that the only difference you hear is one between the quality of the adjacent vowels. Listen to the following pairs:

Drill 1. Vowels *aa* and *a* next to a plain consonant and next to an emphatic. Listen.

taab	'he repented'	→	*ṭaab*	'it became pleasant'
tamm	'it was completed'		*ṭamm*	'he buried'
batt	'he decided'		*baṭṭ*	'ducks'

You are hearing correctly: these vowel differences are physical facts, easily perceptible to English-speakers—the vowels next to the plain consonants sound more like those of *has* or *hat*, and those next to the emphatics more like those of *cause* or *hot*. For an English speaker, this much of a difference in vowel quality is enough to make the difference between one word and another, as is shown by *hat* and *hot*. In these two words there may also be a physical difference between the two final *t* sounds, but such a difference is never enough in the English system to make the difference between two words, and the English-speaker is consequently unaware of it: it is automatic, therefore non-significant, therefore imperceptible to our ears. Now in Iraqi the situation is much the same, but the other way around. It is the difference between a plain and an emphatic *consonant* which is enough to make the difference between two words, as is shown by each of the three pairs in the drill above. There may well also be a physical difference in the quality of the vowels in such pairs, but this difference is completely automatic: certain vowel qualities go with plain consonants, and certain others with emphatics. The vowel differences alone are never enough to make the difference between two words, and therefore Iraqi-speakers are generally unaware of them. In the Iraqi system, the *aa* of *taab* and the *aa* of *ṭaab* are the same vowel, and it is the two consonants which, for an Iraqi, are quite obviously different. English-speakers learning Iraqi must therefore learn to recognize and produce the different sounds of plain and emphatic consonants, since to confuse one with the other would result in another word or a meaningless form; and they must also develop the automatic habit of producing appropriate vowel qualities next to each of the two types of consonants, since this ability will help to give them a natural-sounding, easily understandable accent.

B. Emphatic consonant *ḷ*

As we have said before, the Iraqi emphatic *ḷ* is very similar to the final *l* in such English words as ***bell*** or ***hill***. It is sometimes described as a "heavy" *l*. Say the word ***bell*** very slowly, drawing out each sound as long as possible. The sequence you produce will probably be something like ***beh-eh-eh-eh-uh-uh-uh-l-l-l***; that is, as your tongue gradually move up to begin the sound of *l*, the quality of the vowel slowly changes from the beginning *eh*-sound, as in ***bet***, to an *uh*-sound, as in ***dull***. In normal-speed speech, of course, the change in vowel quality is very rapid, and the speaker is generally not aware of it at all. Now say ***bell*** again, slowly, and hold on to the final *l*-sound. This is the Iraqi emphatic *ḷ*. Here are some examples.

Drill 2. Emphatic *ḷ*. Listen and repeat.

↓ *ʔaḷḷa*	'God'	*gaḷgaḷ*	'he jiggled'
baḷḷa	'please'	*gaḷub*	'heart'
waḷḷa	'really'	*gabuḷ*	'before'
yaḷḷa	'come on'	*gubaḷ*	'straight ahead'
gaḷḷa	'he fried'	*gamuḷ*	'lice'

In the next drill, the words in the left-hand column contain a plain *l*; those in the right-hand column contain an emphatic *ḷ* in the same position, but are otherwise identical or similar to those on the left. Notice the difference in the sound of the plain *l* and the emphatic *ḷ*, and also the effect which each has on the quality of adjacent vowels.

Drill 3. Contrast between plain *l* and emphatic *ḷ*. Listen and repeat.

ballal	'he wet'	→	***baḷḷa***	'please'
walla	'he went away'		***waḷḷa***	'really'
kalla	'sugarloaf'		***yaḷḷa***	'come on'
gal-la	'he told him'		***gaḷḷa***	'he fried'
balbal	'it M trickled'		***gaḷgaḷ***	'he jiggled'
čalib	'dog'		***gaḷub***	'heart'
δibal	'he drooped'		***gubaḷ***	'straight ahead'

C. Emphatic consonant *ṭ*

As you will recall from 3 A, in the production of the Iraqi plain *t* the tip of the tongue touches the area where the upper teeth emerge from the gum. For the emphatic *ṭ*, a slightly larger portion of the tongue touches the gum area; not only the tip but also a little more of the front upper surface. At the same time, the central and back parts of the tongue assume the concave position characteristics of emphatic consonants in general, instead of remaining relaxed and smoothly sloping as for plain consonants (see A above). The whole tongue feels a little tenser, and sometimes gives the impression of filling up the back of the mouth more than for *t*. If you have trouble making your tongue assume the proper position, go back to the final *l* of English *bell,* as in the preceding section: say *bell* slowly and note the position of the tongue for the final *l* sound. This is also approximately the position for the emphatic *ṭ*. Say the word again, holding on to the final *l,* and then put a *t* sound on the end: *bellllllt*. The last sound is probably fairly close in quality to the Iraqi emphatic *ṭ*. One more preliminary exercise is the following. Say several times the English syllable *ult* (as in *ultimate* or *cult*), without any break between but not so fast as to cause stumbling: *ultultultultultult*. Next repeat the sequence, this time whispering it. Whisper it again several times, gradually suppressing the *ul* part of the syllable and concentrating on the sound and the feeling of the *t* alone, until finally all you hear is a succession of whispered *t* sounds: *—t—t—t—t—t*. The important thing here is to end up actually uttering only the *t* sounds, but to continue to *think* the whole syllable *ult* while doing so. In this way you may be able to trick your tongue into assuming the proper position for an emphatic *ṭ,* since it will do so automatically for the "emphatic" English *l* in *ult,* and the position will carry over to the *t*. The final result should be a series of sounds fairly closely approximating the Iraqi emphatic *ṭ*. By way of contrast, whisper a sequence consisting of the English word *tea* repeated several times without pause: *teateateateatea*. Repeat again, gradually suppressing the vowel and concentrating on the sound of the *t* alone: *t—t—t—t—t—*. Now contrast this with the series of *t* sounds resulting from the *ult* exercise. The *tea* exercise should give you a sound more like Iraqi plain *t* (with the differences indicated in 3 A), and the *ult* exercise should give you a sound very much like the Iraqi emphatic *ṭ*.

The main problem for English-speakers in working with *ṭ* is, naturally, to learn to hear the difference between it and the plain *t,* and to learn to produce them so that others will hear the difference. The following drills will therefore concentrate on the contrast between the two sounds. The words on the left illustrate *t;* those on the right, *ṭ*. As you work with these words, remember that in the Iraqi system it is the difference between the two *consonants* which is meaningful, but also notice carefully and imitate as closely as possible the automatic differences in the quality of adjacent vowels.

Drill 4. Contrast between initial plain *t* and emphatic *ṭ*. Listen and repeat.

taab	'he repented'	→	*ṭaab*	'it M became pleasant'
taabuut	'coffin'		*ṭaabuug*	'brick'
tiin	'figs'		*ṭiin*	'mud'
tuub	'repent M'		*ṭuuf*	'walk around M'
teel	'wire'		*ṭeer*	'bird'
toom	'twins'		*ṭoog*	'hoop'
tabsi	'tray'		*ṭabṭab*	'he patted'
tara	'or else'		*ṭari*	'tender M'
tanta	'car top'		*ṭanṭan*	'it M buzzed'
tifal	'he spat'		*ṭifil*	'infant M'
tirak	'he left'		*ṭirag*	'he beat' (eggs)
timman	'rice'		*ṭibbi*	'medical M'
turki	'Turk M'		*ṭubag*	'he closed' (book)
tukki	'mulberries'		*ṭuggi*	'explode F'

Drill 5. Contrast between medial plain *t* and emphatic *ṭ*. Listen and repeat.

watad	'peg'	→	*waṭan*	'country'
kitab	'he wrote'		*šiṭab*	'he crossed out'
šita	'winter'		*niṭa*	'he gave'
banaati	'my daughters'		*naaṭi*	'having given M'
beeruuti	'from Beirut M'		*šuruuṭi*	'my conditions'
faata	'it M passed him'		*ṭamaaṭa*	'tomatoes'
beetuuta	'overnight stay'		*fuuṭa*	'head scarf'

Drill 6. Contrast between double plain *tt* and emphatic *ṭṭ*. Listen and repeat.

fattaan	'tattletale M'	→	*šaṭṭaani*	'by the river M'
sittaat	'sixes'		*maṭṭaaṭ*	'elastic M'
hat-tiin	'these figs'		*haṭ-ṭiin*	'this mud'
šatta	'he put on winter clothes'		*šaṭṭa*	'his river'
jatti	'she came'		*baṭṭi*	'my ducks'

Drill 7. Contrast between final plain *t* and emphatic *ṭ*. Listen and repeat.

batt	'he decided'	→	*baṭṭ*	'ducks'
maat	'he died'		*našaaṭ*	'energy'
moot	'death'		*šooṭ*	'race, heat'
kibriit	'sulphur'		*našiiṭ*	'energetic'
nakkat	'he made jokes'		*naggaṭ*	'it M dripped'
beeruut	'Beirut'		*šabbuuṭ*	(kind of fish)

D. Emphatic consonant *ṣ*

Between plain *s* and its emphatic counterpart *ṣ* there is the same relation as between *t* and *ṭ*. The plain *s* is very much like most occurrences of the English *s* sound, as for example in *see:* the front part of the upper surface of the tongue just behind the tip (for some people, the tip itself) approaches the gum ridge behind the upper teeth and thus forms a narrow channel through which the breathstream passes with the characteristic hissing noise; the rest of the tongue is relaxed and slopes smoothly backward and downward. For the emphatic *ṣ*, on the other hand, the front part of the tongue (not the tip in this case) performs the same action as for *s*, but the central part is depressed and the back part raised a bit, the whole surface assuming a hollow shape, just as it does in the production of the English final *l* as in *bell,* or the *l* in *else*. The *s* sound in this last word, under the influence of the preceding "emphatic" *l,* is probably something like the Iraqi *ṣ*, certainly closer to it than the *s* in *see*. These facts suggest a preliminary exercise which may help you begin the process of learning to distinguish between *s* and *ṣ*. Say the word *see* several times without any pause: *seeseeseeseesee*. Next whisper the same sequence, and gradually suppress everything except the *s* sound *s—s—s—s—s—*. Now go through the same steps with the word *else,* ending up with a sequence *—s—s—s—s—s* in which you continue to *think* the whole syllable *else* but actually produce only the *s* sound audibly. The *see* exercise should give you a sound more like the Iraqi *s,* and the *else* exercise a sound more like *ṣ*.

The following drills illustrate the contrast between *s* and *ṣ*. As in the preceding section, while you are doing these drills, concentrate on hearing and reproducing the difference between the two *consonants,* but also notice and imitate the automatic differences in the quality of adjacent vowels.

Drill 8. Contrast between initial plain *s* and emphatic *ṣ*. Listen and repeat.

saam	'he priced'	→	*ṣaam*	'he fasted'
saad	'he governed'		*ṣaad*	'he hunted'
siir	'march M'		*ṣiir*	'become M'
siin	(letter name)		*ṣiini*	'Chinese M'
suug	'market'		*ṣuum*	'fast M'
suuri	'Syrian'		*ṣuura*	'picture'
seef	'sword'		*ṣeef*	'summer'
seel	'torrent'		*ṣeed*	'hunting'
soof	'wearing out'		*ṣoob*	'side' (of river)
sooda	'black F'		*ṣooda*	'soda'
sadd	'dam'		*ṣadd*	'he repelled'

safra	'trip'	*ṣafra*	'yellow F'
sill	'tuberculosis'	*ṣill*	'adder'
sima	'heaven'	*ṣifa*	'adjective'
sitra	'jacket'	*ṣidfa*	'chance occurrence'
sudus	'one-sixth'	*ṣudug*	'truth'
sukur	'drunkenness'	*ṣubar*	'he waited'

Drill 9. Contrast between medial plain *s* and emphatic *ṣ*. Listen and repeat.

naasi	'having forgotten M'	→	*naaṣi*	'low M'
ˀasaasa	'its M origin'		*riṣaaṣa*	'bullet'
naasuur	'fistula'		*maaṣuul*	'whistle'
nasil	'offspring'		*maṣil*	'serum'
nisab	'he attributed'		*niṣab*	'he wound'

Drill 10. Contrast between double plain *ss* and emphatic *ṣṣ*. Listen and repeat.

hassa	'now'	→	*naṣṣa*	'he bent over'
kassar	'he smashed'		*waṣṣal*	'he transmitted'
bis-siin	'with the letter *siin*'		*biṣ-ṣiin*	'in China'
bis-seef	'with the sword'		*biṣ-ṣeef*	'in the summer'
has-suur	'this fence'		*haṣ-ṣuura*	'this picture'

Drill 11. Contrast between final plain *s* and emphatic *ṣ*. Listen and repeat.

gaas	'he touched'	→	*paaṣ*	'bus'
jaamuus	'water buffalo'		*raaguuṣ*	'dancer M'
jass	'feeling'		*gaṣṣ*	'he cut'
libas	'he put on'		*rigaṣ*	'he danced'
filis	'fils' (Iraqi penny)		*rigiṣ*	'dancing'
sudus	'one-sixth'		*nuṣṣ*	'one-half'

E. Emphatic consonant ẟ̣

As in the case of the other emphatic consonants, the main problem with ẟ̣ is learning to recognize and produce the distinction between it and its plain counterpart ẟ. You will recall from 1 A that the plain ẟ is very similar to the English voiced *th* sound as in *they* or *then:* a voiced interdental spirant. Say the word *they* aloud a few times, then take a deep breath and say the initial *th* sound alone, holding it as long as your breath lasts. (Remember to keep the vocal cords vibrating, as this is a voiced sound, not the voiceless *th* of *thin.*) What you are now producing is in effect a sustained Iraqi δδδδδδδδδ. Notice that the tip of the tongue is lightly touching the edges of both the upper and the lower teeth, probably protruding a little beyond them, and that the rest of the tongue seems to be relaxed. Now for the emphatic δ̣, the vocal cords vibrate in the same way, and the tip of the tongue assumes the same position between the teeth; but the central part of the tongue is slightly depressed and the back part raised, thus forming the concave shape characteristic of all emphatics, and the whole tongue is held somewhat more tensely than for δ. The following drills will illustrate the difference. As before, remember to concentrate on hearing and reproducing the difference between the two *consonants*, but also notice and imitate the automatic differences in the quality of adjacent vowels.

Drill 12. Contrast between initial plain δ and emphatic δ̣. Listen and repeat.

δaab	'it M dissolved'	→	*δ̣aaf*	'he added'
δaak	'that M'		*δ̣aag*	'he tasted'
δiič	'that F'		*δ̣iif*	'add M'
δuub	'dissolve M'		*δ̣uug*	'taste M'
δeel	'tail'		*δ̣eef*	'guest'
δool	'these'		*δ̣ooj*	'boredom'
δabb	'he threw'		*δ̣abb*	'he tightened'
δamm	'he criticized'		*δ̣amm*	'he hid'
δill	'subjugation'		*δ̣idd*	'against'
δikir	'mention'		*δ̣iris*	'molar'
δuhuul	'amazement'		*δuhuur*	'appearance'

Drill 13. Contrast between medial plain δ and emphatic δ̣. Listen and repeat.

haaδa	'this M'	→	*baaδ̣at*	'it F laid an egg'
haaδi	'this F'		*gaaδ̣i*	'having finished off M'
laδiiδ	'delicious M'		*niδ̣iif*	'clean M'
niδar	'he warned'		*niδ̣ar*	'he considered'
čiδab	'he lied'		*hiδ̣am*	'he digested'
muδaakara	'consultation'		*muδ̣aahara*	'demonstration'

Drill 14. Contrast between double plain δδ and emphatic δ̣δ̣. Listen and repeat.

baδδar	'he wasted'	→	*naδ̣δ̣af*	'he cleaned'
haδδab	'he refined'		*naδ̣δ̣am*	'he organized'
biδ-δaat	'personally'		*biδ̣-δ̣abuṭ*	'exactly'

Drill 15. Contrast between final plain ð and emphatic ḍ. Listen and repeat.

nafaað	'used-up state'	→	*faaḍ*	'it M overflowed'
tanfiið	'carrying out'		*tanfiiḍ*	'brushing off'
nufuuð	'influence'		*raakuuḍ*	'runner M'

UNIT 6

A. Primary and secondary emphatics: General comments

The examples in the preceding unit have illustrated, among other things, the influence of emphatic consonants on adjacent vowels: the quality of the *a* in *baṭṭ* 'ducks' is different from that of the *a* in *batt* 'he decided'. In many cases, however, the influence of an emphatic extends not only to adjacent vowels, but also to adjacent consonants, to consonants in the same syllable or an adjacent syllable, or even further, with the result that these other consonants also become emphatic, and that the vowels adjacent to *them* then also have the qualities characteristic of vowels adjacent to emphatics. Consider for example the pair *maktaba* 'library' and *maṣṭaba* 'bench'. In the latter, not only are the first two vowels (those adjacent to the emphatics) different in quality from the two corresponding vowels in the former, but also the *m* and *b* become emphatic, and the vowel following the *b* is different in quality from the corresponding vowel in the former. These facts could be indicated by writing the second word as *ṃaṣṭaḅa,* but since they are automatically predictable from the presence of the *ṣ* and the *ṭ,* we can continue to write simply *maṣṭaba,* and similarly in other such cases.

The three emphatic consonants *ṭ, ṣ,* and *ḍ,* each of which very commonly occurs even when no other emphatic is nearby, are **primary emphatics.** All other emphatic consonants are called **secondary emphatics,** as they occur in most cases only when near some primary emphatic or, as we will see later, near certain combinations of non-emphatic consonants. The emphatic *ḷ,* which was discussed in 5 B, is a secondary emphatic. As between the plain *l* and the emphatic *ḷ,* the latter occurs as a general rule in one of the following environments: near a primary emphatic; in a syllable beginning with *g* (or with one of two other velar consonants to be described later); and in a word in which two nearby consonants are a combination of an emphatic, *g* or one of the other velars, a labial, and *r.* However, the occurrence of *ḷ* as opposed to *l* is not quite so automatically determined by the environment as is the occurrence of the other secondary emphatics—sometimes *l* occurs in the environments just listed, and sometimes *ḷ* occurs in others—and we will therefore write the emphatic as *ḷ* wherever it occurs. Here are some examples.

Notice that when a labial, like *b* or *m*, is near an emphatic *ḷ*, the labial is also emphatic, just as it is when near a primary emphatic.

Drill 1. Emphatic consonant *ḷ*. Listen and repeat.

↓ *laṭiif*	'nice M'	*ṭabuḷ*	'drum'
luṭuf	'kindness'	*gaḷba*	'his heart'
ʔaḷṭaf	'nicer'	*gamḷa*	'louse'
nuṭḷub	'we request'	*ramḷa*	'sandy place'
gḷaaṣ	'glass'	*yaḷḷa*	'come on!'

B. Emphatic consonants *p̣ ḅ f̣ ṃ ẓ*

The first four of the secondary emphatics listed in the heading are labials, and we will consider them first, as a group. The difference between the plain labials *p b f m* and their emphatic counterparts *p̣ ḅ f̣ ṃ* is similar to the difference between plain and emphatic consonants described in Unit 5: for the plain labials, the lips form the basic articulation, and the tongue is relatively relaxed and out of action; while for the emphatic labials, the lips again form the same basic articulation, but the tongue is tenser, depressed in the middle and raised at the back. In addition, labial emphatics are commonly released with a little extra lip-rounding, which makes them sound as though they were followed by a faint *w* sound. This effect is particularly noticeable when there is a vowel *a* following.

As between plain labials and their emphatic counterparts, the latter generally occur automatically near one of the primary emphatics *ṭ ṣ ð̣* or near the secondary emphatic *ḷ*. Here are examples; note again that when the labial is automatically emphatic, as here, we do not write the dot underneath.

Drill 2. Emhatic consonants *p̣ ḅ f̣ ṃ*. Listen and repeat.

↓ *paaṣ*	'bus'	*ṣaffa*	'his class'
ð̣abba	'bunch'	*ʔaṣfar*	'yellow M'
ṭooba	'ball'	*nað̣ð̣ma*	'organize M it M'
baṣiiṭ	'easy M'	*maṣṭaba*	'bench'
mað̣buuṭ	'correct M'	*ṣumaṭ*	'he scalded'

Labial emphatics also occur in a great many words which do not contain a primary emphatic. In most such cases, the occurrence of the labial emphatic (rather than its plain counterpart) is still automatic, but is determined by the presence of certain non-emphatic consonants or combinations of consonants. For example, there is a plain *b* in the words *bass* 'only' and *kitab* 'he wrote', but an emphatic *ḅ* in the words *ḅagg* 'bugs' and *rikaḅ* 'he rode'. These words illustrate the fact that as a general rule the labial emphatics occur automatically in certain environments involving a velar (*k, g,* and certain others), or an *r,* or a combination of these. There are other cases, however, in which their occurrence is not determined by any particular environment but is simply a fact about the word in question, for example *ṃaay* 'water'. We will write the dot underneath in both these types of occurrence. The following drill illustrates the occurrence of labial emphatics in words containing no primary emphatics, and contrasts them with the corresponding plain labials.

Drill 3. Contrast between emphatic labials *p̣ ḅ ṃ f̣* and plain labials *p b m f.* Listen and repeat.

p̣anka	'fan'	→	*pančar*	'flat tire'
ˀawrup̣p̣a	'Europe'		*parda*	'curtain'
ḅagg	'bugs'		*bass*	'only'
ḅaaḅa	'dad'		*baaba*	'his door'
guḅḅa	'room'		*δibba*	'throw M it M out'
šarḅa	'bowl'		*šarbat*	'flavored drink'
rugḅa	'neck'		*nisba*	'relation'
rikaḅ	'he rode'		*kitab*	'he wrote'
f̣akk	'he opened'		*facč*	'jaw'
waagf̣a	'standing F'		*keefa*	'as he wishes'
raf̣raf̣	'it M rippled'		*laflaf*	'he swiped'
ṃara	'woman'		*maši*	'walking'
ṃarga	'sauce'		*malik*	'king'
ṃaay	'water'		*maat*	'he died'
huṃṃa	'they'		*timman*	'rice'
dugṃa	'button'		*ˀisma*	'his name'

The secondary emphatic *ẓ* is less common than the labial emphatics. It is produced in the same way as the primary emphatic *ṣ* (5 D), except that it is voiced. In most instances, *ẓ* occurs near another emphatic, or after *j* in the same syllable. Here are some examples, contrasted with plain *z.*

Drill 4. Emphatic consonant *ẓ* contrasted with plain *z.* Listen and repeat.

ẓumaṭ	'he boasted'	→	*zibil*	'trash'
juẓṃa	'boots'		*wazna*	'his weight'
jaẓẓ	'it M creaked'		*wazz*	'geese'
jiẓdaan	'wallet'		*dizzna*	'send M us'

There are also occasional occurrences of one or two other secondary emphatics, besides the five just described. These will be noted as they occur.

C. Initial consonant clusters

Up to this point all the examples have been words beginning with a single consonant. A great many Iraqi words, however, begin with two consonants. The same thing is true of English, as words like *trip, play,* and *stop* will illustrate; but in English the particular combinations of consonants which occur as initial clusters are quite limited—for example, no word begins with *rt* or *mb*—while in Iraqi most of the theoretically possible combinations actually do occur. When a word beginning with such a cluster occurs at the beginning of an utterance—that is, when it does not immediately follow some other word—the cluster may be preceded by a short vowel sound; for example, one may sometimes hear *nšuuf* 'we see' and sometimes *inšuuf.* This sound, which is usually *i* but in some cases *u,* is called a **helping vowel.** Its occurrence or non-occurrence at the beginning of an utterance is random, and has no effect on meaning; for this reason we do not indicate it in the transcription when the word is given in a list or as the first word in an utterance. Listen to the following examples, and imitate what you hear as closely as you can. Only a few of the many possible combinations are illustrated here.

Drill 5. Initial consonant clusters. Listen and repeat.

↓ *praawa*	'fitting'	*swaag*	'markets'
pwaaši	'veils'	*ṣfuuf*	'classes'
blaam	'rowboats'	*ṣnaadiig*	'boxes'
btida	'he began'	*zbaala*	'trash'
b-gadda	'as much as he'	*štira*	'he bought'
triid	'you M want'	*š-yaakul*	'what does he eat'
tnaffas	'he breathed'	*htamm*	'he was concerned'
ṭwaal	'tall P'	*hnaak*	'there'
druus	'lessons'	*hwaaya*	'much, a lot'
dlaal	'coffee-pots'	*čtuwa*	'he was burned'
kḅaar	'big P'	*čfuuf*	'gloves'
ksaala	'lazy P'	*jraḅḅ*	'it M got mangy'
gbaaḷ	'across from'	*jwaariib*	'socks'
gziiza	'piece of glass'	*mneen*	'from where'
ftiham	'he understood'	*msajjal*	'recorded M'
fraaš	'bed'	*mzaayna*	'barbers'
θmaanya	'eight'	*nšuuf*	'we see'
θneen	'two'	*lsaan*	'tongue'
ḍruuf	'envelopes'	*l-beet*	'the house'
sfanja	'sponge'	*rfuuf*	'shelves'

When the semivowel *w* is the first member of an initial consonant cluster, it has a vowel-like sound, similar to the vowel in English *boot* but varying in length. Similarly, when the semivowel *y* is the first member of an initial consonant cluster, it has a vowel-like sound similar to the vowel in English *beat* but varying in length.

Drill 6. Semivowels *w* and *y* as first members of initial consonant cluster. Listen and repeat.

↓ *wlaaya*	'city'	*ysaafir*	'he goes on a trip'
w-šaafa	'and he saw him'	*ybaddil*	'he changes'
w-jiib	'and bring M'	*yjiib*	'he brings'

D. Initial double consonants

Iraqi words may begin with a double consonant as well as with a cluster of two different consonants, for example *nnaam* 'we sleep'. When a word of this sort occurs at the beginning of an utterance, the initial double consonant, like an initial cluster, is sometimes preceded by a helping vowel, for example *innaam*. This optional helping vowel, as before, is not indicated in the transcription. The following drills illustrate the contrast between an initial single consonant and the corresponding initial double consonant.

Drill 7. Contrast between initial single and double consonants. Listen and repeat.

baalak	'your M mind'	→	*b-baalak*	'in your M mind'
beeti	'my house'		*b-beeti*	'in my house'
tammim	'finish M'		*ttammim*	'you M finish'
tanaka	'can'		*t-tanaka*	'the can'
daari	'take care of M'		*ddaari*	'you M take care of'
daris	'lesson'		*d-daris*	'the lesson'
ṭiir	'fly M'		*ṭṭiir*	'you M fly'
ṭabiib	'doctor'		*ṭ-ṭabiib*	'the doctor'
θawra	'revolution'		*θ-θawra*	'the revolution'
θaaliθ	'third M'		*θ-θaaliθ*	'the third M'
δakkar	'he reminded'		*δδakkar*	'he remembered'
δahab	'gold'		*δ-δahab*	'the gold'

ḍubb	'tighten M'	*ḍḍubb*	'you M tighten'
ḍaabuṭ	'officer'	*ḍ-ḍaabuṭ*	'the officer'
sana	'year'	*s-sana*	'the year'
suug	'market'	*s-suug*	'the market'
ṣooṭ	'voice'	*ṣ-ṣooṭ*	'the voice'
ṣanduug	'box'	*ṣ-ṣanduug*	'the box'
zanjiil	'chain'	*z-zanjiil*	'the chain'
zibid	'butter'	*z-zibid*	'the butter'
šibbaač	'window'	*š-šibbaač*	'the window'
šifit	'you M saw'	*š-šifit*	'what did you M see'
čiis	'bag'	*č-čiis*	'the bag'
čilma	'word'	*č-čilma*	'the word'
jaahil	'child M'	*j-jaahil*	'the child M'
jariida	'newspaper'	*j-jariida*	'the newspaper'
maθθal	'he acted'	*mmaθθal*	'acted M'
maššiṭ	'comb M'	*mmaššiṭ*	'having combed M'
naas	'people'	*n-naas*	'the people'
naam	'he slept'	*nnaam*	'we sleep'
labnaan	'Lebanon'	*l-labnaan*	'to Lebanon'
leela	'night'	*l-leela*	'the night'
raʔiis	'president'	*r-raʔiis*	'the president'
rijil	'leg'	*r-rijil*	'the leg'

When the semivowel *w* occurs doubled in initial position, the first element has a vowel-like sound, similar to the vowel in English *boot,* and the second element has the usual *w* sound as in *well.* Similarly, when the semi-vowel *y* occurs doubled in initial position, the first element has a vowel-like sound, similar to the vowel in English *beat,* and the second element has the usual *y* sound as in *yell.*

Drill 8. Contrast between initial single *w* and *y* and initial double *ww* and *yy*. Listen and repeat.

wannas	'he amused'	→	*w-wannas*	'and he amused'
wučča	'his face'		*w-wučča*	'and his face'
ween	'where?'		*w-ween*	'and where?'
yabbis	'dry M'		*yyabbis*	'he dries'
yaʔʔisni	'discourage M me'		*yyaʔʔisni*	'he discourages me'

UNIT 7

A. Consonant *x*

In the English writing system the letter *x* is used mostly to represent the two sounds *ks* as in *box,* or the two sounds *gz* as in *exert.* In our transcription of Iraqi, however, the symbol *x* is used to represent a single Iraqi sound which does not occur as a distinctive speech sound in English at all. The sound is a **voiceless velar spirant,** which means that (1) it is not accompanied by vibration of the vocal cords, (2) it is produced by moving the back part of the tongue upward until it almost—but not quite—touches the rear part of the roof of the mouth (the soft palate, or **velum**), so that (3) the breath is not completely cut off at any point but passes with a scraping friction noise through the narrow channel between tongue and velum. Although this is not a distinctive speech sound in English like, say, *f* or *s,* English-speakers often produce it in certain exclamations, such as the one usually written *ugh!* or a similar one which might be written *yeuch!.* To those who know German, the sound will be familiar as the "back *ch* sound", as in *Bach, Buch,* and *noch.*

In learning to produce and control the *x,* your main problem will be a tendency to produce a *k* instead. This tendency must be vigorously combatted from the beginning, for if you say *k* where you should say *x* the result will be either a word quite different from the one you intended or a word with no meaning at all, and you will not be understood. The main thing to remember in practicing these two sounds is that *k* results when the back of the tongue *touches* the velum, no matter how briefly, and the breathstream is thus cut off for a split second; whereas *x* results when the back of the tongue *approaches* the velum but never touches, and the air continues to scrape through. The last phrase is important: the sound *k* is a momentary thing, since the very act of making it also ends it; whereas you can keep the sound *x* going as long as your breath holds out. In this respect, *k* is like *p* and *t* (all are stops), and *x* is like *f, θ, s, š* (all are spirants). Some examples follow.

Drill 1. Initial, medial, and final *x.* Listen and repeat.

↓ *xaaf*	'he was afraid'	*naxaḷ*	'palm trees'
xaali	'empty M'	*ˀuxut*	'sister'
xooš	'good'	*laax*	'other M'
xeel	'horses'	*ṭabbaax*	'cook M'
xass	'lettuce'	*čoox*	'felt'
xidma	'service'	*šeex*	'sheik'
xubuz	'bread'	*ˀax*	'brother'
ˀaxuuya	'my brother'	*muxx*	'brains'
raaxi	'loose M'	*lux*	'other F'

Here now are some exercises which may be helpful in the process of learning to produce and control the sound. The first one is designed to show the approximate point at which the back part of the tongue approaches the velum. Say the word *cot.* Now take a deep breath, and put your tongue into position ready to say *cot,* but just hold it there for a few seconds without uttering a sound. You should now be able to feel that the back part of your tongue is touching the velum, closing off the air entirely. This is the position for a *k* sound. Now relax that part of your tongue very slightly, just enough to allow a very small stream of air pass through the opening at that same point where a moment before it was touching. (Don't make any vowel sound along with this; you should hear only the whispered scrape of the breath passing through.) Keep it scraping through as long as your breath lasts: you are now making a continuous *xxxxxx* sound. Try it all over again: deep breath, position for *k,* hold a second, release slightly so that the air starts scraping through, and keep it scraping as long as you have breath. The whole sequence could be represented *kxxxxxx.* (It is important to remember that only the *back* part of the tongue should be involved in the *x* sound. The tip of the tongue should stay relaxed. If you find that the tip of your tongue has a tendency to curl back when you are practicing *x,* press it lightly against the inner surface of the lower teeth and make a point of keeping it there throughout.)

The above exercise, however, is only a preliminary one. The next step is to get rid of the *k* sound at the beginning. This time, instead of starting from a closed position, as for *k,* go at it from the other direction. Take a deep breath and begin to let it out very slowly and lightly, keeping the tip of the tongue pressed against the lower teeth as before, but the back of the tongue relaxed. Now, while continuing to expel breath, gradually raise the back part of your tongue higher and higher toward the *k* position until the passage becomes narrow enough to cause an audible scrape when the air passes through. Now you have a continuous *xxxxxx.* Be careful not to let the tongue rise high enough to touch, or you will get a *k* instead. Repeat this several times, and try to get a feel for the tongue height that will produce the right amount of scrape. Now try it again, and this time see if you can start off with the right tongue height immediately, without having to work up to it; practice it until you can.

The next exercise involves adding a vowel. First make a long continuous *xxxxxx* as before. (Remember to keep the tongue tip out of action by pressing it against the lower teeth.) Repeat, and this time end up with a vowel *aa,* so that you produce something like *xxxxxxxaa.* Bear in mind that the consonant *x* is voiceless, and therefore that until you come to the vowel part you should hear only the sound of the breath scrape and no voice. Now repeat this a number of times, and each time try to shorten the duration of the consonant a little more: *xxxxxxxaa—xxxxxxaa—xxxxxaa—xxxxaa—xxxaa—xxaa—xaa.*

The last sequence represents a normal and quite common Iraqi syllable, consisting of a very brief breath scrape and then the long vowel. The whole sequence has the same length as any voiceless spirant with a long vowel. Compare the following: *faa—θaa—saa—xaa*. Repeat the sequences *saa* and *xaa* three times each without pause: *saasaasaa—xaaxaaxaa*. Again, several times. Now once more, and then replace *aa* with each of the other long vowels, as in the following drill.

Drill 2. Practice exercise: consonants *s* and *x*. Listen and repeat.

saasaasaa	→	*xaaxaaxaa*
soosoosoo		*xooxooxoo*
suusuusuu		*xuuxuuxuu*
seeseesee		*xeexeexee*
siisiisii		*xiixiixii*

In the final exercise you are asked to concentrate on the difference between the consonants *k* and *x*. Remember that for Iraqi *k*, as for the English *k*, the back of the tongue touches the velum and cuts off the breath stream for a brief moment, while for *x* the back of the tongue approaches the velum and the breath continues to pass through with audible friction. Here are contrasts of the two consonants in various positions and with various vowels.

Drill 3. Practice exercise: consonants *k* and *x*. Listen and repeat.

kaakaakaa	→	*xaaxaaxaa*
kookookoo		*xooxooxoo*
kuukuukuu		*xuuxuuxuu*
keekeekee		*xeexeexee*
kiikiikii		*xiixiixiixii*

daaka	→	*daaxa*	*daak*	→	*daax*
dooka		*dooxa*	*dook*		*doox*
duuka		*duuxa*	*duuk*		*duux*
deeka		*deexa*	*deek*		*deex*
diika		*diixa*	*diik*		*diix*

The following drills, containing the words given in Drill 1 and some additional words, illustrate *x* in various positions.

Drill 4. Initial *x*. Listen and repeat.

↓ *xaaf*	'he was afraid'	*xass*	'lettuce'
xaaḷ	'maternal uncle'	*xašš*	'he entered'
xaali	'empty M'	*xamsa*	'five'
xoof	'fear'	*xašim*	'nose'
xooš	'good'	*xidma*	'service'
xuuδa	'helmet'	*xubuz*	'bread'
xeel	'horses'	*xalliini*	'let M me'
xeer	'goodness'	*xaddaama*	'maid'

Drill 5. Final *x*. Listen and repeat.

↓ *laax*	'other M'	*daayix*	'dizzy M'
čoox	'felt'	*čarix*	'wheel'
šeex	'sheik'	*nusax*	'copies'
ˀax	'brother'	*čruux*	'wheels'
muxx	'brains'	*baṭṭiix*	'melons'
lux	'other F'	*ṭabbaax*	'cook M'

Drill 6. Medial single *x* and double *xx*. Listen and repeat.

↓ *maaxiδ*	'having taken M'	*ˀadaxxin*	'I smoke'
dooxa	'dizziness'	*daxxil*	'put in M'
ˀuxut	'sister'	*θaxxan*	'he thickened'
ˀaxaaf	'I am afraid'	*ṣaxxar*	'he sent on an errand'
ˀaxiir	'last M'	*zaxxaat*	'rain showers'
θixiin	'thick M'	*duxxaan*	'smoke'

Drill 7. Consonant *x* in medial and initial clusters. Listen and repeat.

↓ *staxdam*	'he employed'	*ˀaθxan*	'thicker'
maxzan	'store'	*ˀarxaṣ*	'cheaper'
muxtabar	'laboratory'	*nusxa*	'copy'
muxḷiṣ	'sincere M'	*yitxarraj*	'he graduates'
muxtaar	(a local official)	*ˀašxaaṣ*	'persons'
ˀaxbaar	'news'	*txalli*	'you M let'
xtinag	'he choked'	*l-xass*	'the lettuce'
xḍarr	'it M turned green'	*mxarbaṭ*	'messed up M'
xbaabiiz	'bakers'	*nxaan*	'he was betrayed'

B. Consonant *ġ*

This consonant is a **voiced velar spirant.** If you have now gained control of the *x* sound described in the preceding section, you will have taken the first step toward learning *ġ* as well, since the two sounds are alike in every respect but one. Both are velar spirants: the back of the tongue is raised to a position near—but not touching—the velum, and the breath scrapes through this narrow passage with audible friction. The difference is that *x* is voiceless and *ġ* is voiced—the same as the difference between *s* and *z*, to take a more familiar example. If you make a prolonged *ssssss* you hear only the hissing friction noise from an area near the tip of the tongue; while if you make a prolonged *zzzzzz*, your tongue stays in exactly the same position, but the friction noise from that area is joined by the vibrations from the vocal cords, and we generally think of the total effect as a buzzing noise. Similarly, in making a prolonged *xxxxxx* you hear only the scrape of the breath passing between the back of the tongue and the velum, while in a prolonged *ġġġġġġ* you hear both the scrape of the breath and the buzzing vibration of the vocal cords.

This leads us to some exercises. First, to attain conscious control of the vocal cord vibration, make a long *ssssss*, pause, then a long *zzzzzz*, and repeat the sequence several times. Make the pause between the two sounds shorter and shorter, and finally eliminate it altogether, so that you are producing an uninterrupted sequence of alternately voiceless and voiced sound: *sssssszzzzzzsssssszzzzzz* and so on as long as your breath lasts. Next, do the same thing with *x* and *ġ;* that is, first make a long *xxxxxx*, pause, then (keeping your tongue in exactly the same position) turn on the vocal cord vibration for a long *ġġġġġġ*, and repeat the sequence several times. (NOTE: In practicing *ġ*, you may find that the tip of your tongue has even more of a tendency to curl back than in *x*, so make a point of keeping it pressed lightly against the lower teeth until the proper position becomes automatic. Only the back part of the tongue should be in action.) Gradually shorten the pause, and finally eliminate it, so that you are producing an uninterrupted velar spirant, alternately voiceless and voiced: *xxxxxxġġġġġġxxxxxxġġġġġġ* and so on to the end of the breath. Remember that your tongue should stay in exactly the same position throughout, and that the breath should continue to scrape through in the same way during the *x* phase and the *ġ* phase of the exercise. The only change is in the vocal cords, which do not vibrate for *x* but do for *ġ*.

The next step involves adding a vowel. First make a prolonged *xxxxxx* as before, then add the vowel *aa* at the end: *xxxxxxaa*. Now, keeping your tongue in exactly the same position, make a prolonged *ġġġġġġ* and add the vowel at the end of that: *ġġġġġġaa*. Next, always doing *x* first for contrast, gradually shorten the length of the consonant: *xxxxxxaa—ġġġġġaa—xxxxaa—ġġġġaa—xxxaa—ġġġaa—xxaa—ġġaa—xaa—ġaa*. Now repeat the last two syllables several times each: *xaaxaaxaa—ġaaġaaġaa*. Repeat again, and then replace *aa* with each of the other long vowels, as in the following drill.

Drill 8. Practice exercise: consonants *x* and *ġ*. Listen and repeat.

xaaxaaxaa	→	*ġaaġaaġaa*
xooxooxoo		*ġooġooġoo*
xuuxuuxuu		*ġuuġuuġuu*
xeexeexee		*ġeeġeeġee*
xiixiixii		*ġiiġiiġii*

Finally, go through the same sequences again, this time also adding the consonant on at the end, as below.

Drill 9. Practice exercise: consonants *x* and *ġ*. Listen and repeat.

xaaxaaxaax	→	*ġaaġaaġaaġ*
xooxooxoox		*ġooġooġooġ*
xuuxuuxuux		*ġuuġuuġuuġ*
xeexeexeex		*ġeeġeeġeeġ*
xiixiixiix		*ġiiġiiġiiġ*

Given in the following drill are some pairs of words which are identical except that one has *x* and the other *ġ*.

Drill 10. Contrast between *x* and *ġ*. Listen and repeat.

xaali	'empty M'	→	*ġaali*	'expensive M'
xeer	'goodness'		*ġeer*	'other than'
xeema	'tent'		*ġeema*	'cloud'
lixam	'he slapped'		*liġam*	'he mined'
šaaxir	'having snored M'		*šaaġir*	'vacant M'
raxwa	'soft F'		*raġwa*	'suds'
daax	'he got dizzy'		*daaġ*	'it M boiled'

The remaining drills illustrate *ġ* in various positions.

Drill 11. Initial *ġ*. Listen and repeat.

↓ *ġaali*	'expensive M'	*ġada*	'lunch'
ġaayib	'absent M'	*ġanam*	'sheep'
ġooṣ	'diving'	*ġariib*	'strange M'
ġuuṣ	'dive M'	*ġalṭaan*	'mistaken M'
ġeeba	'absence'	*ġurfa*	'room'
ġiiba	'backbiting'	*ġina*	'singing'
ġiira	'jealousy'	*ġisal*	'he washed'

Drill 12. Final *ġ*. Listen and repeat.

↓ *balaaġ*	'proclamation'	*farraġ*	'he emptied'
damaaġ	'brain'	*mablaġ*	'amount'
ṣbaabiiġ	'painters'	*ṣaayiġ*	'goldsmith'
madbuuġ	'tanned M'	*ṣubuġ*	'paint'

Drill 13. Medial single *ġ* and double *ġġ*. Listen and repeat.

↓ *šaaġir*	'vacant M'	*ʔaġaati*	(form of address)
baġaḷ	'mule'	*maġaara*	'cave'
luġa	'language'	*raġġaḅ*	'he interested'
šuġuḷ	'work'	*šaġġaḷ*	'he employed'
šaaġuuḷ	'hard worker'	*waġġaf*	'he made foamy'

Drill 14. Consonant *ġ* in medial and initial clusters. Listen and repeat.

↓ *raġḅa*	'wish'	*ʔadġam*	'gloomy'
šaġḷa	'errand'	*burġi*	'screw'
taġyiir	'change'	*yilġi*	'he cancels'
baġdaad	'Baghdad'	*bġaaḷ*	'mules'
ġmaaj	'deep P'	*mġaṭṭa*	'covered M'

C. Short vowel *o*

This short vowel, which is much less common than the other three, occurs mainly in words which have been borrowed from other languages. It sounds somewhat like the English vowel at the end of the words *window* and *yellow,* but it is shorter, and does not have any of the diphthongal glide (into the sound of the vowel of *boot*) which the English vowel has. Here are the most common examples.

Drill 15. Short vowel *o*. Listen and repeat.

banyo	'bathtub'
ṃaayo	'bathing-suit'
raadyo	'radio'
pyaano	'piano'
gaaziino	(kind of cafe)

D. Diphthongs *eew, ooy,* and *iw*

These three diphthongs are far less common than those described in 3 D and 4 D. The first, *eew,* consists of the Iraqi long vowel *ee* (the first variant described in 1 G) followed smoothly by a glide into a vowel sound like that of English *boot.* The second, *ooy,* consists of the Iraqi long vowel *oo* followed smoothly by a glide into a vowel sound like that of English *feet;* and the third, *iw,* consists of a short vowel sound like that of English *fit* followed very quickly by a glide into a vowel sound like that of English *boot.* The second and third are extremely rare, occurring in only one or two words each. Examples follow.

Drill 16. Diphthongs *eew, ooy,* and *iw.* Listen and repeat.

↓ *geewti*	'my slippers'	*booy*	'boy, waiter'
jreew	'puppy'	*stiwṭaan*	'settling down'

UNIT 8

A. Consonant *q*

In the English writing system the letter *q* is usually followed by *u,* and this combination of letters represents the two sounds *kw.* In our transcription of Iraqi, however, the symbol *q* represents a single consonant sound, different from anything in English. This sound is a **voiceless uvular stop.** It differs from the voiceless velar stop *k* only in the point at which the closure occurs. For *k,* as we have noted earlier, the back of the tongue cuts off the breathstream momentarily by touching the velum (soft palate). For *q,* the extreme back of the tongue cuts off the breathstream by touching a point noticeably farther back than for *k,* in the region of the **uvula.** The uvula is the small appendage which hangs down in the center of the mouth, at the very back of the velum; you can easily see it in a mirror if you open your mouth wide and keep your tongue relaxed.

The closest English sound to *q* is *k*, and for this reason you may find that in trying to produce a *q* you are producing a *k* instead; in fact at first you may even have difficulty hearing any difference between them. It is therefore important to remember that Iraqi has both a *k* and a *q*, and that for Iraqi-speakers the two are just as different as, say, *k* and *t*. The first step in learning to distinguish *k* and *q* is to observe the points at which the tongue touches the roof of the mouth for each sound. With a little effort you can see this in a mirror. Take a deep breath, open the jaws fairly wide, and say the syllable *kaa* several times. (Keep the tip of the tongue out of action by pressing it against the lower teeth.) In the mirror, observe how the back of the tongue moves up and touches the roof of the mouth for every successive *k* sound, and note that the point of contact is about at the borderline between the hard and the soft palate. Now stretch the jaws open as wide as possible, if necessary bracing them in that position with your fingers, and try to repeat *kaakaakaa*. This time, if you are doing it right, the extreme back of your tongue will make contact at a point much farther back than for *k*, and you will actually be saying *qaaqaaqaa*. Keep practicing while watching in the mirror until you have acquired a sense of the proper contact point and can make your tongue touch there at will. You should be able to see the uvula itself being flattened by the tongue when it makes contact for the *q*. In the following drill, the two sounds *k* and *q* are contrasted. Listen carefully to the distinction, and notice also that *q* has somewhat the same effect on the quality of adjacent vowels as emphatic consonants do.

Drill 1. Contrast between *k* and *q*. Listen and repeat.

kaasa	'bowl' →	*qaasa*	'he measured it M'
kaanuun	(part of month name)	*qaanuun*	'law'
stikaan	'tea-glass'	*stiqaal*	'he resigned'
mukawwi	'presser'	*muqawwi*	'strengthener'
malak	'angel'	*malaq*	'flattery'

Here now are drills illustrating *q* in various positions.

Drill 2. Initial *q*. Listen and repeat.

↓ *qaas*	'he measured'	*qalam*	'pencil'
qaanuun	'law'	*qarrar*	'he decided'
qaamuus	'dictionary'	*qadiim*	'ancient M'
qaari	'having read M'	*qurʔaan*	'Koran'
qooqat	'she cackled'	*qundara*	'shoes'
quuzi	'baby lamb'	*qibal*	'he accepted'
quuri	'teapot'	*qisim*	'part'
qiima	'value'	*qira*	'he read'

Drill 3. Final *q*. Listen and repeat.

↓ *saaq*	'he drove'	*malaq*	'flattery'
sibaaq	'race'	*waraq*	'paper'
fariiq	'team'	*funduq*	'hotel'
ṣadiiq	'friend'	*fariq*	'difference'
ṭariiq	'road'	*waaθiq*	'confident M'

Drill 4. Medial single *q* and double *qq*. Listen and repeat.

↓ *buqa*	'he stayed'	*šiqqa*	'apartment'
raqam	'number'	*traqqa*	'he advanced'
laqab	'surname'	*θaqqaf*	'he educated'
ṣiqaṭ	'he failed'	*waqqaf*	'he arrested'
faqiir	'poor M'	*daqqaq*	'he examined'

Drill 5. Consonant *q* in medial and initial clusters. Listen and repeat.

↓ *staqbal*	'he went to meet'	*ʔabqa*	'I stay'
nuqṭa	'point'	*ʔačqal*	'cross-eyed'
tiqra	'you M read'	*šarqi*	'eastern M'
qwaari	'teapots'	*tqassim*	'you M divide'
qmaaš	'cloth'	*mqarrar*	'decided M'

B. Final consonant clusters; automatic stress (4)

In English, a great many words end in a cluster of two, three, or even more different consonant sounds; this sentence itself contains several illustrations. In Iraqi, however, no words end in a cluster of more than two consonants, and very few even in a cluster of two. Some examples of the latter type are shown in the following drill. As you will note here and elsewhere, the first consonant in such final clusters is in the great majority of cases *m, n, l, r, w,* or *y*.

Drill 6. Final consonant clusters. Listen and repeat.

↓ *kamp*	(part of place-name)	*silk*	'wire'
band	'clause'	*karx*	(part of place-name)
banj	'anesthetic'	*šarq*	'east'
pang	'bank'	*ġarb*	'west'
hind	(girl's name)	*qaws*	'bow'
ʔalf	'thousand'	*jayš*	'army'

However, some words in which *w* or *y* is the first consonant in the final cluster, and the cluster is preceded by *a,* have variant pronunciations in which *aw* or *ay* is replaced by *oo* or *ee* respectively, for example *jeeš* 'army'. Also, some words in which one of the other consonants listed above is the first consonant in the final cluster have variant pronunciations in which a short vowel *i* or *u* occurs between the last two consonants, for example *silik* 'wire'.

If a word of two or more syllables ends in a consonant cluster, the last syllable is a long syllable and is therefore automatically stressed (see automatic stress rule, 3 F). There are not many words of this sort; here are three examples.

Drill 7. Automatic stress on last syllable. Listen and repeat.

↓ *naarinj*	(kind of fruit)
šiṭranj	'chess'
kabang	'shop shutter'

C. Final double consonants; automatic stress (5)

As we pointed out in the note in 2 A, some words are written with a single consonant letter at the end, and some with a double consonant letter, and there is no difference at all as far as the sound itself is concerned. For example, the *d* at the end of *ˀaswad* 'black M' and the *dd* at the end of *yiswadd* 'he turns black' both represent the same sound *d*. However, in words of more than one syllable, the presence of a double consonant at the end of a word affects the *stress* of the word in a way that a single consonant does not: it causes the stress to fall on the last syllable, since that is a long syllable (see 3 F). Examples are given in the drill below. The words in the left-hand column end in a short vowel followed by a single consonant, and in these the stress is automatically on the next-to-last syllable. The words in the right-hand column end in a short vowel followed by a double consonant, and in these the stress is automatically on the last syllable.

Drill 8. Stress contrast between final single and final double consonants. Listen and repeat.

ˀaswad	'black M'	→	*yiswadd*	'he turns black'
kitab	'he wrote'		*statabb*	'it M settled down'
namil	'ants'		*mumill*	'boring M'
šitam	'he cursed'		*yištamm*	'he smells'

nahim	'greedy M'	*muhimm*	'important M'
ˀamtan	'bigger around'	*mimtann*	'grateful M'
ˀazrag	'blue M'	*mizragg*	'having turned blue M'
barid	'coldness'	*yistiridd*	'he gets back'
baddil	'change M'	*tistidill*	'she infers'

UNIT 9

A. Consonant *c*

The two consonants to be described in this unit are produced by the action of the **pharynx,** which is the upper part of the throat, above the larynx; and they are therefore called pharyngeal consonants. There are no similar speech sounds in English. The first is *c,* which is a **voiceless pharyngeal spirant.** In the production of this sound, the muscles of the pharynx are tightened so that the throat passage becomes smaller and narrower than it is in a relaxed state, and the breath passes through this narrowed channel with a friction noise which differs in quality from that of ordinary breathing and is much more audible. In addition, the root of the tongue (the part which is too far down in the throat to see in a mirror) is drawn back slightly so as to form part of the front wall of the narrowed passage (but no part of the tongue approaches the velum as for *x* or touches the uvula area as for *q*). It is a voiceless sound: there is no accompanying vibration of the vocal cords. It is a spirant: the breathstream is never completely cut off at any point, but continues to scrape through for the duration of the sound. Here, for listening purposes only, are some examples of words beginning with *c*.

Drill 1. Initial *c*. Listen.

↓ *caal*	'condition'	*cabil*	'rope'
cooš	'house'	*cači*	'talk'
cuuta	'whale'	*curr*	'free M'
ceewa	'quince'	*cilu*	'sweet M'
ciira	'perplexity'	*ciss*	'voice'

At first you may have some difficulty in distinguishing this sound from the Iraqi *h,* which is very much like English *h;* and even after you have learned to hear the difference you may find it difficult to produce a distinctive *c* yourself. Nevertheless it is very important to learn to make a clear *c* from the beginning. For Iraqi-speakers, the two sounds are just as different as any other two consonants, and if you produce *h* when you mean *c,* you will often be misunderstood. Moreover, *c* is a good deal more common than *h*, so it is well worth while to devote a considerable amount of time and effort to the task of mastering it now, rather than have it continue to cause troubles whenever you speak. The main difference between the two sounds is that for *h* the throat passage is relaxed and relatively wide open, so that the breath passes through with no perceptible noise except a slight friction in the area of the glottis, very much as in normal breathing; while for *c* the throat muscles are tightened, so that the passage is narrowed, and the breath sets up a clearly audible and distinctive friction noise as it passes through this constriction. There are quite a few pairs of words which are identical except that one contains *h* and the other *c*. Some of these are given in the drill below. Listen to the contrast, and try to reproduce it.

Drill 2. Contrast between *h* and *c* in various positions. Listen and repeat.

↓ *haak*	'here, take M'	*caak*	'he knitted'
hooš	'cattle'	*cooš*	'house'
habb	'it M blew'	*cabb*	'he liked'
hanna	'he congratulated'	*canna*	(man's name)
hiba	'gift'	*ciba*	'he crawled'
himal	'he neglected'	*cimal*	'he carried'
sihal	'it M became easy'	*sical*	'he dragged'
liham	'he gobbled up'	*licam*	'he welded'
šabah	'similarity'	*šabac*	'ghost'
šarih	'greedy M'	*šaric*	'explanation'

As you can observe, control of the pharyngeal muscles is essential in the production of *c*. Since these muscles play virtually no role in the production of English speech sounds, however, it will take some effort to learn to tighten and relax them at will. As the first step in this task, the following exercise may be useful. Breathe in and out several times through the mouth, not very deeply, and note the very slight friction noise of the outgoing breath in the region of the glottis. Each expiration is in effect a long *h* sound. Now clasp the front of your neck with one hand, the palm over the Adam's apple, and tighten the neck muscles until you can feel them bunch under your hand; the interior throat muscles will probably tighten along with those of the neck. Holding all these muscles as tense as you can, breathe in and out again several times through the open mouth. This time you should be able to hear—and feel—considerable friction coming with each expiration from the upper throat region, and this is the *c* sound. It is well to remember that this is exclusively a *throat* sound: the tongue is out of action (except for the root, which is too far down to observe). Specifically, there are two tendencies which should be guarded against in practicing *c*. One is the tendency of the tongue tip to curl up and back; to prevent this, if necessary, press it lightly against the back of the upper teeth. The other is the tendency of the back part of the tongue to rise and touch, or almost touch, the velum or the uvula, which will result in a *k, x,* or *q* as the case may be. If you find this happening, try taking a slightly deeper breath and opening the jaws wider. For a good *c,* there should be no noise from the back of the mouth at all, but only from the throat, and the noise from there should not be gurgly, but dry and breathy.

The exercise involving the neck muscles is only a first step, of course, as the ultimate goal is to be able to control the contraction of the throat muscles alone. You can observe some of the process in a mirror. Open the mouth wide, keeping the tongue well down, and look down your throat as far as you can. If you now work your neck and throat muscles, you can see the upper opening of the throat passage contract and relax. At first these movements will seem random and uncoordinated, but practice will gradually bring a degree of voluntary control. The following drills provide examples of *c* in various positions.

Drill 3. Initial *c*. Listen and repeat.

↓ *caaja*	'necessity'	*cabba*	'seed'
ciira	'perplexity'	*cassan*	'he improved'
cuuk	'knit M'	*cadiid*	'iron'
cooš	'house'	*cidd*	'sharpen M'
ceel	'hard'	*ciss*	'voice'
call	'he solved'	*cukk*	'scratch M'
cafla	'party'	*cukuuma*	'government'

Drill 4. Final *c*. Listen and repeat.

↓ *raac*	'he went'	*gacc*	'he coughed'
looc	'boards'	*fattac*	'he opened'
ruuc	'go M'	*ʔasmac*	'I permit'
fallaac	'farmer'	*sibac*	'he swam'
muriic	'comfortable M'	*jaric*	'wound'
masmuuc	'permitted M'	*ribic*	'profit'

Drill 5. Medial single *Ċ* and double *ĊĊ*. Listen and repeat.

↓ *saaĊa*	'yard'	*maĊĊad*	'no one'
waaĊid	'one M'	*waĊĊad*	'he unified'
looĊa	'board'	*laĊĊag*	'he caught up'
ruuĊi	'go F'	*ṣiĊĊa*	'health'
muĊaami	'lawyer'	*guĊĊi*	'cough F'
raĊiim	'merciful M'	*baĊĊaar*	'sailor'
maĊall	'place'	*faĊĊaam*	'charcoal-seller'

Drill 6. Consonant *Ċ* in medial and initial clusters. Listen and repeat.

↓ *ʔaĊmar*	'red M'	*ʔafĊaṣ*	'I examine'
zaĊma	'trouble'	*yibĊaθ*	'he discusses'
maĊkama	'court'	*l-baarĊa*	'yesterday'
tiĊči	'she speaks'	*miĊtaaj*	'needing M'
liĊya	'beard'	*yinĊall*	'it M is solved'
Ċmarr	'he turned red'	*tĊammal*	'he endured'
Ċwaaš	'houses'	*fĊuula*	'males'

B. Consonant *Ɛ*

This consonant is a **voiced pharyngeal spirant,** and is thus the voiced counterpart of *Ċ*. It is produced, like *Ċ*, by a constriction of the muscles of the upper throat, but differs from *Ċ* in being accompanied by vibration of the vocal cords. It also differs in another way: *Ċ* is basically an expiration of breath through a narrowed pharynx, and gives the impression of being a breathy sound, whereas *Ɛ* is produced with a much less forceful expiration of breath, and gives the impression of being a somewhat strangled or squeezed sound. Here, for listening purposes only, are some examples of words containing *Ɛ*.

Drill 7. Initial, medial, and final *Ɛ*. Listen.

↓ *Ɛaal*	'excellent'	*baƐad*	'yet'
Ɛeen	'eye'	*fiƐil*	'action'
Ɛiid	'feast'	*baaƐ*	'he sold'
Ɛuuda	'stick'	*beeƐ*	'selling'
Ɛalam	'flag'	*biiƐ*	'sell M'
Ɛinab	'grapes'	*nooƐ*	'sort, kind'
Ɛumur	'age'	*juuƐ*	'hunger'

When practicing *ε*, as in the case of *ḥ*, remember that it is a sound produced entirely in the throat, and that the tongue should not curl up or back. Again, if necessary to prevent this, press the tongue tip against the back of the upper teeth. As a first exercise, say the syllable *baa,* and hold the long vowel sound for a moment: *baaaaa.* Now repeat, and this time, when you come to the end of the long-drawn-out vowel, suddenly tighten your neck and throat muscles, so that you get the impression of having choked off the sound in your throat. This is in effect a *ε*, probably a good deal exaggerated at first, but basically the sound you are trying to acquire: *baaaaaε*. Repeat this several times, and each time shorten the vowel a bit: *baaaε—baaaε—baaε*. The last is a normal Iraqi syllable, and in fact is a real word, which appears in the list above. Try it all again, and then replace *aa* with each of the other long vowels, as in the drill below.

Drill 8. Practice exercise: consonant *ε*. Listen and repeat.

baaaaε - *baaaε* - *baaε*
booooε - *boooε* - *booε*
buuuuε - *buuuε* - *buuε*
beeeeε - *beeeε* - *beeε*
biiiiε - *biiiε* - *biiε*

The next step is to add another vowel to the end of these syllables. First, take a deep breath and start out with the original long-drawn-out syllable *baaaaaε*. Now, while holding the long vowel sound, alternately tighten and relax the throat muscles, remembering to keep the tongue entirely out of action, and also to keep the vocal cords vibrating throughout, so that there is an uninterrupted stream of voiced—not whispered—noise. The result should be a series of long *aaaaa* sounds separated by *ε* sounds, the latter probably overly long and exaggerated, something like *baaaaεεεaaaaaεεεaaaaa*. Repeat the sequence several times, concentrating on the alternate squeezing and relaxing sensations in the throat. Repeat several times again, and now try to reduce the exaggeration of the *ε* sounds; that is, keep the *aaaaa* sounds long, but try to reduce the intervening *εεε* sounds to a single momentary squeeze: *baaaaaεaaaaaεaaaaaεaaaaa*. Next, repeat the sequence, now gradually reducing the length of the vowel as well, with the end result of a sequence like *baaεaaεaaεaaεaa*. Finally, eliminate the initial *b* and try to start off with a squeeze, immediately relaxing it into a vowel: *εaaεaaεaaεaa*. Now go through the whole procedure with each of the other long vowels.

Most English-speaking students, when encountering the *ε* for the first time, have difficulty in distinguishing it from certain other consonant sounds, or find that it gives them the impression of a vowel sound of some kind, or are unable to hear it at all. This is quite natural, since no similar distinctions exist in the English sound system, and consequently English-speakers are not accustomed to hearing them or making them. Practice will overcome many of these initial difficulties. The following drills contain words illustrating some of the troublesome contrasts.

Drill 9. Contrast between initial ʔ and initial ε. Listen and repeat.

ʔaani	'I'	→	*εaani*	(family name)
ʔalam	'pain'		*εalam*	'flag'
ʔamal	'hope'		*εamal*	'act'
ʔajjil	'postpone M'		*εajjil*	'speed up M'
ʔiid	'hand'		*εiid*	'feast'
ʔila	'to him'		*εila*	'he rose higher'
ʔimal	'he hoped'		*εimal*	'he acted'
ʔuḅar	'needles'		*εuḅar*	'he crossed'

Drill 10. Contrast between medial ʔ and medial ε. Listen and repeat.

raʔi	'opinion'	→	*raεi*	'grazing'
suʔaal	'question'		*suεaal*	'coughing'
maʔuuna	'supplies'		*maεuuna*	'assistance'
masaaʔi	'of evening M'		*masaaεi*	'efforts'

Drill 11. Contrast between medial *aa* and medial *aεa*. Listen and repeat.

taab	'he repented'	→	*taεab*	'tiredness'
zaal	'he removed'		*zaεal*	'anger'
naal	'he acquired'		*naεal*	'sole'
naam	'he slept'		*naεam*	'yes'

Drill 12. Contrast between final *a* and final *aε*. Listen and repeat.

jaa	'he came'	→	*jaaε*	'he starved'
jawwa	'under'		*jawwaε*	'he starved out'
lamma	'when'		*lammaε*	'he polished'
difa	'it M got warm'		*difaε*	'he paid'
sima	'heaven'		*simaε*	'he heard'
buqa	'he stayed'		*buqaε*	'stains'

The following drills illustrate ε in various positions.

Drill 13. Initial *ε*. Listen and repeat.

↓ *εaal*	'excellent'	*εašra*	'ten'
εaadil	'just M'	*εallam*	'he taught'
εaadatan	'usually'	*εajiib*	'strange M'
εaalam	'world'	*εilba*	'can'
εeeb	'defect'	*εilim*	'science'
εeen	'eye'	*εiraf*	'he knew'
εiid	'feast'	*εumur*	'age'
εuuda	'stick'	*εušur*	'one-tenth'

Drill 14. Final *ε*. Listen and repeat.

↓ *gaaε*	'floor'	*wugaε*	'he fell'
bayyaaε	'salesman'	*rijaε*	'he returned'
beeε	'selling'	*ʔismaε*	'listen M'
ʔasaabiiε	'weeks'	*jaamiε*	'mosque'
sariiε	'fast M'	*šaariε*	'street'
nooε	'sort, kind'	*rubuε*	'one-fourth'
mamnuuε	'forbidden M'	*subuε*	'one-seventh'

Drill 15. Medial single *ε* and double *εε*. Listen and repeat.

↓ *taεab*	'tiredness'	*taεεab*	'he tired'
zaεal	'anger'	*zaεεal*	'he angered'
saaεad	'he helped'	*jaεεad*	'he curled'
taεaazi	'condolences'	*naεεas*	'he was sleepy'
biεiid	'far M'	*naεεal*	'he shoed'
maaεuun	'plate'	*laεεaaba*	'toy'
juuεaan	'hungry M'	*gaεεadhum*	'he seated them'

Drill 16. Consonant *ε* in medial and initial clusters. Listen and repeat.

↓ *maεna*	'meaning'	*sabεa*	'seven'
maεhad	'institute'	*maṭεam*	'restaurant'
staεmal	'he used'	*ʔasεaar*	'prices'
naεsaan	'sleepy M'	*šabεaan*	'full M' (of food)
maεluum	'of course'	*tisεiin*	'ninety'
εtiqad	'he thought'	*tεallam*	'he learned'
εyuun	'eyes'	*mεabbis*	'frowning M'

C. Non-automatic stress

Previous sections on stress have dealt with the automatic type only, that is, with words in which the position of stress is automatically determined by—and thus predictable from—the phonological structure of the word, the arrangement of its consonants and vowels. The great majority of Iraqi words have predictable stress of this type. There are some words, however, in which stress is not predictable by the same criteria. This does not mean that in these cases the position of stress has to be learned for each individual word, but rather that stress is determined by—and thus predictable from—the grammatical structure of the word instead of the phonological structure. This means that words with non-automatic stress fall into a relatively small number of classes, each class characterized by a certain grammatical feature with which a certain kind of stress is associated. As you proceed through the book learning points of grammar, you will gradually meet these classes and become familiar with the way the stress falls in each class. For now we will give only one example. In words ending in the suffix *-a* which corresponds in meaning to the English object pronoun 'him or 'it M', stress falls on the syllable preceding that suffix, regardless of whether stress in that position conforms to the automatic stress rule or not. When it does not (that is, when stress is non-automatic) we indicate the position of stress by an acute accent mark, as in the examples on the right below.

Drill 17. Non-automatic stress. Listen and repeat.

tirak	'he left'	→	*tiráka*	'he left him'
ˀaxδat	'she took'		*ˀaxδáta*	'she took it M'
baddal	'he changed'		*baddála*	'he changed it M'
darrsat	'she taught'		*darrsáta*	'she taught him'
saaƐad	'he helped'		*saaƐáda*	'he helped him'
tarjam	'he translated'		*tarjáma*	'he translated it M'

UNIT 10

All the individual sounds of Iraqi have now been described and illustrated. The examples thus far given have been single words, each word illustrating sounds which occur in that word as it would be spoken in isolation, that is, not preceded or followed by any other words, and perhaps pronounced a little more slowly than usual. In normal speech, however, words are uttered not in isolation, with a pause before and after each one, but in a fast uninterrupted stream. In this flow of normal-speed speech, it often happens that an individual sound is modified or changed to something else by the influence of adjacent sounds, whether in the same word or not, and also that the form of a whole element (word, prefix, or suffix) is influenced by the form of a preceding or following element. In this unit we discuss the main types of this kind of modification in Iraqi. We also present, in the last section of the unit, complete charts of the consonants, the vowels, and the diphthongs.

A. Assimilation

A sound, under the influence of another (usually adjacent) sound, may become more like the other in some respect, or identical to it; this kind of modification is **assimilation.** In Iraqi, a stop, affricate, or spirant may assimilate to another consonant in any of these categories as to voice (in this case it is usually the first of the two which assimilates to the second): a voiceless consonant followed by a voiced consonant tends to become voiced, and a voiced consonant followed by a voiceless consonant tends to become voiceless. For example, the word ***sudus*** 'one-sixth' begins with an *s,* which is voiceless. In the plural of this word, ***ˀasdaas*** 'sixths', the *s* in question is immediately followed by *d,* which is voiced, so the *s* assimilates to the *d* by becoming voiced, which makes it a *z*. Thus the word which we write as *ˀasdaas* is normally pronounced *"ˀazdaas"*. Nevertheless, in this and similar cases we continue to write the unassimilated form (here *ˀasdaas*), because doing so makes clearer the relationship between the word in question and related words in which there is no assimilation (here *sudus*), and because the assimilated pronunciation is in any event quite automatic. Some other examples:

mašġuuḷ	'busy M'	is pronounced	*"mažġuuḷ"*
ˀaṣdiqaaˀ	'friends'	" "	*"ˀaẓdiqaaˀ"*
maδkuur	'mentioned M'	" "	*"maθkuur"*
libsat	'she wore'	" "	*"lipsat"*

A consonant may also assimilate to another as to the feature of emphasis, a plain consonant becoming emphatic when either followed or preceded by an emphatic (or even, as we saw in 6 A, when an emphatic is not adjacent but nearby). For example, there is a suffix *-ti* which occurs in past-tense verb-forms: ***kitabti*** 'you F wrote'. When this suffix is added to a stem ending in an emphatic, the *t* of the suffix may assimilate to the emphatic by becoming emphatic *ṭ,* as in ***xuḅaṭṭi*** 'you F mixed'. For other examples see 6 A and B.

In addition to the two general cases just described, there are several special types of assimilation involving particular consonants, as follows:

l followed by *n* becomes *n*:
  ʔil- 'to' plus *-na* 'us' gives *ʔinna* 'to us'
n followed by *r* becomes *n*:
  (*da-* '-ing') *n-* 'we' plus *-ruuC* 'go' gives *da-rruuC* 'we're going'
n followed by *b* becomes *m*:
  (*da-* 'ing') *n-* 'we' plus *-biiČ* 'sell' gives *da-mbiiČ* 'we're selling'
n followed by *m* becomes *m*:
  da- '-ing') *n-* 'we' plus *-muut* 'die' gives *da-mmuut* 'we're dying'

In the four special cases just mentioned, you may also occasionally hear the unassimilated sequences, but in normal-speed speech the assimilated forms are more common.

B. Loss of initial ʔ

When a word beginning with the glottal stop ʔ (see 4 C) is not the first element in an utterance, but is immediately preceded by a prefix or by another word, the initial ʔ is quite commonly dropped altogether:

ʔiidi	'my hand'	*b-iidi*	'in my hand'
ʔašuufa	'I see him'	*ma-ašuufa*	'I don't see him'
ʔaxuuya	'my brother'	*wiyya axuuya*	'with my brother'
ʔaruuC	'I go'	*ʔagdar aruuC*	'I can go'

C. Helping vowel

In 6 C and D we noted that a helping vowel may optionally occur before an initial consonant cluster or double consonant, when the word in question is at the beginning of an utterance. If the word is not the first element in the utterance, but is immediately preceded by a prefix or another word, then there is no option, but rather the following statement automatically applies: If the preceding element ends in a vowel, there is never a helping vowel; and if the preceding element ends in a consonant, there is always a helping vowel. Examples:

štira	'he bought'	*ma-štira*	'he didn't buy'
		ˀibni štira	'my son bought'
		ˀibnak ištira	'your son bought'
		baʕdeen ištira	'then he bought'
ktaab	'book'	*štira ktaab*	'he bought a book'
		haaδa ktaab	'this is a book'
		hal-iktaab	'this book'
		štireet iktaab	'I bought a book'
nnaam	'we sleep'	*ma-nnaam*	'we don't sleep'
		xalliina nnaam	'let us sleep'
		raḥ-innaam	'we're going to sleep'
		nigdar innaam	'we can sleep'

These examples illustrate an important general fact about Iraqi, which is that (with very rare exceptions) clusters of more than two consonants do not occur, whether within a single word or from one word to another in an uninterrupted utterance. Thus in any utterance there is always a helping vowel whenever its absence would result in a cluster of more than two consonants. The position of the helping vowel is between the first and second of three consonants, and between the second and third of four.

D. Loss of stem vowel

A stem vowel is a short vowel followed by a single consonant at the end of a word, for example the last *a* of *šahar* 'month', the last *i* of *ˀisim* 'name', and the *u* of *gabuḷ* 'before'. When a word containing such a stem vowel is immediately followed in an utterance by a word beginning with a vowel (either a helping vowel as in C above or the vowel that is left in initial position when a *ˀ* is dropped as in B above), the stem vowel may be dropped as long as the result is no more than two consonants in sequence. This is not to say that all stem vowels are invariably dropped under these circumstances—you will hear considerable variation—but the dropping is common in normal-speed speech.

šahar	'month'	*šahr iθ-θaaliθ*	'the third month'
ˀisim	'name'	*ˀism axuuya*	'my brother's name'
gabuḷ	'before'	*gabḷ isbuuʕ*	'a week ago'
laazim	'must'	*laazm aruuḥ*	'I must go'
baʕad	'after'	*baʕd išwayya*	'after a while'
činit	'I was'	*čint ihnaak*	'I was there'
xaabur	'call up'	*xaabr il-muḥaami*	'call up the lawyer'

E. Double consonants

In Iraqi, there are only two situations in which a double consonant sound ever occurs. We have had many examples of the first, which is

(1) When followed by a vowel in the same word:

dazza	'he sent him'
dazz-ilha	'he sent to her'

The second is

(2) When followed by a vowel at the beginning of the next word, if that word follows the first with no pause:

dazz il-maktuub	'he sent the letter'

In all other situations only a single consonant sound *can* occur, namely:

(3) When followed by another consonant in the same word:

dazzha	'he sent her'
dazz-la	'he sent to him'

(4) When followed by another consonant at the beginning of the next word:

dazz maktuub	'he sent a letter'

(5) When followed by a pause; that is, by at least a brief second of complete silence:

dazz	'he sent'

Thus, in (3), (4), and (5), the syllable written *dazz* is pronounced *daz,* and indeed cannot be pronounced any other way. We *write* a double consonant in this and similar cases, however, as a convenient way of indicating the presence of a potentially double consonant, one which is automatically pronounced double in the situations described in (1) and (2), and automatically pronounced single in the other three situations. Here are some other examples:

Double consonant sound		**Single consonant sound**	
dazzeet	'I sent'	*dazzhum*	'he sent them'
ɛabba	'seed'	*ɛabb*	'seeds'
baddil	'change M'	*baddlat*	'she changed'
sinn il-walad	'the boy's tooth'	*sinn θaani*	'another tooth'
sidd il-baab	'close M the door'	*siddha*	'close M it F'

As the examples in (3) and (4) and in the right-hand column above show, a written sequence consisting of a double consonant letter followed by another consonant letter, for example ***zzh, zz-l,*** or ***zz m,*** represents a spoken sequence consisting of a single consonant sound followed by another (single) consonant sound. Such a sequence is a cluster of only two consonant sounds, and is therefore permissible.

F. Charts

As a final summary of the sounds of Iraqi, all the consonants, vowels, and diphthongs are shown below in chart form.

Consonants

	LABIAL	INTERDENTAL	DENTAL	PALATAL	VELAR	UVULAR	PHARYNGEAL	GLOTTAL
STOPS Voiceless Voiced	 *p ṗ* *b ḅ*		 *t ṭ* *d*		 *k* *g*	 *q*		 *ʔ*
SPIRANTS Voiceless Voiced	 *f f̣* *v*	 *θ* *δ δ̣*	 *s ṣ* *z ẓ*	 *š* *ž*	 *x* *ġ*		 *ħ* *ʕ*	 *h*
AFFRICATES Voiceless Voiced				 *č* *j*				
NASALS	*m ṃ*		*n*					
LATERALS			*l ḷ*					
FLAP			*r*					
SEMIVOWELS	*w*			*y*				

Notes: 1. Emphatic consonants, marked with a dot underneath, are shown to the right of their respective plain counterparts.

2. In the LABIAL column, the spirants (*f ḟ v*) are labiodental; the others, bilabial.

3. The two voiced spirants *v* and *ž* are very rare.

4. The nasals, laterals, flap, and semivowels are all usually voiced, but voiceless varieties may be heard in certain environments.

Vowels

LONG	FRONT Unrounded	CENTRAL Unrounded	BACK Rounded
HIGH	*ii*		*uu*
MID	*ee*		*oo*
LOW		*aa*	

SHORT	FRONT Unrounded	CENTRAL Unrounded	BACK Rounded
HIGH	*i*		*u*
MID			*o*
LOW		*a*	

Notes: 1. The labels are not absolute but relative. This means, for example, that the central vowels may also have fronted or backed qualities, but are always lower, or more central, or both, than the mid front and mid back vowels; and that the high front vowels may also have centralized qualities, but are always more front than the high back vowels.

2. The short vowel *o* is rare.

Diphthongs

	With glide to *y*	With glide to *w*
High vowel		*iw*
Mid vowels	*ooy*	*eew*
Low vowels	*aay* *ay*	*aaw* *aw*

Note: The diphthongs *iw* and *ooy* are extremely rare, the diphthong *eew* slightly more common, and the others very common.

UNIT 11

A. DIALOGUE

Two men happen to meet on a street in downtown Baghdad. They are old friends but haven't seen each other for some time.

ʔabu zuheer	Abu Zuhayr
marḥaba	hello
šloonak	how are you M
1. *marḥaba, ʔabu xaalid! šloonak?*	Hello, Abu Khalid! How are you?

ʔabu xaalid	Abu Khalid
zeen	good, well M
lḥamdilla	praise to God
ʔinta	you M
2. *zeen ilḥamdilla. ʔinta šloonak?*	Fine, thanks. How're you?

ʔabu zuheer	Abu Zuhayr
yaaba	(form of address; see Notes)
haay	this F
weenak	where are you M
ma-da-nšuufak	we are not seeing you M

3. *lCamdilla zeen.*
yaaba haay weenak,
ma-da-nšuufak?

Fine, thanks. Where've you been all this time, that we don't ever see you?

ʔabu xaalid	Abu Khalid
waḷḷa	really, honestly
mašġuuḷ	busy M
l-maCruusiin	the children
šloonhum	how are they

4. *waḷḷa mašġuuḷ.*
l-maCruusiin išloonhum?

Well, I've been busy. How're the children?

ʔabu zuheer	Abu Zuhayr
zeeniin	good, well P
ybuusuun	they kiss
ʔiidak	your M hand
gul-li	tell M me
šloon	how
š-šuġuḷ	the work, the business
hal-ayyaam	these days

5. *zeeniin ilCamdilla,*
ybuusuun ʔiidak.
gul-li,
šloon iš-šuġuḷ hal-ayyaam?

They're fine, thanks. Tell me, how's business these days?

ʔabu xaalid	Abu Khalid
maaši	walking, going along M
ṃarra	a time; sometimes
muu zeen	not good, bad M

6. *maaši lCamdilla.*
ṃarra zeen, ṃarra muu zeen.

Going along. Sometimes good, sometimes bad.

NOTES ON DIALOGUE

1. Polite formulas. Like all forms of Arabic, Iraqi is rich in words and expressions used automatically in certain social situations, for example on meeting or taking leave of someone. Some of these polite formulas lend themselves quite well to translation into English: *šloonak,* for example, corresponds in meaning to *How are you?* and is used in just about the same way. Others, however, may present problems. In certain situations, both the Iraqi and the English-speaker normally use some sort of polite formula, but the two expressions may not have the same literal meaning; or, in certain other situations, the Iraqi may habitually use a polite formula where the English-speaker would normally say nothing at all. When an Iraqi polite formula occurs in a dialogue in this book, we show its approximate literal meaning in the indented breakdowns, but in the translation of the numbered sentence we give the expression that an English-speaker would normally use in the same situation (or no equivalent at all, if that would be normal). In any case, it is best to learn every polite formula as a whole, associating it with the situations in which it is used, and not to be too concerned about its literal meaning. In these Notes we will give a brief comment on each new polite formula and list some of the situations in which it is used.

marƈaba — An informal phrase of greeting, corresponding approximately to English *hello*. Said on meeting an acquaintance.

šloonak — The most common enquiry about health, corresponding closely to English *How are you?* This form is used only in addressing a male person; for other forms see B below.

lƈamdilla — A frequently used expression, meaning literally 'praise to God'. It is used: (1) as a favorable reply to any enquiry about health, either alone or with some word meaning 'well, good' (such as *zeen*). In this context the English equivalent is *Fine, thank you* or the like. (2) In general, any time something good happens, or something turns out in a desirable way. In this context the equivalent might be *Good, Thank goodness,* or *Thank God,* depending on the seriousness of the matter. Besides the form shown here, other slightly differing forms may be heard, for example *ƈamdilla, lƈamdillaa,* or the Classical Arabic *ʔal-ƈamdu lillaah.*

ybuusuun ˀiidak	Literal meaning: 'they kiss your M hand'. Said immediately after answering a question about the health of one's children. Implies that the children send their polite respects to the enquirer. No English equivalent. This form is used only in addressing a male person; for other forms see B below.

2. Forms of address

ˀabu	A male acquaintance who has children is usually addressed or referred to by a form consisting of the word *ˀabu* followed by the name of his eldest son (or, if he has no sons, by that of his eldest daughter), for example *ˀabu xaalid,* which means literally 'father of Khalid'. The same man's wife, similarly, is called *ˀumm xaalid* 'mother of Khalid'.
yaaba	A friendly form of address, used most commonly—but not exclusively—among males. No precise equivalent.
3. *l-maƐruusiin*	This term means literally 'the guarded ones', and is used to refer to someone else's children, the implication being that they are guarded by God.

B. GRAMMAR

1. Pronoun suffixes: Second person

Note the ending *-ak* in the following examples from the dialogue:

šloonak	how are you M
weenak	where are you M
ma-da-nšuufak	we are not seeing you M
ybuusuun ˀiidak	they kiss your M hand

This ending is a **pronoun suffix.** It never occurs alone, as an independent word, but always attached to some other form. When attached to a noun, as in the last example above, it corresponds in meaning to English *your M*: *ˀiid* 'hand', *ˀiidak* 'your M hand'. When attached to a verb, as in the third example, it corresponds to *you M* as the object of the verb: *ma-da-nšuuf* 'we are not seeing', *ma-da-nšuufak* 'we are not seeing you M'. It may also occur attached to a very few words other than nouns and verbs, as in the first two examples, and may then correspond to *you M* as the subject: *šloon* 'how', *šloonak* 'how (are) you M'.

The pronoun suffix *-ak,* however, is used only in addressing one male person. The corresponding pronoun suffix used in addressing one female person is *-ič,* as in the following examples:

šlooni č	'how are you F'
weeni č	'where are you F'
ma-da-nšuufič	'we are not seeing you F'
ybuusuun ˀiidič	'they kiss your F hand'

In addressing two or more persons, regardless of their sex, the corresponding pronoun suffix is *-kum,* as follows:

šloonkum	'how are you P'
weenkum	'where are you P'
ma-da-nšuufkum	'we are not seeing you P'
ybuusuun ˀiidkum	'they kiss your P hand'

Since the English forms *you* and *your* do not reflect the gender-number distinctions indicated by the Iraqi forms *-ak, ič,* and *-kum,* we use the letters M, F, and P (for masculine, feminine, and plural) in all the English translations in order to show which Iraqi form is involved. The following table summarizes these second-person pronoun suffix forms:

M	*-ak*	'you, your M'
F	*-ič*	'you, your F'
P	*-kum*	'you, your P'

2. Independent personal pronouns: Second person

Note the word *ˀinta* in the following exchange from the dialogue:

Abu Zuhayr:	*šloonak?*	'How are you M?'
Abu Khalid:	*zeen ilɛamdilla.*	'Fine, thanks.
	ˀinta šloonak?	How're you M?'

Besides the pronoun suffixes, Iraqi also has personal pronoun forms which are independent words, one corresponding to each pronoun suffix. The form *ˀinta* in the example above is the second-person masculine independent personal pronoun, equivalent in meaning to English *you M*. The second-person feminine and plural forms are *ˀinti* 'you F' and *ˀintu* 'you P'.

These independent personal pronoun forms are used much less in Iraqi than are the corresponding pronouns in English. The example above illustrates one typical use: for contrastive emphasis. After answering the question about his own health, Abu Khalid then asks *ˀinta šloonak?* The use of the independent pronoun form *ˀinta* 'you M', along with the corresponding pronoun suffix form *-ak* 'you M', indicates a change of the focus of attention, a shift from one subject to another. The same kind of contrastive emphasis is often indicated in English by extra stress on the pronoun, so that Abu Khalid's enquiry might be translated 'How are *you*?'

The table below shows the second-person independent personal pronouns and also the corresponding pronoun suffixes.

Independent pronouns			Pronoun suffixes		
M	*ˀinta*	'you M'	M	*-ak*	'you, your M'
F	*ˀinti*	'you F'	F	*-ič*	'you, your F'
P	*ˀintu*	'you P'	P	*-kum*	'you, your P'

3. Adjectives: Masculine, feminine, and plural forms

In English, an adjective has the same form whether it refers to a male, a female, or two or more persons, for example the adjective *fine* in *he's fine, she's fine,* and *they're fine.* In Iraqi, on the other hand, most adjectives have several different forms. One is a **masculine** form, used when the adjective refers to one male person; one is a **feminine** form, used when the adjective refers to one female person; one is a **masculine plural** form, used when the adjective refers to two or more persons of whom at least one is male; and one is a **feminine plural** form, used when the adjective refers to two or more persons of whom all are females. (In this last case, however, the masculine plural is sometimes used instead.) The different forms of an adjective are known as **inflections.**

In Sentences 2 and 3 of the dialogue, note the word *zeen* 'good, well M', which is an adjective in its masculine form. In each of these sentences, the speaker uses the masculine form because he is applying the adjective to himself, and he is a man. If a woman were speaking, she would use the feminine form, which is *zeena.* In Sentence 5, the speaker uses the masculine plural form *zeeniin* because he is now referring to two or more persons, namely his children. If his children were all girls, he might use the same form *zeeniin,* or the feminine plural form *zeenaat.* The following table shows the four inflectional forms of *zeen* and of *mašġuul̩* 'busy M'. (In the translations of adjectives we write M, F, MP, or FP after the English word to indicate the distinctions made by the Iraqi forms.)

Masculine	*zeen*	*mašġuuḷ*
Feminine	*zeena*	*mašġuuḷa*
Masculine plural	*zeeniin*	*mašġuuḷiin*
Feminine plural	*zeenaat*	*mašġuuḷaat*

This table illustrates some facts which are true of many adjectives: the masculine form is usually the simplest, without any ending; the feminine form bears the ending *-a*; the masculine plural form, *-iin*; and the feminine plural form, *-aat*.

C. DRILLS

Drill 1. Repeat the utterance, replacing the underlined name with each of the new names given, and making any other necessary changes.

marCaba ʔabu <u>xaalid!</u> šloonak?	Hello, Abu <u>Khalid!</u> How are you M?
zuheer	Zuhayr
samiira	Samira
muṣṭafa	Mustafa
mCammad	Muhammad
xaalid	Khalid

Drill 2. Repeat the utterance, replacing the underlined name with each of the new names given, and making any other necessary changes.

marCaba ʔumm <u>xaalid!</u> šloonič?	Hello, Umm <u>Khalid!</u> How are you F?
zuheer	Zuhayr
samiira	Samira
muṣṭafa	Mustafa
mCammad	Muhammad
xaalid	Khalid

Drill 3. The following utterances are addressed to a man. Say them as you would to a woman.

šloonak?	*šloonič?*
marCaba! šloonak?	*marCaba! šloonič?*
haay weenak?	*haay weenič?*
ma-da-nšuufak.	*ma-da-nšuufič.*
haay weenak, ma-da-nšuufak?	*haay weenič, ma-da-nšuufič?*
ybuusuun ʔiidak.	*ybuusuun ʔiidič.*

Drill 4. The following utterances are addressed to a woman. Say them as you would to a group.

šloonič?
marḥaba! šloonič?
haay weenič?
ma-da-nšuufič.
haay weenič, ma-da-nšuufič?

šloonkum?
marḥaba! šloonkum?
haay weenkum?
ma-da-nšuufkum.
haay weenkum, ma-da-nšuufkum?

Drill 5. The following utterances are addressed to a group. Say them as you would to a man.

šloonkum?
marḥaba! šloonkum?
haay weenkum?
ma-da-nšuufkum.
haay weenkum, ma-da-nšuufkum?

šloonak?
marḥaba! šloonak?
haay weenak?
ma-da-nšuufak.
haay weenak, ma-da-nšuufak?

Drill 6. The following utterances are addressed to a man. Say them as you would to a group.

šloonak?
marḥaba! šloonak?
haay weenak?
ma-da-nšuufak.
haay weenak, ma-da-nšuufak?

šloonkum?
marḥaba! šloonkum?
haay weenkum?
ma-da-nšuufkum.
haay weenkum, ma-da-nšuufkum?

Drill 7. The following utterances are addressed to a group. Say them as you would to a woman.

šloonkum?
marḥaba! šloonkum?
haay weenkum?
ma-da-nšuufkum.
haay weenkum, ma-da-nšuufkum?

šloonič?
marḥaba! šloonič?
haay weenič?
ma-da-nšuufič.
haay weenič, ma-da-nšuufič?

Drill 8. The following utterances are addressed to a woman. Say them as you would to a man.

šloonič?
marḥaba! šloonič?
haay weenič?
ma-da-nšuufič.
haay weenič, ma-da-nšuufič?
ybuusuun ʔiidič.

šloonak?
marḥaba! šloonak?
haay weenak?
ma-da-nšuufak.
haay weenak, ma-da-nšuufak?
ybuusuun ʔiidak.

Drill 9. Repeat the utterance, replacing the underlined independent pronoun with each of the other independent pronouns given, and making whatever other changes may then be necessary.

ʔinta šloonak?	*ʔinta šloonak?*
ʔinti	*ʔinti šlooničʔ*
ʔintu	*ʔintu šloonkum?*
ʔinti	*ʔinti šlooničʔ*
ʔinta	*ʔinta šloonak?*
ʔintu	*ʔintu šloonkum?*
ʔinta	*ʔinta šloonak?*

Drill 10. Respond to the following questions by saying *zeen ilḥamdilla* if you are male, or *zeena lḥamdilla* if you are female, or *zeeniin ilḥamdilla* if the question is addressed to a group. If you are male, do not respond to questions addressed to a female, and vice versa.

šloonak?	(M)	*zeen ilḥamdilla.*
šlooničʔ	(F)	*zeena lḥamdilla.*
šloonkum?		*zeeniin ilḥamdilla.*
marḥaba! šlooničʔ	(F)	*zeena lḥamdilla.*
marḥaba! šloonkum?		*zeeniin ilḥamdilla.*
marḥaba! šloonak?	(M)	*zeen ilḥamdilla.*
ʔinta šloonak?	(M)	*zeen ilḥamdilla.*
ʔinti šlooničʔ	(F)	*zeena lḥamdilla.*
ʔintu šloonkum?		*zeeniin ilḥamdilla.*

UNIT 12

A. DIALOGUE

Abu Zuhayr and Abu Khalid continue their conversation.

ʔabu zuheer	Abu Zuhayr
ween	where
raayiḥ	going M
ʕindak	on, with you M
1. *ween raayiḥ, ʔabu xaalid?* *ʕindak šuġuḷ?*	Where are you going, Abu Khalid? Have you got something you have to do?

ʔabu xaalid	Abu Khalid
laa	no
kullši	everything; anything
ma-ʕindi	not on me, not with me
2. *laa waḷḷa, kullši ma-ʕindi.*	No, I haven't anything.
ʔabu zuheer	Abu Zuhayr
laʕad	then, in that case
xal-da-rruuḥ	let's be going
lil-gahwa	to the coffee-house
nišrab	we drink
fadd	a, an
stikaan	glass (small, used for tea)
čaay	tea
suwa	together
3. *zeen laʕad, xal-da-rruuḥ lil-gahwa nišrab fadd istikaan čaay suwa.*	All right, then, let's go to the coffee-house and have a glass of tea together.
ʔabu xaalid	Abu Khalid
ʕaal	fine, excellent
ʔaku	there is, there are
b-hal-manṭiqa	in this area
ʕajab	wonder
4. *ʕaal! ʔaku gahwa b-hal-manṭiqa ʕajab?*	Fine. Is there a coffee-house in this area, I wonder?
ʔabu zuheer	Abu Zuhayr
ʔii	yes
yamm	by, next to
l-ḅang	the bank
5. *ʔii, ʔaku gahwa zeena yamm il-ḅang.*	Yes, there's a good coffee-house next to the bank.
ʔabu xaalid	Abu Khalid
6. *zeen laʕad, xal-da-rruuḥ.*	All right, then, let's go.

NOTES ON DIALOGUE

1. **The coffee-house.** In Iraq, as in most parts of the Middle East, the coffee-house is a flourishing institution. Men go there to sip a drink, talk to their friends, play cards or other games, read the newspaper, and in general relax. Women never go. Some coffee-houses serve only tea and coffee; some offer a few other kinds of beverages such as yoghurt or bottled soft drinks. Tables are outside when the weather permits.

B. GRAMMAR

1. Pronoun suffixes: First person

In Sentence 2 of the dialogue, note the ending *-i* in the form *ma-ɛindi.* This is the first-person singular pronoun suffix, corresponding in most cases to English *my* or *me.* Here are two other examples:

ˀiidi	'my hand'
yammi	'next to me'

There is no masculine-feminine distinction in the forms of the first-person singular pronoun suffix, as there is in those of the second-person singular; in the first person the only distinction is between singular and plural. The form *-i,* however, is only one of three forms, or **alternants,** of the first-person singular pronoun suffix (the others will be given later). The alternant *-i* is attached to certain nouns and prepositions, but not to verbs.

The first-person plural pronoun suffix is *-na,* corresponding in most cases to English *our* or *us,* for example:

šuġuḷna	'our work'
yammna	'next to us'

This pronoun suffix has the form *-na* wherever it occurs.

2. The preposition *ɛind*

The form *ɛind,* which occurs (with attached pronoun suffixes) in Sentences 1 and 2 of the dialogue, is a preposition. For the sake of brevity, it is translated in the breakdowns as 'on, with'. The fact is, however, that neither this nor any other Iraqi preposition corresponds exactly to any English preposition, and therefore such translations should be taken as convenient labels rather than indications of a full range of meaning, and the various uses of each Iraqi preposition should be learned in their own contexts. There are two main uses of *ɛind*. One expresses the idea 'at the house of' or 'at the place of business of', as in *at Khalid's house, at the barber's, at the doctor's*. Examples of this use will occur in later lessons. The second main use, illustrated in this dialogue, is in expressing the idea which in English is expressed by the verb *to have;* in this use the preposition generally has an attached pronoun suffix. Thus, *ɛindi šuğuḷ* may be translated 'I have work', but remember that *ɛindi* is not a verb form meaning literally 'I have', but a preposition plus a pronoun suffix.

This preposition has two alternants, depending on what follows. With a pronoun suffix beginning with a vowel, it is *ɛind-;* with a pronoun suffix beginning with a consonant, it is *ɛid-*. Following is a table of forms consisting of this preposition with the pronoun suffixes we have so far discussed, namely those of the second and first person:

Second person		
Masculine	*ɛindak*	'you M have'
Feminine	*ɛindič*	'you F have'
Plural	*ɛidkum*	'you P have'
First person		
Singular	*ɛindi*	'I have'
Plural	*ɛidna*	'we have'

3. Noun gender and adjective agreement

Every Iraqi noun, whether it refers to a human being, an animal, an inanimate object, or an abstraction, belongs to one or the other of two great classes, called **masculine** and **feminine.** A noun's membership in one of these classes is its **gender.** In the case of human beings and some of the larger animals, nouns referring to males are masculine in gender and those referring to females are feminine; but in the other cases the terms "masculine" and "feminine" are purely grammatical labels and have nothing to do with sex.

The form of a noun in the singular will often provide a clue as to its gender, since most feminine nouns end in *-a* and most masculine nouns do not. For example, of the nouns we have had so far, *šuğuḷ* 'work', *stikaan* 'glass', *čaay* 'tea', and *ḅang* 'bank' are masculine; *ṃarra* 'time', *gahwa* 'coffee-house', and *manṭiqa* 'area' are feminine. This is not foolproof, however, because there are also some masculine nouns which end in *-a* and some very common feminine nouns which do not; in these cases we will indicate the gender of each noun as it occurs.

The importance of all this lies in the fact that the gender of a noun, along with its **number** (for example, whether it is singular or plural), determines the inflectional form of any adjective or pronoun which refers to it. In Sentence 5 of the dialogue, for example, note the phrase *gahwa zeena* 'good coffee-house'. The noun in this phrase is a feminine (singular) noun, and therefore the adjective *zeena* which refers to it is in its feminine (singular) form. (Note also that, unlike English, the adjective in such a phrase always *follows* the noun.) If the noun were masculine (singular) instead, the adjective would be in its masculine (singular) form, for example *þang zeen* 'good bank'. This relationship between the gender and number of a noun, and the form of an adjective referring to it, is called **agreement.** When the noun is singular, agreement is a simple matter: masculine noun—masculine form of adjective; feminine noun—feminine form of adjective. When the noun is plural, the type of agreement depends on various factors, which will be discussed as they arise.

4. Iraqi equivalents of English indefinite article

There is no one Iraqi form which always corresponds exclusively to the English indefinite article *a* or *an,* but there are two main ways to express the same general idea. One is by the use of the noun alone, as in Sentences 4 and 5 of the dialogue: *gahwa* 'a coffee-house'. The other is by the use of the word *fadd* preceding the noun, as in Sentence 3: *fadd istikaan* 'a glass'. There are some contexts in which it is more natural to use the noun alone, others in which it is more natural to use *fadd,* and still others in which the two possibilities would be equally natural. You should imitate what you hear in each case, and you will gradually develop a fairly accurate feeling for the use of one or the other. Bear in mind, in addition, that *fadd* is also used in other ways, when it does not correspond to *a* or *an.*

5. The article prefix *l-/D-*

The Iraqi equivalent of the English definite article *the* is not an independent word, as in English, but a prefix attached to the noun. This prefix has two alternants, depending on the first sound of the following noun. One alternant is a prefixed *l-*, used if the noun to which it is attached begins with one of the following sounds or their emphatic counterparts:

ʔ	*x*	*f*	*m*	*y*
b	*ε*	*q*	*h*	*p*
ħ	*ġ*	*k*	*w*	*g*

Note that these are all sounds which are *not* produced by action of the tongue tip. Examples:

ʔiid	'hand'	*l-ʔiid*	'the hand'
ḅang	'bank'	*l-ḅang*	'the bank'
maħruusiin	'children'	*l-maħruusiin*	'the children'
manṭiqa	'area'	*l-manṭiqa*	'the area'
ṃarra	'time'	*l-ṃarra*	'the time'
gahwa	'coffee-house'	*l-gahwa*	'the coffee-house'

The second alternant is a prefix consisting of the same sound as the initial sound of the noun to which it is attached; that is, with a noun beginning with *t*, the prefix is *t;* with a noun beginning with *θ*, the prefix is *θ;* and so on. This is really a whole group of different alternants rather than just one, but they all work on the same principle and it is useful to think of the whole group as a single type, which we may symbolize as the alternant *D-* (for "doubled"). This alternant is used when the noun begins with one of the following sounds or their emphatic counterparts:

t	*d*	*z*	*l*
θ	*δ*	*s*	*n*
j	*r*	*š*	*č*

Note that these are all sounds which *are* produced by action of the tongue tip. Examples:

šuġuḷ	'work'	*š-šuġuḷ*	'the work'
čaay	'tea'	*č-čaay*	'the tea'

However, if the noun begins with a cluster of any two consonants, including those in the second group above, the prefix is generally *l-*, and a helping vowel occurs before the initial cluster of the noun:

stikaan	'tea-glass'	*l-istikaan*	'the tea-glass'

6. The demonstrative prefix: *hal-/haD-*

The Iraqi equivalent of the English demonstratives *this* and *these* (and in some contexts *that* and *those* as well) is a prefix consisting of the element *ha-* combined with the article prefix just described. This prefix therefore also has two alternants, *hal-* and *haD-*, and the use of these is exactly parallel to the use of the two alternants of the article prefix. Examples:

ʔayyaam	'days'	*hal-ayyaam*	'these days'
manṭiqa	'area'	*hal-manṭiqa*	'this area'
gahwa	'coffee-house'	*hal-gahwa*	'this coffee-house'
stikaan	'tea-glass'	*hal-istikaan*	'this tea-glass'
šuġuḷ	'work'	*haš-šuġuḷ*	'this work'
čaay	'tea'	*hač-čaay*	'this tea'

An initial *ʔ*, in an unstressed syllable, as in the first item above, is generally dropped when a prefix or another word immediately precedes it.

C. DRILLS

Drill 1. New words. Listen and repeat.

εindak beet?	Do you M have a house?
εindak qalam?	Do you M have a pencil?
εindak talafoon?	Do you M have a telephone?
εindak sayyaara?	Do you M have a car?
εindak šiqqa?	Do you M have an apartment?
εindak xariiṭa?	Do you M have a map?
εidkum beet?	Do you P have a house?
εidkum qalam?	Do you P have a pencil?
εidkum talafoon?	Do you P have a telephone?
εidkum sayyaara?	Do you P have a car?
εidkum šiqqa?	Do you P have an apartment?
εidkum xariiṭa?	Do you P have a map?
ma-εidna beet.	We don't have a house.
ma-εidna qalam.	We don't have a pencil.
ma-εidna talafoon.	We don't have a telephone.
ma-εidna sayyaara.	We don't have a car.
ma-εidna šiqqa.	We don't have an apartment.
ma-εidna xariiṭa.	We don't have a map.

Drill 2. Repeat the utterance, replacing the underlined portion with each of the items given.

ma-ɛindak beet?	Don't you M have a house?
šiqqa	an apartment
sayyaara	a car
talafoon	a telephone
šuġuḷ	work
xariiṭa	a map
qalam	a pencil
čaay	tea
stikaan	a tea-glass
beet	a house

Drill 3. Repeat the utterance, replacing the underlined portion with each of the items given.

ma-ɛindi beet.	I don't have a house.
talafoon	a telephone
čaay	tea
šuġuḷ	work
šiqqa	an apartment
stikaan	a tea-glass
qalam	a pencil
sayyaara	a car
xariiṭa	a map
beet	a house

Drill 4. Repeat the utterance, replacing the underlined portion with each of the items given.

ɛindi beet zeen.	I have a good house.
čaay zeen	good tea
šuġuḷ zeen	good work
stikaan zeen	a good tea-glass
qalam zeen	a good pencil
šiqqa zeena	a good apartment
sayyaara zeena	a good car
xariiṭa zeena	a good map
beet zeen	a good house

Drill 5. Repeat the utterance, replacing the underlined portion with each of the items given.

ʕidna <u>beet zeen.</u>	We have <u>a good house.</u>
šiqqa zeena	a good apartment
šuġuḷ zeen	good work
stikaan zeen	a good tea-glass
sayyaara zeena	a good car
čaay zeen	good tea
xariiṭa zeena	a good map
beet zeen	a good house

Drill 6. The following utterances are addressed to a man. Say them as you would to a woman.

šloonak?	*šlooničʔ*
ybuusuun ʔiidak.	*ybuusuun ʔiidič.*
ʕindak talafoon?	*ʕindič talafoon?*
ʕindak beet zeen?	*ʕindič beet zeen?*
ma-ʕindak šuġuḷ?	*ma-ʕindič šuġuḷ?*
ma-ʕindak sayyaara zeena?	*ma-ʕindič sayyaara zeena?*
kullši ma-ʕindak.	*kullši ma-ʕindič.*
haay weenak?	*haay weenič?*
ween beetak?	*ween beetič?*

Drill 7. The following utterances are addressed to a woman. Say them as you would to a group.

šloonič?	*šloonkum?*
haay weenič?	*haay weenkum?*
ma-da-nšuufič.	*ma-da-nšuufkum.*
ʕindič beet zeen?	*ʕidkum beet zeen?*
ʕindič beet ib-hal-manṭiqa?	*ʕidkum beet ib-hal-manṭiqa?*
ween beetič?	*ween beetkum?*
ma-ʕindič sayyaara zeena?	*ma-ʕidkum sayyaara zeena?*
kullši ma-ʕindič.	*kullši ma-ʕidkum.*

Drill 8. Change the first-person singular pronoun suffix *-i* to the first-person plural pronoun suffix *-na,* and make whatever other changes may then be necessary.

ʕindi beet.	*ʕidna beet.*
ma-ʕindi beet.	*ma-ʕidna beet.*
ʕindi beet zeen.	*ʕidna beet zeen.*
ʕindi beet ib-hal-manṭiqa?	*ʕidna beet ib-hal-manṭiqa.*
ʕindi talafoon.	*ʕidna talafoon.*
ma-ʕindi šuġuḷ.	*ma-ʕidna šuġuḷ.*
ʕindi sayyaara zeena.	*ʕidna sayyaara zeena.*
kullši ma-ʕindi.	*kullši ma-ʕidna.*

Drill 9. Replace the underlined portion with each of the items given, making whatever changes in the form of the article prefix may then be necessary.

šloon il-maʕruusiin?	*šloon il-maʕruusiin?*
beet	*šloon il-beet?*
qalam	*šloon il-qalam?*
gahwa	*šloon il-gahwa?*
xariiṭa	*šloon il-xariiṭa?*
šuġuḷ	*šloon iš-šuġuḷ?*
šiqqa	*šloon iš-šiqqa?*
čaay	*šloon ič-čaay?*
sayyaara	*šloon is-sayyaara?*

Drill 10. Change each sentence as in the following example:

Cue:	*ʕindak beet?*	Have you M a house?
Response:	*ween il-beet?*	Where's the house?

ʕindak qalam?	*ween il-qalam?*
ʕindak xariiṭa?	*ween il-xariiṭa?*
ʕindak čaay?	*ween ič-čaay?*
ʕindak ḅang?	*ween il-ḅang?*
ʕindak sayyaara?	*ween is-sayyaara?*
ʕindak talafoon?	*ween it-talafoon?*
ʕindak šiqqa?	*ween iš-šiqqa?*

Drill 11. Answer each question negatively, as in the following example:

Question:	*hal-beet zeen?*	Is this house all right?
Answer:	*laa, hal-beet muu zeen.*	No, this house is not good.

hal-qalam zeen?	*laa, hal-qalam muu zeen.*
hal-ƀang zeen?	*laa, hal-ƀang muu zeen.*
hal-istikaan zeen?	*laa, hal-istikaan muu zeen.*
hal-xariiṭa zeena?	*laa, hal-xariiṭa muu zeena.*
hal-gahwa zeena?	*laa, hal-gahwa muu zeena.*
haš-šuġuḷ zeen?	*laa, haš-šuġuḷ muu zeen.*
hač-čaay zeen?	*laa, hač-čaay muu zeen.*
has-sayyaara zeena?	*laa, has-sayyaara muu zeena.*
haš-šiqqa zeena?	*laa, haš-šiqqa muu zeena.*

Drill 12. Answer each question affirmatively, as in the example. If the question is addressed to one person, use the first-person singular pronoun suffix in your answer; however, if you are male, do not respond to questions addressed to a female, and vice versa. If the question is addressed to a group, use the first-person plural pronoun suffix in your answer.

Question:	*ʕindak beet?*	Have you M a house?
Answer:	*ʔii, ʕindi beet.*	Yes, I have a house.

ʕindak qalam?	(M)	*ʔii, ʕindi qalam.*
ʕindič qalam?	(F)	*ʔii, ʕindi qalam.*
ʕidkum qalam?		*ʔii, ʕidna qalam.*
ʕindič čaay?	(F)	*ʔii, ʕindi čaay.*
ʕidkum xariiṭa?		*ʔii, ʕidna xariiṭa.*
ʕindak šuġuḷ?	(M)	*ʔii, ʕindi šuġuḷ.*
ʕindič sayyaara?	(F)	*ʔii, ʕindi sayyaara.*
ʕindak ƀang zeen?	(M)	*ʔii, ʕindi ƀang zeen.*
ʕindič talafoon?	(F)	*ʔii, ʕindi talafoon.*
ʕidkum sayyaara zeena?		*ʔii, ʕidna sayyaara zeena.*
ʕindak beet zeen?	(M)	*ʔii, ʕindi beet zeen.*
ʕidkum šiqqa zeena?		*ʔii, ʕidna šiqqa zeena.*

UNIT 13

A. DIALOGUE

Abu Zuhayr and Abu Khalid sit down at a table at the coffee-house, and a waiter comes to take their order.

l-booy	The waiter
š-itħibbuun	what do you P like
ššurbuun	you P drink
ʔixwaan	brothers (see Notes)
ʔajiib-ilkum	I bring to you P
šii	thing, something
ħaarr	hot M
loo	or
baarid	cold M
1. *š-itħibbuun iššurbuun ixwaan? ʔajiib-ilkum šii ħaarr loo baarid?*	What would you like to drink, gentlemen? Shall I bring you something hot or cold?

ʔabu zuheer	Abu Zuhayr
liban	yoghurt (see Notes)
l-yoom	the day; today
2. *ʕidkum liban il-yoom?*	Do you have yoghurt today?

l-booy	The waiter
bali	yes
ħaamuð̣	sour M; lemon-tea (see Notes)
gahwa	coffee (see Notes)
3. *bali, ʕidna liban, čaay, ħaamuð̣, gahwa . . .*	Yes, we have yoghurt, tea, lemon-tea, coffee . . .

ʔabu zuheer	Abu Zuhayr
ṭayyib	good M; all right
nṭiini	give M me
gḷaaṣ	glass
rajaaʔan	please

4. *ṭayyib, inṭiini fadd iglaaṣ liban baarid, rajaaˀan.* — All right, give me a glass of cold yoghurt, please.

l-booy — The waiter

w-inta — and you M
ˀaxi — (form of address; see Notes)
š-itḥibb — what do you M like

5. *w-inta ˀaxi, š-itḥibb?* — And you, sir, what would you like?

ˀabu xaalid — Abu Khalid

ˀaani — I
jiib-li — bring M to me
ḥilwa — sweet F

6. *ˀaani jiib-li fadd gahwa ḥilwa.* — Bring me a sweet coffee.

NOTES ON DIALOGUE

1. Forms of address

ˀaxi — The word *ˀax* means 'brother'. The form *ˀaxi* means 'my brother', but is used only in a figurative sense. (The form *ˀaxuuya* is used for 'my brother' in the literal sense.) The form *ˀaxi* is one of the most common modes of address among men. It is used with friends, acquaintances, and strangers, as well as by—and sometimes to—persons performing services or selling goods. In some situations it may correspond to English *sir*, but is generally warmer and friendlier in tone and lacks any connotation of subservience.

ˀixwaan — This is the plural of *ˀax* in its figurative sense. As a form of address it is used in speaking to two or more men in generally the same situations in which *ˀaxi* would be used in speaking to one.

2. Drinks

liban — This is yoghurt, a preparation made of fermented milk. It is usually sold as a fairly thick liquid, somewhere between the consistency of buttermilk and mayonnaise, but in coffee-houses it is diluted with water and served in glasses as a beverage. In this form it is often called *šiniina.*

čaay — Tea. Served hot in small glases. You put sugar in it, but nothing else. In some establishments you can get a cup of tea with milk in it by specifying *čaay Ɛaliib* 'milk tea'.

Ɛaamuδ̣ — Although this is translated 'lemon-tea' as a convenient label, it actually contains neither lemon nor tea. It is a hot drink, thin and clear, made by pouring boiling water over small flaky particles obtained by pounding dried *nuumi baṣra,* a kind of citrus fruit. Sometimes called *čaay Ɛaamuδ̣* 'sour tea'.

gahwa — Coffee. Coffee-houses usually serve one kind of coffee free at regular intervals to everyone there; this is *gahwa murra* 'bitter coffee', served in very small cups with no handles, containing only a sip or two of very black sugarless coffee. You may order—and pay for—*gahwa Ɛilwa* 'sweet coffee' (also called *gahwa šakarli* 'sugar coffee'), which is what we think of as Turkish coffee. You can specify how sweet you want it.

B. GRAMMAR

1. Pronoun suffixes: First person pronoun suffix *-ni*

In Sentence 4 of the dialogue, note the ending *-ni* in the form *nṭiini* 'give M me'. This ending is one of the three alternants of the first-person singular pronoun suffix (see 12 B 1). The alternant *-ni* is attached directly to verb stems, and corresponds in meaning to the English pronoun *me*. The alternant *-i,* which we took up in Unit 12, is used with nouns and prepositions, but not with verbs. Of all the pronoun suffixes, it is only this first-person singular suffix which has a different alternant for use with verbs.

2. Independent personal pronouns: First person

In Sentence 6 of the dialogue, the word *ʔaani* is the first-person singular independent personal pronoun, meaning 'I'. Here again, although the independent pronoun is not essential to the grammatical structure of the sentence, it is used for contrastive emphasis. One person has already ordered a drink, and Abu Khalid is saying in effect, "As for *me,* bring me . . .", implying that someone else has ordered, or will order, something different. In English the same purpose may be served by extra stress on a certain word: "*I*'ll have . . ." If Abu Khalid were alone at the table, he would simply start off *jiib-li,* without *ˀaani.*

The first-person plural independent personal pronoun is *ˀiḥna* 'we'.

3. Preposition suffix *-l-* 'to, for'

In Sentence 6, the form *jiib-li* is composed of a masculine imperative verb form *jiib* 'bring M', the preposition suffix *-l-* 'to, for', and the first-person singular pronoun suffix *-i* 'me'. (Note that the pronoun suffix has the alternant *-i,* not *-ni,* because it is not attached directly to the verb form but rather to the preposition suffix.) In Sentence 1, similarly, the form *ˀajiib-ilkum* is composed of the verb form *ˀajiib* 'I bring', the preposition suffix *-l-,* and the second-person plural pronoun suffix *-kum* 'you P'; the short vowel *i* preceding the preposition suffix is the helping vowel which occurs automatically whenever a sequence of three consonants would otherwise result (see 10 C). The preposition suffix *-l-* always occurs attached to some verbal form, and it always has a pronoun suffix attached to it. In meaning, the combination of *-l-* and its pronoun suffix may correspond to an English prepositional phrase consisting of *to* or *for* with a pronoun object, as in *he sent the money to me* or *he bought some books for us;* or it may correspond to an English pronoun functioning as an indirect object with no preposition, as in *he sent me the money* or *he bought us some books.* The table below shows the forms of *-l-* with the three second-person pronoun suffixes, the whole combination attached for illustrative purposes to the verb form *ˀajiib* 'I bring':

2 M	*ˀajiib-lak*	'I bring to you M'
F	*ˀajiib-lič*	'I bring to you F'
P	*ˀajiib-ilkum*	'I bring to you P'

The next table shows the forms of *-l-* with the two first-person pronoun suffixes, attached to the imperative verb form *jiib* 'bring M':

1 S	*jiib-li*	'bring M to me'
P	*jiib-ilna*	'bring M to us'

In the combination *-ilna,* as in the last form above, the *l* usually assimilates to the *n* (see 10 A): *jiib-inna.*

There are some verbs with which the suffix *-l-* is not used, regardless of what the English translation might lead us to expect. Note these two sentences:

jiib-li fadd iglaaṣ liban.	'Bring M me a glass of yoghurt.'
nṭiini fadd iglaaṣ liban.	'Give M me a glass of yoghurt.'

The two English sentences are structurally identical, each consisting of a verb form, followed by an objective-case pronoun in first position (indirect object) and a noun phrase in second position (direct object). The corresponding Iraqi sentences, however, are structurally different in that *jiib* is followed by *-l-* and a pronoun suffix, while *nṭii-* is followed immediately by a pronoun suffix without *-l-*. All this merely illustrates one fact to be learned about the Iraqi verb meaning 'to give' (and several other verbs as well): it does not take *-l-*. Note also that in *nṭiini* the pronoun suffix has the alternant *-ni,* not *-i,* because it is attached directly to the verb form.

4. Prefix *š-* 'what'

There are several Iraqi forms corresponding to the English interrogative *what;* one of these is a prefix *š-*. This form may be attached to a verb, serving as the subject or, as in the following examples, as the object:

š-ajiib-ilkum?	'What shall I bring you P?'
š-itḥibbuun?	'What would you P like?'
š-nišrab?	'What shall we drink?'

It may also be attached to certain other forms, for example to *ʔaku* 'there is, there are' or the preposition *ʕi(n)d*:

š-aku?	'What is there?' 'What's up?' 'What's going on?'
š-ʕindak?	'What do you have?'

Associated with this prefix *š-* is an intonational feature which you may already have noticed: there is usually a relatively high pitch and a slight extra stress on the next vowel after *š-,* regardless of the normal stress the word in question would have without *š-*.

5. Prefix *w-* 'and'

The Iraqi equivalent of the English conjunction *and* is a prefix *w-,* which can be attached to any kind of word. When it is attached to a word beginning with the article prefix, we write the two prefixes together without a hyphen, as in the second and fourth examples below.

gahwa w-čaay	'coffee and tea'
l-beet wiš-šiqqa	'the house and the apartment'
Ɛaarr w-baarid	'hot and cold'
ˀinta wil-maƐruusiin	'you M and the children'
ˀaani w-inta	'you M and I'

Note in the last example that the word for *I* usually comes first, the reverse of the usual English order.

6. Adjective inflection: Stem changes

A **stem** is an element to which a prefix or suffix is or can be added. For example, in the left-hand table in 11 B 3 above, the feminine, plural, and feminine plural adjective forms consist of the stem *zeen-* and the endings *-a, -iin,* and *-aat* respectively. Note that the form of the stem to which these endings are added is identical with the form of the masculine adjective *zeen;* in other words, the endings are added to the masculine form (which then becomes a stem) without any change in the latter. This fact is true of the two adjectives illustrated in 11 B 3 and of many others as well. In the case of some adjectives, however, a slight change does take place when the endings are added. The most common type of change is loss of the **stem vowel,** which is defined as a short vowel preceding a final single consonant, for example the *i* in *baarid* 'cold M'. When one of the three endings above is added to this stem, the stem vowel *i* is dropped, and the stem becomes *baard-*. Thus the four forms of this adjective are as follows:

Masculine	*baarid*
Feminine	*baarda*
Plural	*baardiin*
Feminine plural	*baardaat*

(This adjective is most often used to refer to things, and not to people in the sense of the English "I'm cold", so the two plural forms are relatively rare.)

A second type of stem change is one involving a short **final vowel,** for example the *u* in *Ɛilu* 'sweet M'. In this adjective the final *u* is changed to *w* when one of the endings above is added, as follows:

Masculine	*Ɛilu*
Feminine	*Ɛilwa*
Plural	*Ɛilwiin*
Feminine plural	*Ɛilwaat*

C. DRILLS

Drill 1. New words. Listen and repeat.

nṭiini fadd igḷaaṣ ṃaay, rajaaʔan.	Give me a glass of water, please.
nṭiini fadd igḷaaṣ ɛaliib, rajaaʔan.	Give me a glass of milk, please.
nṭiini fadd igḷaaṣ biira, rajaaʔan.	Give me a glass of beer, please.
nṭiini fadd igḷaaṣ šarbat, rajaaʔan.	Give me a glass of sherbet,[1] please.
ɛidkum ɛaliib il-yoom?	Do you have milk today?
ɛidkum biira l-yoom?	Do you have beer today?
ɛidkum šarbat il-yoom?	Do you have sherbet today?
ɛidkum ṃaay il-yoom?	Do you have water today?
šloon il-biira?	How's the beer?
šloon il-ṃaay?	How's the water?
šloon iš-šarbat?	How's the sherbet?
šloon il-ɛaliib?	How's the milk?
l-ɛaliib muu zeen.	The milk isn't good.
l-ṃaay muu zeen.	The water isn't good.
š-šarbat muu zeen.	The sherbet isn't good.
l-biira muu zeena.	The beer isn't good.

Drill 2. Repeat the utterance, replacing the underlined portion with each of the items given.

jiib-li fadd gahwa, rajaaʔan.	Bring me a coffee, please.
čaay	tea
šarbat	sherbet
biira	beer
stikaan	tea-glass
stikaan čaay	glass of tea
gḷaaṣ	glass
gḷaaṣ liban	glass of yoghurt
gḷaaṣ ṃaay	glass of water
gahwa	coffee

Drill 3. Repeat the utterance, replacing the underlined portion with each of the items given.

[1] This word is used here only as a convenient translation. The Iraqi *šarbat* is not at all like our concept of sherbet, but rather a thin liquid drink made from flavored syrup.

jiib-inna l-gahwa.	Bring us the coffee.
l-ṃaay	the water
l-biira	the beer
l-ḥaliib	the milk
š-šarbat	the sherbet
č-čaay	the tea
l-igḷaaṣ	the glass
l-istikaan	the tea-glass
l-qalam	the pencil
l-xariiṭa	the map
l-gahwa	the coffee

Drill 4. Change each statement to the negative, as in the following example:

Cue:	*hal-ṃaay baarid.*	This water is cold.
Response:	*hal-ṃaay muu baarid.*	This water isn't cold.

hal-ḥaliib baarid.	*hal-ḥaliib muu baarid.*
hal-gahwa baarda.	*hal-gahwa muu baarda.*
hač-čaay baarid.	*hač-čaay muu baarid.*
hal-biira baarda.	*hal-biira muu baarda.*
hal-liban ḥaarr.	*hal-liban muu ḥaarr.*
hal-gahwa ḥaarra.	*hal-gahwa muu ḥaarra.*
hal-istikaan zeen.	*hal-istikaan muu zeen.*
hal-xariiṭa zeena.	*hal-xariiṭa muu zeena.*
haš-šarbat ḥilu.	*haš-šarbat muu ḥilu.*
hal-gahwa ḥilwa.	*hal-gahwa muu ḥilwa.*

Drill 5. In each of the following utterances, change the word *čaay* to the word *gahwa,* and make whatever other changes may then be necessary.

jiib-li fadd čaay ḥilu.	*jiib-li fadd gahwa ḥilwa.*
jiib-li fadd čaay ḥaarr.	*jiib-li fadd gahwa ḥaarra.*
hač-čaay baarid.	*hal-gahwa baarda.*
hač-čaay muu zeen.	*hal-gahwa muu zeena.*
jiib-li fadd čaay zeen.	*jiib-li fadd gahwa zeena.*
ma-εidkum čaay ḥaarr?	*ma-εidkum gahwa ḥaarra?*
nṭiini fadd čaay ḥaarr.	*nṭiini fadd gahwa ḥaarra.*
nṭiini fadd čaay ḥilu.	*nṭiini fadd gahwa ḥilwa.*
hač-čaay muu baarid.	*hal-gahwa muu baarda.*
tḥibbuun čaay ḥaarr?	*tḥibbuun gahwa ḥaarra?*

Drill 6. In each of the following utterances, change *nṭiini* to *jiib-li.*

nṭiini šii Caarr.	*jiib-li šii Caarr.*
nṭiini šii baarid.	*jiib-li šii baarid.*
nṭiini šii Cilu.	*jiib-li šii Cilu.*
nṭiini šii zeen.	*jiib-li šii zeen.*
nṭiini fadd igḷaaṣ.	*jiib-li fadd igḷaaṣ.*
nṭiini fadd igḷaaṣ liban.	*jiib-li fadd igḷaaṣ liban.*
nṭiini fadd igḷaaṣ liban baarid.	*jiib-li fadd igḷaaṣ liban baarid.*
nṭiini fadd igḷaaṣ biira.	*jiib-li fadd igḷaaṣ biira.*
nṭiini fadd igḷaaṣ biira baarda.	*jiib-li fadd igḷaaṣ biira baarda.*
nṭiini fadd igḷaaṣ ṃaay.	*jiib-li fadd igḷaaṣ ṃaay.*
nṭiini fadd igḷaaṣ ṃaay baarid.	*jiib-li fadd igḷaaṣ ṃaay baarid.*
nṭiini fadd gahwa.	*jiib-li fadd gahwa.*
nṭiini fadd gahwa Caarra.	*jiib-li fadd gahwa Caarra.*
nṭiini šii Caarr.	*jiib-li šii Caarr.*

Drill 7. Repeat the utterance, replacing the underlined portion with each of the items given, and making whatever other changes may then be necessary.

ween il-gahwa?	*ween il-gahwa?*
Caliib	*ween il-Caliib?*
biira	*ween il-biira?*
ṃaay	*ween il-ṃaay?*
maCruusiin	*ween il-maCruusiin?*
ḅang	*ween il-ḅang?*
talafoon	*ween it-talafoon?*
sayyaara	*ween-is-sayyaara?*
stikaan	*ween l-istikaan?*
gḷaaṣ	*ween l-igḷaaṣ?*
beet	*ween il-beet?*
šiqqa	*ween iš-šiqqa?*
liban	*ween il-liban?*
šarbat	*ween iš-šarbat?*
qalam	*ween il-qalam?*
xariiṭa	*ween il-xariiṭa?*
gahwa	*ween il-gahwa?*

Drill 8. The following utterances are addressed to a man. Say them as you would to a group.

marḥaba, šloonak?
haay weenak, ma-da-nšuufak?
ʕindak šuġuḷ?
ʕindak sayyaara?
ʕindak gahwa zeena?
š-ʕindak il-yoom?
ʕindak šarbat il-yoom?
ʔajiib-lak šii ḥaarr?
ʔajiib-lak šii baarid, ʔaxi?
ʔajiib-lak šii ḥaarr loo baarid?
š-ajiib-lak il-yoom?

marḥaba, šloonkum?
haay weenkum, ma-da-nšuufkum?
ʕidkum šuġuḷ?
ʕidkum sayyaara?
ʕidkum gahwa zeena?
š-ʕidkum il-yoom?
ʕidkum šarbat il-yoom?
ʔajiib-ilkum šii ḥaarr?
ʔajiib-ilkum šii baarid, ʔixwaan?
ʔajiib-ilkum šii ḥaarr loo baarid?
š-ajiib-ilkum il-yoom?

Drill 9. The following utterances are addressed to a group. Say them as you would to a woman.

marḥaba, šloonkum?
haay weenkum, ma-da-nšuufkum?
ʕidkum talafoon?
ʕidkum sayyaara zeena?
ʕidkum ḥaamuð̣ il-yoom?
ma-ʕidkum liban il-yoom?
š-ʕidkum il-yoom?
š-ajiib-ilkum?
ʔajiib-ilkum ḥaamuð̣?
ʔajiib-ilkum šii ḥilu?
ʔajiib-ilkum gahwa ḥilwa?
š-ajiib-ilkum il-yoom?

marḥaba, šloonič?
haay weenič, ma-da-nšuufič?
ʕindič talafoon?
ʕindič sayyaara zeena?
ʕindič ḥaamuð̣ il-yoom?
ma-ʕindič liban il-yoom?
š-ʕindič il-yoom?
š-ajiib-lič?
ʔajiib-lič ḥaamuð̣?
ʔajiib-lič šii ḥilu?
ʔajiib-lič gahwa ḥilwa?
š-ajiib-lič il-yoom?

Drill 10. The following utterances are addressed to a woman. Say them as you would to a man.

marḥaba, šloonič?
haay weenič, ma-da-nšuufič?
ween beetič?
ʕindič šuġuḷ il-yoom?
ʕindič qalam zeen?
ʕindič šiqqa zeena?

marḥaba, šloonak?
haay weenak, ma-da-nšuufak?
ween beetak?
ʕindak šuġuḷ il-yoom?
ʕindak qalam zeen?
ʕindak šiqqa zeena?

εindič ḥaamuð̣ il-yoom?	*εindak ḥaamuð̣ il-yoom?*
ma-εindič liban il-yoom?	*ma-εindak liban il-yoom?*
š-εindič il-yoom?	*š-εindak il-yoom?*
ʔajiib-lič fadd istikaan čaay?	*ʔajiib-lak fadd istikaan čaay?*
ʔajiib-lič fadd igḷaaṣ šarbat?	*ʔajiib-lak fadd igḷaaṣ šarbat?*
ʔajiib-lič fadd igḷaaṣ ṃaay baarid?	*ʔajiib-lak fadd igḷaaṣ ṃaay baarid?*
š-ajiib-lič?	*š-ajiib-lak?*

Drill 11. Change each sentence so that it begins with the interrogative prefix *š-*, as in the following example:

Cue:	*tḥibbuun čaay?*	Would you P like tea?
Response:	*š-itḥibbuun?*	What would you P like?

tḥibbuun gahwa?	*š-itḥibbuun?*
tḥibbuun gahwa l-yoom?	*š-itḥibbuun il-yoom?*
tḥibbuun iššurbuun gahwa?	*š-itḥibbuun iššurbuun?*
tḥibbuun iššurbuun gahwa l-yoom?	*š-itḥibbuun iššurbuun il-yoom?*
ʔaku gahwa?	*š-aku?*
ʔaku ḥaamuð̣ il-yoom?	*š-aku l-yoom?*
εindak šuğuḷ?	*š-εindak?*
εidkum liban il-yoom?	*š-εidkum il-yoom?*
εindič čaay?	*š-εindič?*
ʔajiib-lič šii ḥilu?	*š-ajiib-lič?*
ʔajiib-ilkum šii baarid?	*š-ajiib-ilkum?*
ʔajiib-lak fadd čaay il-yoom?	*š-ajiib-lak il-yoom?*
nišrab fadd čaay?	*š-nišrab?*
nišrab šii ḥaarr il-yoom?	*š-nišrab il-yoom?*

Drill 12. Repeat each utterance, and then expand it by adding the prefix *w-* with the item given, as in the example:

Cue:	*εindak liban?*	Do you have yoghurt?
Response:	*εindak liban?*	Do you have yoghurt?
Cue:	*šarbat.*	Sherbet.
Response:	*εindak liban w-šarbat?*	Do you have yoghurt and sherbet?

εidkum čaay?	*εidkum čaay?*
gahwa.	*εidkum čaay w-gahwa?*
ma-εidkum gahwa?	*ma-εidkum gahwa?*
čaay.	*ma-εidkum gahwa w-čaay?*
jiib-inna liban, rajaaʔan.	*jiib-inna liban, rajaaʔan.*

šarbat.	*jiib-inna liban w-šarbat, rajaaʔan*
ʔaku ṃaay.	*ʔaku ṃaay.*
ɛaliib.	*ʔaku ṃaay w-ɛaliib.*
ʔaku ḅang ib-hal-manṭiqa?	*ʔaku ḅang ib-hal-manṭiqa?*
gahwa.	*ʔaku ḅang w-gahwa b-hal-manṭiqa?*
ween zuheer?	*ween zuheer?*
xaalid.	*ween zuheer w-xaalid?*
ween muṣṭafa?	*ween muṣṭafa?*
zuheer.	*ween muṣṭafa w-zuheer?*
ween il-ṃaay?	*ween il-ṃaay?*
l-ɛaliib.	*ween il-ṃaay wil-ɛaliib?*
jiib-li č-čaay.	*jiib-li č-čaay.*
l-gahwa.	*jiib-li č-čaay wil-gahwa.*
jiib-inna l-liban.	*jiib-inna l-liban.*
š-šarbat.	*jiib-inna l-liban wiš-šarbat.*
nṭiini l-qalam.	*nṭiini l-qalam.*
l-xariiṭa.	*nṭiini l-qalam wil-xariiṭa.*

UNIT 14

A. DIALOGUE

A friend sees Abu Zuhayr and Abu Khalid sitting at the coffee-house and comes up to speak to them.

ʔabu samiira	Abu Samira
s-salaamu ɛalaykum	the peace upon you P
1. *s-salaamu ɛalaykum!*	Good morning!
ʔabu xaalid	Abu Khalid
ɛalaykum is-salaam	upon you P the peace
2. *ɛalaykum is-salaam!*	Hello, how're you?
ʔabu samiira	Abu Samira
šinu	what
š-jaabkum	what brought you P
3. *haay šinu? š-jaabkum il-yoom lil-gahwa?*	What's this? What brings you to the coffee-house today?

ʔabu zuheer	Abu Zuhayr
jeena	we came
tfaḏḏal	be pleased M
stiriiḥ	rest M
4. *jeena waḷḷa.*	We just came, that's all.
tfaḏḏal, stiriiḥ.	Here, have a seat.

ʔabu xaalid	Abu Khalid
ʔaḷḷaa bil-xeer	God keep you well
5. *ʔaḷḷaa bil-xeer.*	— — — — — — —

ʔabu samiira	Abu Samira
šgadd	how much, how long
ṣaar-ilkum	it M became for you P
gaaʕdiin	sitting P
hnaa	here
6. *ʔaḷḷaa bil-xeer.*	— — — — — — —
šgadd ṣaar-ilkum gaaʕdiin ihnaa?	How long have you been sitting here?

ʔabu zuheer	Abu Zuhayr
ma-ṣaar-inna	it M did not become for us
hwaaya	much, a lot
š-raḥ-tišrab	what are you M going to drink
triid	you M want
7. *ma-ṣaar-inna hwaaya.*	It hasn't been long. What are
š-raḥ-tišrab, ʔabu samiira?	you going to drink, Abu Samira?
triid gahwa, čaay?	Do you want coffee, tea?

ʔabu samiira	Abu Samira
raḥ-ašrab-li	I'm going to drink for myself
šukran	thanks, thank you
8. *raḥ-ašrab-li fadd čaay, šukran.*	I'm going to have tea, thanks.

NOTES ON DIALOGUE

1. Polite formulas

s-salaamu ɛalaykum	A greeting, meaning literally 'the peace upon you P'. Said by someone arriving at a place to those already present. Although the ending *-kum* is a second-person *plural* pronoun suffix, the phrase is said in just this form to a man or a woman alone as well as to a group.
ɛalaykum is-salaam	The standard reply to the foregoing greeting. This too is said to one person or more than one.
M *tfaḍḍal* F *tfaḍḍali* P *tfaḍḍalu*	These are imperative verb forms, said respectively to a man, to a woman, and to two or more people. The literal meaning is something like 'be pleased' (to do something) or 'be so good' (as to do something). Said when offering something, for example food, a cigarette, or a seat, or when urging someone to go first, for example through a door.
M *stiriiḥ* F *stiriiḥi* P *stiriiḥu*	These too are imperative verb forms, meaning 'rest' or 'have a rest'. Said when inviting someone to sit down. Usually preceded by the corresponding form of *tfaḍḍal*.
ʔaḷḷaa bil-xeer	The word *ʔaḷḷaa* or *ʔaḷḷa* means 'God'; *bil-xeer* means 'in the (state of) prosperity'; the whole phrase conveys the idea 'God keep you well and prosperous'. Said to a newcomer who sits down with you. The reply is the same: *ʔaḷḷaa bil-xeer*.
šukran	Means 'thank you' and is used in much the same way.

B. GRAMMAR

1. Interrogative *šinu* 'what'

Besides the prefix form *š-* described in 13 B 4, there is an independent form *šinu*, also corresponding to the English interrogative *what*. This form usually functions as the subject of an equational sentence (see 2 below), for example:

šinu haaδaʔ	'What's this?'
šinu šuġḷakʔ	'What's your business?'

It may also function as a one-word question *šinuʔ*, corresponding to English 'What?', 'What is it?', and the like.

2. Equational sentences

One of the three main types of sentence in Iraqi is the **equational sentence.** This is a sentence composed of two major elements, a **subject** and a **predicate,** the one following the other directly without any verb between them. Equational sentences most commonly correspond to English sentences in which the subject and the predicate are linked by a present-tense form of the verb *to be,* that is, sentences of the general formula *X am Y, X is Y,* or *X are Y* (or the corresponding questions *am X Yʔ, is X Yʔ,* or *are X Yʔ*), for example *I am here, the coffee is hot, my brother is a doctor, the books are on the table, am I lateʔ, is the coffee readyʔ, are you busyʔ, are the children wellʔ.* The corresponding Iraqi sentences are equational sentences, all of the general formula *X Y*. In such sentences there is no word corresponding to the English *am, is,* or *are.* Examples:

ʔaani mašġuuḷ.	'I am busy.'
l-gahwa baarda.	'The coffee is cold.'
l-maCruusiin zeeniin.	'The children are well.'
l-gahwa baardaʔ	'Is the coffee cold?'
l-maCruusiin zeeniinʔ	'Are the children well?'
ʔinta mašġuuḷʔ	'Are you M busy?'

In some equational sentences, mainly those beginning with an interrogative, the subject is last, for example:

ween-il-ḅaṇgʔ	'Where is the bank?'
šinu haaδaʔ	'What is this?'

3. General demonstrative pronoun: Masculine and feminine forms

Shown below are the masculine and feminine forms of the general demonstrative pronoun.

Masculine	*haaδa*	'this (one), that (one) M'
Feminine	*haaδi* / *haay*	'this (one), that (one) F'

This is called the general demonstrative because it sometimes indicates something near at hand and then corresponds to English *this* or *this one,* and sometimes indicates something farther away and then corresponds to English *that* or *that one.*

The masculine form *haaδa* is used in referring to a masculine singular noun, whether that noun is actually mentioned in the same sentence, or is one which has previously been mentioned, or is one which the speaker has in mind, for example:

haaδa čaay.	'This is tea.'
haaδa ḅang.	'That's a bank.'
haaδa muu zeen.	'This one M is no good.'
nṭiini haaδa.	'Give me that one M.'

This form is also normally used in referring to some object not yet identified:

šinu haaδa?	'What's this?'

The feminine form *haaδi,* or its common variant *haay,* is used in referring to a feminine singular noun, for example:

haaδi / *haay* *xariiṭa.*	'This is a map.'
haaδi / *haay* *gahwa.*	'That's a coffee-house.'
haaδi / *haay* *muu zeena.*	'This one F is no good.'
nṭiini *haaδi.* / *haay.*	'Give me that one F.'

The form *haay* is also commonly used in referring, not to a concrete object or some specific noun, but to a situation or event:

šinu haay?	'What is this?' (in the sense:
haay šinu?	'What's going on here?')

4. Preposition prefix *l-/D-* 'to, for'

The Iraqi equivalent of the English prepositions *to* and *for* is a prefix attached to a following noun (or demonstrative pronoun; but for pronoun suffixes see 13 B 3). This prefix has two alternants: one is *l-*, and the other consists of the same sound as the initial sound of the following noun. In other words, this preposition prefix is identical in form with the article prefix (12 B 5), and its two alternants are used in exactly the same way. However, this identity of form rarely causes any confusion, since noun-forms which have the preposition prefix alone usually cannot have the article prefix anyway; for example the proper noun *baġdaad* never has an article prefix, so *l-baġdaad* unambiguously means 'to Baghdad'; and the noun-form *beeti* 'my house', with the pronoun suffix *-i* 'my', cannot also have the article prefix, so *l-beeti* unambiguously means 'to my house'. Of course, a form like *l-beet* cited alone could mean either 'the house' or 'to a house', but in such cases the context will usually resolve the ambiguity. Here are further examples of words with this preposition prefix, first some in which the prefix alternant is *l-*. (Whether the appropriate English translation is 'to' or 'for', or even some other word, depends on the context; here we shall use 'to' for all.)

xaalid	'Khalid'	*l-xaalid*	'to Khalid'
ʔabu xaalid	'Abu Khalid'	*l-abu xaalid*	'to Abu Khalid'
mčammad	'Muhammad'	*l-imčammad*	'to Muhammad'
haaδa	'this one M'	*l-haaδa*	'to this one M'
beetak	'your M house'	*l-beetak*	'to your M house'
hal-manṭiqa	'this area'	*l-hal-manṭiqa*	'to this area'

Next, some examples in which the prefix alternant is *D-*, that is, the same consonant as the first consonant in the following word:

zuheer	'Zuhayr'	*z-zuheer*	'to Zuhayr'
samiira	'Samira'	*s-samiira*	'to Samira'
šuġḷak	'your M work'	*š-šuġḷak*	'to your M work'

This preposition prefix is frequently attached to a form which already has the article prefix, the two prefixes then corresponding to English *to the* or *for the*. In such cases the preposition prefix always has the alternant *l-*, while the article prefix has whichever of its two alternants is called for by the initial sound of the following form. The helping vowel *i* occurs between the two prefixes. The whole combination is thus *lil-* or *liD-*. Here are examples:

l-beet	'the house'	*lil-beet*	'the the house'
l-manṭiqa	'the area'	*lil-manṭiqa*	'to the area'
l-istikaan	'the tea-glass'	*lil-istikaan*	'to the tea-glass'
s-sayyaara	'the car'	*lil-sayyaara*	'to the car'
š-šiqqa	'the apartment'	*liš-šiqqa*	'the the apartment'
t-talafoon	'the telephone'	*lit-talafoon*	'to the telephone'

5. Imperfect tense: First-person forms

Iraqi verbs have two tenses, **perfect** and **imperfect.** In a general way, the former corresponds to the English past tense and the latter to the English present tense or future construction, but the correspondence is not exact, and details will be given as required. Within each tense, a verb has eight inflectional forms, corresponding to the person-gender-number categories listed below. (The abbreviations shown are those which will be used henceforth to label verb forms. You will also see later that there is good reason to list the forms in this order, with the third person first.)

3 M	Third-person masculine (singular)
F	Third-person feminine (singular)
P	Third-person (masculine or feminine) plural
2 M	Second-person masculine (singular)
F	Second-person feminine (singular)
P	Second-person (masculine or feminine) plural
1 S	First-person (masculine or feminine) singular
P	First-person (masculine or feminine) plural

In this section we take up the two first-person forms of the imperfect tense.

A first-person verb form in the imperfect tense consists of a prefix and a verb stem. The first-person singular prefix with verb stems beginning with a consonant (almost all do) is *ˀa-*, for example:

Prefix *ˀa-*	**Verb stem**	**Verb form**	
	-šuuf	*ˀašuuf*	'I see'
	-ruuḥ	*ˀaruuḥ*	'I go'
	-jiib	*ˀajiib*	'I bring'
	-riid	*ˀariid*	'I want'
	-ḥibb	*ˀaḥibb*	'I like'
	-šrab	*ˀašrab*	'I drink'

The first-person plural singular prefix with verb stems beginning with two consonants is *ni-* (or, in some cases to be taken up later, *nu-*) for example:

Prefix *ni-*	**Verb stem**	**Verb form**	
	-šrab	*nišrab*	'we drink'

With all other verb stems the prefix is *n-*, for example:

Prefix *n-*	**Verb stem**	**Verb form**	
	-šuuf	*nšuuf*	'we see'
	-ruuc	*nruuc*	'we go'
	-jiib	*njiib*	'we bring'
	-riid	*nriid*	'we want'
	-cibb	*ncibb*	'we like'

When this prefix *n-* is attached to a verb stem beginning with *r*, as in the second and fourth examples above, it may assimilate to the *r*, becoming an *r* itself (see 10 A): *rruuc* 'we go' and *rriid* 'we want'. This kind of assimilation is particularly common when a vowel immediately precedes, for example in *xal-da-rruuc* 'let's go' or *ma-rriid* 'we don't want'. Hereafter we shall give the unassimilated forms in verb conjugations or isolated citations, and elsewhere whichever form would be more natural.

Note that in English the personal pronoun subject of a verb is normally expressed by a separate word (I drink, we drink), whereas in Iraqi the corresponding information is indicated by the verb form alone (*ʔašrab, nišrab*). There are, of course, independent personal pronoun forms in Iraqi (see 11 B 2 and 13 B 2), and they *may* be used together with verb forms, but such use indicates special emphasis or contrast. This kind of special emphasis is often indicated in English by extra-loud stress on the pronoun. Thus, the verb form *nišrab* alone would usually correspond to English 'we drink', whereas the combination *ʔicna nišrab* would correspond to '*we* drink', as for example in 'You always drink tea, but *we* drink coffee'.

6. Imperfect tense: Second-person forms

A second-person masculine verb form in the imperfect tense consists of a prefix and a verb stem. With verb stems beginning with two consonants the prefix is *ti-* (or, in some cases to be taken up later, *tu-*), for example:

Prefix *ti-*	**Verb stem**	**Verb form**	
	-šrab	*tišrab*	'you M drink'

With other verb stems the prefix is basically *t-*. However, when this prefix *t-* is attached to verb stems beginning with certain (single) consonants, it assimilates in certain ways to them; for example, in the third verb form in the list below, the *t-* assimilates to the following *j* as to voice, becoming *d-*.

Prefix *t-*	**Verb stem**	**Verb form**	
	-šuuf	*tšuuf*	'you M see'
	-ruuɛ	*truuɛ*	'you M go'
	-jiib	*djiib*	'you M bring'
	-riid	*triid*	'you M want'
	-ɛibb	*tɛibb*	'you M like'

Assimilations of the sort illustrated by *djiib* above are automatic, and we shall write such items in their assimilated forms wherever they occur. The prefix *t-* may also assimilate to certain following consonants in other ways; for example, in the first item in the list above, the *t-* may assimilate completely to the following *š*, itself becoming *š-*: *ššuuf* 'you M see'. Assimilations of this sort are less automatic and consistent, although they are quite common when a vowel immediately precedes, for example in *ma-ššuuf* 'you M do not see'. For such cases we shall give the unassimilated forms in verb conjugations or isolated citations, and elsewhere whichever form would be more natural.

A second-person feminine verb form in the imperfect tense consists of a prefix, a verb stem, and a suffix. The prefix is the same as for the second-person masculine forms just described: *ti* or *tu-* with verb stems beginning with two consonants, and *t-* (assimilated in some cases) with other stems. The suffix is always *-iin*. Thus, in many cases, the feminine form can be obtained simply by adding *-iin* to the masculine form. Here are examples:

Prefix *t-*	**Verb stem**	**Suffix** *-iin*	**Verb form**	
	-šuuf-		*tšuufiin*	'you F see'
	-ruuɛ-		*truuɛiin*	'you F go'
	-jiib-		*djiibiin*	'you F bring'
	-riid-		*triidiin*	'you F want'
	-ɛibb-		*tɛibbiin*	'you F like'

Some types of verb stems undergo certain changes when the suffix is added. If the verb stem has the shape -CCvC (that is, consists of two consonants, a short vowel, and another consonant), the vowel is **shifted** to a position between the first and second consonant when the suffix is added, so that the new shape of the stem is -CvCC-. Before shifting, the short vowel in question is ***a*** in some verbs, ***i*** in others, and ***u*** in others; but after shifting, it is always ***i*** or ***u***. For example, the stem *-šrab* in *tišrab* 'you M drink' becomes *-šurb-* in *tšurbiin* 'you F drink'. This new stem begins with one consonant, not two, and the prefix is accordingly *t-* rather than *ti-*:

Prefix *t-*	Verb stem	Suffix *-iin*	Verb form	
	-šurb-		*tšurbiin*	'you F drink'

A second-person plural verb form in the imperfect tense also consists of a prefix, a verb stem, and a suffix. It is exactly like the second-person feminine form just described, except that the suffix is *-uun*. Examples:

Prefix *t-*	Verb stem	Suffix *-uun*	Verb form	
	-šuuf-		*tšuufuun*	'you P see'
	-ruuC-		*truuCuun*	'you P go'
	-jiib-		*djiibuun*	'you P bring'
	-riid-		*triiduun*	'you P want'
	-Cibb-		*tCibbuun*	'you P like'
	-šurb-		*tšurbuun*	'you P drink'

Two of the verbs illustrated in the foregoing lists have two second-person feminine and two second-person plural forms each. One is the form given in the lists above, and the other is a shorter form. Both are acceptable, but the shorter is probably more common in normal-speed speech. The two forms are shown below:

2 F	*truuCiin* or *tirCiin*	'you F go'
2 P	*truuCuun* or *tirCuun*	'you P go'
2 F	*triidiin* or *tirdiin*	'you F want'
2 P	*triiduun* or *tirduun*	'you P want'

7. Future prefix *raC-*

The prefix *raC-* occurs with imperfect-tense verb forms, and indicates future action. It often corresponds to English *going to* or *will*. When it is prefixed to a first-person singular verb form, the initial ˀ of that form is usually dropped (see 10 B). When it is prefixed to a verb form beginning with two consonants, a helping vowel occurs before those two consonants (see 10 C). Examples:

ˀašuuf	'I see'	*raC-ašuuf*	'I'm going to see'
ˀajiib	'I bring'	*raC-ajiib*	'I'm going to bring'
ˀašrab	'I drink'	*raC-ašrab*	'I'm going to drink'

nšuuf	'we see'	*raC-inšuuf*	'we're going to see'
njiib	'we bring'	*raC-injiib*	'we're going to bring'
nišrab	'we drink'	*raC-nišrab*	'we're going to drink'
tšuuf	'you M see'	*raC-itšuuf*	'you're M going to see'
djiib	'you M bring'	*raC-idjiib*	'you're M going to bring'
tišrab	'you M drink'	*raC-tišrab*	'you're M going to drink'
tšuufiin	'you F see'	*raC-itšuufiin*	'you're F going to see'
djiibiin	'you F bring'	*raC-idjiibiin*	'you're F going to bring'
tšurbiin	'you F drink'	*raC-itšurbiin*	'you're F going to drink'
tšuufuun	'you P see'	*raC-itšuufuun*	'you're P going to see'
djiibuun	'you P bring'	*raC-idjiibuun*	'you're P going to bring'
tšurbuun	'you P drink'	*raC-itšurbuun*	'you're P going to drink'

A variant form *raaC-*, with a long vowel, is also common.

C. DRILLS

Drill 1. New words. Listen and repeat.

ʔaku ʔuuteel ib-hal-manṭiqa?	Is there a hotel in this area?
ʔaku maṭaar ib-hal-manṭiqa?	Is there an airport in this area?
ʔaku gaaziino b-hal-manṭiqa?	Is there a gaaziino [1] in this area?
ʔaku daaʔira b-hal-manṭiqa?	Is there an office in this area?
ʔaku safaara b-hal-manṭiqa?	Is there an embassy in this area?
ʔaku suug ib-hal-manṭiqa?	Is there a market [2] in this area?
ween il-uuteel?	Where's the hotel?
ween il-maṭaar?	Where's the airport?
ween il-gaaziino?	Where's the gaaziino?
ween id-daaʔira?	Where's the office?
ween is-safaara?	Where's the embassy?
ween is-suug?	Where's the market?
xal-da-rruuC lil-uuteel.	Let's go to the hotel.
xal-da-rruuC lil-maṭaar.	Let's go to the airport.
xal-da-rruuC lil-gaaziino.	Let's go to the gaaziino.

[1] We use the Iraqi word here because there is no exact English equivalent. A gaaziino is a place where soft drinks, ice-cream, and some kinds of snacks are served. Although most nouns ending in *o* are masculine, the noun *gaaziino* is feminine.

[2] The word *suug* may refer to a particular concentration of merchants and craftsmen, sometimes in a large shed-like building, or to a shopping area in general.

xal-da-rruuc lid-daaʔira.	Let's go to the office.
xal-da-rruuc lis-safaara.	Let's go to the embassy.
xal-da-rruuc lis-suug.	Let's go to the market.
š-jaabkum il-yoom lil-uuteel?	What brought you P to the hotel today?
š-jaabkum il-yoom lil-maṭaar?	What brought you P to the airport today?
š-jaabkum il-yoom lil-gaaziino?	What brought you P to the gaaziino today?
š-jaabkum il-yoom lid-daaʔira?	What brought you P to the office today?
š-jaabkum il-yoom lis-safaara?	What brought you P to the embassy today?
š-jaabkum il-yoom lis-suug?	What brought you P to the market today?

Drill 2. Answer each question affirmatively, as in the following example:

Cue:	*haaδa ʔuuteel?*	Is this a hotel?
Response:	*bali, haaδa ʔuuteel.*	Yes, this is a hotel.

haaδa ḅang?	*bali, haaδa ḅang.*
haaδa suug?	*bali, haaδa suug.*
haaδa maṭaar?	*bali, haaδa maṭaar.*
haaδa stikaan?	*bali, haaδa stikaan.*
haaδa čaay?	*bali, haaδa čaay.*
haaδi gahwa?	*bali, haaδi gahwa.*
haaδi gaaziino?	*bali, haaδi gaaziino.*
haaδi xariiṭa?	*bali, haaδi xariiṭa.*
haaδi biira?	*bali, haaδi biira.*
haaδi sayyaara?	*bali, haaδi sayyaara.*

Drill 3. Answer each question negatively, as in the following example:

Cue:	*haaδa qalam?*	Is this a pencil?
Response:	*laa, haaδa muu qalam.*	No, this is not a pencil.

haaδa ʔuuteel?	*laa, haaδa muu ʔuuteel.*
haaδa liban?	*laa, haaδa muu liban.*
haaδa caliib?	*laa, haaδa muu caliib.*
haaδa šarbat?	*laa, haaδa muu šarbat.*
haaδa ṃaay?	*laa, haaδa muu ṃaay.*
haaδa talafoon?	*laa, haaδa muu talafoon.*
haaδa caamuḍ?	*laa, haaδa muu caamuḍ.*
haaδa ḅang?	*laa, haaδa muu ḅang.*
haaδa ʔabu zuheer?	*laa, haaδa muu ʔabu zuheer.*
haaδa ʔabu xaalid?	*laa, haaδa muu ʔabu xaalid.*

Drill 4. In each of the following utterances, change *haaδi* to *haay.*

haaδi sayyaara?	*haay sayyaara?*
haaδi sayyaara zeena?	*haay sayyaara zeena?*
haaδi biira.	*haay biira.*
haaδi biira baarda.	*haay biira baarda.*
haaδi gahwa.	*haay gahwa.*
haaδi gahwa cilwa.	*haay gahwa cilwa.*
haaδi gaaziino?	*haay gaaziino?*
bali, haaδi gaaziino.	*bali, haay gaaziino.*
haaδi gaaziino zeena.	*haay gaaziino zeena.*
haaδi ʔumm zuheer?	*haay ʔumm zuheer?*
laa, haaδi muu ʔumm zuheer.	*laa, haay muu ʔumm zuheer.*

Drill 5. Change each sentence as in the following example:

Cue:	*ween il-uuteel?*	Where's the hotel?
Response:	*xal-da-rruuc lil-uuteel.*	Let's go to the hotel.

ween il-beet?	*xal-da-rruuc lil-beet.*
ween il-gahwa?	*xal-da-rruuc lil-gahwa.*
ween id-daaʔira?	*xal-da-rruuc lid-daaʔira.*
ween il-ḅang?	*xal-da-rruuc lil-ḅang.*
ween is-sayyaara?	*xal-da-rruuc lis-sayyaara.*
ween is-safaara?	*xal-da-rruuc lis-safaara.*
ween il-maṭaar?	*xal-da-rruuc lil-maṭaar.*
ween iš-šiqqa?	*xal-da-rruuc liš-šiqqa.*
ween il-uuteel?	*xal-da-rruuc lil-uuteel.*

Drill 6. Change each sentence as in the following example:

Cue:	*ʔaku gahwa b-hal-manṭiqa?*	Is there a coffee-house in this area?
Response:	*ʔinta raayic lil-gahwa?*	Are you going to the coffee-house?

ʔaku gaaziino b-hal-manṭiqa?	*ʔinta raayic lil-gaaziino?*
ʔaku ʔuuteel ib-hal-manṭiqa?	*ʔinta raayic lil-uuteel?*
ʔaku beet ib-hal-manṭiqa?	*ʔinta raayic lil-beet?*
ʔaku safaara b-hal-manṭiqa?	*ʔinta raayic lis-safaara?*
ʔaku daaʔira b-hal-manṭiqa?	*ʔinta raayic lid-daaʔira?*
ʔaku suug ib-hal-manṭiqa?	*ʔinta raayic lis-suug?*
ʔaku ḅang ib-hal-manṭiqa?	*ʔinta raayic lil-ḅang?*
ʔaku talafoon ib-hal-manṭiqa?	*ʔinta raayic lit-talafoon?*
ʔaku gahwa b-hal-manṭiqa?	*ʔinta raayic lil-gahwa?*

Drill 7. Repeat the utterance, replacing the underlined portion with each of the items given.

tCibbuun iššurbuun <u>gahwa</u>?	Would you P like to drink <u>coffee</u>?
čaay	*tCibbuun iššurbuun čaay?*
liban	*tCibbuun iššurbuun liban?*
Caamuð̣	*tCibbuun iššurbuun Caamuð̣?*
ṃaay	*tCibbuun iššurbuun maay?*
Caliib	*tCibbuun iššurbuun Caliib?*
biira	*tCibbuun iššurbuun biira?*
šarbat	*tCibbuun iššurbuun šarbat?*

Drill 8. Repeat the utterance, replacing the underlined portion with each of the items given.

tCibb tišrab <u>gahwa</u>?	Would you M like to drink <u>coffee</u>?
gahwa Cilwa	*tCibb tišrab gahwa Cilwa?*
gahwa Caarra	*tCibb tišrab gahwa Caarra?*
gahwa baarda	*tCibb tišrab gahwa baarda?*
biira baarda	*tCibb tišrab biira baarda?*
gḷaaṣ biira	*tCibb tišrab gḷaaṣ biira?*
gḷaaṣ liban	*tCibb tišrab gḷaaṣ liban?*
stikaan čaay	*tCibb tišrab istikaan čaay?*

Drill 9. Repeat the utterance, replacing the underlined portion with each of the items given.

tCibbiin iššurbiin <u>gahwa</u>?	Would you F like to drink <u>coffee</u>?
čaay Caarr	*tCibbiin iššurbiin čaay Caarr?*
čaay Cilu	*tCibbiin iššurbiin čaay Cilu?*
stikaan čaay	*tCibbiin iššurbiin istikaan čaay?*
gḷaaṣ šarbat	*tCibbiin iššurbiin igḷaaṣ šarbat?*
gḷaaṣ ṃaay	*tCibbiin iššurbiin igḷaaṣ ṃaay?*
ṃaay baarid	*tCibbiin iššurbiin ṃaay baarid?*
gahwa Cilwa	*tCibbiin iššurbiin gahwa Cilwa?*

Drill 10. In the following utterances, change the 2 M verb forms to 2 F forms, as in the example.

Cue:	*tCibb čaay?*	Would you M like tea?
Response:	*tCibbiin čaay?*	Would you F like tea?

tCibb čaay?	*tCibbiin čaay?*
tišrab čaay?	*tšurbiin čaay?*
tCibb tišrab čaay?	*tCibbiin iššurbiin čaay?*
triid čaay?	*tirdiin čaay?*
triid tišrab čaay?	*tirdiin iššurbiin čaay?*
raC-tišrab čaay?	*raC-iššurbiin čaay?*
ma-raC-tišrab čaay?	*ma-raC-iššurbiin čaay?*
ma-triid tišrab čaay?	*ma-tirdiin iššurbiin čaay?*

Drill 11. In the following utterances, change the 2 F verb forms to 2 P forms, as in the example.

Cue:	*tCibbiin gahwa?*	Would you F like coffee?
Response:	*tCibbuun gahwa?*	Would you P like coffee?

tCibbiin gahwa?	*tCibbuun gahwa?*
tšurbiin gahwa?	*tšurbuun gahwa?*
ma-ššurbiin gahwa?	*ma-ššurbuun gahwa?*
ma-tCibbiin iššurbiin gahwa?	*ma-tCibbuun iššurbuun gahwa?*
raC-iššurbiin gahwa?	*raC-iššurbuun gahwa?*
ma-raC-iššurbiin gahwa?	*ma-raC-iššurbuun gahwa?*
ma-tirdiin iššurbiin gahwa?	*ma-tirduun iššurbuun gahwa?*

Drill 12. In the following utterances, change the 2 P verb forms to 2 M forms, as in the example.

Cue:	*raC-iššurbuun il-biira?*	Are you P going to drink the heer?
Response:	*raC-tišrab il-biira?*	Are you M going to drink the beer?

raC-iššurbuun il-biira?	*raC-tišrab il-biira?*
ma-raC-iššurbuun il-biira?	*ma-raC-tišrab il-biira?*
ma-tCibbuun il-biira?	*ma-tCibb il-biira?*
tCibbuun biira?	*tCibb biira?*
tCibbuun iššurbuun biira?	*tCibb tišrab biira?*
tirduun biira?	*triid biira?*
ma-tirduun biira?	*ma-triid biira?*
ma-tirduun iššurbuun biira?	*ma-triid tišrab biira?*
ma-tirduun iššurbuun il-biira?	*ma-triid tišrab il-biira?*

UNIT 15

A. NARRATIVE

yšuuf	he sees
ṣadiiqa	his friend
biš-šaariƐ	in/on the street
ysallim Ɛalee	he greets him

1. *ˀabu zuheer yšuuf ṣadiiqa ˀabu xaalid biš-šaariƐ w-ysallim Ɛalee.* — Abu Zuhayr sees his friend Abu Khalid on the street and greets him.

ysiˀla	he asks him
šuġḷa	his work
yruuC	he goes

2. *w-ysiˀla šloon šuġḷa w-ween yruuC.* — He asks him how his work is and where he's going.

baƐdeen	then; afterward
yirCuun	they go

3. *w-baƐdeen yirCuun lil-gahwa suwa.* — Then they go to the coffee-house together.

yisˀalhum	he asks them
yCibbuun	they would like
yšurbuun	they drink

4. *wil-booy yisˀalhum š-yCibbuun yšurbuun.* — The waiter asks them what they would like to drink.

ṣadiiqhum	their friend
yšuufhum	he sees them
hnaak	there
yugƐud	he sits
wiyyaahum	with them

5. *w-ṣadiiqhum ˀabu samiira yšuufhum ihnaak w-yugƐud wiyyaahum.* — Their friend Abu Samira sees them there and sits with them.

baɛad-ma	after (conjunction)
yiɛčuun	they talk
mudda	period of time, (a) while
yguumuun	they get up; they begin
yiqruun	they read
jaraayid	newspapers
6. *w-baɛad-ma yiɛčuun fadd mudda yguumuun yiqruun jaraayid.*	And after they talk for a while they begin to read newspapers.

B. GRAMMAR

1. Preposition prefix *b-* 'in'

The prefix *b-*, which often corresponds in meaning to the English preposition 'in', is attached to nouns or to the first word in certain noun phrases, and is pronounced as part of the word to which it is attached, for example:

beetak	'your M house'	*b-beetak*	'in your M house'
šuġḷak	'your M work'	*b-šuġḷak*	'in your M work'
stikaan	'tea-glass'	*b-istikaan*	'in a tea-glass'
hal-manṭiqa	'this area'	*b-hal-manṭiqa*	'in this area'
fadd gahwa	'a coffee-house'	*b-fadd gahwa*	'in a coffee-house'

This preposition prefix is often attached to a form which already has the article prefix, in which case the helping vowel *i* occurs between the two prefixes, and the whole combination has the form *bil-* or *biD-*, for example:

l-beet	'the house'	*bil-beet*	'in the house'
l-gahwa	'the coffee-house'	*bil-gahwa*	'in the coffee-house'
s-sayyaara	'the car'	*bis-sayyaara*	'in the car'
j-jariida	'the newspaper'	*bij-jariida*	'in the newspaper'

2. Imperfect tense: Third-person forms

A third-person masculine or feminine verb form in the imperfect tense consists of a prefix and a verb stem. With verb stems beginning with two consonants the prefix for the masculine form is *yi-* or *yu-*, and for the feminine form *ti-* or *tu-*. (The alternants *yu-* and *tu-* occur in a somewhat smaller number of cases than the others, and these cases must be learned as they arise.) With other verb stems the prefix for the masculine form is *y-*, and for the feminine form *t-*. The latter is subject to the same types of assimilation as described for the second-person masculine suffix *t-* in 14 B 6; in fact, in every verb the second-person masculine and the third-person feminine forms are identical. Examples:

Prefix	**Verb stem**	**Verb form**	
yi-	*-šrab*	*yišrab*	'he drinks'
ti-		*tišrab*	'she drinks'
yi-	*-qra*	*yiqra*	'he reads'
ti-		*tiqra*	'she reads'
yu-	*-gƐud*	*yugƐud*	'he sits'
tu-		*tugƐud*	'she sits'
y-	*-šuuf*	*yšuuf*	'he sees'
t-		*tšuuf*	'she sees'
y-	*-jiib*	*yjiib*	'he brings'
t-		*djiib*	'she brings'

A third-person plural verb form in the imperfect tense consists of a prefix, a verb stem, and the suffix *-uun*. With verb stems beginning with two consonants the prefix is *yi-* or *yu-*; with other verb stems the prefix is *y-*. If the verb stem ends in a vowel, that vowel is dropped when the suffix *-uun* is added. If the verb stem ends in a sequence -DDvC (that is, a double consonant followed by a short vowel and another (different) consonant), the vowel is normally dropped when a suffix beginning with a vowel is added. Examples:

Prefix	**Verb stem**	**Suffix** *-uun*	**Verb form**	
yi-	*-qr(a)-*		*yiqruun*	'they read'
yi-	*-Ɛč(i)-*		*yiƐčuun*	'they talk'
y-	*-sall(i)m-*		*ysallmuun*	'they greet'
y-	*-šuuf*		*yšuufuun*	'they see'
y-	*-jiib*		*yjiibuun*	'they bring'
y-	*-ruuƐ*		*yruuƐuun*	'they go'
y-	*-riid*		*yriiduun*	'they want'

Besides the forms *yruuƐuun* 'they go' and *yriiduun* 'they want' shown above, there are shorter (and more common) forms based on the stems *-rƐ-* and *-rd-*: *yirƐuun* 'they go' and *yirduun* 'they want'. These are parallel to the alternant forms for the second-person feminine and plural forms of these verbs described in 14 B 6.

As in the case of the second-person plural verb forms (14 B 6), stems which have the shape -CCvC when not followed by a suffix (for example the stems *-šrab* as in *yišrab* 'he drinks' and *-gɛud* as in *yugɛud* 'he sits') have the shape -CvCC- when followed by a suffix beginning with a vowel. That is, the vowel of the stem is shifted from a position between the second and third consonants to a position between the first and second. After shifting, the vowel is either *i* or *u*, even if it is *a* before shifting. The new stem begins with one consonant rather than two, and the prefix is accordingly *y-*. Below, on the left, are examples of third-person masculine verb forms, which have stems of the shape -CCvC (unshifted), and, on the right, the corresponding third-person plural verb forms, which have stems of the shape -CvCC (shifted):

Unshifted stem	**Verb form**		**Shifted stem**	**Verb form**	
-sʔal	*yisʔal*	'he asks'	*-siʔl-*	*ysiʔluun*	'they ask'
-šrab	*yišrab*	'he drinks'	*-šurb-*	*yšurbuun*	'they drink'
-gɛud	*yugɛud*	'he sits'	*-guɛd-*	*yguɛduun*	'they sit'

3. Summary of imperfect-tense verb forms

The first table below shows all the personal prefixes and, where applicable, suffixes, of the imperfect tense. Prefixes ending in *i* or *u* are used with verb stems beginning with two consonants; which of the two vowels occurs is a matter to be learned in each case, but the former is more common. The prefixes *y-*, *t-*, and *n-* are used with verb stems beginning with a single consonant (or with a vowel, of which no examples have yet occurred). The first-person singular prefix *ʔa-* is used with all verb stems except those beginning with a vowel, for which the alternant *ʔ-* is used.

PERSONAL AFFIXES OF THE IMPERFECT TENSE

3	M	*yi-/yu-/y-*	'he'
	F	*ti-/tu-/t-*	'she'
	P	*yi-/yu-/y . . . -uun*	'they'
2	M	*ti-/tu-/t-*	'you M'
	F	*ti-/tu-/t- . . . -iin*	'you F'
	P	*ti-/tu-/t- . . . -uun*	'you P'
1	S	*ʔa/ʔ-*	'I'
	P	*ni-/nu-/n-*	'we'

The following tables show all inflectional forms for the various types of verb stems which have thus far appeared in the imperfect tense. The tables are arranged according to the kind of change, if any, undergone by the verb stem when a suffix beginning with a vowel (i.e., *-uun* or *-iin*) is added.

No stem change

3	M	*yšuuf*	'he sees'	*yjiib*	'he brings'
	F	*tšuuf*	'she sees'	*djiib*	'she brings'
	P	*yšuufuun*	'they see'	*yjiibuun*	'they bring'
2	M	*tšuuf*	'you M see'	*djiib*	'you M bring'
	F	*tšuufiin*	'you F see'	*djiibiin*	'you F bring'
	P	*tšuufuun*	'you P see'	*djiibuun*	'you P bring'
1	S	*ʔašuuf*	'I see'	*ʔajiib*	'I bring'
	P	*nšuuf*	'we see'	*njiib*	'we bring'

Optional stem change of unique type (these three verbs only)

3	M	*yruuḥ*	'he goes'	*yriid*	'he wants'
	F	*truuḥ*	'she goes'	*triid*	'she wants'
	P	*yruuḥuun* *yirḥuun*	'they go'	*yriiduun* *yirduun*	'they want'
2	M	*truuḥ*	'you M go'	*triid*	'you M want'
	F	*truuḥiin* *tirḥiin*	'you F go'	*triidiin* *tirdiin*	'you F want'
	P	*truuḥuun* *tirḥuun*	'you P go'	*triiduun* *tirduun*	'you P want'
1	S	*ʔaruuḥ*	'I go'	*ʔariid*	'I want'
	P	*nruuḥ*	'we go'	*nriid*	'we want'

3	M	*yguul*	'he says'
	F	*tguul*	'she says'
	P	*yguuluun* *yugluun*	'they say'
2	M	*tguul*	'you M say'
	F	*tguuliin* *tugliin*	'you F say'
	P	*tguuluun* *tugluun*	'you P say'

1 S	*ʔaguul*	'I say'
P	*nguul*	'we say'

Stem change involving final double consonant

This kind of change is not apparent from the written form of words, but it is an important matter of pronunciation: A final (written) double consonant letter, as in *yCibb* 'he likes', is pronounced exactly like a single consonant; but if a suffix beginning with a vowel is added, as in *yCibbuun* 'they like', the double consonant is between two vowels and must be pronounced as a double consonant sound (see 10 E). This kind of stem change is completely automatic, and occurs not only in verb forms but throughout the language; therefore it will not be mentioned again after this paragraph.

3 M	*yCibb*	'he likes'
F	*tCibb*	'she likes'
P	*yCibbuun*	'they like'
2 M	*tCibb*	'you M like'
F	*tCibbiin*	'you F like'
P	*tCibbuun*	'you P like'
1 S	*ʔaCibb*	'I like'
P	*nCibb*	'we like'

Stem vowel is dropped

The **stem vowel** is defined as the short vowel before the final consonant of a stem. In stems in which it is preceded by a double consonant and followed by a different consonant, as in the example below, it is normally dropped when a suffix beginning with a vowel is added. (Sometimes, in rather deliberate speech, it is retained, so you may hear it both ways, but in this book we shall present only the forms in which it is dropped.) Note that a (written) double consonant letter immediately preceding another consonant, as in *ysallmuun,* is pronounced exactly like a single consonant, but a double consonant between two vowels, as in *ysallim,* must be pronounced as a double consonant sound (see 10 E).

3 M	*ysallim* (*Calee*)	'he greets (him)'
F	*tsallim*	'she greets'
P	*ysallmuun*	'they greet'

2	M	*tsallim*	'you M greet'
	F	*tsallmiin*	'you F greet'
	P	*tsallmuun*	'you P greet'
1	S	*ˀasallim*	'I greet'
	P	*nsallim*	'we greet'

Stem vowel is shifted (see B 2 above)

3	M	*yisˀal*	'he asks'	*yišrab*	'he drinks'
	F	*tisˀal*	'she asks'	*tišrab*	'she drinks'
	P	*ysiˀluun*	'they ask'	*yšurbuun*	'they drink'
2	M	*tisˀal*	'you M ask'	*tišrab*	'you M drink'
	F	*tsiˀliin*	'you F ask'	*tšurbiin*	'you F drink'
	P	*tsiˀluun*	'you P ask'	*tšurbuun*	'you P drink'
1	S	*ˀasˀal*	'I ask'	*ˀašrab*	'I drink'
	P	*nisˀal*	'we ask'	*nišrab*	'we drink'

3	M	*yugƐud*	'he sits'
	F	*tugƐud*	'she sits'
	P	*yguƐduun*	'they sit'
2	M	*tugƐud*	'you M sit'
	F	*tguƐdiin*	'you F sit'
	P	*tguƐduun*	'you P sit'
1	S	*ˀagƐud*	'I sit'
	P	*nugƐud*	'we sit'

In verbs like those illustrated above, you may occasionally hear two kinds of variation. The first is that the stem may remain unshifted even when a suffix beginning with a vowel is added, for example *yugƐuduun* 'they sit' instead of *yguƐduun*. The second is that even when the stem is shifted, the prefix may retain its vowel, for example *yuguƐduun* instead of *yguƐduun*. In this book, however, we shall present only forms like those given in the tables above.

Final vowel is dropped

If the verb stem ends in a vowel, as in *yiqra* 'he reads', that final vowel is invariably dropped when a suffix beginning with a vowel is added.

3	M	*yiqra*	'he reads'	*yiḥči*	'he talks'
	F	*tiqra*	'she reads'	*tiḥči*	'she talks'
	P	*yiqruun*	'they read'	*yiḥčuun*	'they talk'
2	M	*tiqra*	'you M read'	*tiḥči*	'you M talk'
	F	*tiqriin*	'you F read'	*tiḥčiin*	'you F talk'
	P	*tiqruun*	'you P read'	*tiḥčuun*	'you P talk'
1	S	*ʔaqra*	'I read'	*ʔaḥči*	'I talk'
	P	*niqra*	'we read'	*niḥči*	'we talk'

4. Pronoun suffixes: Third person

In Sentences 1 and 2 of the dialogue, note the ending *-a* in the following forms:

ṣadiiqa	'his friend'
šuġḷa	'his work'
ysiʔla	'he asks him'

This ending *-a* is one alternant of the third-person masculine pronoun suffix, which when attached to a noun often corresponds to English *his,* and when attached to a verb or preposition to English *him.* This alternant is used only with stems ending in a consonant; the other will be described later. Additional examples:

beet	'house'	*beeta*	'his house'
ʔiid	'hand'	*ʔiida*	'his hand'
yamm	'beside, next to'	*yamma*	'beside him'
ʕind	'on, with'	*ʕinda*	'on, with him; he has'
yšuuf	'he sees'	*yšuufa*	'he sees him'
tḥibb	'she likes'	*tḥibba*	'she likes him'

The third-person masculine suffix may also refer to an inanimate masculine noun (see 12 B 3), and in that case it corresponds to English *its* or *it,* as in:

yamm	'beside, next to'	*yamma*	'beside it M'
yšuuf	'he sees'	*yšuufa*	'he sees it M'

Some stems undergo changes when this ending is added. Many nouns and prepositions of the shape CvCvC lose their stem vowel:

šuġuḷ	'work, business'	*šuġḷa*	'his work'
baʕad	'after'	*baʕda*	'after him/it M'

And verb stems ending in -CCvC undergo shift to -CvCC, just as they do when one of the verbal endings *-iin* or *-uun* is added:

yisˀal	'he asks'	*ysiˀla*	'he asks him'
yišrab	'he drinks'	*ysurba*	'he drinks it M'

The third-person feminine pronoun suffix is *-ha,* corresponding to the English possessive *her* or the objective *her.* It is also used in referring to an inanimate feminine noun, and then corresponds to English *its* or *it.* The third-person plural pronoun suffix is *-hum,* corresponding to English *their* or *them.* Examples:

beet	'house'	*beetha*	'her house'
		beethum	'their house'
šuġuḷ	'work'	*šuġuḷha*	'her work'
		šuġuḷhum	'their work'
yamm	'beside'	*yammha*	'beside her'
		yammhum	'beside them'
yšuuf	'he sees'	*yšuufha*	'he sees her'
		yšuufhum	'he sees them'
yisˀal	"he asks'	*yisˀalha*	'he asks her'
		yisˀalhum	'he asks them'

5. Summary of pronoun suffix forms used with consonant stems

Following is a table summarizing the forms of pronoun suffixes thus far given. Those that begin with a consonant, namely *-ha, -hum, -kum, -ni,* and *-na,* are invariable, and are used both with consonant stems (stems ending in a consonant) and with vowel stems (stems ending in a vowel). The pronoun suffix forms that begin with a vowel, however, namely *-a, -ak, -ič,* and *-i,* are used only with consonant stems. (Each of these has an alternant used with vowel stems, which we shall take up later.)

3	M	*-a*	'his/its M; him/it M'
	F	*-ha*	'her/its F; her/it F'
	P	*-hum*	'their; them'
2	M	*-ak*	'your M; you M'
	F	*-ič*	'your F; you F'
	P	*-kum*	'your P; you P'
1	S	*-i*	'my; me' (with noun and preposition stems)
		-ni	'me' (with verb stems)
	P	*-na*	'our; us'

The following tables show these pronoun suffix forms attached to a noun, a preposition, and a verb. (In the English translations of words containing the third-person masculine suffix *-a* and feminine suffix *-ha,* we will use only 'his', 'him', and 'her', but remember that when they refer to inanimate nouns the translation would be 'its' or 'it'.)

With a noun stem

		beet	'house'
3	M	*beeta*	'his house'
	F	*beetha*	'her house'
	P	*beethum*	'their house'
2	M	*beetak*	'your M house'
	F	*beetič*	'your F house'
	P	*beetkum*	'your P house'
1	S	*beeti*	'my house'
	P	*beetna*	'our house'

With a preposition stem

		yamm	'beside, next to'
3	M	*yamma*	'beside him'
	F	*yammha*	'beside her'
	P	*yammhum*	'beside them'
2	M	*yammak*	'beside you M'
	F	*yammič*	'beside you F'
	P	*yammkum*	'beside you P'
1	S	*yammi*	'beside me'
	P	*yammna*	'beside us'

With a verb stem

		yšuuf	'he sees'
3	M	*yšuufa*	'he sees him'
	F	*yšuufha*	'he sees her'
	P	*yšuufhum*	'he sees them'
2	M	*yšuufak*	'he sees you M'
	F	*yšuufič*	'he sees you F'
	P	*yšuufkum*	'he sees you P'
1	S	*yšuufni*	'he sees me'
	P	*yšuufna*	'he sees us'

6. Verb strings

Note the underlined portions of the following sentences from Units 13 and 15:

š-it<u>حibbuun iššurbuun</u> ixwaanʔ	'What <u>would you like to drink,</u> gentlemen?'
wil-booy yisʔalhum š-<u>yحibbuun yšurbuun</u>.	'The waiter asks them what <u>they would like to drink.</u>'
w-baعad-ma yiحčuun fadd mudda <u>yguumuun yiqruun</u> jaraayid.	'And after they talk for a while <u>they begin to read</u> newspapers.'

In Iraqi there is no separate verb form corresponding to English infinitives like *to drink* and *to read*. The meaning expressed by an English phrase like *they begin to read* is expressed in Iraqi by two verb forms, one right after the other, and both in the same person, gender, and number. Such a sequence is called a **verb string.** Thus ***yحibbuun*** 'they like' and ***yšurbuun*** 'they drink' may occur together in a string ***yحibbuun yšurbuun,*** meaning 'they like (*or* would like) to drink'. Strings consisting of two verbs are the most common, but strings of three or even more also occur. In any string, the first verb may be in the imperfect, perfect, or imperative, but any verb thereafter is always in the imperfect. Additional examples:

yriid yišrab	'he wants to drink'
triid tišrab	'she wants to drink'
yriiduun yšurbuun *yirduun yšurbuun*	'they want to drink'
tحibb tiحči	'you M (would) like to talk'
tحibbiin tiحčiin	'you F (would) like to talk'
tحibbuun tiحčuun	'you P (would) like to talk'
ʔaguum ʔaqra	'I begin to read'
nguum niqra	'we begin to read'

Note: The verb translated 'begin' above has that meaning only when followed by another verb in a string, as in the examples. Otherwise it generally means 'get up'.

C. DRILLS

Drill 1. Repeat the utterance, replacing the underlined portion with each of the items given.

ˀabu zuheer	Abu Zuhayr
yšuuf ṣadiiqa bil-ḅang.	sees his friend in the bank.
bis-sayyaara	in the car
bil-maṭaar	at the airport
bil-beet	at home
b-beeta	at his house
b-hal-uuteel	at this hotel
bil-uuteel	at the hotel
bil-manṭiqa	in the area
bis-suug	at the market
bil-gaaziino	at the gaaziino

Drill 2. Repeat the utterance, replacing the underlined portion with each of the items given, and making whatever other changes may then be necessary.

ˁinda šuġuḷ bil-ḅang il-yoom.	He has business at the bank today.
daaˀira	*ˁinda šuġuḷ bid-daaˀira l-yoom.*
maṭaar	*ˁinda šuġuḷ bil-maṭaar il-yoom.*
gahwa	*ˁinda šuġuḷ bil-gahwa l-yoom.*
ˀuuteel	*ˁinda šuġuḷ bil-uuteel il-yoom.*
safaara	*ˁinda šuġuḷ bis-safaara l-yoom.*
šiqqa	*ˁinda šuġuḷ biš-šiqqa l-yoom.*
beet	*ˁinda šuġuḷ bil-beet il-yoom.*

Drill 3. Repeat the utterance, replacing the underlined portion with each of the items given, and making whatever other changes may then be necessary.

ˁidha šuġuḷ bil-ḅang il-yoom?	Does she have business at the bank today?
manṭiqa	*ˁidha šuġuḷ bil-manṭiqa l-yoom?*
safaara	*ˁidha šuġuḷ bis-safaara l-yoom?*
ˀuuteel	*ˁidha šuġuḷ bil-uuteel il-yoom?*
daaˀira	*ˁidha šuġuḷ bid-daaˀira l-yoom?*
maṭaar	*ˁidha šuġuḷ bil-maṭaar il-yoom?*
suug	*ˁidha šuġuḷ bis-suug il-yoom?*
gaaziino	*ˁidha šuġuḷ bil-gaaziino l-yoom?*

Drill 4. Repeat the utterance, replacing the underlined portion with each of the items given, and making whatever other changes may then be necessary.

εidhum daaʔira b-hal-uuteel.	They have an office in this hotel.
maṭaar	*εidhum daaʔira b-hal-maṭaar.*
safaara	*εidhum daaʔira b-has-safaara.*
šaariε	*εidhum daaʔira b-haš-šaariε.*
gahwa	*εidhum daaʔira b-hal-gahwa.*
beet	*εidhum daaʔira b-hal-beet.*
šiqqa	*εidhum daaʔira b-haš-šiqqa.*
manṭiqa	*εidhum daaʔira b-hal-manṭiqa.*
ʔuuteel	*εidhum daaʔira b-hal-uuteel.*

Drill 5. The following sentences illustrate third-person verb forms. Listen and repeat.

ʔabu zuheer yšuuf muṣṭafa biš-šaariε.	Abu Zuhayr sees Mustafa on the street.
ʔumm zuheer itšuuf muṣṭafa biš-šaariε.	Umm Zuhayr sees Mustafa on the street.
zuheer w-xaalid yšuufuun muṣṭafa biš-šaariε.	Zuhayr and Khalid see Mustafa on the street.
ʔabu zuhayr ma-yišrab biira.	Abu Zuhayr doesn't drink beer.
ʔumm zuhayr ma-tišrab biira.	Umm Zuhayr doesn't drink beer.
zuheer-w-xaalid ma-yšurbuun biira.	Zuhayr and Khalid don't drink beer.
ʔabu zuheer yugεud wiyyaahum bil-beet.	Abu Zuhayr sits with them at home.
ʔumm zuheer tugεud wiyyaahum bil-beet.	Umm Zuhayr sits with them at home.
zuheer w-xaalid yguεduun wiyyaahum bil-beet.	Zuhayr and Khalid sit with them at home.
ʔabu zuheer yšuuf ʔabu muṣṭafa w-ysallim εalee.	Abu Zuhayr sees Abu Mustafa and greets him.
ʔumm zuheer itšuuf ʔabu muṣṭafa w-itsallim εalee.	Umm Zuhayr sees Abu Mustafa and greets him.
zuheer w-xaalid yšuufuun ʔabu muṣṭafa w-ysallmuun εalee.	Zuhayr and Khalid see Abu Mustafa and greet him.

ʔabu zuheer raḥ-yiḥči wiyyaahum.	Abu Zuhayr is going to talk with them.
ʔumm zuheer raḥ-tiḥči wiyyaahum.	Umm Zuhayr is going to talk with them.
zuheer w-xaalid raḥ-yiḥčuun wiyyaahum.	Zuhayr and Khalid are going to talk with them.
ʔabu zuheer raḥ-yisʔal il-booy.	Abu Zuhayr is going to ask the waiter.
ʔumm zuheer raḥ-tisʔal il-booy.	Umm Zuhayr is going to ask the waiter.
zuheer w-xaalid raḥ-ysiʔluun il-booy.	Zuhayr and Khalid are going to ask the waiter.
ʔabu zuheer yḥibb yruuḥ lis-suug.	Abu Zuhayr likes to go to the market.
ʔumm zuheer itḥibb itruuḥ lis-suug.	Umm Zuhayr likes to go to the market.
zuheer w-xaalid yḥibbuun yirḥuun lis-suug.	Zuhayr and Khalid like to go to the market.
ʔabu zuheer ma-yriid yjiib is-sayyaara.	Abu Zuhayr doesn't want to bring the car.
ʔumm zuheer ma-triid idjiib is-sayyaara.	Umm Zuhayr doesn't want to bring the car.
zuheer w-xaalid ma-yirduun yjiibuun is-sayyaara.	Zuhayr and Khalid don't want to bring the car.

Drill 6. Change the 3 M verb forms to 3 F forms, as in the example.

Cue:	*yšuuf xaalid biš-šaariʕ.*	He sees Khalid on the street.
Response:	*tšuuf xaalid biš-šaariʕ.*	She sees Khalid on the street.

yšuuf ʔabu xaalid bil-ḅang.	*tšuuf ʔabu xaalid bil-ḅang.*
yšuuf ʔabu xaalid bis-sayyaara.	*tšuuf ʔabu xaalid bis-sayyaara.*
yruuḥ lis-suug wiyyaahum.	*truuḥ lis-suug wiyyaahum.*
yruuḥ lil-maṭaar wiyyaahum.	*truuḥ lil-maṭaar wiyyaahum.*
raḥ-yjiib il-gahwa.	*raḥ-idjiib il-gahwa.*
raḥ-yjiib-li stikaan čaay.	*raḥ-idjiib-li stikaan čaay.*
ma-yišrab ḥaliib il-yoom.	*ma-tišrab ḥaliib il-yoom.*
ma-yišrab šarbat il-yoom.	*ma-tišrab šarbat il-yoom.*
ween raḥ-yugʕud?	*ween raḥ-tugʕud?*

raħ-yugʕud ihnaak?	*raħ-tugʕud ihnaak?*
yriid gḷaaṣ ṃaay.	*triid gḷaaṣ ṃaay.*
yriid gḷaaṣ liban.	*triid gḷaaṣ liban.*
yriid yisʔal muṣṭafa.	*triid tisʔal muṣṭafa.*
yriid yisʔal zuheer.	*triid tisʔal zuheer.*
ma-yħibb haš-šiqqa hwaaya.	*ma-tħibb haš-šiqqa hwaaya.*
ma-yħibb has-sayyaara hwaaya.	*ma-tħibb has-sayyaara hwaaya.*
yħibb yruuħ lil-beet.	*tħibb itruuħ lil-beet.*
yħibb yruuħ lid-daaʔira.	*tħibb itruuħ lid-daaʔira.*
raħ-yiħči wiyyaahum il-yoom.	*raħ-tiħči wiyyaahum il-yoom.*
raħ-yiħči wiyyaahum baʕdeen.	*raħ-tiħči wiyyaahum baʕdeen.*

Drill 7. Change the subject from *ʔabu zuheer* to *ʔumm zuheer,* and make the necessary changes in the verb forms.

Cue:	*ʔabu zuheer yšuuf xaalid.*	Abu Zuhayr sees Khalid.
Response:	*ʔumm zuheer itšuuf xaalid.*	Umm Zuhayr sees Khalid.

ʔabu zuheer yišrab čaay.	*ʔumm zuheer tišrab čaay.*
ʔabu zuheer yħibb yišrab čaay.	*ʔumm zuheer itħibb tišrab čaay.*
ʔabu zuheer yugʕud bis-sayyaara.	*ʔumm zuheer tugʕud bis-sayyaara.*
ʔabu zuheer yriid yugʕud bis-sayyaara.	*ʔumm zuheer itriid tugʕud bis-sayyaara.*
ʔabu zuheer yiħči hwaaya.	*ʔumm zuheer tiħči hwaaya.*
ʔabu zuheer yħibb yiħči hwaaya.	*ʔumm zuheer itħibb tiħči hwaaya.*
ʔabu zuheer yšuuf xaalid w-ysallim ʕalee.	*ʔumm zuheer itšuuf xaalid w-itsallim ʕalee.*
ʔabu zuheer raħ-yšuuf xaalid w-ysallim ʕalee.	*ʔumm zuheer raħ-itšuuf xaalid w-itsallim ʕalee.*
ʔabu zuheer yiqra jaraayid.	*ʔumm zuheer tiqra jaraayid.*
ʔabu zuheer yguum yiqra jaraayid.	*ʔumm zuheer itguum tiqra jaraayid.*
ʔabu zuheer yiħči bit-talafoon.	*ʔumm zuheer tiħči bit-talafoon.*
ʔabu zuheer yħibb yiħči bit-talafoon.	*ʔumm zuheer itħibb tiħči bit-talafoon.*
ʔabu zuheer ma-yruuħ il-hal-manṭiqa.	*ʔumm zuheer ma-truuħ il-hal-manṭiqa.*
ʔabu zuheer ma-yriid yruuħ il-hal-manṭiqa.	*ʔumm zuheer ma-triid itruuħ il-hal-manṭiqa.*
ʔabu zuheer raħ-yjiib-lak gḷaaṣ ṃaay.	*ʔumm zuheer raħ-idjiib-lak gḷaaṣ ṃaay.*
ʔabu zuheer yħibb yjiib-lak gḷaaṣ ṃaay.	*ʔumm zuheer itħibb idjiib-lak gḷaaṣ ṃaay.*

Drill 8. Change the 3 M verb forms to 3 P forms, as in the example.

Cue:	*yšuuf xaalid biš-šaariƐ.*	He sees Khalid on the street.
Response:	*yšuufuun xaalid biš-šaariƐ.*	They see Khalid on the street.

yšuuf ʔabu xaalid bil-maṭaar.	*yšuufuun ʔabu xaalid bil-maṭaar.*
yšuuf ʔabu xaalid bil-gahwa.	*yšuufuun ʔabu xaalid bil-gahwa.*
baƐdeen yruuC lis-safaara.	*baƐdeen yirCuun lis-safaara.*
baƐdeen yruuC lil-gaaziino.	*baƐdeen yirCuun lil-gaaziino.*
raC-yišrab fadd istikaan čaay.	*raC-yšurbuun fadd istikaan čaay.*
raC-yišrab fadd gahwa Cilwa.	*raC-yšurbuun fadd gahwa Cilwa.*
ma-yCibb biira hwaaya.	*ma-yCibbuun biira hwaaya.*
ma-yCibb haš-šuġuḷ ihwaaya.	*ma-yCibbuun haš-šuġuḷ ihwaaya.*
raC-yjiib ij-jaraayid lil-uuteel.	*raC-yjiibuun ij-jaraayid lil-uuteel.*
raC-yjiib ij-jaraayid lid-daaʔira.	*raC-yjiibuun ij-jaraayid lid-daaʔira.*
ma-yriid hal-qalam.	*ma-yirduun hal-qalam.*
ma-yriid hal-xariiṭa.	*ma-yirduun hal-xariiṭa.*
ma-yriid yruuC wiyyaahum.	*ma-yirduun yirCuun wiyyaahum.*
ma-yriid yiCči wiyyaahum.	*ma-yirduun yiCčuun wiyyaahum.*
yugƐud w-yiqra jaraayid.	*yguƐduun w-yiqruun jaraayid.*
yugƐud w-yišrab gahwa.	*yguƐduun w-yšurbuun gahwa.*

Drill 9. Change the subject from *muṣṭafa* to *zuheer w-muṣṭafa,* and make the necessary changes in the verb forms.

Cue:	*muṣṭafa yšuuf xaalid biš-šaariƐ.*	Mustafa sees Khalid on the street.
Response:	*muṣṭafa w-zuheer yšuufuun xaalid biš-šaariƐ.*	Mustafa and Zuhayr see Khalid on the street.

muṣṭafa yšuuf xaalid w-ysallim Ɛalee.	*muṣṭafa w-zuheer yšuufuun xaalid w-ysallmuun Ɛalee.*
muṣṭafa yruuC lid-daaʔira.	*muṣṭafa w-zuheer yirCuun lid-daaʔira.*
muṣṭafa yriid gḷaaṣ ṃaay.	*muṣṭafa w-zuheer yirduun gḷaaṣ ṃaay.*
muṣṭafa yguul "ʔaḷḷaa bil-xeer".	*muṣṭafa w-zuheer yugluun "ʔaḷḷaa bil-xeer".*
muṣṭafa yisʔal "ween raayiC?"	*muṣṭafa w-zuheer ysiʔluun "ween raayiC?"*
muṣṭafa yCibb haš-šuġuḷ ihwaaya.	*muṣṭafa w-zuheer yCibbuun haš-šuġuḷ ihwaaya.*
muṣṭafa yiCči wiyyaahum bil-gahwa.	*muṣṭafa w-zuheer yiCčuun wiyyaahum bil-gahwa.*
muṣṭafa ma-yCibb yiCči wiyyaahum.	*muṣṭafa w-zuheer ma-yCibbuun yiCčuun wiyyaahum.*

muṣṭafa ma-raC-yugCud wiyyaahum.	*muṣṭafa w-zuheer ma-raC-yguCduun wiyyaahum.*
muṣṭafa yugCud w-yiqra jaraayid.	*muṣṭafa w-zuheer yguCduun w-yiqruun jaraayid.*
muṣṭafa yugCud bid-daaˀira w-yiCči.	*muṣṭafa w-zuheer yguCduun bid-daaˀira w-yiCčuun.*
muṣṭafa yguum yiCči wiyyaahum.	*muṣṭafa w-zuheer yguumuun yiCčuun wiyyaahum.*
muṣṭafa yriid yisˀal xaalid ween raayiC.	*muṣṭafa w-zuheer yirduun ysiˀluun xaalid ween raayiC.*
muṣṭafa ma-yCibb yišrab ihwaaya.	*muṣṭafa w-zuheer ma-yCibbuun yšurbuun ihwaaya.*
muṣṭafa raC-yjiib is-sayyaara.	*muṣṭafa w-zuheer raC-yjiibuun is-sayyaara.*

Drill 10. Change the third-person masculine pronoun suffix *-a* to the third-person feminine pronoun suffix *-ha,* and make any other necessary changes.

Cue:	*ween beetaˀ*	Where's his house?
Response:	*ween beethaˀ*	Where's her house?

šloonaˀ	*šloonhaˀ*
šloon beetaˀ	*šloon beethaˀ*
weenaˀ	*weenhaˀ*
haay weena, ma-da-nšuufaˀ	*haay weenha, ma-da-nšuufhaˀ*
Cinda šuġuḷˀ	*Cidha šuġuḷˀ*
Cinda šuġuḷ bid-daaˀiraˀ	*Cidha šuġuḷ bid-daaˀiraˀ*
laa, kullši ma-Cinda.	*laa, kullši ma-Cidha.*
Cinda sayyaaraˀ	*Cidha sayyaaraˀ*
bali, Cinda sayyaara zeena.	*bali, Cidha sayyaara zeena.*
šloon šuġḷaˀ	*šloon šuġuḷhaˀ*
raC-ašuufa l-yoom.	*raC-ašuufha l-yoom.*
ˀariid ˀagCud yamma.	*ˀariid ˀagCud yammha.*
ˀajiib-la šii baaridˀ	*ˀajiib-ilha šii baaridˀ*
jiib-la fadd igḷaaṣ liban rajaaˀan.	*jiib-ilha fadd igḷaaṣ liban rajaaˀan.*

Drill 11. Change the third-person masculine pronoun suffix *-a* to the third-person plural pronoun suffix *-hum,* and make any other necessary changes.

Cue:	*ween beetaˀ*	Where's his house?
Response:	*ween beethumˀ*	Where's their house?

weenaʔ
ma-da-nšuufa.
ma-tḥibbaʔ
laa, ma-aḥibba hwaaya.
š-jaaba lil-gahwa l-yoomʔ
šgadd ṣaar-la hnaakʔ
šgadd ṣaar-la bil-gahwaʔ
xaalid raḥ-ysiʔla ween beeta.
xaalid ma-yriid ysiʔla.
ʔabu samiira raḥ-yugɛud yamma.
samiira raḥ-tugɛud yamma.
ɛinda šuġuḷ bil-maṭaarʔ
laa, ma-ɛinda šuġuḷ il-yoom.
š-raḥ-idjiib-laʔ
raḥ-ajiib-la šii ḥaarr.

weenhumʔ
ma-da-nšuufhum.
ma-tḥibbhumʔ
laa, ma-aḥibbhum ihwaaya.
š-jaabhum lil-gahwa l-yoomʔ
šgadd ṣaar-ilhum ihnaakʔ
šgadd ṣaar-ilhum bil-gahwaʔ
xaalid raḥ-yisʔalhum ween beethum.
xaalid ma-yriid yisʔalhum.
ʔabu samiira raḥ-yugɛud yammhum.
samiira raḥ-tugɛud yammhum.
ɛidhum šuġuḷ bil-maṭaarʔ
laa, ma-ɛidhum šuġuḷ il-yoom.
š-raḥ-idjiib-ilhumʔ
raḥ-ajiib-ilhum šii ḥaarr.

Drill 12. Answer each question as in the following examples, using the appropriate pronoun suffix.

Cue:	*ʔinta raḥ-itšuuf xaalid il-yoomʔ*	Are you going to see Khalid today?
Response:	*laa, ma-raḥ-ašuufa.*	No, I'm not going to see him.

ʔinta raḥ-itšuuf zuheer il-yoomʔ	*laa, ma-raḥ-ašuufa.*
ʔinta raḥ-itšuuf ʔumm xaalid il-yoomʔ	*laa, ma-raḥ-ašuufha.*
ʔinta raḥ-itšuuf zuheer w-xaalid il-yoomʔ	*laa, ma-raḥ-ašuufhum.*
ʔinta raḥ-itšuuf samiira l-yoomʔ	*laa, ma-raḥ-ašuufha.*
ʔinta raḥ-itšuuf ʔabu xaalid il-yoomʔ	*laa, ma-raḥ-ašuufa.*
ʔinta raḥ-itšuuf il-beet il-yoomʔ	*laa, ma-raḥ-ašuufa.*
ʔinta raḥ-itšuuf ʔumm zuheer il-yoomʔ	*laa, ma-raḥ-ašuufha.*
ʔinta raḥ-itšuuf iš-šiqqa l-yoomʔ	*laa, ma-raḥ-ašuufha.*
ʔinta raḥ-itšuuf il-maḥruusiin il-yoomʔ	*laa, ma-raḥ-ašuufhum.*

Cue:	*xaalid š-yḥibb yišrabʔ*	What would Khalid like to drink?
Response:	*raḥ-asiʔla š-yḥibb.*	I'll ask him what he'd like.

ʔabu zuheer š-yḥibb yišrabʔ	*raḥ-asiʔla š-yḥibb.*
ʔumm zuheer š-itḥibb tišrabʔ	*raḥ-asʔalha š-itḥibb.*
zuheer w-xaalid š-yḥibbuun yšurbuunʔ	*raḥ-asʔalhum š-yḥibbuun.*
ʔumm samiira š-itḥibb tišrabʔ	*raḥ-asʔalha š-itḥibb.*
ʔabu xaalid š-yḥibb yišrabʔ	*raḥ-asiʔla š-yḥibb.*
l-maḥruusiin š-yḥibbuun yšurbuunʔ	*raḥ-asʔalhum š-yḥibbuun.*

zuheer w-samiira š-yCibbuun yšurbuun?	*raC-as?alhum š-yCibbuun.*
mCammad š-yCibb yišrab?	*raC-asi?la š-yCibb.*
mCammad w-muṣṭafa š-yCibbuun yšurbuun?	*raC-as?alhum š-yCibbuun.*
?umm muṣṭafa š-itCibb tišrab?	*raC-as?alha š-itCibb.*
?abu muṣṭafa š-yCibb yišrab?	*raC-asi?la š-yCibb.*

UNIT 16

A. DIALOGUE

The three men are still sitting in the coffee-house. Abu Zuhayr prepares to leave.

?abu zuheer	Abu Zuhayr
?astarxiṣ	I ask permission
yaa	(particle of address; see Notes)
jamaaCa	group (of people)
laazim	necessary M; must, have to
1. *?astarxiṣ, yaa jamaaCa, laazim aruuC.*	Excuse me, gentlemen, I have to go.

?abu xaalid	Abu Khalid
š-aku	what is there?
mistaCjil	urgent M; in a hurry M
baCad	still, yet
wakit	time
2. *š-aku mistaCjil? muu baCad wakit?*	What's the hurry? It's still early, you know.

?abu zuheer	Abu Zuhayr
mawCid	appointment, engagement
s-saaCa	the hour; the clock, the watch
xamsa	five
3. *Cindi mawCid wiyya fadd ṣadiiq is-saaCa xamsa.*	I have an appointment with a friend at five o'clock.

ʔabu xaalid	Abu Khalid
ruuC	go M
gubaḷ	straight ahead
la-tidfaƐ	don't pay M
Csaabak	your M bill, check, account
Ɛalayya	on me
4. *zeen laƐad, ruuC gubaḷ, la-tidfaƐ kullši. Csaabak Ɛalayya.*	All right then, but go straight out, don't pay for anything. Your check's on me.

ʔabu zuheer	Abu Zuhayr
ma-yṣiir	it M does not happen
raC-adfaƐ	I'm going to pay
Csaabkum	your P bill, check, account
kull	all, every, any
Cači	talk
ma-aku	there isn't, there aren't
5. *laa, ma-yṣiir. ʔaani raC-adfaƐ iCsaabkum w-kull Cači ma-aku.*	No, absolutely not. I'm going to pay your checks, and there isn't going to be any discussion.

ʔabu xaalid	Abu Khalid
keefak	your M wish, feeling
ma-tiswa	it F isn't worth
6. *keefak, yaaba, ma-tiswa. šukran.*	Whatever you say. I won't argue. Thank you.

ʔabu zuheer	Abu Zuhayr
fiimaanillaa	in the protection of God
7. *fiimaanillaa.*	Good-bye.

ʔabu xaalid	Abu Khalid
ʔaḷḷa wiyyaak	God be with you M
8. *ʔaḷḷa wiyyaak.*	Good-bye.

NOTES ON DIALOGUE

1. Polite formulas

ˀastarxiṣ	A first-person singular imperfect verb form, meaning literally 'I ask permission'. Said by someone about to leave.
fiimaanillaa	From the Classical phrase *fii ˀamaani llaahi* 'in the protection of God'. One of several common expressions generally corresponding to English *good-bye*.
M *ˀaḷḷa wiyyaak* F *ˀaḷḷa wiyyaač* P *ˀaḷḷa wiyyaakum*	Literally 'God with you'; another expression corresponding to *good-bye*. Said respectively to a male, a female, and to two or more. Usually said to, not by, the one(s) departing.

2. Forms of address

yaa jamaaƐa	The word *jamaaƐa* is a common noun meaning 'group' or 'gang', and usually refers to a group of friends or associates. The word *yaa* is a particle of address; it usually precedes common nouns, and may precede proper names, when they are used as forms of address. In calling to people it may serve as a sort of attention-getter, somewhat like English *oh* or *hey,* for example *yaa muṣṭafa* 'oh Mustafa!; hey, Mustafa!; but in most contexts it has no English equivalent. The phrase *yaa jamaaƐa* itself might correspond to various English terms. It lies somewhere between the somewhat formal *gentlemen* and the very informal *you guys*. As a form of address it is much more commonly used by males than by females.

3. The friendly squabble about paying the check is typical. It would be thought impolite not to offer to pay at all, and among all but the closest friends the argument would usually go on for a little longer than in the dialogue before one or the other gives in.

B. GRAMMAR

1. *laazim* 'must'

The Iraqi equivalent of such English phrases as *I must go, we have to take, Khalid has to bring,* and the like, is a construction consisting of the word *laazim* (the masculine form of an adjective meaning 'necessary') followed by a verb form in the imperfect tense: *laazim aruuC* 'I must go' or 'I have to go'. The word *laazim* in such a construction is invariable, but the verb form varies according to the subject. Additional examples:

laazim inruuC	'we must go'
laazim itruuC	'you M/she must go'
laazim yirCuun	'they must go'
laazim yjiib	'he must bring'
laazim idjiibiin	'you F must bring'
laazim idjiibuun	'you P must bring'

The negative of such constructions is formed by attaching the negative prefix *ma-* to *laazim.* Note that such a negative usually corresponds to English *does/do not have to,* and not to *must not.*

ma-laazim itruuC	'you M don't have to go'
ma-laazim yjiib	'he doesn't have to bring'

2. Imperative forms (1)

In the imperfect tense, Iraqi verbs have not only the eight indicative forms described in the preceding units, but also three second-person **imperative** forms: a masculine form used in addressing one male person, a feminine form used in addressing one female, and a plural form used in addressing two or more persons. It is important to note from the beginning that these forms are used only in giving a *positive* command, that is, in telling a person to do something. (For negative commands—telling a person *not* to do something—see B 3 below.) In this unit we will take up the imperative forms of some of the verbs that have occurred so far, and leave the others until later.

Note the forms *jiib* and *ruuC* in the following sentences from Dialogues 13 and 16:

ˀaani jiib-li fadd gahwa Cilwa.	'Bring me a sweet coffee.'
zeen laCad, ruuC gubaḷ . . .	'All right, then, (but) go straight (out) . . .

These are masculine singular (2 M) imperative forms; they consist of the verb stem alone, with no prefix and no suffix. The corresponding feminine singular (2 F) form consists of the stem and the suffix *-i*, and the plural (2 P) form consists of the stem and the suffix *-u*. All verbs with imperfect stems of the pattern -CvvC form their imperative in the same way. In the tables below, the left-hand side shows second-person indicative forms for the sake of contrast, and the right-hand shows the corresponding imperative forms.

	Indicative		Imperative	
2 M	*djiib*	'you M bring'	*jiib*	'bring M'
F	*djiibiin*	'you F bring'	*jiibi*	'bring F'
P	*djiibuun*	'you P bring'	*jiibu*	'bring P'
2 M	*truuC*	'you M go'	*ruuC*	'go M'
F	*truuCiin* / *tirCiin*	'you F go'	*ruuCi*	'go F'
P	*truuCuun* / *tirCuun*	'you P go'	*ruuCu*	'go P'
2 M	*tšuuf*	'you M see'	*šuuf*	'see, look M'
F	*tšuufiin*	'you F see'	*šuufi*	'see, look F'
P	*tšuufuun*	'you P see'	*šuufu*	'see, look P'
2 M	*tguum*	'you M get up'	*guum*	'get up M'
F	*tguumiin*	'you F get up'	*guumi*	'get up F'
P	*tguumuun*	'you P get up'	*guumu*	'get up P'
2 M	*tbuus*	'you M kiss'	*buus*	'kiss M'
F	*tbuusiin*	'you F kiss'	*buusi*	'kiss F'
P	*tbuusuun*	'you P kiss'	*buusu*	'kiss P'
2 M	*tguul*	'you M say'	*guul*	'say, tell M'
F	*tguuliin*	'you F say'	*guuli*	'say, tell F'
P	*tguuluun*	'you P say'	*guulu*	'say, tell P'

3. Negative commands

Note the following from Sentence 4 of the dialogue:

la-tidfaC kullši. 'Don't pay for anything.'

The form *la-tidfaC* is an example of a negative command (or request), which is expressed by the regular second-person *indicative* verb form, preceded by the negative prefix *la-*. In the examples below, note the contrast between the verb forms used in a positive command (imperative forms) and those used in a negative command (indicative forms preceded by *la-*):

	Positive command		Negative command	
2 M	*jiib*	'bring M'	*la-djiib*	'don't bring M'
F	*jiibi*	'bring F'	*la-djiibiin*	'don't bring F'
P	*jiibu*	'bring P'	*la-djiibuun*	'don't bring P'
2 M	*guum*	'get up M'	*la-tguum*	'don't get up M'
F	*guumi*	'get up F'	*la-tguumiin*	'don't get up F'
P	*guumu*	'get up P'	*la-tguumuun*	'don't get up P'

In the following examples note also that a negative command differs from a negative statement (or a negative question) only in the negative prefix, which is *ma-* for the latter but *la-* for the former:

	Negative statement		Negative command	
2 M	*ma-tišrab*	'you M don't drink'	*la-tišrab*	'don't drink M'
F	*ma-tšurbiin*	'you F don't drink'	*la-tšurbiin*	'don't drink F'
P	*ma-tšurbuun*	'you P don't drink'	*la-tšurbuun*	'don't drink P'
2 M	*ma-tidfaʕ*	'you M don't pay'	*la-tidfaʕ*	'don't pay M'
F	*ma-ddifʕiin*	'you F don't pay'	*la-ddifʕiin*	'don't pay F'
P	*ma-ddifʕuun*	'you P don't pay'	*la-ddifʕuun*	'don't pay P'

4. Pronoun suffix forms used with vowel stems

In 15 B 5 a summary was given of all the pronoun suffix forms used with stems ending in a consonant, and it was noted that those suffixes which begin with a consonant (namely *ha-, -hum, -kum, -ni,* and *-na*) are also used with stems ending in a vowel. The others, however, have two alternants each, one used with consonant stems, as shown in 15 B 5, and one used with vowel stems. The table below shows all these forms together.

	With consonant stems	With all stems	With vowel stems	
3 M	*-a*		*-ø*	'his/its M; him/it M'
F		*-ha*		'her/its F; her/it F'
P		*-hum*		'their/them'

2 M	*-ak*		*-k*	'your M; you M'
F	*-ič*		*-č*	'your F; you F'
P		*-kum*		'your P; you P'
1 S	*-i*		*-ya*	'my; me' (noun and preposition stems)
		-ni		'me' (verb stems)
P		*-na*		'our; us'

As an example of a vowel stem let us consider the preposition *wiyya* 'with'. This is the **independent form** of the word, used when no suffix is added, for example in *wiyya xaalid* 'with Khalid'. If a suffix is added, however, the final vowel is lengthened, and thus the **suffixing stem** becomes *wiyyaa-*. This is a vowel stem, and the appropriate forms of the pronoun suffixes—those in the middle and right-hand columns above—must be used with it, for example *wiyyaak* 'with you M', as in Sentence 8 of the dialogue.

The symbol *-ø* at the top of the right-hand column above is to be read "zero", and means that the alternant of the 3 M pronoun suffix used with vowel stems is *no suffix at all.* Thus a word containing this alternant has the same form as the stem (not the independent form) alone, for example:

Independent form	Suffixing stem	Pronoun suffix	Stem and suffix
wiyya 'with'	*wiyyaa-*	*-ø*	*wiyyaa* 'with him'

A vowel stem always differs in some way from its independent form, so no confusion arises between the latter and a word consisting of the stem with the zero alternant of the 3 M suffix. In many cases, as above, the difference is one of short versus long final vowel and thus also of stress, but other differences also occur (see B 5 below).

Shown in the following table are all the forms of the preposition *wiyya* 'with' (suffixing stem *wiyyaa-*) and pronoun suffixes:

3	M	*wiyyaa*	'with him'
	F	*wiyyaaha*	'with her'
	P	*wiyyaahum*	'with them'
2	M	*wiyyaak*	'with you M'
	F	*wiyyaač*	'with you F'
	P	*wiyyaakum*	'with you P'
1	S	*wiyyaaya*	'with me'
	P	*wiyyaana*	'with us'

5. Vowel stems

All vowel stems end in a *long* vowel. Also, as noted in the preceding section, they all differ in some way from their independent forms, and can be classified according to the way in which they differ. Two of the main types are as follows:

a. The independent form ends in a short vowel, and the suffixing stem ends in the corresponding long vowel. Of this type, in addition to some prepositions like *wiyya* 'with' shown above, are all verb forms, including imperatives, which end in a short vowel. Here are some examples:

yiqra 'he reads'

(suffixing stem *yiqraa-*)

yiqraa 'he reads it M'
yiqraaha 'he reads it F'

niqra 'we read'

(suffixing stem *niqraa-*)

niqraa 'we read it M'
niqraaha 'we read it F'

jiibi 'bring F'

(suffixing stem *jiibii-*)

jiibii 'bring him'
jiibiiha 'bring her'

jiibu 'bring P'

(suffixing stem *jiibuu-*)

jiibuu 'bring him'
jiibuuha 'bring her'

šuufi 'look (at) F'

(suffixing stem *šuufii-*)

šuufii 'look at him'
šuufiiha 'look at her'
šuufiini 'look at me'
šuufiina 'look at us'

šuufu 'look (at) P'

(suffixing stem *šuufuu-*)

šuufuu 'look at him'
šuufuuha 'look at her'
šuufuuni 'look at me'
šuufuuna 'look at us'

b. Verb forms of the imperfect tense which end in *-uun* or *-iin* (3 P, 2 F, and 2 P) have suffixing stems without the final *-n,* that is, ending in *-uu-* and *-ii-* respectively.

yCibbuun 'they like'

(suffixing stem *yCibbuu-*)

yCibbuu 'they like him'
yCibbuuha 'they like her'
yCibbuuhum 'they like them'

yCibbuuk 'they like you M'
yCibbuuč 'they like you F'
yCibbuukum 'they like you P'

yCibbuuni 'they like me'
yCibbuuna 'they like us'

tčibbiin	'you F like'	*la-tšuufuun*	'don't look (at) P'
(suffixing stem *tčibbii-*)		(suffixing stem *tšuufuu-*)	
tčibbii	'you like him'	*la-tšuufuu*	'don't look at him'
tčibbiiha	'you like her'	*la-tšuufuuha*	'don't look at her'
tčibbiini	'you like me'	*la-tšuufuuni*	'don't look at me'
tčibbiina	'you like us'	*la-tšuufuuna*	'don't look at us'

6. The preposition *ɛala* 'on'

This preposition has an irregular suffixing stem *ɛalee-*, which changes to *ɛalay-* before the 1 S pronoun suffix *-ya* 'me'. All the forms are shown below:

ɛalee	'on him'
ɛaleeha	'on her'
ɛaleehum	'on them'
ɛaleek	'on you M'
ɛaleeč	'on you F'
ɛaleekum	'on you P'
ɛalayya	'on me'
ɛaleena	'on us'

In preceding units there have been two examples of the uses of this preposition. One was in the polite formula *s-salaamu ɛalaykum* 'the peace upon you P', and the response *ɛalaykum is-salaam* 'upon you P the peace' (Unit 14, Sentences 1 and 2 of the dialogue). Here, as in many polite formulas, the Classical form *ɛalaykum* is usually heard instead of the colloquial form *ɛaleekum,* but some people use the latter even in these expressions. The other use of *ɛala* was in the phrase *ysallim ɛalee* 'he greets him' (Unit 15, Sentence 1). In English, certain verbs require certain prepositions to express a particular meaning, for example *to care for* or *to look at;* and the same is true in Iraqi, although of course the verbs which require prepositions are not necessarily the same in the two languages. In Iraqi, one such verb is *ysallim* (and all its other forms), which in the meaning 'to greet' requires the preposition *ɛala*:

ysallim ɛala xaalid	'He greets Khalid.'
ysallim ɛalee.	'He greets him.'
nsallim ɛala samiira.	'We greet Samira.'
nsallim ɛaleeha.	'We greet her.'

ysallmuun *Cala zuheer w-xaalid.*	'They greet Zuhayr and Khalid.'
ysallmuun Caleehum.	'They greet them.'
ysallmuun Caleek.	'They greet you M'.
ysallmuun Calayya.	'They greet me.'

'In addition to the meaning 'on', as in phrases like 'on the table' or 'on the floor', the preposition *Cala* may have the meaning 'about, concerning', for example:

yiCčuun Cala Csaabhum. 'They talk about their check.'

When the object of *Cala* is a person, there may be a connotation of 'against', for example:

yiCčuun Cala ṣadiiqhum. 'They talk about their friend.' (They say unfavorable things about him.)

When *Cala* in any of these senses is followed by a noun with the article prefix, it has a special shortened form *Ca-*, which combines with the consonant of the article prefix. Examples:

Cal-gahwa	'about the coffee'
Caṣ-ṣadiiq	'about the friend'
Cad-daaʔira	'about the office'

C. DRILLS

Drill 1. Change each utterance by inserting *laazim*, as in the example:

Cue:	*xaalid yruuC lis-suug.*	Khalid goes to the market.
Response:	*xaalid laazim yruuC lis-suug.*	Khalid has to go to the market.

xaalid yruuC bis-sayyaara.	*xaalid laazim yruuC bis-sayyaara.*
yruuC wiyya ṣadiiqa zuheer.	*laazim yruuC wiyya ṣadiiqa zuheer.*
yšuuf ṣadiiqa zuheer il-yoom.	*laazim yšuuf ṣadiiqa zuheer il-yoom.*
samiira tišrab ihwaaya čaay.	*samiira laazim tišrab ihwaaya čaay.*
tišrab iglaaṣ ṃaay.	*laazim tišrab iglaaṣ ṃaay.*
djiib-li glaaṣ šarbat.	*laazim idjiib-li glaaṣ šarbat.*
zuheer w-xaalid yiqruun jaraayid.	*zuheer w-xaalid laazim yiqruun jaraayid.*
yiCčuun wiyya xaalid.	*laazim yiCčuun wiyya xaalid.*
ysiʔluu ween raayiC.	*laazim ysiʔluu ween raayiC.*

ˀinta tguum is-saaʕa xamsa?	*ˀinta laazim itguum is-saaʕa xamsa?*
djiib is-sayyaara lil-uuteel.	*laazim idjiib is-sayyaara lil-uuteel.*
tsallim ʕala ṣadiiqak.	*laazim itsallim ʕala ṣadiiqak.*

Drill 2. Change *raḥ-* to *laazim,* as in the example:

Cue:	*ˀinti raḥ-itšuufiiha l-yoom?*	Are you F going to see her today?
Response:	*ˀinti laazim itšuufiiha l-yoom?*	Do you F have to see her today?

ˀinti raḥ-itguʕdiin yamm samiira?	*ˀinti laazim itguʕdiin yamm samiira?*
ma-raḥ-itsallmiin ʕaleeha?	*ma-laazim itsallmiin ʕaleeha?*
raḥ-tiḥčiin wiyyaana l-yoom.	*laazim tiḥčiin wiyyaana l-yoom.*
ˀintu š-raḥ-itšuufuun il-yoom?	*ˀintu š-laazim itšuufuun il-yoom?*
raḥ-itšurbuun istikaan čaay wiyyaana.	*laazim itšurbuun istikaan čaay wiyyaana.*
raḥ-idjiibuun ij-jaraayid lil-beet.	*laazim idjiibuun ij-jaraayid lil-beet.*
ˀaani raḥ-ašuuf fadd ṣadiiq.	*ˀaani laazim ašuuf fadd ṣadiiq.*
raḥ-ašuufa s-saaʕa xamsa.	*laazim ašuufa s-saaʕa xamsa.*
raḥ-ašrab-li šii baarid.	*laazim ašrab-li šii baarid.*
ˀiḥna raḥ-nugʕud wiyya ṣadiiqna.	*ˀiḥna laazim nugʕud wiyya ṣadiiqna.*
raḥ-nisˀal ˀabu zuheer š-yḥibb.	*laazim nisˀal ˀabu zuheer š-yḥibb.*
baʕdeen raḥ-insallim ʕala xaalid.	*baʕdeen laazim insallim ʕala xaalid.*

Drill 3. Change the 2 M imperative forms to 2 F, and then to 2 P, as in the example:

Cue:	*jiib fadd qalam zeen.*	Bring M a good pencil.
Response 1:	*jiibi fadd qalam zeen.*	Bring F a good pencil.
Response 2:	*jiibu fadd qalam zeen.*	Bring P a good pencil.

jiib xariiṭa zeena.	*jiibi xariiṭa zeena.* *jiibu xariiṭa zeena.*
jiib fadd iglaaṣ rajaaˀan.	*jiibi fadd iglaaṣ rajaaˀan.* *jiibu fadd iglaaṣ rajaaˀan.*
jiib is-sayyaara lil-uuteel.	*jiibi s-sayyaara lil-uuteel.* *jiibu s-sayyaara lil-uuteel.*
ruuḥ lil-uuteel is-saaʕa xamsa.	*ruuḥi lil-uuteel is-saaʕa xamsa.* *ruuḥu lil-uuteel is-saaʕa xamsa.*
ruuḥ lid-daaˀira s-saaʕa xamsa.	*ruuḥi lid-daaˀira s-saaʕa xamsa.* *ruuḥu lid-daaˀira s-saaʕa xamsa.*
ruuḥ wiyya zuheer bis-sayyaara.	*ruuḥi wiyya zuheer bis-sayyaara.* *ruuḥu wiyya zuheer bis-sayyaara.*

šuuf zuheer bis-sayyaara!	*šuufi zuheer bis-sayyaara!*
	šuufu zuheer bis-sayyaara!
šuuf, ʔaku gaaziino yamm il-uuteel.	*šuufi, ʔaku gaaziino yamm il-uuteel.*
	šuufu, ʔaku gaaziino yamm il-uuteel.
šuuf is-sayyaara yamm is-safaara!	*šuufi s-sayyaara yamm is-safaara!*
	šuufu s-sayyaara yamm is-safaara!

Drill 4. Change the *laazim* phrase to the corresponding imperative form:

Cue:	*laazim idjiib is-sayyaara l-yoom.*	You M have to bring the car today.
Response:	*jiib is-sayyaara l-yoom.*	Bring M the car today.

laazim idjiib is-sayyaara lil-beet.	*jiib is-sayyaara lil-beet.*
laazim idjiibiin is-sayyaara lil-beet.	*jiibi s-sayyaara lil-beet.*
laazim idjiibuun is-sayyaara lil-beet.	*jiibu s-sayyaara lil-beet.*
laazim idjiib il-xariiṭa wiyyaak.	*jiib il-xariiṭa wiyyaak.*
laazim idjiibiin il-xariiṭa wiyyaač.	*jiibi l-xariiṭa wiyyaač.*
laazim idjiibuun il-xariiṭa wiyyaakum.	*jiibu l-xariiṭa wiyyaakum.*
laazim itruuε lis-suug wiyyaahum.	*ruuε lis-suug wiyyaahum.*
laazim tirεiin lis-suug wiyyaahum.	*ruuεi lis-suug wiyyaahum.*
laazim tirεuun lis-suug wiyyaahum.	*ruuεu lis-suug wiyyaahum.*
laazim itruuε lid-daaʔira baεdeen.	*ruuε lid-daaʔira baεdeen.*
laazim tirεiin lid-daaʔira baεdeen.	*ruuεi lid-daaʔira baεdeen.*
laazim tirεuun lid-daaʔira baεdeen.	*ruuεu lid-daaʔira baεdeen.*
laazim itguum is-saaεa xamsa.	*guum is-saaεa xamsa.*
laazim itguumiin is-saaεa xamsa.	*guumi s-saaεa xamsa.*
laazim itguumuun is-saaεa xamsa.	*guumu s-saaεa xamsa.*
laazim itbuus ʔiida.	*buus ʔiida.*
laazim itbuusiin ʔiida.	*buusi ʔiida.*
laazim itbuusuun ʔiida.	*buusu ʔiida.*
laazim itšuuf l-iεsaab.	*šuuf l-iεsaab.*
laazim itšuufiin l-iεsaab.	*šuufi l-iεsaab.*
laazim itšuufuun l-iεsaab.	*šuufu l-iεsaab.*

Drill 5. Change the various verb phrases to the corresponding negative command.

Cue:	*ma-laazim itruuε il-yoom.*	You M don't have to go today.
Response:	*la-truuε il-yoom.*	Don't go today.

ma-laazim itruuε lid-daaʔira.	*la-truuε lid-daaʔira.*
ma-laazim tirεiin lid-daaʔira.	*la-tirεiin lid-daaʔira.*

ma-laazim tirḥuun lid-daaʔira.
ma-raḥ-itšuuf l-iḥsaab.
ma-raḥ-itšuufiin l-iḥsaab.
ma-raḥ-itšuufuun l-iḥsaab.
ma-raḥ-tidfaʕ l-iḥsaab.
ma-raḥ-iddifʕiin l-iḥsaab.
ma-raḥ-iddifʕuun l-iḥsaab.
ma-laazim tiḥči hwaaya l-yoom.
ma-laazim tiḥčiin ihwaaya l-yoom.
ma-laazim tiḥčuun ihwaaya l-yoom.
ma-raḥ-tišrab gahwa l-yoom.
ma-raḥ-itšurbiin gahwa l-yoom.
ma-raḥ-itšurbuun gahwa l-yoom.
ma-laazim tiqra jaraayid bid-daaʔira.
ma-laazim tiqriin jaraayid bid-daaʔira.
ma-laazim tiqruun jaraayid bid-daaʔira.

la-tirḥuun lid-daaʔira.
la-tšuuf l-iḥsaab.
la-tšuufiin l-iḥsaab.
la-tšuufuun l-iḥsaab.
la-tidfaʕ l-iḥsaab.
la-ddifʕiin l-iḥsaab.
la-ddifʕuun l-iḥsaab.
la-tiḥči hwaaya l-yoom.
la-tiḥčiin ihwaaya l-yoom.
la-tiḥčuun ihwaaya l-yoom.
la-tišrab gahwa l-yoom.
la-tšurbiin gahwa l-yoom.
la-tšurbuun gahwa l-yoom.
la-tiqra jaraayid bid-daaʔira.
la-tiqriin jaraayid bid-daaʔira.
la-tiqruun jaraayid bid-daaʔira.

Drill 6. Respond as in the examples, using the appropriate form of ***wiyya*** with a pronoun suffix.

Cue: *muṣṭafa raayiḥ lis-suug.* — Mustafa's going to the market.
Response: *laazim aruuḥ wiyyaa.* — I have to go with him.

muṣṭafa raayiḥ lil-ḅang.
ʔumm zuheer raayḥa lil-ḅang.
xaalid w-zuheer raayḥiin lil-ḅang.
samiira raayḥa lil-beet.
zuheer w-samiira raayḥiin lil-beet.
ʔabu xaalid raayiḥ lil-beet.
ʔinta raayiḥ lil-maṭaar?
ʔinti raayḥa lil-maṭaar?
ʔintu raayḥiin lil-maṭaar?

laazim aruuḥ wiyyaa.
laazim aruuḥ wiyyaaha.
laazim aruuḥ wiyyaahum.
laazim aruuḥ wiyyaaha.
laazim aruuḥ wiyyaahum.
laazim aruuḥ wiyyaa.
laazim aruuḥ wiyyaak.
laazim aruuḥ wiyyaač.
laazim aruuḥ wiyyaakum.

Cue: *ʔaani raayiḥ lis-suug.* — I'm going to the market.
Response: *tḥibb itruuḥ wiyyaaya?* — Would you M like to go with me?

ʔaani raayiḥ lid-daaʔira.
ʔiḥna raayḥiin lid-daaʔira.
zuheer w-xaalid raayḥiin lid-daaʔira.
ʔumm xaalid raayḥa lil-gaaziino.
ʔaani raayiḥ lil-maṭaar.
ʔiḥna raayḥiin lil-uuteel.

tḥibb itruuḥ wiyyaaya?
tḥibb itruuḥ wiyyaana?
tḥibb itruuḥ wiyyaahum?
tḥibb itruuḥ wiyyaaha?
tḥibb itruuḥ wiyyaaya?
tḥibb itruuḥ wiyyaana?

ˀumm zuheer w-zuheer raayCiin lil-beet.	*tCibb itruuC wiyyaahum?*
muṣṭafa raayiC lil-ḅang.	*tCibb itruuC wiyyaa?*
samiira raayCa lis-safaara.	*tCibb itruuC wiyyaaha?*

Drill 7. Respond as in the example, using the appropriate form of *Cala* with a pronoun suffix.

Cue:	*ˀabu xaalid gaaCid bil-gahwa.*	Abu Khalid's sitting in the coffee-house.
Response:	*ma-raC-itsallim Calee?*	Aren't you M going to say hello to him?

ˀabu xaalid gaaCid bil-beet.	*ma-raC-itsallim Calee?*
ˀumm xaalid gaaCda bis-sayyaara.	*ma-raC-itsallim Caleeha?*
samiira w-muṣṭafa gaaCdiin bis-sayyaara.	*ma-raC-itsallim Caleehum?*
ˀiCna gaaCdiin ihnaa bis-sayyaara.	*ma-raC-itsallim Caleena?*
ˀaani gaaCda hnaa bis-sayyaara.	*ma-raC-itsallim Calayya?*
ˀiCna gaaCdiin ihnaa bil-uuteel.	*ma-raC-itsallim Caleena?*
mCammad gaaCid ihnaak bil-gahwa.	*ma-raC-itsallim Calee?*
samiira gaaCda hnaak bid-daaˀira.	*ma-raC-itsallim Caleeha?*
ˀaani gaaCid ihnaa bid-daaˀira.	*ma-raC-itsallim Calayya?*
zuheer w-imCammad gaaCdiin bil-gahwa.	*ma-raC-itsallim Caleehum?*

Drill 8. Respond as in the example, using the appropriate form of the 2 F imperative *jiibi* and pronoun suffix.

Cue:	*ween il-xariiṭa?*	Where's the map?
Response:	*jiibiiha lil-beet.*	Bring it home.

ween is-sayyaara?	*jiibiiha lil-beet.*
ween il-qalam?	*jiibii lil-beet.*
ween imCammad?	*jiibii lil-beet.*
ween samiira?	*jiibiiha lil-beet.*
ween ˀabu xaalid?	*jiibii lil-beet.*
ween il-xariiṭa?	*jiibiiha lil-beet.*
ween il-maCruusiin?	*jiibiihum lil-beet.*
ween ˀumm xaalid?	*jiibiiha lil-beet.*
ween ˀummič?	*jiibiiha lil-beet.*
ween zuheer w-imCammad?	*jiibiihum lil-beet.*
ween muṣṭafa?	*jiibii lil-beet.*

Drill 9. Respond as in the example, using the appropriate form of the 2 M imperative *jiibu* and pronoun suffix.

Cue:	*mεammad raayiε lil-ḅang.*	Muhammad's going to the bank.
Response:	*jiibuu lis-safaara baεdeen.*	Bring P him to the embassy afterward.

zuheer raayiε lis-suug.	*jiibuu lis-safaara baεdeen.*
zuheer w-xaalid raayεiin lil-beet.	*jiibuuhum lis-safaara baεdeen.*
ʔumm zuheer raayεa lid-daaʔira.	*jiibuuha lis-safaara baεdeen.*
ʔummkum raayεa lis-suug.	*jiibuuha lis-safaara baεdeen.*
ʔabu xaalid raayiε lil-uuteel.	*jiibuu lis-safaara baεdeen.*
mεammad w-muṣṭafa raayεiin lil-maṭaar.	*jiibuuhum lis-safaara baεdeen.*
zuheer w-ṣadiiqa raayεiin lil-gaaziino.	*jiibuuhum lis-safaara baεdeen.*
ʔumm xaalid raayεa lil-beet.	*jiibuuha lis-safaara baεdeen.*
ṣadiiqna zuheer raayiε il-beetkum.	*jiibuu lis-safaara baεdeen.*

Drill 10. In the following negative commands, change the noun object to the corresponding pronoun suffix, making the necessary changes in the verb stem.

Cue:	*la-tšurbiin il-gahwa.*	Don't drink F the coffee.
Response:	*la-tšurbiiha.*	Don't drink F it F.

la-tšurbiin il-biira.	*la-tšurbiiha.*
la-tšurbuun il-biira.	*la-tšurbuuha.*
la-tšurbiin ič-čaay.	*la-tšurbii.*
la-tšurbuun ič-čaay.	*la-tšurbuu.*
la-tšurbiin il-εaliib.	*la-tšurbii.*
la-tšurbuun il-εaliib.	*la-tšurbuu.*
la-tšurbiin il-gahwa.	*la-tšurbiiha.*
la-tšurbuun il-gahwa.	*la-tšurbuuha.*
la-djiibiin il-gahwa.	*la-djiibiiha.*
la-djiibuun il-gahwa.	*la-djiibuuha.*
la-djiibiin iš-šarbat.	*la-djiibii.*
la-djiibuun iš-šarbat.	*la-djiibuu.*

Drill 11. The following utterances include statements, questions, and positive commands. In each, change the noun object to the corresponding pronoun suffix, making the necessary changes in the verb stem and elsewhere.

Cue:	*raħ-itšuuf zuheer il-yoom?*	Are you M going to see Zuhayr today?
Response:	*raħ-itšuufa l-yoom?*	Are you M going to see him today?

raħ-itšuuf musṭafa l-yoom?	*raħ-itšuufa l-yoom?*
raħ-itšuufiin musṭafa l-yoom?	*raħ-itšuufii l-yoom?*
raħ-itšuufuun musṭafa l-yoom?	*raħ-itšuufuu l-yoom?*
laazim idjiib zuheer wiyyaak.	*laazim idjiiba wiyyaak.*
laazim idjiibiin zuheer wiyyaač.	*laazim idjiibii wiyyaač.*
laazim idjiibuun zuheer wiyyaakum.	*laazim idjiibuu wiyyaakum.*
jiib ʔumm xaalid bis-sayyaara.	*jiibha bis-sayyaara.*
jiibi ʔumm xaalid bis-sayyaara.	*jiibiiha bis-sayyaara.*
jiibu ʔumm xaalid bis-sayyaara.	*jiibuuha bis-sayyaara.*
ma-tħibb samiira?	*ma-tħibbha?*
ma-tħibbiin samiira?	*ma-tħibbiiha?*
ma-tħibbuun samiira?	*ma-tħibbuuha?*

Drill 12. Change the noun object first to the 1 S pronoun suffix *-ni* 'me', and then to the 1 P pronoun suffix *na-* 'us', making the necessary changes in the verb stem.

Cue:	*zuheer yšuuf xaalid biš-šaariɛ.*	Zuhayr sees Khalid on the street.
Response 1:	*zuheer yšuufni biš-šaariɛ.*	Zuhayr sees me on the street.
Response 2:	*zuheer yšuufna biš-šaariɛ.*	Zuhayr sees us on the street.

yšuuf ṣadiiqa biš-šaariɛ.	*yšuufni biš-šaariɛ.*
	yšuufna biš-šaariɛ.
yšuufuun imħammad bil-gahwa.	*yšuufuuni bil-gahwa.*
	yšuufuuna bil-gahwa.
ʔinti ma-tħibbiin zuheer?	*ʔinti ma-tħibbiini?*
	ʔinti ma-tħibbiina?
raħ-yjiibuun zuheer wiyyaahum.	*raħ-yjiibuuni wiyyaahum.*
	raħ-yjiibuuna wiyyaahum.
la-tisʔal ʔabu xaalid.	*la-tisʔalni.*
	la-tisʔalna.
la-tsiʔliin ʔabu xaalid.	*la-tsiʔliini.*
	la-tsiʔliina.
la-tsiʔluun ʔabu xaalid.	*la-tsiʔluuni.*
	la-tsiʔluuna.

UNIT 17

A. DIALOGUE

Abu Zuhayr goes up to the coffee-house proprietor to pay for himself and his friends.

ˀabu zuheer	Abu Zuhayr
ˀusṭa	master (see Notes)
1. *šgadd iḥsaabna, ˀusṭa?*	How much is our check?
l-gahawči	The coffee-house proprietor
čam	how many
waaḥid	one M
čam waaḥid	how many (persons, things)
sayyidna	sir (see Notes)
2. *čam waaḥid ˀintu, sayyidna?*	How many are you, sir?
ˀabu zuheer	Abu Zuhayr
ˀixwaan	gentlemen (see Notes)
θneen	two
jawwa	under
p̣anka	fan
3. *ˀaani wil-ixwaan l-iθneen il-gaaʕdiin jawwa l-p̣anka.*	Myself and the two gentlemen sitting under the fan.
l-gahawči	The coffee-house proprietor
ysawwi	he makes, does
sittiin	sixty
filis	fils (see Notes)
4. *ḥsaabkum ysawwi sittiin filis.*	Your check comes to sixty fils.
ˀabu zuheer	Abu Zuhayr
5. *ṭayyib. tfaḍḍal.*	All right. Here.

l-gahawči	The coffee-house proprietor
mamnuun	grateful M (see Notes)
ɛammi	my (paternal) uncle (see Notes)
maɛa s-salaama	with the safety (see Notes)
6. *mamnuun ɛammi. maɛa s-salaama.*	Thank you, sir. Good-bye.

NOTES ON DIALOGUE

1. Forms of address

ˀusṭa — A noun meaning 'master' (of a trade). Used in addressing master craftsmen (weavers, goldsmiths, etc.), foremen of construction gangs, coffee-house proprietors, and the like.

sayyidna — A term of respect, corresponding approximately to English *sir*, commonly used by tradesmen in addressing a customer. The word *sayyid*, generally followed by the first name rather than the family name, is a somewhat formal way of addressing a new aquaintance: *sayyid zuheer*. In speaking politely *of* another man, the article prefix is attached: *s-sayyid zuheer*. Both these phrases correspond generally to the English form *Mr.* with a surname.

l-ixwaan — This form (literally 'the brothers'; see Notes in Unit 13) may be used in referring politely to two or more men without mentioning their names; the English equivalent is *the gentlemen*. In referring to one man, either *l-ˀax* or, a little more formally, *s-sayyid* may be used, both corresponding to *the gentleman*.

ɛammi — The word *ɛamm* means '(paternal) uncle', and *ɛammi* 'my (paternal) uncle' as a form of address indicates a certain respect. It is used by servants to an employer, by tradespeople to a customer, by children to a grown man, and also by anyone to an older man.

2. Polite formulas

M *mamnuun* F *mamnuuna* P *mamnuuniin*	This word is an adjective with the literal meaning 'grateful' or 'obliged'. It refers to the speaker: a male speaker uses the masculine form; a female speaker, the feminine; and a speaker referring to one or more others along with himself, the plural. It is said in two main situations: (1) on being given something or having something done for you; it then corresponds to English *thank you;* and (2) as a reply to various other expressions of thanks, such as *šukran;* it then corresponds to English *not at all, my pleasure, you're welcome,* and the like.
maʕa s-salaama	Literal meaning 'with the safety'. (The word *maʕa* 'with' is Classical, and occurs in Iraqi only in a few standardized phrases such as this one.) Another of the several common expressions corresponding to English *good-bye,* usually said to, rather than by, the person departing.

3. Iraqi money

The basic Iraqi unit of currency is the dinar, which at the time of this writing has the value of one pound sterling, or about $2.80. The dinar is divided into one thousand fils. Thus one fils is worth a little over a quarter of a cent; ten fils, not quite three cents; and a hundred fils, about 28 cents. The Iraqi words are *diinaar,* plural *danaaniir* or *dnaaniir;* and *filis,* plural *fluus.* The form *fluus* also means 'money'.

B. GRAMMAR

1. Interrogatives *šgadd* 'how much' and *čam* 'how many'

These two interrogatives differ both as to the kind of answer they call for and as to the way they can function in a sentence. First, *šgadd* is used to ask about the amount or the quantity of something, and generally refers to things that exist in bulk or mass form, such as money, coffee, or sugar, for example:

šgadd ifluus Ċindak?	'How much money have you got?'
šgadd gahwa aku bil-beet?	'How much coffee is there in the house?'

The noun in such questions need not follow *šgadd* directly, as above, but may be separated from it by one or more other words:

šgadd Ċindak ifluus?	'How much money have you got?'
šgadd aku gahwa bil-beet?	'How much coffee is there in the house?'

On the other hand, *čam* is used only to ask about the specific number of individual items involved, for example houses, books, or glasses. It is followed directly by a *singular* form, not a plural as in English:

čam beet laazim inšuuf?	'How many houses do we have to see?'
čam iglaaṣ itriid?	'How many glasses do you want?'
čam gahwa aku b-hal-manṭiqa?	'How many coffee-houses are there in this area?'
čam gahwa tirduun ixwaan?	'How many coffees do you want, gentlemen?' (i.e., how many individual cups of coffee?)

Second, *šgadd* may occur without a noun; that is, it may function like a pronoun, serving for example as the object of a verb or preposition, or as one of the elements of an equational sentence:

šgadd itriid?	'How much do you want?'
šgadd iĊsaabna?	'How much is our check?'

On the other hand, again, *čam* alone does not function in this way. If it is not followed by a noun, as above, it is followed by the numeral *waaĊid* (masculine) or *wiĊda* (feminine) 'one':

čam waaĊid itriid?	'How many do you want?' (referring to something masculine, for example *qalam* 'pencil')
čam wiĊda triid?	'How many do you want?' (referring to something feminine, for example *xariiṭa* 'map')
čam waaĊid ʔintu?	'How many are you?' (i.e., how many of you are there?—referring to a group including at least one male person)

2. The numerals 'one' and 'two'

The numerals meaning 'one' and 'two' are different from all other Iraqi numerals in that they have both a masculine and a feminine form, used according to whether they modify, or refer to, a masculine or a feminine noun:

Masculine	Feminine	
waacid	*wicda*	'one'
θneen	*θinteen*	'two'

The numeral 'one' is an adjective, and therefore follows the noun it modifies, the masculine form after a masculine noun and the feminine form after a feminine:

qalam waacid	'one pencil'	*xariiṭa wicda*	'one map'
yoom waacid	'one day'	*saaεa wicda*	'one hour'

Similarly, when this numeral does not modify an immediately preceding noun, but rather refers to some noun previously mentioned, or apparent from the situation, it agrees in gender with the noun referred to:

(*čam qalam εindak?*	'How many pencils do you have?')
εindi waacid.	'I have one.'
or *waacid.*	'One.'
(*čam xariiṭa εindak?*	'How many maps do you have?')
εindi wicda.	'I have one.'
or *wicda.*	'One.'

In Iraqi there are several common ways of expressing the idea indicated in English by phrases like *two pencils* or *two maps*. One is a phrase consisting of the plural form of the noun, followed by *θneen* if the noun is masculine. If the noun is feminine it may be followed by either *θneen* or *θinteen,* but in this book we shall use only the latter. Examples:

ʔixwaan iθneen	'two gentlemen'	*jaraayid θinteen*	'two newspapers'

To express *the* in such phrases, the article prefix, in the appropriate form (see 12 B 5), is attached to both the noun and the numeral:

l-ixwaan l-iθneen	'the two gentlemen'	*j-jaraayid iθ-θinteen*	'the newspapers'

If the numeral refers to some previously mentioned noun, gender agreement is as described above:

	(*čam qalam Ɛindak?*)	('How many pencils do you have?')
	Ɛindi θneen.	'I have two.'
or	*θneen.*	'Two.'
	(*čam xariiṭa Ɛindak?*)	('How many maps do you have?')
	Ɛindi θinteen.	'I have two.'
or	*θinteen.*	'Two.'

In counting and arithmetical figuring, the masculine forms are used:

waaƐid, θneen . . .	'One, two . . .'
waaƐid w-waaƐid iθneen.	'One and one is two.'
waaƐid min iθneen waaƐid.	'One from two is one.'

3. Noun-adjective phrases: Agreement in definiteness (1)

A **noun-adjective phrase** in its simplest form consists of a noun followed immediately by a modifying adjective, the whole phrase functioning within the sentence in the same way as a noun alone might function, for example as subject or object of a verb, as subject or predicate of an equational sentence, or as object of a preposition. There have already been numbers of instances of noun-adjective phrases in which the noun is indefinite, for example *čaay Ɛaarr* 'hot tea' and *gahwa Ɛaarra* 'hot coffee'; and it has been noted that after a masculine singular noun the adjective is in its masculine form, and after a feminine singular noun the adjective is in its feminine form, as in the examples just cited. Besides this gender agreement, an adjective in a noun-adjective phrase also must agree with the noun in **definiteness**: if the noun is definite, the adjective must also be definite. There are several ways in which a noun can be definite; the most common is by having the article prefix: *čaay* 'tea' and *gahwa* 'coffee' are indefinite, while *č-čaay* 'the tea' and *l-gahwa* 'the coffee' are definite. An adjective is made definite only by the article prefix. Examples:

Indefinite		**Definite**	
čaay Ɛaarr	'hot tea'	*č-čaay il-Ɛaarr*	'the hot tea'
gahwa Ɛaarra	'hot coffee'	*l-gahwa l-Ɛaarra*	'the hot coffee'
qalam zeen	'a good pencil'	*l-qalam iz-zeen*	'the good pencil'
sayyaara zeena	'a good car'	*s-sayyaara z-zeena*	'the good car'
liban baarid	'cold yoghurt'	*l-liban il-baarid*	'the cold yoghurt'
biira baarda	'cold beer'	*l-biira l-baarda*	'the cold beer'

Note carefully the distinction between the two types of constructions illustrated below:

(1)	*l-gahwa l-ḥaarra*	'the hot coffee'
(2)	*l-gahwa ḥaarra.*	'The coffee is hot.'

The first is a noun-adjective phrase. The adjective agrees with the noun not only in gender but also in definiteness. This is a phrase, not a complete sentence, but the whole phrase may function as one of the elements of a complete sentence, for example *ween il-gahwa l-ḥaarra?* 'Where's the hot coffee?' or *la-tišrab il-gahwa l-ḥaarra.* 'Don't drink the hot coffee.' The second item above is itself a complete sentence. It is an equational sentence (see 14 B 2), in which *l-gahwa* is the subject, and *ḥaarra* the predicate. When an adjective is the predicate of an equational sentence, it agrees with its subject as to gender in the same way as it does in a noun-adjective phrase, but not as to definiteness: it does not have the article prefix.

C. DRILLS

Drill 1. Repeat the utterance, replacing the underlined word with each of the items given.

šgadd εindak <u>ifluus</u> il-yoom?	How much <u>money</u> do you M have today?
šuġuḷ	work
wakit	time
gahwa	coffee
liban	yoghurt
ḥaamuð̣	lemon-tea
čaay	tea
biira	beer
šarbat	sherbet

Drill 2. Repeat the utterance, replacing the underlined word with each of items given.

čam <u>beet</u> ʔaku b-hal-manṭiqa?	How many <u>houses</u> are there in this area?
ḅang	banks
ʔuuteel	hotels
gahwa	coffee-houses
gaaziino	gaaziinos
daaʔira	offices
safaara	embassies
maṭaar	airports

Drill 3. Answer the question as in the example.

Cue:	*šgadd liban ʕidna bil-beet?*	How much yoghurt do we have in the house?
Response:	*ma-ʕidna liban ihwaaya l-yoom.*	We don't have much yoghurt today.

šgadd gahwa ʕidna bil-beet?	*ma-ʕidna gahwa hwaaya l-yoom.*
šgadd šarbat ʕidna bil-beet?	*ma-ʕidna šarbat ihwaaya l-yoom.*
šgadd ḥaamuð̣ ʕidna bil-beet?	*ma-ʕidna šarbat ihwaaya l-yoom.*
šgadd čaay ʕidna bil-beet?	*ma-ʕidna čaay ihwaaya l-yoom.*
šgadd ḥaliib ʕidna bil-beet?	*ma-ʕidna ḥaliib ihwaaya l-yoom.*
šgadd biira ʕidna bil-beet?	*ma-ʕidna biira hwaaya l-yoom.*
šgadd liban ʕidna bil-beet?	*ma-ʕidna liban ihwaaya l-yoom.*

Drill 4. Answer the question as in the example, using the form *waaḥid* or *wiḥda* as appropriate.

Cue:	*čam beet ʔaku hnaak?*	How many houses are there there?
Response:	*ʔaku beet waaḥid ihnaak.*	There's one house there.

čam qalam ʔaku hnaak?	*ʔaku qalam waaḥid ihnaak.*
čam sayyaara ʔaku hnaak?	*ʔaku sayyaara wiḥda hnaak.*
čam xariiṭa ʔaku hnaak?	*ʔaku xariiṭa wiḥda hnaak.*
čam maṭaar ʔaku hnaak?	*ʔaku maṭaar waaḥid ihnaak.*
čam gahwa ʔaku hnaak?	*ʔaku gahwa wiḥda hnaak.*
čam istikaan ʔaku hnaak?	*ʔaku stikaan waaḥid ihnaak.*
čam gaaziino ʔaku hnaak?	*ʔaku gaaziino wiḥda hnaak.*
čam safaara ʔaku hnaak?	*ʔaku safaara wiḥda hnaak.*
čam igḷaaṣ ʔaku hnaak?	*ʔaku gḷaaṣ waaḥid ihnaak.*

Drill 5. Answer the question as in the example, using the form *θneen* or *θinteen* as appropriate.

Cue:	*čam beet itriid itšuuf?*	How many houses do you M want to see?
Response:	*ʔariid ašuuf iθneen.*	I want to see two.

čam ḅang itriid itšuuf?	*ʔariid ašuuf iθneen.*
čam xariiṭa triid itšuuf?	*ʔariid ašuuf θinteen.*
čam gahwa triid itšuuf?	*ʔariid ašuuf θinteen.*
čam ṣadiiq itriid itšuuf?	*ʔariid ašuuf iθneen.*
čam sayyaara triid itšuuf?	*ʔariid ašuuf θinteen.*
čam šaariʕ itriid itšuuf?	*ʔariid ašuuf iθneen.*
čam maṭaar itriid itšuuf?	*ʔariid ašuuf iθneen.*
čam uuteel itriid itšuuf?	*ʔariid ašuuf iθneen.*
čam šiqqa triid itšuuf?	*ʔariid ašuuf θinteen.*

Drill 6. New words. Listen and repeat.

ʕidhum beet čibiir.	They have a big house.
ʕidhum šiqqa čibiira.	They have a big apartment.
ʕidhum beet iṣġayyir.	They have a small house.
ʕidhum šiqqa ṣġayyra.	They have a small apartment.
ʕidhum beet jidiid.	They have a new house.
ʕidhum šiqqa jidiida.	They have a new apartment.
ʕidhum beet ʕatiig.	They have an old house.
ʕidhum šiqqa ʕatiiga.	They have an old apartment.
ween il-beet ič-čibiir?	Where's the big house?
ween iš-šiqqa č-čibiira?	Where's the big apartment?
ween il-beet l-iṣġayyir?	Where's the small house?
ween iš-šiqqa l-iṣġayyra?	Where's the small apartment?
ween il-beet ij-jidiid?	Where's the new house?
ween iš-šiqqa j-jidiida?	Where's the new apartment?
ween il-beet il-ʕatiig?	Where's the old house?
ween iš-šiqqa l-ʕatiiga?	Where's the old apartment?

Drill 7. Replace the underlined portion with the items given.

ʕinda beet čibiir yamm il-uuteel.	He has a big house next to the hotel.
jidiid	new
ṣġayyir	small
ʕatiig	old
ḥilu	pretty
waaḥid	one
jidiid	new
čibiir	big
ʕatiig	old
ṣġayyir	small

Drill 8. Replace the underlined portion with the items given.

ʔaku xariiṭa čibiira bid-daaʔira.	There's a big map in the office.
jidiida	new
ḥilwa	pretty
ʕatiiga	old
ṣġayyra	small
wiḥda	one
čibiira	big
zeena	good
jidiida	new
ʕatiiga	old
ṣġayyra	small

Drill 9. Add the article prefix to the noun and the adjective, as in the example.

Cue:	*nṭiini qalam jidiid.*	Give me a new pencil.
Response:	*nṭiini l-qalam ij-jidiid.*	Give me the new pencil.

jiib-li gahwa caarra.	*jiib-li l-gahwa l-caarra.*
rac-yšurbuun biira baarda.	*rac-yšurbuun l-biira l-baarda.*
la-tšurbiin čaay baarid.	*la-tšurbiin ič-čaay il-baarid.*
laazim ašuuf beet jidiid.	*laazim ašuuf il-beet ij-jidiid.*
zuheer gaaɛid jawwa p̣anka ɛatiiga.	*zuheer gaaɛid jawwa l-p̣anka l-ɛatiiga.*
rac-ajiib igḷaaṣ čibiir.	*rac-ajiib l-iġlaaṣ ič-čibiir.*
nriid inruuc ib-sayyaara ṣġayyra.	*nriid inruuc bis-sayyaara l-iṣġayyra.*
laazim idjiib-li csaab jidiid.	*laazim idjiib-li l-icsaab ij-jidiid.*
ɛindi mawɛid ib-gahwa jidiida.	*ɛindi mawɛid bil-gahwa j-jidiida.*
ɛidna daaʔira b-uuteel iṣġayyir.	*ɛidna daaʔira bil-uuteel l-iṣġayyir.*

Drill 10. Change each sentence as in the example.

Cue:	*ʔaku gahwa jidiida hnaak.*	There's a new coffee-house there.
Response:	*ʔaani raayic lil-gahwa j-jidiida.*	I'm going to the new coffee-house.

ʔaku gaaziino jidiida hnaak.	*ʔaani raayic lil-gaaziino j-jidiida.*
ʔaku beet ɛatiig ihnaak.	*ʔaani raayic lil-beet il-ɛatiig.*
ʔaku ʔuuteel čibiir ihnaak.	*ʔaani raayic lil-uuteel ič-čibiir.*
ʔaku daaʔira čibiira hnaak.	*ʔaani raayic lid-daaʔira č-čibiira.*
ʔaku gahwa ɛatiiga hnaak.	*ʔaani raayic lil-gahwa l-ɛatiiga.*
ʔaku safaara jidiida hnaak.	*ʔaani raayic lis-safaara j-jidiida.*
ʔaku maṭaar iṣġayyir ihnaak.	*ʔaani raayic lil-maṭaar l-iṣġayyir.*
ʔaku gaaziino ṣġayyra hnaak.	*ʔaani raayic lil-gaaziino l-iṣġayyra.*
ʔaku ʔuuteel ɛatiig ihnaak.	*ʔaani raayic lil-uuteel il-ɛatiig.*
ʔaku ḅang jidiid ihnaak.	*ʔaani raayic lil-ḅang ij-jidiid.*

Drill 11. Respond as in the example.

Cue:	*šgadd icsaaba?*	How much is his bill?
Response:	*csaaba ysawwi sittiin filis.*	His bill amounts to sixty fils.

šgadd icsaabna?	*csaabna ysawwi sittiin filis.*
šgadd icsaabha?	*csaabha ysawwi sittiin filis.*
šgadd icsaabhum?	*csaabhum ysawwi sittiin filis.*
šgadd l-icsaab?	*l-icsaab ysawwi sittiin filis.*
šgadd l-icsaab ij-jidiid?	*l-icsaab ij-jidiid ysawwi sittiin filis.*
šgadd icsaabha?	*csaabha ysawwi sittiin filis.*
šgadd icsaabhum?	*csaabhum ysawwi sittiin filis.*
šgadd icsaaba?	*csaaba ysawwi sittiin filis.*
šgadd l-icsaab ij-jidiid?	*l-icsaab ij-jidiid ysawwi sittiin filis.*

Drill 12. Change the verb form *yšuuf* so that it corresponds to the cue given, as in the example. Do not repeat the cue.

	laazim yšuuf id-daaʔira j-jidiida.	He must see the new office.
Cue:	*ʔumm samiira*	
Response:	*laazim itšuuf id-daaʔira j-jidiida*	She must see the new office.

zuheer w-xaalid	*laazim yšuufuun id-daaʔira j-jidiida.*
ʔabu muṣṭafa	*laazim yšuuf id-daaʔira j-jidiida.*
ʔaani	*laazim ašuuf id-daaʔira j-jidiida.*
ʔiḥna	*laazim inšuuf id-daaʔira j-jidiida.*
samiira	*laazim itšuuf id-daaʔira j-jidiida.*
ʔinta	*laazim itšuuf id-daaʔira j-jidiida.*
ʔinti	*laazim itšuufiin id-daaʔira j-jidiida.*
ʔintu	*laazim itšuufuun id-daaʔira j-jidiida.*
muṣṭafa w-abu zuheer	*laazim yšuufuun id-daaʔira j-jidiida.*
ʔiḥna	*laazim inšuuf id-daaʔira j-jidiida.*
ʔumm xaalid	*laazim itšuuf id-daaʔira j-jidiida.*
ʔaani	*laazim ašuuf id-daaʔira j-jidiida.*

UNIT 18

A. DIALOGUE

At a bus stop, Abu Zuhayr asks a bus conductor for information.

ʔabu zuheer	Abu Zuhayr
hal-paaṣ	this bus
yooṣal	he arrives
lil-karraada	to (the) Karrada (see Notes)
loo laa	or not (see Notes)
sayyid	mister (see Notes)
1. *hal-paaṣ yooṣal lil-karraada loo laa, sayyid?*	Does this bus go to Karrada, conductor?

j-jaabi	The conductor
2. *laa ʔaxi, ma-yooṣal.*	No sir, it doesn't.

ʔabu zuheer	Abu Zuhayr
yaa	which
ʔagdar	I can
ʔaaxuδ	I take
3. *laƐad yaa paaṣ agdar aaxuδ rajaaʔan?*	Then which bus can I take, please?
j-jaabi	The conductor
ʔuxuδ	take (M)
raqam	number
tlaaθa	three
minnaa	from here
l-baab iš-šarji	to Bab ish-Sharji (see Notes)
minnaak	from there
baddil	change (M)
4. *ʔuxuδ paaṣ raqam itlaaθa minnaa l-baab iš-šarji, w-minnaak baddil.*	Take bus number three from here to Bab ish-Sharji, and change there.
ʔabu zuheer	Abu Zuhayr
ʔarkab	I ride, get on
5. *b-yaa raqam arkab minnaak?*	What number do I get on there?
j-jaabi	The conductor
ʔirkab	ride, get on M
sitta	six
huwwa	he, it M
ywaṣṣlak	he conveys you M
6. *ʔirkab raqam sitta w-huwwa ywaṣṣlak.*	Get on number six; that'll get you there.

NOTES ON DIALOGUE

1. Karrada is a mainly residential section of Baghdad, located in the southern part of the city, on the east bank of the Tigris.

2. The phrase *loo laa* 'or not' is often used in questions to which the answer is yes or no. In English, the use of 'or not' in such questions suggests some impatience on the part of the speaker, or implies that the question has been previously asked and unsatisfactorily answered. As these implications are not necessarily present in the Iraqi phrase, *loo laa* is often best left untranslated.

3. The word *sayyid* 'mister' is a polite form used in addressing a man, especially one whose name is unknown. Sometimes it may correspond to English *sir* (but with no connotation of subservience), and sometimes to an occupational name like *conductor* or *driver;* sometimes it is best left untranslated.

4. Bab ish-Sharji is an area near the center of present-day Baghdad, on the east bank of the Tigris. In this area, not far from the river, is a large square where a number of major bus lines intersect, and sometimes the square itself is called Bab ish-Sharji. Literally the name means 'East Gate', but the place is often called South Gate in English.

B. GRAMMAR

1. Imperfect verb stems beginning with a vowel

In preceding units we have had only verbs with imperfect stems beginning with consonants (one or two), and in fact the great majority of Iraqi verbs are of that type. However, there are also a dozen or so verbs with stems beginning with a vowel (always long), and among these are several of the most common verbs of the language. Two occur in this unit: the verb meaning 'to arrive', which has the imperfect stem *-ooṣal,* and the verb meaning 'to take', which has the imperfect stem *-aaxuδ*. Inflectional prefixes occurring with such stems have the alternants which consist of a consonant alone (see table in 15 B 3): *y-, t-, ˀ-, n-*. When one of the inflectional suffixes *-iin* or *-uun* also occurs, the stem vowel is dropped. Following are all the imperfect forms of these verbs:

3	M	*yooṣal*	'he arrives'	*yaaxuδ*	'he takes
	F	*tooṣal*	'she arrives'	*taaxuδ*	'she takes'
	P	*yooṣluun*	'they arrive'	*yaaxδuun*	'they take'
2	M	*tooṣal*	'you M arrive'	*taaxuδ*	'you M take'
	F	*tooṣliin*	'you F arrive'	*taaxδiin*	'you F take'
	P	*tooṣluun*	'you P arrive'	*taaxδuun*	'you P take'
1	S	*ˀooṣal*	'I arrive'	*ˀaaxuδ*	'I take'
	P	*nooṣal*	'we arrive'	*naaxuδ*	'we take'

2. Imperative forms (2)

The imperative forms of verbs like those above have a prefix *ˀ-*. The masculine imperative form consists of the prefix and the stem; the feminine form consists of the prefix, the stem, and the suffix *-i;* and the plural form consists of the prefix, the stem, and the suffix *-u*. When one of the suffixes occurs, the stem vowel is dropped. Here are the imperative forms of the two verbs shown above (the imperative stem *-uxuδ* is irregular):

2 M	*ˀooṣal*	'arrive M'	*ˀuxuδ*	'take M'
F	*ˀooṣli*	'arrive F'	*ˀuxδi*	'take F'
P	*ˀooṣlu*	'arrive P'	*ˀuxδu*	'take P'

Verbs with imperfect stems beginning with one consonant have no prefix in their imperative forms. The masculine imperative form consists of the stem alone; the feminine form consists of the stem and the suffix *-i*; and the plural form consists of the stem and the suffix *-u*. The imperative forms of one group of verbs in this category, those with stems of the shape -CvvC, have already been described (16 B 2); but one set is given below again for review and comparison. The imperfect indicative forms are shown on the left, and the imperative forms on the right. Note in all cases that the imperfect stem is what remains if the inflectional prefix *t-, ti-,* or *tu-* is removed from the 2 M indicative form.

	Indicative		**Imperative**	
2 M	*tguum*	'you M get up'	*guum*	'get up M'
F	*tguumiin*	'you F get up'	*guumi*	'get up F'
P	*tguumuun*	'you P get up'	*guumu*	'get up P'

If the stem begins with one consonant and has a stem vowel, the stem vowel is dropped when a suffix beginning with a vowel is added:

2 M	*tbaddil*	'you M change'	*baddil*	'change M'
F	*tbaddliin*	'you F change'	*baddli*	'change F'
P	*tbaddluun*	'you P change'	*baddlu*	'change P'
2 M	*twaṣṣil*	'you M convey'	*waṣṣil*	'convey M'
F	*twaṣṣliin*	'you F convey'	*waṣṣli*	'convey F'
P	*twaṣṣluun*	'you P convey'	*waṣṣlu*	'convey P'

If the stem begins with one consonant and has a final vowel, that vowel is dropped when a suffix beginning with a vowel is added:

2 M	*tsawwi*	'you M do'	*sawwi*	'do M'
F	*tsawwiin*	'you F do'	*sawwi*	'do F'
P	*tsawwuun*	'you P do'	*sawwu*	'do P'

In verbs with imperfect stems of the shape -CCvC (see 15 B 2), the masculine imperative form consists of a prefix *ʔi-* or *ʔu-*, and the stem, the vowel of the prefix being the same as in the corresponding 2 M indicative form. The feminine and plural imperative forms may consist of the prefix, the stem, and the suffix *-i* and *-u* respectively; or they may consist of the stem and the suffix only. In this book we shall use mainly the forms without the prefix. Whether the prefix is present or not, the stem vowel shifts when one of the suffixes *-i* or *-u* is added, just as it does in the indicative when one of the suffixes *-iin* or *-uun* is added, so that the stem has the shape -CvCC-. Here are examples:

	Indicative		**Imperative**	
2 M	*tisʔal*	'you M ask'	*ʔisʔal*	'ask M'
F	*tsiʔliin*	'you F ask'	*siʔli*	'ask F'
P	*tsiʔluun*	'you P ask'	*siʔlu*	'ask P'
2 M	*tidfaɛ*	'you M pay'	*ʔidfaɛ*	'pay M'
F	*ddifɛiin*	'you F pay'	*difɛi*	'pay F'
P	*ddifɛuun*	'you P pay'	*difɛu*	'pay P'
2 M	*tišrab*	'you M drink'	*ʔišrab*	'drink M'
F	*tšurbiin*	'you F drink'	*šurbi*	'drink F'
P	*tšurbuun*	'you P drink'	*šurbu*	'drink P'
2 M	*tirkab*	'you M ride'	*ʔirkab*	'ride M'
F	*trukbiin*	'you F ride'	*rukbi*	'ride F'
P	*trukbuun*	'you P ride'	*rukbu*	'ride P'
2 M	*tugɛud*	'you M sit'	*ʔugɛud*	'sit M'
F	*tguɛdiin*	'you F sit'	*guɛdi*	'sit F'
P	*tguɛduun*	'you P sit'	*guɛdu*	'sit P'

Verbs with imperfect stems of the shape -CCv have imperative forms consisting of a prefix *ʔi-* (*ʔu-* in a few verbs) and the stem. The feminine and plural imperative forms also have the suffixes *-i* and *-u* respectively; when one of these suffixes is added, the final vowel of the stem is dropped. Examples:

		Indicative		Imperative	
2	M	*tiqra*	'you M read'	*ˀiqra*	'read M'
	F	*tiqriin*	'you F read'	*ˀiqri*	'read F'
	P	*tiqruun*	'you P read'	*ˀiqru*	'read P'
2	M	*tiḥči*	'you M speak'	*ˀiḥči*	'speak M'
	F	*tiḥčiin*	'you F speak'	*ˀiḥči*	'speak P'
	P	*tiḥčuun*	'you P speak'	*ˀiḥču*	'speak P'

3. Verb 'to be able, can'

The imperfect forms of the verb meaning 'to be able, can' are:

3	M	*yigdar*	'he can'
	F	*tigdar*	'she can'
	P	*ygidruun*	'they can'
2	M	*tigdar*	'you M can'
	F	*tgidriin*	'you F can'
	P	*tgidruun*	'you P can'
1	S	*ˀagdar*	'I can'
	P	*nigdar*	'we can'

This verb most commonly occurs as the first verb in a string (15 B 6), as for example in Sentence 3 of the dialogue: *ˀagdar ˀaaxuδ* 'I can take' (a *ˀ* at the beginning of a word is often dropped in normal-speed speech, except at the beginning of a sentence). Other examples:

yigdar yaaxuδ paaṣ raqam sitta.	'He can take a number six bus.'
tigdar idjiib-lak gahwa.	'She can bring you M coffee.'
ma-ygidruun yiqruun zeen.	'They can't read well.'
tigdar itruuḥ wiyyaaya?	'Can you M go with me?'
ma-tgidriin iššurbiin čaay?	'Can't you F drink tea?'
š-itgidruun idjiibuun?	'What can you P bring?'
ma-agdar ašuufa l-yoom.	'I can't see him today.'
nigdar nisˀal ṣadiiqna xaalid.	'We can ask our friend Khalid.'

4. *minnaa* and *minnaak*

The preposition *min* 'from' combines with the particles *hnaa* 'here' and *hnaak* 'there' to form the words *minnaa* 'from here' and *minnaak* 'from there'. Note that the latter two forms are sometimes used in Iraqi when the simple words 'here' or 'there' are used in English, as in Sentence 4 of the dialogue.

5. The numerals from 'three' to 'ten'

Following are the Iraqi numerals from 'three' to 'ten'. Note that these numerals, unlike those for 'one' and 'two', do not have different masculine and feminine forms.

tlaaθa	'three'	*sabƐa*	'seven'
ˀarbaƐa	'four'	*θmaanya*	'eight'
xamsa	'five'	*tisƐa*	'nine'
sitta	'six'	*Ɛašra*	'ten'

The forms listed above are the **independent forms** of these numerals. They are used in counting, in arithmetical figuring, alone, and when following a noun. (They are not used immediately before a noun, in constructions equivalent to English *three pencils, five days,* and so on; in such constructions slightly different forms of these numerals are used which will be taken up later.) Examples:

waaƐid, θneen, tlaaθa, ˀarbaƐa . . .	'One, two, three, four . . .'
xamsa w-waaƐid sitta.	'Five and one is six.'
tlaaθa w-sitta tisƐa.	'Three and six is nine.'
θmaanya min Ɛašra θneen.	'Eight from ten is two.'
ˀarbaƐa min sabƐa tlaaθa.	'Four from seven is three."
(*čam qalam Ɛindak?*)	('How many pencils do you have?')
Ɛindi tlaaθa.	'I have three.'
tlaaθa.	'Three.'
(*čam xariiṭa Ɛindak?*)	('How many maps do you have?')
Ɛindi tlaaθa.	'I have three.'
tlaaθa.	'Three.'
ˀuxuδ raqam ˀarbaƐa.	'Take number four.'
Ɛindi mawƐid is-saaƐa ˀarbaƐa.	'I have an appointment at four o'clock.'

6. Independent personal pronouns: Third person and summary

The form *huwwa* in Sentence 6 of the dialogue is the third-person masculine singular independent personal pronoun. It corresponds to English *he* when referring to a person, or to *it* when referring to an inanimate thing for which the Iraqi noun is masculine. The feminine singular form is *hiyya* 'she, it F', and the plural form is *hum̩m̩a* 'they'. Below is a table recapitulating all the independent personal pronouns.

3	M	*huwwa*	'he, it M'
	F	*hiyya*	'she, it F'
	P	*huṃṃa*	'they'
2	M	*ˀinta*	'you M'
	F	*ˀinti*	'you F'
	P	*ˀintu*	'you P'
1	S	*ˀaani*	'I'
	P	*ˀiḥna*	'we'

C. DRILLS

Drill 1. Replace the underlined portion by the items given.

hal-paaṣ yooṣal lil-karraada?	Does this bus go to Karrada?
l-baab iš-šarji	to Bab ish-Sharji
lil-uuteel	to the hotel
l-uuteelna	to our hotel
lil-beet	to the house
l-beetkum	to your P house
lil-maṭaar	to the airport
lil-maṭaar ij-jidiid	to the new airport
lis-safaara j-jidiida	to the new embassy
l-baab iš-šarji	to Bab ish-Sharji
lil-karraada	to Karrada

Drill 2. Replace the underlined portion by the items given.

ˀuxuð paaṣ raqam itlaaθa minnaa l-baab iš-sarji.	Take bus number three from here to Bab ish-Sharji.
l-beethum	to their house
l-uuteelkum	to your P hotel
lil-uuteel	to the hotel
lil-karraada	to Karrada
lis-safaara	to the embassy
lis-safaara l-ʕatiiga	to the old embassy
lil-gaaziino č-čibiira	to the big gaaziino
lil-paŋg ič-čibiir	to the big bank
lil-paŋg il-iṣġayyir	to the little bank
lil-karraada	to Karrada
l-baab iš-šarji	to Bab ish-Sharji

Drill 3. Replace the underlined portion with the items given.

ʔuxuδ paaṣ raqam itlaaθa minnaa l-baab iš-šarji.	Take bus number three from here to Bab ish-Sharji.
ʔarbaʕa	four
xamsa	five
sitta	six
sabʕa	seven
θmaanya	eight
tisʕa	nine
ʕašra	ten
waaḥid	one
θneen	two
tlaaθa	three

Drill 4. Replace the underlined portion with the items given.

ʔirkab raqam sitta w-huwwa ywaṣṣlak.	Get on number six and that'll get you there.
sabʕa	seven
θmaanya	eight
tisʕa	nine
ʕašra	ten
waaḥid	one
θneen	two
tlaaθa	three
ʔarbaʕa	four
xamsa	five
sitta	six

Drill 5. Replace the underlined portion with the items given.

ʕindi mawʕid wiyya fadd ṣadiiq is-saaʕa xamsa.	I have an appointment with a friend at five o'clock.
ʕašra	ten
sabʕa	seven
wiḥda	one
θmaanya	eight
θinteen	two
ʔarbaʕa	four
tisʕa	nine
sitta	six
tlaaθa	three
xamsa	five

Drill 6. Repeat the original sentence, then replace the underlined portion by the items given, making the necessary changes in the verb form.

<u>ʔabu zuheer</u> raħ-yooṣal is-saaʕa sitta.	<u>Abu Zuhayr</u> will arrive at six o'clock.
ʔumm zuheer	*ʔumm zuheer raħ-tooṣal is-saaʕa sitta.*
l-maħruusiin	*l-maħruusiin raħ-yooṣluun is-saaʕa sitta.*
ʔaani	*ʔaani raħ-ooṣal is-saaʕa sitta.*
ʔiħna	*ʔiħna raħ-nooṣal is-saaʕa sitta.*
ʔumm xaalid	*ʔumm xaalid raħ-tooṣal is-saaʕa sitta.*
ʔinta	*ʔinta raħ-tooṣal is-saaʕa sitta.*
ʔinti	*ʔinti raħ-tooṣliin is-saaʕa sitta.*
ʔintu	*ʔintu raħ-tooṣluun is-saaʕa sitta.*
ʔiħna	*ʔiħna raħ-nooṣal is-saaʕa sitta.*
ʔabu xaalid	*ʔabu xaalid raħ-yooṣal is-saaʕa sitta.*
zuheer	*zuheer raħ-yooṣal is-saaʕa sitta.*
samiira	*samiira raħ-tooṣal is-saaʕa sitta.*
xaalid w-samiira	*xaalid w-samiira raħ-yooṣluun is-saaʕa sitta.*

Drill 7. Repeat the original sentence, then change the verb form to correspond with each of the cue items given. Do not repeat the cues.

laazim <u>yooṣal</u> lid-daaʔira s-saaʕa tisʕa.	<u>He</u> has to arrive at the office at nine o'clock.
hiyya	*laazim tooṣal lid-daaʔira s-saaʕa tisʕa.*
humma	*laazim yooṣluun lid-daaʔira s-saaʕa tisʕa.*
huwwa	*laazim yooṣal lid-daaʔira s-saaʕa tisʕa.*
muṣṭafa w-zuheer	*laazim yooṣluun lid-daaʔira s-saaʕa tisʕa.*
ʔumm xaalid	*laazim tooṣal lid-daaʔira s-saaʕa tisʕa.*
ʔabu mħammad	*laazim yooṣal lid-daaʔira s-saaʕa tisʕa.*
ʔaani	*laazim ooṣal lid-daaʔira s-saaʕa tisʕa.*
ʔinta	*laazim tooṣal lid-daaʔira s-saaʕa tisʕa.*
ʔiħna	*laazim nooṣal lid-daaʔira s-saaʕa tisʕa.*
ʔaani w-inta	*laazim nooṣal lid-daaʔira s-saaʕa tisʕa.*
ʔinti	*laazim tooṣliin lid-daaʔira s-saaʕa tisʕa.*
ʔintu	*laazim tooṣluun lid-daaʔira s-saaʕa tisʕa.*
mħammad	*laazim yooṣal lid-daaʔira s-saaʕa tisʕa.*

Drill 8. Change the *laazim* construction to the corresponding imperative.

laazim tooṣal is-saaεa ʔarbaεa.
laazim tooṣliin is-saaεa ʔarbaεa.
laazim tooṣluun is-saaεa ʔarbaεa.
laazim taaxuδ paaṣ raqam sabεa.
laazim taaxδiin paaṣ raqam sabεa.
laazim taaxδuun paaṣ raqam sabεa.
laazim tirkab paaṣ il-baab iš-šarji.
laazim itrukbiin paaṣ il-baab iš-šarji.
laazim itrukbuun paaṣ il-baab iš-šarji.
baεdeen laazim tisʔal ij-jaabi.
baεdeen laazim issiʔliin ij-jaabi.
baεdeen laazim issiʔluun ij-jaabi.
laazim tišrab istikaan čaay.
laazim iššurbiin istikaan čaay.
laazim iššurbuun istikaan čaay.

ʔooṣal is-saaεa ʔarbaεa.
ʔooṣli s-saaεa ʔarbaεa.
ʔooṣlu s-saaεa ʔarbaεa.
ʔuxuδ paaṣ raqam sabεa.
ʔuxδi paaṣ raqam sabεa.
ʔuxδu paaṣ raqam sabεa.
ʔirkab paaṣ il-baab iš-šarji.
rukbi paaṣ il-baab iš-šarji.
rukbu paaṣ il-baab iš-šarji.
baεdeen ʔisʔal ij-jaabi.
baεdeen siʔli j-jaabi.
baεdeen siʔlu j-jaabi.
ʔišrab istikaan čaay.
šurbi stikaan čaay.
šurbu stikaan čaay.

Drill 9. Change the negative command to the corresponding imperative.

la-tidfaε hal-iḥsaab.
la-ddifεiin hal-iḥsaab.
la-ddifεuun hal-iḥsaab.
la-tugεud bis-sayyaara.
la-tguεdiin bis-sayyaara.
la-tguεduun bis-sayyaara.
la-tiqra jaraayid bid-daaʔira.
la-tiqriin jaraayid bid-daaʔira.
la-tiqruun jaraayid bid-daaʔira.
la-tiḥči wiyyaahum il-yoom.
la-tiḥčiin wiyyaahum il-yoom.
la-tiḥčuun wiyyaahum il-yoom.

ʔidfaε hal-iḥsaab.
difεi hal-iḥsaab.
difεu hal-iḥsaab.
ʔugεud bis-sayyaara.
guεdi bis-sayyaara.
guεdu bis-sayyaara.
ʔiqra jaraayid bid-daaʔira.
ʔiqri jaraayid bid-daaʔira.
ʔiqru jaraayid bid-daaʔira.
ʔiḥči wiyyaahum il-yoom.
ʔiḥči wiyyaahum il-yoom.
ʔiḥču wiyyaahum il-yoom.

Drill 10. Change the verb string to the imperative of the final verb.

tigdar itbaddil minnaak.
tgidriin itbaddliin minnaak.
tgidruun itbaddluun minnaak.

baddil minnaak.
baddli minnaak.
baddlu minnaak.

ma-tħibb itruuħ lis-suug? — *ruuħ lis-suug.*
ma-tħibbiin itruuħiin lis-suug? — *ruuħi lis-suug.*
ma-tħibbuun itruuħuun lis-suug? — *ruuħu lis-suug.*
triid itwaṣṣil samiira lil-beet? — *waṣṣil samiira lil-beet.*
tirdiin itwaṣṣliin samiira lil-beet? — *waṣṣli samiira lil-beet.*
tirduun itwaṣṣluun samiira lil-beet? — *waṣṣlu samiira lil-beet.*
ma-tigdar issallim εaleehum? — *sallim εaleehum.*
ma-tgidriin issallmiin εaleehum? — *sallmi εaleehum.*
ma-tgidruun issallmuun εaleehum? — *sallmu εaleehum.*

Drill 11. Change the masculine imperative to the corresponding feminine.

ʔuxuδ paaṣ raqam iθmaanya. — *ʔuxδi paaṣ raqam iθmaanya.*
ʔirkab raqam sitta lil-karraada. — *rukbi raqam sitta lil-karraada.*
ʔisʔal zuheer ween raayiħ. — *siʔli zuheer ween raayiħ.*
baεdeen baddil. — *baεdeen baddli.*
sawwi kullši l-yoom. — *sawwi kullši l-yoom.*
ʔiqra j-jaraayid bil-beet. — *ʔiqri j-jaraayid bil-beet.*
ʔiħĉi wiyya ʔumm xaalid. — *ʔiħči wiyya ʔumm xaalid.*
ʔiŝrab hal-ṃaay. — *šurbi hal-ṃaay.*
ʔugεud yammna fadd mudda. — *guεdi yammna fadd mudda.*
guum is-saaεa θinteen. — *guumi s-saaεa θinteen.*

Drill 12. Change *laazim* to the appropriate form of *yigdar*.

laazim yruuħ bis-sayyaara. — *yigdar yruuħ bis-sayyaara.*
laazim ašuufhum il-yoom. — *ʔagdar ašuufhum il-yoom.*
laazim itruuħ lil-ḅang wiyyaaya. — *tigdar itruuħ lil-ḅang wiyyaaya.*
laazim nišrab istikaan čaay suwa. — *nigdar nišrab istikaan čaay suwa.*
laazim iddifεiin l-iħsaab il-yoom. — *tgidriin iddifεiin l-iħsaab il-yoom.*
laazim issawwuun kullši bid-daaʔira. — *tgidruun issawwuun kullši bid-daaʔira.*
laazim taaxuδ paaṣ raqam waaħid. — *tigdar taaxuδ paaṣ raqam waaħid.*
laazim itwaṣṣluun ʔumm xaalid il-beetha. — *tgidruun itwaṣṣluun ʔumm xaalid il-beetha.*
laazim ajiib il-xariiṭa lil-uuteel. — *ʔagdar ajiib il-xariiṭa lil-uuteel.*
laazim yooṣal is-saaεa tlaaθa. — *yigdar yooṣal is-saaεa tlaaθa.*

UNIT 19

A. DIALOGUE

Abu Zuhayr gets on a bus and sits down, and the conductor comes along to collect the fare.

ʔabu zuheer	**Abu Zuhayr**
b-eeš	for what, how much
biṭaaqa	ticket
1. *b-eeš il-biṭaaqa, sayyid?*	How much is the ticket, conductor?
j-jaabi	**The conductor**
2. *ween itriid itruuħ, ʔaxi, l-baab iš-šarji?*	Where do you want to go, sir, to Bab ish-Sharji?
ʔabu zuheer	**Abu Zuhayr**
3. *laa, lil-karraada.*	No, to Karrada.
j-jaabi	**The conductor**
tguṣṣ	you M cut; you M buy (tickets)
maal	of, belonging to, for
manṭiqteen	two areas, two zones
4. *zeen, laʕad laazim itguṣṣ biṭaaqa maal manṭiqteen.*	All right, then you'll have to buy a two-zone ticket.
ʔabu zuheer	**Abu Zuhayr**
5. *ṭayyib, b-eeš il-biṭaaqa maal manṭiqteen?*	All right, how much is the two-zone ticket?
j-jaabi	**The conductor**
θmunṭaʕaš	eighteen
6. *θmunṭaʕaš filis, ʔaxi. tfaððal. šukran.*	Eighteen fils, sir. Here you are. Thank you.

NOTES ON DIALOGUE

The Baghdad bus system

There are several ways in which the bus system in Baghdad differs from the usual American system. First of all, you do not pay as you board, but rather you get on and sit down, and shortly the conductor—every bus has both a conductor and a driver—comes to you to collect the fare. He then gives you a small slip of paper—the ticket—which you keep until you get off as proof that you have paid. Second, most buses have first-class and second-class sections; the former is in the front part of the bus and has slightly more comfortable seats. The basic fare is ten fils for the second-class section and fifteen for the first. Finally, for the basic fare you can ride any distance within one bus zone (*manṭiqa*), but if you are still on the bus when it crosses into another zone you have to pay another fare. However, if you know in advance that your trip will take you into another zone, you can save a little money by asking for a "two-zone ticket" when you first pay; this costs two fils less, in either first or second class, than would two separate tickets.

B. GRAMMAR

1. Interrogative *-eeš* 'what'; *b-eeš* 'how much'

As we have seen before, the Iraqi equivalent of the English interrogative *what* has several different forms, or alternants. The prefix alternant *š-* 'what' was described in 13 B 4, and the independent alternant *šinu* 'what' in 14 B 1. There is also a suffix alternant, which occurs, among other places, as the object of a preposition. Its form is *-eeš* after a consonant, and *-weeš* after a vowel, for example:

yamm-eeš	'next to what'
minn-eeš	'of what, from what'
b-eeš	'with what, in what, for what'
ʕala-weeš	'on what, about what'

Thus the form *b-eeš* in Sentences 1 and 5 of the dialogue is composed of two elements, the preposition prefix *b-* and the suffix form *-eeš* of the interrogative, and in certain contexts has the literal meaning shown in the list above. It is also very commonly used in two situations where the English equivalent is quite different. The first is in asking the price of something, where it corresponds to English 'How much (is/are) . . .', for example:

b-eeš il-biṭaaqa?	'How much is the ticket?'
b-eeš ij-jaraayid?	'How much are the newspapers?'

The second situation is in asking the time:

b-eeš is-saaƹa? *s-saaƹa b-eeš?*	'What time is it?'

Sometimes instead of *b-eeš* the form *b-beeš* is used.

2. The dual

An Iraqi noun may have not only a singular and a plural form, as in English, but also a **dual** form, meaning 'two (of the items indicated)'. (See 17 B 2 for another way of expressing the same meaning.) A noun is made dual by adding the suffix *-een* to the singular stem:

Singular		**Dual**	
beet	'house'	***beeteen***	'two houses'
yoom	'day'	***yoomeen***	'two days'
diinaar	'dinar'	***diinaareen***	'two dinars'

A stem vowel *i* or *u* is usually dropped when *-een* is added, but not if the result would be a sequence of more than two consonants:

	filis	'fils'	*filseen*	'two fils'
	šaariƹ	'street'	*šaarƹeen*	'two streets'
but	*mawƹid*	'appointment'	*mawƹideen*	'two appointments'

A stem vowel *a* is dropped in some words but not in others; the facts must be learned for each word:

	raqam	'number'	*raqmeen*	'two numbers'
but	*qalam*	'pencil'	*qalameen*	'two pencils'

Dual forms ending in *-een* may have non-automatic stress (see 9 C). From the automatic stress rule (3 F), one would expect the stress in these words always to fall on the ending *-een,* since that is the long syllable nearest the end of the word. In fact, however, the stress often falls on the next-to-last syllable in two-syllable words and on the third-from-last in others, for example *yóomeen, díinaareen.* Variation between this non-automatic type of stress and the automatic type with the stress on *-een* depends largely on the overall intonation of the sentence in which the dual form occurs. The presence of the ending *-een* is enough to alert you to the possibility of this stress variation, and we shall not use the stress mark in these words.

3. Feminine *-t-* stems

Feminine nouns ending in *a* have two special **suffixing stems,** used whenever the dual suffix *-een* or any of the pronoun suffixes is added. The **consonant suffixing stem,** used with suffixes beginning with a consonant, is formed by adding *-t-* to the singular form, for example *sayyaara* 'car', consonant suffixing stem *sayyaarat-,* as in *sayyaaratna* 'our car'. The **vowel suffixing stem,** used with suffixes beginning with a vowel, is formed in many nouns by dropping the stem vowel *a* from the consonant suffixing stem, for example *sayyaart-,* as in *sayyaarteen* 'two cars' and *sayyaarta* 'his car'. (In some nouns the dropping of the stem vowel would result in a cluster of more than two different consonants, and in such cases the vowel suffixing stem is formed in different ways to be taken up later.) Following are two examples of feminine nouns with all the pronoun suffixes. Note the regular alternation between the consonant suffixing stem and the vowel suffixing stem, according to whether the suffix begins with a consonant or a vowel.

sayyaara	'car'	*šiqqa*	'apartment'
sayyaarta	'his car'	*šiqqta*	'his apartment'
sayyaaratha	'her car'	*šiqqatha*	'her apartment'
sayyaarathum	'their car'	*šiqqathum*	'their apartment'
sayyaartak	'your M car'	*šiqqtak*	'your M apartment'
sayyaartič	'your F car'	*šiqqtič*	'your F apartment'
sayyaaratkum	'your P car'	*šiqqatkum*	'your P apartment'
sayyaarti	'my car'	*šiqqti*	'my apartment'
sayyaaratna	'our car'	*šiqqatna*	'our apartment'

Following are examples of feminine nouns and their dual forms.

sayyaara	'car'	*sayyaarteen*	'two cars'
šiqqa	'apartment'	*šiqqteen*	'two apartments'
m̡arra	'time'	*m̡arrteen*	'two times, twice'
saaƐa	'hour; clock, watch'	*saaƐteen*	'two hours; two clocks, watches'
manṭiqa	'area, zone'	*manṭiqteen*	'two areas, zones'

The noun *gahwa* 'coffee; coffee-house', and all other feminine nouns ending in *-wa* preceded by a consonant, have regularly formed consonant suffixing stems, for example *gahwat-,* but have vowel suffixing stems in which the final *-wat-* is changed to *-uut-*. Examples:

gahwatna	'our coffee-house'	*gahuuta*	'his coffee-house'
gahwatkum	'your P coffee-house'	*gahuuteen*	'two coffee-houses'

4. The numerals from 'eleven' to 'nineteen'

Following is a list of the Iraqi numerals from 'eleven' to 'nineteen'. Note that these all end in *-aĉaš* or *-ṭaĉaš*, and that the first part of most of them contains emphatic consonants not occurring in the corresponding simple numerals under 'ten'.

daĉaš	'eleven'	*xṃuṣṭaĉaš*	'fifteen'
θṇaĉaš	'twelve'	*ṣiṭṭaĉaš*	'sixteen'
ṭḷaṭṭaĉaš	'thirteen'	*ṣḅaaṭaĉaš*	'seventeen'
ˀarḅaaṭaĉaš	'fourteen'	*θṃunṭaĉaš*	'eighteen'
		ṭṣaaṭaĉaš	'nineteen'

When a noun follows any number higher than ten, it is in the ***singular*** form, not in the plural as in English. Examples:

yoom	'day'	*daĉaš yoom*	'eleven days'
saaĉa	'hour'	*θṇaĉaš saaĉa*	'twelve hours'
filis	'fils'	*xṃuṣṭaĉaš filis*	'fifteen fils'
diinaar	'dinar'	*ṣiṭṭaĉaš diinaar*	'sixteen dinars'
safaara	'embassy'	*θṃunṭaĉaš safaara*	'eighteen embassies'

C. DRILLS

Drill 1. Change the phrase consisting of a noun plus the numeral 'one' to the dual form of the noun.

Cue:	*ĉidhum qalam waaĉid ihnaak.*	They have one pencil there.
Response:	*ĉidhum qalameen ihnaak.*	They have two pencils there.

ĉidhum beet waaĉid ihnaak.	*ĉidhum beeteen ihnaak.*
ĉidhum ṣadiiq waaĉid ihnaak.	*ĉidhum ṣadiiqeen ihnaak.*
ĉidhum filis waaĉid ihnaak.	*ĉidhum filseen ihnaak.*
ĉidhum diinaar waaĉid ihnaak.	*ĉidhum diinaareen ihnaak.*
ĉidhum yoom waaĉid ihnaak.	*ĉidhum yoomeen ihnaak.*
ĉidhum igḷaaṣ waaĉid ihnaak.	*ĉidhum igḷaaṣeen ihnaak.*
ĉidhum qalam waaĉid ihnaak.	*ĉidhum qalameen ihnaak.*
ĉidhum sayyaara wiĉda hnaak.	*ĉidhum sayyaarteen ihnaak.*

ʕidhum saaʕa wiḥda hnaak.	*ʕidhum saaʕteen ihnaak.*
ʕidhum safaara wiḥda hnaak.	*ʕidhum safaarteen ihnaak.*
ʕidhum daaʔira wiḥda hnaak.	*ʕidhum daaʔirteen ihnaak.*
ʕidhum šiqqa wiḥda hnaak.	*ʕidhum šiqqteen ihnaak.*
ʕidhum gahwa wiḥda hnaak.	*ʕidhum gahuuteen ihnaak.*

Drill 2. Change the first noun to the dual form.

Cue:	*ʔaku gahwa yamm il-uuteel.*	There's a coffee-house next to the hotel.
Response:	*ʔaku gahuuteen yamm il-uuteel.*	There are two coffee-houses next to the hotel.

ʔaku beet yamm is-suug.	*ʔaku beeteen yamm is-suug.*
ʔaku safaara b-hal-manṭiqa.	*ʔaku safaarteen ib-hal-manṭiqa.*
ʔaku qalam yamm it-talafoon.	*ʔaku qalameen yamm it-talafoon.*
ʔaku sayyaara biš-šaariʕ.	*ʔaku sayyaarteen biš-šaariʕ.*
ʔaku šiqqa b-hal-beet.	*ʔaku šiqqteen ib-hal-beet.*
ʔaku gahwa yamm il-gaaziino.	*ʔaku gahuuteen yamm il-gaaziino.*
ʔaku ʔuuteel ib-hal-manṭiqa.	*ʔaku ʔuuteeleen ib-hal-manṭiqa.*
ʔaku xariiṭa b-daaʔiratna.	*ʔaku xariiṭteen ib-daaʔiratna.*
ʔaku biṭaaqa jawwa t-talafoon.	*ʔaku biṭaaqteen jawwa t-talafoon.*

Drill 3. Answer the questions, using the dual form of the appropriate noun. In your answers, incorporate as much of the material in the questions as possible.

Cue:	*čam beet aku hnaak?*	How many houses are there there?
Response:	*ʔaku beeteen ihnaak.*	There are two houses there.

čam qalam ʕindak?	*ʕindi qalameen.*
čam sayyaara ʕidhum?	*ʕidhum sayyaarteen.*
čam safaara ʔaku b-hal-manṭiqa?	*ʔaku safaarteen ib-hal-manṭiqa.*
šgadd ʕindak ifluus?	*ʕindi diinaareen.*
čam iglaaṣ laazim yjiib?	*laazim yjiib iglaaṣeen.*
čam xariiṭa tirdiin iššuufiin?	*ʔariid ašuuf xariiṭteen.*
čam biṭaaqa laazim inguṣṣ?	*laazim itguṣṣuun biṭaaqteen.*
šgadd ʕidhum ifluus?	*ʕidhum diinaareen.*
šgadd iḥsaabna?	*ḥsaabkum ysawwi diinaareen.*
šgadd ṣaar-ilkum gaaʕdiin ihnaa?	*ṣaar-inna saaʕteen gaaʕdiin ihnaa.*
šgadd raḥ-yguʕduun ihnaak?	*raḥ-yguʕduun saaʕteen ihnaak.*
čam gahwa ʔaku b-hal-manṭiqa?	*ʔaku gahuuteen ib-hal-manṭiqa.*
čam ṃarra laazim abaddil?	*laazim itbaddil ṃarrteen.*

Drill 4. Change each question as in the example.

Cue:	*triid gahwa l-yoom?*	Do you M want coffee today?
Response:	*b-eeš il-gahwa l-yoom?*	How much is the coffee today?

triid čaay il-yoom?	*b-eeš ič-čaay il-yoom?*
tirdiin ɛaliib il-yoom?	*b-eeš il-ɛaliib il-yoom?*
triid biira l-yoom?	*b-eeš il-biira l-yoom?*
tirduun šarbat il-yoom?	*b-eeš iš-šarbat il-yoom?*
triid ɛaamuḍ il-yoom?	*b-eeš il-ɛaamuḍ il-yoom?*
tirdiin gahwa l-yoom?	*b-eeš il-gahwa l-yoom?*

Drill 5. Change the article prefix to the 2 M pronoun suffix, making the necessary change in the stems.

Cue:	*ween is-sayyaara?*	Where's the car?
Response:	*ween sayyaartak?*	Where's your M car?

ween id-daa?ira?	*ween daa?irtak?*
ween iš-šiqqa?	*ween šiqqtak?*
ween is-safaara?	*ween safaartak?*
ween il-gahwa?	*ween gahuutak?*
ween is-saaɛa?	*ween saaɛtak?*
ween il-biṭaaqa?	*ween biṭaaqtak?*
ween il-xariiṭa?	*ween xariiṭtak?*
ween is-sayyaara?	*ween sayyaartak?*

Drill 6. Change the demonstrative prefix to the 3 P pronoun suffix, making the necessary change in the stem.

Cue:	*has-sayyaara čbiira.*	This car is big.
Response:	*sayyaarathum čibiira.*	Their car is big.

haš-šiqqa čbiira.	*šiqqathum čibiira.*
hal-xariiṭa čbiira.	*xariiṭathum čibiira.*
had-daa?ira čbiira.	*daa?irathum čibiira.*
has-safaara čbiira.	*safaarathum čibiira.*
hal-gahwa čbiira.	*gahwathum čibiira.*
has-saaɛa čbiira.	*saaɛathum čibiira.*
has-sayyaara čbiira.	*sayyaarathum čibiira.*

Drill 7. Change each sentence as in the example.

Cue:	*ɛidhum sayyaara jidiida.*	They have a new car.
Response:	*sayyaarathum jidiida.*	Their car is new.

εidha sayyaara jdiida.	*sayyaaratha jdiida.*
εidha šiqqa jdiida.	*šiqqatha jdiida.*
εinda šiqqa jdiida.	*šiqqta jdiida.*
εinda saaεa jdiida.	*saaεta jdiida.*
εidkum saaεa jdiida.	*saaεatkum jidiida.*
εidkum xariiṭa jdiida.	*xariiṭatkum jidiida.*
εindi xariiṭa jdiida.	*xariiṭti jdiida.*
εindi biṭaaqa jdiida.	*biṭaaqti jdiida.*
εidna biṭaaqa jdiida.	*biṭaaqatna jdiida.*
εidna safaara jdiida.	*safaaratna jdiida.*
εidkum safaara jdiida.	*safaaratkum jidiida.*
εidkum gahwa jdiida.	*gahwatkum jidiida.*
εindak gahwa jdiida.	*gahuutak jidiida.*
εindak saaεa jdiida.	*saaεtak jidiida.*
εindič saaεa jdiida.	*saaεtič jidiida.*
εindič sayyaara jdiida.	*sayyaartič jidiida.*
εidhum sayyaara jdiida.	*sayyaarathum jidiida.*

Drill 8. Replace the underlined portion by the items given.

laazim tidfaε daεaš diinaar.	You M have to pay eleven dinars.
θṇaεaš	twelve
ṭḷaṭṭaεaš	thirteen
ʔarḅaaṭaεaš	fourteen
xṃuṣṭaεaš	fifteen
ṣiṭṭaεaš	sixteen
ṣḅaaṭaεaš	seventeen
θṃunṭaεaš	eighteen
ṭṣaaṭaεaš	nineteen

Drill 9. Replace the underlined portion by the items given.

ṣaar-inna xṃuṣṭaεaš yoom ihnaa.	We've been here fifteen days.
θṇaεaš	twelve
ṣiṭṭaεaš	sixteen
ʔarḅaaṭaεaš	fourteen
ṣḅaaṭaεaš	seventeen
daεaš	eleven
ṭṣaaṭaεaš	nineteen
ṭḷaṭṭaεaš	thirteen
θṃunṭaεaš	eighteen

Drill 10. Answer the first question using the numeral *daεaš* 'eleven', the next using the numeral *θṇaεaš* 'twelve', and so on.

čam qalam εindak?	*εindi daεaš qalam.*
čam safaara ʔaku b-hal-manṭiqa?	*ʔaku θṇaεaš safaara b-hal-manṭiqa.*
čam xariiṭa εidhum bid-daaʔira?	*εidhum ṭḷaṭṭaεaš xariiṭa bid-daaʔira.*
čam yoom ṣaar-ilhum ihnaak?	*ṣaar-ilhum arḅaaṭaεaš yoom ihnaak.*
čam saaεa ṣaar-ilkum gaaεdiin ihnaa?	*ṣaar-inna xṃuṣṭaεaš saaεa gaaεdiin ihnaa.*
čam igḷaaṣ εidna bil-beet?	*εidna ṣiṭṭaεaš igḷaaṣ bil-beet.*
čam istikaan tigdar idjiib?	*ʔagdar ajiib iṣḅaaṭaεaš istikaan.*
čam talafoon ʔaku bil-uuteel?	*ʔaku θṃunṭaεaš talafoon bil-uuteel.*
čam sayyaara ʔaku biš-šaariε?	*ʔaku ṭṣaaṭaεaš sayyaara biš-šaariε.*

Drill 11. Change the 2 M imperative forms first to 2 F and then to 2 P imperative forms.

Cue:	*ʔuxuδ ṗaaṣ raqam daεaš.*	Take M bus number eleven.
Response 1:	*ʔuxδi ṗaaṣ raqam daεaš.*	Take F bus number eleven.
Response 2:	*ʔuxδu ṗaaṣ raqam daεaš.*	Take P bus number eleven.

ʔuxuδ ṗaaṣ raqam iθṇaεaš.	*ʔuxδi ṗaaṣ raqam iθṇaεaš.* *ʔuxδu ṗaaṣ raqam iθṇaεaš.*
ʔirkab ṗaaṣ raqam iṭḷaṭṭaεaš.	*rukbi ṗaaṣ raqam iṭḷaṭṭaεaš.* *rukbu ṗaaṣ raqam iṭḷaṭṭaεaš.*
ʔidfaε arḅaaṭaεaš diinaar.	*difεi ʔarḅaaṭaεaš diinaar.* *difεu ʔarḅaaṭaεaš diinaar.*
nṭiini xṃuṣṭaεaš filis.	*nṭiini xṃuṣṭaεaš filis.* *nṭuuni xṃuṣṭaεaš filis.*
jiib-li ṣiṭṭaεaš istikaan.	*jiibii-li ṣiṭṭaεaš istikaan.* *jiibuu-li ṣiṭṭaεaš istikaan.*
jiib-ilha ṣḅaaṭaεaš igḷaaṣ.	*jiibii-lha ṣḅaaṭaεaš igḷaaṣ.* *jiibuu-lha ṣḅaaṭaεaš igḷaaṣ.*
guṣṣ iθṃunṭaεaš biṭaaqa.	*guṣṣi θṃunṭaεaš biṭaaqa.* *guṣṣu θṃunṭaεaš biṭaaqa.*
ʔirkab raqam iṭṣaaṭaεaš w-baεdeen baddil.	*rukbi raqam iṭṣaaṭaεaš w-baεdeen baddli.* *rukbu raqam iṭṣaaṭaεaš w-baεdeen baddlu.*
guum is-saaεa daεaš.	*guumi s-saaεa daεaš.* *guumu s-saaεa daεaš.*

Drill 12. Add each pair of numbers and give the total, as in the example.

Cue:	*xamsa w-sitta*	five and six
Response:	*xamsa w-sitta daεaš.*	Five and six is eleven.

xamsa w-sabεa	*xamsa w-sabεa θṇaεaš.*
sitta w-sabεa	*sitta w-sabεa ṭḷaṭṭaεaš.*
tisεa w-xamsa	*tisεa w-xamsa ʔarḅaaṭaεaš.*
xamsa w-εašra	*xamsa w-εašra xṃuṣṭaεaš.*
θmaanya w-iθmaanya	*θmaanya w-iθmaanya ṣiṭṭaεaš.*
xṃuṣṭaεaš w-iθneen	*xṃuṣṭaεaš w-iθneen ṣḅaaṭaεaš.*
ʔarḅaaṭaεaš w-arbaεa	*ʔarḅaaṭaεaš w-arbaεa θṃunṭaεaš.*
εašra w-tisεa	*εašra w-tisεa ṭṣaaṭaεaš.*
εašra w-waaꞒid	*εašra w-waaꞒid daεaš.*

UNIT 20

A. NARRATIVE

mnij-jamaaεa	from the group
ʔilla	except
rubuε	fourth, quarter
1. *ʔabu zuheer yistarxiṣ*	Abu Zuheer takes his leave
imnij-jamaaεa	from the group
s-saaεa xamsa ʔilla rubuε	at quarter to five,
2. *w-yidfaε iꞒsaabhum bil-gahwa.*	and pays their check at the coffee-house.
mawqif	stopping place
3. *w-yruuꞒ il-mawqif il-paaṣ,*	He goes to the bus stop,
4. *w-yisʔal fadd jaabi*	and asks a conductor
šloon yooṣal lil-karraada.	how to get to Karrada.
5. *w-yirkab paaṣ il-baab iš-šarji.*	He rides a bus to Bab ish-Sharji.

ġeer	other, different
6. *w-baċdeen yirkab ġeer paaṣ lil-karraada,*	Then he rides another bus to Karrada,
nuṣṣ	half
7. *w-yooṣal ihnaak saaċa xamsa w-nuṣṣ.*	and arrives there at five-thirty.

B. GRAMMAR

1. Forms of preposition *min* 'from, of'

This preposition has several different forms, depending on what follows it. The independent form *min* occurs when the following word begins with a single consonants:

min beetna	'from our house'
min daa'iratkum	'from your P office'
min baab iš-šsarji	'from Bab ish-Sharji'

When the following word begins with two consonants, either *min* or (perhaps more commonly) a shorter form *mn-* may occur. In either case the helping vowel (10 C) occurs at the beginning of the following word.

mn-iċsaabna	'from our bill'
mn-iθṇaċaš diinaar	'from twelve dinars'

When the following word begins with the article prefix, *min* regularly combines with the latter to form a compound prefix consisting of *mni-* plus the appropriate consonant of the article:

mnil-paaṣ	'from the bus'
mnil-maṭaar	'from the airport'
mnis-safaara	'from the embassy'
mnid-daa'ira	'from the office'

When pronoun suffixes are attached, the stem form is *min-* before those beginning with a consonant, but *minn-* before those beginning with a vowel:

minna	'from him'	*minnak*	'from you M'
minha	'from her'	*minnič*	'from you F'
minhum	'from them'	*minkum*	'from you P'

minni	'from me'
(*minna*)	'from us'

(The form in parentheses above is rarely used, as it is indistinguishable from *minna* 'from him'. The phrase *min Ɛidna* 'from us' is used instead.) Finally, *min* combines with several other forms in special ways, as follows:

hnaa	'here'	*minnaa*	'from here'
hnaak	'there'	*minnaak*	'from there'
-eeš	'what'	*minneeš*	'from what'
ween	'where'	*mneen*	'from where'

2. The numerals from 'twenty' to 'ninety-nine'

Following is a list of the numerals which are multiples of ten, from 'twenty' to 'ninety':

Ɛišriin	'twenty'	*sittiin*	'sixty'
tlaaθiin	'thirty'	*sabƐiin*	'seventy'
ʔarbaƐiin	'forty'	*θmaaniin*	'eighty'
xamsiin	'fifty'	*tisƐiin*	'ninety'

Numbers between these multiples of ten, from 'twenty-one' to 'ninety-nine', are expressed by phrases consisting of the units numeral (in the masculine form in the case of 'one' and 'two') followed by the tens numeral, the latter with the prefix *w-* 'and'. Some examples:

waaƐid w-Ɛišriin	'twenty-one'	*tlaaθa w-xamsiin*	'fifty-three'
θneen w-Ɛišriin	'twenty-two'	*sitta w-xamsiin*	'fifty-six'
tlaaθa w-Ɛišriin	'twenty-three'	*xamsa w-sittiin*	'sixty-five'
ʔarbaƐa w-Ɛišriin	'twenty-four'	*sabƐa w-sittiin*	'sixty-seven'
xamsa w-Ɛišriin	'twenty-five'	*ʔarbaƐa w-sabƐiin*	'seventy-four'
waaƐid w-itlaaθiin	'thirty-one'	*θmaanya w-sabƐiin*	'seventy-eight'
θneen w-itlaaθiin	'thirty-two'	*waaƐid w-iθmaaniin*	'eighty-one'
sitta w-itlaaθiin	'thirty-six'	*xamsa w-iθmaaniin*	'eighty-five'
tlaaθa w-arbaƐiin	'forty-three'	*θneen w-tisƐiin*	'ninety-two'
tisƐa w-arbaƐiin	'forty-nine'	*tisƐa w-tisƐiin*	'ninety-nine'

Remember that when a noun follows *any* number higher than ten (19 B 4), it is in the singular form, not the plural. Examples:

yoom	'day'	*tlaaθiin yoom*	'thirty days'
saaʕa	'hour'	*ʔarbaʕa w-ʕišriin saaʕa*	'twenty-four hours'
diinaar	'dinar'	*sitta w-iθmaaniin diinaar*	'eighty-six dinars'

3. Telling time

As mentioned in 19 B 1, two common ways of asking for the time are:

b-eeš is-saaʕa?
s-saaʕa b-eeš? } 'What time is it?'

The article prefix in the second construction is not essential; one may also say:

saaʕa b-eeš? 'What time is it?'

There are also two main ways of stating the time, as shown below for all twelve on-the-hour times. In the left-hand column, the first word is given each time as *s-saaʕa,* but in this construction the article prefix is not essential: one may also say *saaʕa wiḥda, saaʕa θinteen,* and so on. In the construction shown in the right-hand column, note that the numerals 'three', 'eight', and 'twelve' have slightly different forms when preceded by the article prefix. In both columns, note that the numerals 'one' and 'two' are in their feminine forms.

s-saaʕa wiḥda.	*s-saaʕa bil-wiḥda.*	'It's one o'clock.'
s-saaʕa θinteen.	*s-saaʕa biθ-θinteen.*	'It's two o'clock.'
s-saaʕa tlaaθa.	*s-saaʕa biθ-θilaaθa.*	'It's three o'clock.'
s-saaʕa ʔarbaʕa.	*s-saaʕa bil-arbaʕa.*	'It's four o'clock.'
s-saaʕa xamsa.	*s-saaʕa bil-xamsa.*	'It's five o'clock.'
s-saaʕa sitta.	*s-saaʕa bis-sitta.*	'It's six o'clock.'
s-saaʕa sabʕa.	*s-saaʕa bis-sabʕa.*	'It's seven o'clock.'
s-saaʕa θmaanya.	*s-saaʕa biθ-θimaanya.*	'It's eight o'clock.'
s-saaʕa tisʕa.	*s-saaʕa bit-tisʕa.*	'It's nine o'clock.'
s-saaʕa ʕašra.	*s-saaʕa bil-ʕašra.*	'It's ten o'clock.'
s-saaʕa daʕaš.	*s-saaʕa bid-daʕaš.*	'It's eleven o'clock.'
s-saaʕa θṇaʕaš.	*s-saaʕa biθ-θiṇaʕaš.*	'It's twelve o'clock.'

All times other than those listed above are more commonly expressed by constructions like those in the left-hand column, and only this type will be shown below. In all these, as before, the article prefix of *s-saaʕa* is optional.

The following fractions are used in expressions involving time:

nuṣṣ	'half'
θiliθ	'third'
rubuɛ	'fourth, quarter'

In time expressions, these words refer respectively to a half-hour (thirty minutes), one-third of an hour (twenty minutes), and one-quarter of an hour (fifteen minutes). Times between a given hour and the following half-hour (including the latter) are expressed by phrases consisting of the hour and the appropriate fraction, the latter preceded by the prefix *w-* 'and', as follows:

s-saaɛa xamsa.	'It's five o'clock.'
s-saaɛa xamsa w-rubuɛ.	'It's quarter past five.'
s-saaɛa xamsa w-θiliθ.	'It's twenty past five.'
s-saaɛa xamsa w-nuṣṣ.	'It's five-thirty.'

Times between a given hour and the preceding half-hour (but not including the latter) are expressed by phrases consisting of the hour and the appropriate fraction, the latter preceded by the word *ʔilla* 'except, but, less', as follows:

s-saaɛa sitta ʔilla θiliθ.	'It's twenty to six.'
s-saaɛa sitta ʔilla rubuɛ.	'It's quarter to six.'
s-saaɛa sitta.	'It's six o'clock.'

Times involving numbers of minutes other than those represented by the above fractions are expressed by phrases consisting of the hour and a numeral representing the appropriate number of minutes (in the feminine form in the case of 'one' and 'two'), the latter preceded by the prefix *w-* or the word *ʔilla* as the case may be, as follows:

s-saaɛa sitta w-wiɛda.	'It's one past six.'
s-saaɛa sitta w-θinteen.	'It's two past six.'
s-saaɛa sitta w-itlaaθa.	'It's three past six.'
s-saaɛa sitta w-arbaɛa.	'It's four past six.'
s-saaɛa sitta w-xamsa.	'It's five past six.'
s-saaɛa sitta w-ɛašra.	'It's ten past six.'
s-saaɛa sabɛa ʔilla ɛašra.	'It's ten to seven.'
s-saaɛa sabɛa ʔilla xamsa.	'It's five to seven.'

Times involving twenty-five minutes after or before the hour may be expressed in two ways each:

s-saaɛa sitta w-xamsa w-ɛišriin. *s-saaɛa sitta w-nuṣṣ ʔilla xamsa.*	'It's twenty-five past six.'
s-saaɛa sitta w-nuṣṣ w-xamsa. *s-saaɛa sabɛa ʔilla xamsa w-ɛišriin.*	'It's twenty-five to seven.'

The concept '*at* such-and-such a time' is expressed by exactly the same constructions as all those shown on the left above, the article prefix again being optional. Examples:

ċindi mawċid is-saaċa xamsa.	'I have an appointment at five o'clock.'
raċ-yooṣal ihnaak saaċa xamsa w-nuṣṣ.	'He'll arrive there at five thirty.'

4. Pre-nouns: *ġeer* and *fadd*

Regardless of what the English translation might suggest, the word *ġeer* in Iraqi is not an adjective, since it is not inflected for gender and does not follow the noun it modifies. Rather it belongs to a small group of words which may function as modifiers of nouns or pronouns (some may also function in other ways), but have no gender inflection, and precede the word they modify. These may be termed **pre-nouns.** When *ġeer* precedes an indefinite noun it means 'another', not in the sense 'in addition to the first' but in the sense 'different from the first'. Examples:

ġeer paaṣ	'another bus'
ġeer sayyaara	'another car'
l-ġeer bang	'to another bank'
b-ġeer manṭiqa	'in another area'
ġeer yoom	'another day, some other day'
ġeer šii	'another thing, something else'
ġeer waaċid	'another one, someone else'

Another pre-noun is *fadd,* which often corresponds, as we have already seen, to the English indefinite article *a* or *an*. It may also correspond to *some,* not in the sense 'an amount of, a portion of' as in *some tea* or *some money,* but in the sense 'some (item or person) or other', for example:

raċ-yruuċuun il-fadd ˀuuteel.	'They're going to go to some hotel.'
laazim tisˀal fadd jaabi.	'You M have to ask some conductor.'

Here are some common *fadd* phrases and their English equivalents:

fadd šii	'a thing, something'
fadd waaċid	'someone'
fadd mudda	'a while'
fadd marra	'a time, one time'
fadd yoom	'a day, one day, some day'

C. DRILLS

Drill 1. Replace the underlined portion by the items given.

raħ-yjiib il-xariiṭa <u>min beeta</u>.	He's going to bring the map <u>from his house</u>.
mnil-beet	from the house
min daaʔirtak	from your M office
mnid-daaʔira	from the office
min baab iš-šarji	from Bab ish-Sharji
mnil-karraada	from Karrada
min safaaratkum	from your P embassy
mnis-safaara	from the embassy
min gahuuta	from his coffee-house
mnil-gahwa	from the coffee-house
min šiqqti	from my apartment
mniš-šiqqa	from the apartment
min hal-uuteel	from this hotel
minnaa	from here
min beetkum	from your P house
minnaak	from there

Drill 2. Repeat the original sentence, then replace the underlined portion by the items given, using the appropriate form of the preposition *min*.

laazim taaxδuun paaṣ min <u>daaʔiratkum</u> lil-karraada.	You P have to take a bus from <u>your P office</u> to Karrada.
s-safaara	*laazim taaxδuun paaṣ imnis-safaara lil-karraada.*
baab iš-šarji	*laazim taaxδuun paaṣ min baab iš-šarji lil-karraada.*
l-maṭaar	*laazim taaxδuun paaṣ imnil-maṭaar lil-karraada.*
hnaa	*laazim taaxδuun paaṣ minnaa lil-karraada.*
hal-manṭiqa	*laazim taaxδuun paaṣ min hal-manṭiqa lil-karraada.*
l-mawqif ihnaak	*laazim taaxδuun paaṣ imnil-mawqif ihnaak lil-karraada.*
beetna	*laazim taaxδuun paaṣ min beetna lil-karraada.*
l-uuteel ij-jidiid	*laazim taaxδuun paaṣ imnil-uuteel ij-jidiid lil-karraada.*
hnaak	*laazim taaxδuun paaṣ minnaak lil-karraada.*
min haš-šaariɛ	*laazim taaxδuun paaṣ min haš-šaariɛ lil-karraada.*
l-ḅang	*laazim taaxδuun paaṣ imnil-ḅang lil-karraada.*

Drill 3. Replace the underlined portion with the items given.

ħsaabkum ysawwi <u>sittiin</u> filis.	Your P check comes to <u>sixty</u> fils.
Ꞓišriin	twenty
tlaaθiin	thirty
ʔarbaꞒiin	forty
xamsa w-arbaꞒiin	forty-five
xamsiin	fifty
sittiin	sixty
xamsa w-sittiin	sixty-five
sabꞒiin	seventy
θmaaniin	eighty
tisꞒiin	ninety
xamsa w-tisꞒiin	ninety-five

Drill 4. Replace the underlined portion with the items given.

laazim nidfaꞒ <u>sabꞒiin</u> diinaar il-yoom.	We have to pay <u>seventy</u> dinars today.
θneen w-sabꞒiin	seventy-two
ʔarbaꞒiin	forty
sitta w-arbaꞒiin	forty-six
tisꞒiin	ninety
waaħid w-tisꞒiin	ninety-one
xamsiin	fifty
θmaanya w-xamsiin	fifty-eight
tlaaθiin	thirty
tlaaθa w-tlaaθiin	thirty-three
sittiin	sixty
ʔarbaꞒa w-sittiin	sixty-four
Ꞓišriin	twenty
sabꞒa w-Ꞓišriin	twenty-seven
θmaaniin	eighty
xamsa w-iθmaaniin	eighty-five

Drill 5. Repeat the sentences, but make every number exactly ten higher than the one given.

Cue:	*ʔariid xamsiin diinaar.*	I want fifty dinars.
Response:	*ʔariid sittiin diinaar.*	I want sixty dinars.

ṣaar-li θneen w-Ꞓišriin saaꞒa hnaa.	*ṣaar-li θneen w-itlaaθiin saaꞒa hnaa.*
jiibi θṃunṭaꞒaš istikaan min beetič.	*jiibi θmaanya w-Ꞓišriin istikaan min beetič.*
tigdar tidfaꞒ sabꞒiin diinaar?	*tigdar tidfaꞒ iθmaaniin diinaar?*

nṭiini ˀarbaƐiin filis, rajaaˀan.	*nṭiini xamsiin filis, rajaaˀan.*
mneen raC-injiib itlaaθiin diinaar?	*mneen raC-injiib arbaƐiin diinaar?*
ṣaar-inna tlaaθa w-xamsiin yoom ihnaa.	*ṣaar-inna tlaaθa w-sittiin yoom ihnaa.*
Csaabna ysawwi θmaaniin filis.	*Csaabna ysawwi tisƐiin filis.*
tgidruun idjiibuun ṣiṭṭaƐaš qalam?	*tgidruun idjiibuun sitta w-Ɛišriin qalam?*
ˀaku ˀarbaƐa w-arbaƐiin safaara hnaak.	*ˀaku ˀarbaƐa w-xamsiin safaara hnaak.*
raC-ašuuf waaCid w-sittiin beet il-yoom.	*raC-ašuuf waaCid w-sabƐiin beet il-yoom.*

Drill 6. Replace the underlined portion with the items given.

raC-nooṣal ihnaak saaƐa <u>xamsa w-nuṣṣ</u>. — We'll arrive there at <u>five-thirty</u>.

xamsa w-rubuƐ	quarter past five
Ɛašra w-rubuƐ	quarter past ten
Ɛašra ˀilla rubuƐ	quarter to ten
sabƐa ˀilla rubuƐ	quarter to seven
sabƐa ˀilla θiliθ	twenty to seven
sabƐa w-θiliθ	twenty past seven
sabƐa w-nuṣṣ	seven-thirty
daƐaš w-nuṣṣ	eleven-thirty
daƐaš w-rubuƐ	quarter past eleven
daƐaš w-θiliθ	twenty past eleven
daƐaš ˀilla θiliθ	twenty to eleven
daƐaš ˀilla rubuƐ	quarter to eleven

Drill 7. Replace the underlined portion with the items given.

laazim awaṣṣilha lil-beet saaƐa <u>sitta w-xamsa</u>. — I have to take her home at <u>five past six</u>.

sitta w-Ɛašra	ten past six
θmaanya w-Ɛašra	ten past eight
θmaanya w-nuṣṣ ˀilla xamsa	twenty-five past eight
θmaanya w-nuṣṣ w-xamsa	twenty-five to nine
ˀarbaƐa w-nuṣṣ w-xamsa	twenty-five to five
xamsa ˀilla Ɛašra	ten to five
θinteen ˀilla Ɛašra	ten to two
θinteen ˀilla xamsa	five to two
θṇaƐaš ˀilla xamsa	five to twelve
θṇaƐaš w-xamsa	five past twelve
θṇaƐaš w-Ɛašra	ten past twelve

Drill 8. Repeat the sentence, but make the times exactly five minutes later than those given.

Cue: *jiib is-sayyaara lil-uuteel saaƐa sabƐa w-Ɛašra.* — Bring M the car to the hotel at ten past seven.

Response: *jiib is-sayyaara lil-uuteel saaƐa sabƐa w-rubuƐ.* — Bring M the car to the hotel at quarter past seven.

jiib is-sayyaara lil-uuteel
saaƐa wiƐda.
jiib is-sayyaara lil-uuteel
saaƐa θinteen w-xamsa.
jiib is-sayyaara lil-uuteel
saaƐa tlaaθa w-Ɛašra.
jiib is-sayyaara lil-uuteel
saaƐa ˀarbaƐa w-rubuƐ.
jiib is-sayyaara lil-uuteel
saaƐa xamsa w-θiliθ.
jiib is-sayyaara lil-uuteel
saaƐa sitta w-nuṣṣ ˀilla xamsa.
jiib is-sayyaara lil-uuteel
saaƐa sabƐa w-nuṣṣ.

jiib is-sayyaara lil-uuteel
saaƐa wiƐda w-xamsa.
jiib is-sayyaara lil-uuteel
saaƐa θinteen w-Ɛašra.
jiib is-sayyaara lil-uuteel
saaƐa tlaaθa w-rubuƐ.
jiib is-sayyaara lil-uuteel
saaƐa ˀarbaƐa w-θiliθ.
jiib is-sayyaara lil-uuteel
saaƐa xamsa w-nuṣṣ ˀilla xamsa.
jiib is-sayyaara lil-uuteel
saaƐa sitta w-nuṣṣ.
jiib is-sayyaara lil-uuteel
saaƐa sabƐa w-nuṣṣ w-xamsa.

Drill 9. Repeat the sentence, but make the times exactly five minutes later than those given.

Cue: *zuheer laazim yruuƐ lid-daaˀira saaƐa tlaaθa w-Ɛašra.* — Zuhayr has to go to the office at ten past three.

Response: *zuheer laazim yruuƐ lid-daaˀira saaƐa tlaaθa w-rubuƐ.* — Zuhayr has to go to the office at quarter past three.

zuheer laazim yruuƐ lid-daaˀira
saaƐa θmaanya w-nuṣṣ w-xamsa.
zuheer laazim yruuƐ lid-daaˀira
saaƐa θmaanya ˀilla θiliθ.
zuheer laazim yruuƐ lid-daaˀira
saaƐa tisƐa ˀilla rubuƐ.
zuheer laazim yruuƐ lid-daaˀira
saaƐa Ɛašra ˀilla Ɛašra.
zuheer laazim yruuƐ lid-daaˀira
saaƐa daƐaš ˀilla xamsa.
zuheer laazim yruuƐ lid-daaˀira
saaƐa θṇaƐaš.

zuheer laazim yruuƐ lid-daaˀira
saaƐa tisƐa ˀilla θiliθ.
zuheer laazim yruuƐ lid-daaˀira
saaƐa θmaanya ˀilla rubuƐ.
zuheer laazim yruuƐ lid-daaˀira
saaƐa tisƐa ˀilla Ɛašra.
zuheer laazim yruuƐ lid-daaˀira
saaƐa Ɛašra ˀilla xamsa.
zuheer laazim yruuƐ lid-daaˀira
saaƐa daƐaš.
zuheer laazim yruuƐ lid-daaˀira
saaƐa θṇaƐaš w-xamsa.

Drill 10. Replace the pre-noun *fadd* 'a, an' with the pre-noun *ġeer* 'another'.

Cue:	*εindi mawεid wiyya fadd waaħid.*	I have an appointment with someone.
Response:	*εindi mawεid wiyya ġeer waaħid.*	I have an appointment with someone else.

jiib-li fadd qalam.	*jiib-li ġeer qalam.*
laazim inruuħ il-fadd ʔuuteel.	*laazim inruuħ il-ġeer ʔuuteel.*
laazim tiħči wiyya fadd waaħid ihnaak.	*laazim tiħči wiyya ġeer waaħid ihnaak.*
tigdar tirkab fadd paaṣ minnaak.	*tigdar tirkab ġeer paaṣ minnaak.*
raħ-ašuufhum fadd yoom bis-safaara.	*raħ-ašuufhum ġeer yoom bis-safaara.*
zuheer yriid yiħči εala fadd šii.	*zuheer yriid yiħči εala ġeer šii.*
ma-tħibbuun iššurbuun fadd šii?	*ma-tħibbuun iššurbuun ġeer šii?*
laazim inwaṣṣilhum il-fadd gahwa.	*laazim inwaṣṣilhum il-ġeer gahwa.*
laazim tisʔal fadd waaħid bid-daaʔira.	*laazim tisʔal ġeer waaħid bid-daaʔira.*
xal-da-rruuħ il-fadd gaaziino.	*xal-da-rruuħ il-ġeer gaaziino.*

Drill 11. Change all the 3 M verb forms to 3 P forms.

yistarxiṣ imnij-jamaaεa s-saaεa xamsa ʔilla rubuε.	*yistarxiṣuun imnij-jamaaεa s-saaεa xamsa ʔilla rubuε.*
w-yidfaε iħsaabhum bil-gahwa.	*w-ydifεuun iħsaabhum bil-gahwa.*
w-yruuħ il-mawqif il-paaṣ.	*w-yruuħuun il-mawqif il-paaṣ.*
w-yisʔal fadd jaabi šloon yooṣal lil-karraada.	*w-ysiʔluun fadd jaabi šloon yooṣluun lil-karraada.*
w-yirkab paaṣ il-baab iš-šarji.	*w-yrukbuun paaṣ il-baab iš-šarji.*
w-baεdeen yirkab ġeer paaṣ lil-karraada.	*w-baεdeen yrukbuun ġeer paaṣ lil-karraada.*
w-yooṣal ihnaak saaεa xamsa w-nuṣṣ.	*w-yooṣluun ihnaak saaεa xamsa w-nuṣṣ.*

Drill 12. Change the 3 M suffixes to 1 S pronoun suffixes.

ʔabu zuheer yšuufa biš-šaariε.	*ʔabu zuheer yšuufni biš-šaariε.*
ʔabu zuheer yšuufa w-ysallim εalee.	*ʔabu zuheer yšuufni w-ysallim εalayya.*
ʔabu zuheer ysallim εalee w-ysiʔla fadd šii.	*ʔabu zuheer ysallim εalayya w-yisʔalni fadd šii.*
ʔabu zuheer ysiʔla šloon šuġḷa.	*ʔabu zuheer yisʔalni šloon šuġḷi.*
baεdeen yruuħ lil-gahwa wiyyaa.	*baεdeen yruuħ lil-gahwa wiyyaaya.*

wil-booy yjiib-la fadd gahwa čilwa.	*wil-booy yjiib-li fadd gahwa čilwa.*
w-ṣadiiqa ʔabu samiira yšuufa hnaak.	*w-ṣadiiqi ʔabu samiira yšuufni hnaak.*
w-ṣadiiqa ʔabu samiira yugčud wiyyaa.	*w-ṣadiiqi ʔabu samiira yugčud wiyyaaya.*
ʔabu samiira yugčud yamma w-yiččí wiyyaa.	*ʔabu samiira yugčud yammi w-yiččí wiyyaaya.*

UNIT 21

A. DIALOGUE

Abu Khalid and Abu Samira are still at the coffee-house, talking.

ʔabu xaalid	Abu Khalid
1. *ween raċ-itruuċ baċad-ma nguum imnil-gahwa?*	Where're you going after we leave the coffee-house?
ʔabu samiira	Abu Samira
bahiija	Bahija (girl's name)
madrasa	school
2. *waḷḷa laazim aruuċ ajiib bahiija mnil-madrasa.*	I have to go and get Bahija from school.
ʔabu xaalid	Abu Khalid
hassa	now
wuṣḷat	she arrived
diraasa	study, studies
3. *gul-li, bahiija hassa ween wuṣḷat ib-diraasatha?*	Tell me, where has Bahija got to in her studies now?
ʔabu samiira	Abu Samira
sana	year
ʔinšaḷḷa	if God wills (see Notes)
titxarraj	she graduates
xaamis	fifth M
4. *has-sana ʔinšaḷḷa titxarraj imnil-xaamis.*	This year she graduates from the fifth grade.

ʔabu xaalid	Abu Khalid
maašaaḷḷaa	whatever God wills (see Notes)
5. *maašaaḷḷaa, maašaaḷḷaa, wiš-raC-issawwi baCdeen?*	Wonderful, wonderful, and what's she going to do afterward?

ʔabu samiira	Abu Samira
txušš	she enters
ṭibbiyya	medical science, (study of) medicine
txaḷḷiṣ	she finishes
6. *triid itxušš biṭ-ṭibbiyya baCad-ma txaḷḷiṣ.*	She wants to go into medicine after she finishes.

NOTES ON DIALOGUE

1. The extremely common expression *ʔinšaḷḷa* is a shorter form of the Classical Arabic phrase *ʔin šaaʔa ḷḷaah,* meaning literally 'if God wills'. It is often used in, or as a response to, sentences telling of some pleasant or desirable event to take place in the future. Sometimes it may correspond to English phrases like "I hope"; sometimes it is best left untranslated. Besides the form *ʔinšaḷḷa* as shown in the dialogue, some speakers use the Classical phrase in its original form, as above, or other forms such as *ʔinšaaḷḷa, ʔinšaaḷḷaa,* or *nšaḷḷa.*

2. The expression *maašaaḷḷaa* is a shorter form of the Classical Arabic phrase *maa šaaʔa ḷḷaah,* meaning 'whatever God wills', with the connotation of "What hath God wrought!" It expresses happy amazement or admiration, and might be translated as "Wonderful!", "Good for you (him, her, etc.)", "Bravo!", or the like.

B. GRAMMAR

1. Conjunctions: Prepositions plus suffix *-ma*

A number of rather common words are formed by the addition of the suffix *-ma* to certain prepositions. The words thus formed have functions in the sentence very much like those of subordinating conjunctions in English, and can be called *conjunctions*. Three of the most common are the following:

Preposition		Conjunction	
baεad	'after'	*baεad-ma*	'after'
gabuḷ	'before'	*gabuḷ-ma*	'before'
miθil	'like, similar to'	*miθil-ma*	'as, in the way that'

In some cases, as in the first two examples above, the English word which functions as a preposition is identical to the English word which functions as a conjunction, but in Iraqi the two forms are distinct. Remember that the preposition is followed immediately by a noun or a pronoun, or has an attached pronoun suffix, while the conjunction is followed (usually immediately) by a verb form. Examples:

baεad šuġḷak	'after your work'
baεad sana	'after a year, a year from now, in a year'
baεad haaδa	'after this'
baεdak	'after you M'
gabuḷ mawεidha	'before her appointment'
gabuḷ yoomeen	'before two days, two days ago'
gabḷi	'before me'
miθil haaδa	'like this one'
miθil beetak	'like your M house'
miθli	'like me'

baεad-ma yiḥčuun fadd mudda	'after they talk a while'
baεad-ma atxarraj	'after I graduate'
baεad-ma nguum	'after we get up'
baεad-ma txaḷḷiṣ	'after she finishes'
gabuḷ-ma yruuḥ lil-beet	'before he goes home'
gabuḷ-ma yooṣḷuun	'before they arrive'
gabuḷ-ma tšuufni	'before she sees me'
miθil-ma triid	'as you wish'
miθil-ma yguuluun	'as they say'
miθil-ma asawwiiha	'the way I do it'

2. Forms of verb stems used with preposition suffix *-l-* 'to, for'

The forms of verb stems used with the preposition suffix *-l-* 'to, for' (13 B 3) are exactly the same in each case as those used with a pronoun suffix. Thus the particular stem changes described in 16 B 5 also apply when *-l-* is added: If the independent form of the verb ends in a short vowel, as in *yiqra* 'he reads', the vowel is lengthened to form the suffixing stem, for example the stem *yiqraa-* as in *yiqraa-li* 'he reads to me' or *yiqraa-lhum* 'he reads to them'. Also, if the independent verb form is an imperfect tense form ending in *-uun* or *-iin* (3 P, 2 F, and 2 P), as in *yiqruun* 'they read', the final *n* is dropped to form the suffixing stem, for example the stem *yiqruu-* as in *yiqruu-lak* 'they read to you M' or *yiqruu-lha* 'they read to her'.

3. Special forms of the verb 'to say' used with preposition suffix *-l-* 'to, for' (1)

The verb 'to say' has some special forms which are used when the preposition suffix *-l-* 'to, for' is added. In the imperfect and the imperative, the forms which otherwise end in *-guul* (*yguul* 'he says', *tguul* 'she says' or 'you M say', *ˀaguul* 'I say', *nguul* 'we say', and *guul* 'say M') have special forms ending in *-gul-* (before a consonant) or *-gull-* (before a vowel). Following is a table showing the forms of *yguul* 'he says' when *-l-* is attached. The other forms listed above are exactly like it.

yguul	'he says'
ygul-la	'he says to him, he tells him'
ygul-lha or *ygull-ilha*	'he says to her, he tells her'
ygul-lhum or *ygull-ilhum*	'he says to them, he tells them'
ygul-lak	'he says to you M, he tells you M'
ygul-lič	'he says to you F, he tells you F'
ygul-lkum or *ygull-ilkum*	'he says to you P, he tells you P'
ygul-li	'he says to me, he tells me'
ygul-lna or *ygull-ilna*	'he says to us, he tells us'

Note: (1) Forms written with two *l*'s followed by a consonant are pronounced exactly as though written with a single *l* followed by a consonant (see 10 E); for example, *ygul-lha* is pronounced *"ygulha"*. (Hyphens are used to indicate certain grammatical divisions and may be ignored in considering matters of pronunciation.) (2) In normal-speed speech, the *l* in a sequence *ln* (or the *ll* in a sequence *lln*) is usually pronounced *n* by assimilation (see 10 A). Thus *ygul-na* and *ygull-ilna* are most commonly pronounced *"ygunna"* and *"ygullinna"*.

Forms of this verb which otherwise end in *-uun, -iin, -i,* or *-u* (*yguuluun* 'they say', *tguuluun* 'you P say', *tguuliin* 'you F say', *guuli* 'say F', and *guulu* 'say P') may remain the same when *-l-* is added (except for the standard dropping of the final *n* or lengthening of the final vowel; see 2 above), or the sequence *-guul-* may change to *-gull-*. Following is a table showing the two variants (both are acceptable) for *yguuluun* 'they say' and *guuli* 'say F'. The other forms listed above behave respectively in the same way.

yguuluun	'they say'
yguuluu-la or *ygulluu-la*	'they say to him, they tell him'
yguuluu-lha or *ygulluu-lha*	'they say to her, they tell her'

yguuluu-lhum or *ygulluu-lhum*	'they say to them, they tell them'
yguuluu-lak or *ygulluu-lak*	'they say to you M, they tell you M'
yguuluu-lič or *ygulluu-lič*	'they say to you F, they tell you F'
yguuluu-lkum or *ygulluu-lkum*	'they say to you P, they tell you P'
yguuluu-li or *ygulluu-li*	'they say to me, they tell me'
yguuluu-lna or *ygulluu-lna*	'they say to us, they tell us'
guuli	'say F'
guulii-la or *gullii-la*	'say F to him, tell F him'
guulii-lha or *gullii-lha*	'say F to her, tell F her'
guulii-lhum or *gullii-lhum*	'say F to them, tell F them'
guulii-li or *gullii-li*	'say F to me, tell F me'
guulii-lna or *gullii-lna*	'say F to us, tell F us'

C. DRILLS

Drill 1. Replace the phrase after *baƐad-ma* with the items given.

gul-li, zuheer, ween raC-itruuC baƐad-ma tišrab il-gahwa? — Tell me, Zuhayr, where are you going after you drink the coffee?

tišrab iš-šaay — *toosal il-baġdaad*
txallis iš-šuġul — *tidfaƐ l-iCsaab*
djiib bahiija mnil-madrasa — *tiqra j-jaraayid*
titxarraj imnil-madrasa — *tiCči wiyya sadiiqak*

Drill 2. Replace the phrase after *gabul-ma* with the items given.

laazim itxallsiin šuġlič gabul-ma truuCiin lis-suug. — You F have to finish your work before you go to the market.

tšurbiin šaay — *tguƐdiin ihnaa*
tiCčiin wiyya bahiija — *tguumiin minnaa*
tiqriin ij-jaraayid — *titxarrjiin imnil-xaamis*
tsawwiin haaδa — *truuCiin lil-beet*

Drill 3. Add *-li* 'to me, for me' to the verb in each of the following, making any necessary changes in the stems.

Cue:	*raC-yjiibuun ij-jaraayid.*	They're going to bring the newspapers.
Response:	*raC-yjiibuu-li j-jaraayid.*	They're going to bring me the newspapers.

tigdar issawwi haaδa?
jiibi fadd istikaan čaay.
xalḷṣu haš-šuġuḷ.
ma-tgidruun idjiibuun is-sayyaara?
ma-raḥ-yiqra j-jaraayid hassa.
la-djiibiin il-gahwa hassa.
laazim iddifʕuun l-iḥsaab.
ma-ygidruun yguuluun haaδa.

Drill 4. Add *-lhum* 'to them, for them' to the verb in each of the following, making any necessary changes in the stems.

Cue:	*raḥ-yjiibuun ij-jaraayid.*	They're going to bring the newspapers.
Response:	*raḥ-yjiibuu-lhum ij-jaraayid.*	They're going to bring them the newspapers.

ma-tgidruun idjiibuun is-sayyaara?
laazim adfaʕ l-iḥsaab.
ma-tgidriin itguuliin haaδa.
xalḷṣi haš-šuġuḷ hassa.
ma-nigdar insawwi haaδa.
baʕdeen raḥ-tiqra j-jaraayid.
jiibi l-xariiṭa, rajaaʔan.
ma-raḥ-yjiibuun il-gahwa?

Drill 5. Add *-la* 'to him' to the verb, making the necessary stem changes.

Cue:	*ma-yigdar yguul haaδa.*	He can't say that.
Response:	*ma-yigdar ygul-la haaδa.*	He can't tell him that.

š-raḥ-itguul hassa?
gul š-itriid.
ʔumm samiira ma-raḥ-itguul haaδa.
baʕdeen nigdar inguul kullši.
guuli š-tirdiin.
guulu š-tirduun.
ma-yguuluun ween yirḥuun.
ma-tgidriin itguuliin šukran?

Drill 6. In the sentences below, change the verb forms to correspond to the cue. Do not repeat the cue itself.

a. *laazim aruuḥ ajiib bahiija mnil-madrasa.* — I have to go and get Bahija from school.

Cue:	*huwwa*	he
Response:	*laazim yruuḥ yjiib bahiija mnil-madrasa.*	He has to go and get Bahija from school.

hiyya	*ʔintu*	*ʔinti*
ʔiḥna	*ʔaani*	*humṃa*
ʔinta	*zuheer w-xaalid*	*ṣadiiqi*
muṣṭafa		*samiira*

b. *has-sana titxarraj imnil-xaamis.* — This year she graduates from the fifth grade.

c. *wiš-raḥ-issawwi baʕdeen?* — And what's she going to do afterward?

d. *triid itxušš biṭ-ṭibbiyya baʕad-ma txalliṣ.* — She wants to go into medicine after she finishes.

UNIT 22

A. DIALOGUE

Abu Khalid asks about Abu Samira's oldest daughter.

ʔabu xaalid	Abu Khalid
sʔaltak	I asked you
ʔaxbaar	news
baʕad	after, since
zawaaj	marriage
1. *gul-li ʔabu samiira, ʔaani ma-sʔaltak, šinu ʔaxbaar samiira, w-išloonha baʕd iz-zawaaj?*	Tell me, Abu Samiira, I haven't asked you, what's the news of Samiira? How is she since the marriage?

ʔabu samiira	Abu Samira
tbayyin	she seems
kulliš	very
mirtaaḥ	happy, contented
2. *zeena lḥamdilla. tbayyin kulliš mirtaaḥa b-zawaajha.*	She's fine, thank you. She seems very happy in her marriage.

ʔabu xaalid	Abu Khalid
ṣaar ʕidha jihaal	it has become (that) she has children
3. *ṣaar ʕidha jihaal loo laa?*	Has she had children?

ʔabu samiira	Abu Samira
waladeen	two boys
bnayya	girl
4. *ʔii, ʕidha waladeen w-ibnayya.*	Yes, she has two boys and a girl.

ʔabu xaalid	Abu Khalid
ʔaḷḷa yxalliihum	God leave them (see Notes)
baʕadhum	they (are) still
gaaʕdiin	sitting P; living P
karradat maryam	Karradat Maryam (section of Baghdad)
tʕawwlaw	they moved
5. *maašaaḷḷaa, ʔaḷḷa yxalliihum. w-baʕadhum gaaʕdiin ib-karradat maryam loo tʕawwlaw?*	Wonderful; God protect them. Are they still living in Karradat Maryam or have they moved?

ʔabu samiira	Abu Samira
6. *laa waḷḷa, baʕadhum ihnaak.*	No, they're still there.

NOTE ON DIALOGUE

Polite formula

ʔaḷḷa yxalliihum This common expression is often used on hearing how many children someone has. It means literally 'God leave them' and implies the wish that God may save the children from danger or death and leave them safely with their parents. If only one boy is involved, the form is *ʔaḷḷa yxallii;* if only one girl, *ʔaḷḷa yxalliiha.*

B. GRAMMAR

1. Perfect tense: Sound verbs (1)

As was stated in 14 B 5, Iraqi verbs have two tenses, perfect and imperfect. We have already seen the forms and some of the uses of the imperfect tense.

The perfect tense generally corresponds to the English simple past (as in *they moved* or *did they move?*) or to the English compound past (as in *they have moved* or *have they moved?*). A verb in the perfect has eight inflectional forms, corresponding to the person-gender-number categories listed in 14 B 5, just as it does in the imperfect. One important difference between the forms of the two tenses is that while the inflections of a verb in the imperfect are characterized by prefixes (and only in some cases also by suffixes), those of a verb in the perfect are characterized solely by suffixes. Following, as an illustration, is the complete perfect tense of the verb 'to ask' and, on the right, a table of the perfect-tense suffixes, which are the same for all verbs.

3	M	*siʔal*	'he asked'	3	M	-ø
	F	*siʔlat*	'she asked'		F	*-at*
	P	*siʔlaw*	'they asked'		P	*-aw*
2	M	*siʔálit*	'you M asked'	2	M	-(*i*)*t*
	F	*siʔalti*	'you F asked'		F	*-ti*
	P	*siʔaltu*	'you P asked'		P	*-tu*
1	S	*siʔálit*	'I asked'	1	S	-(*i*)*t*
	P	*siʔalna*	'we asked'		P	*-na*

The following comments may be made about perfect-tense verb forms:

a. Each form consists of a verb stem and a suffix, except the 3 M form which consists of the stem alone. (In other words, it has no suffix at all, or "zero" suffix, symbolized in the table by -ø.) Thus the 3 M form is the simplest one of all, and the other forms are more or less built on this one. It is for that reason that in conjugations of Arabic verbs the third person is usually given first. Also, the 3 M perfect-tense form of an Arabic verb is the form used to refer to the verb as a whole, in the same way as the infinitive is used in English. Thus in English we speak of the verb *to ask,* but in Arabic one speaks of the verb *siʔal.* The latter form of course literally means 'he asked', but when it is used to refer to the verb as a whole, as in discussing points of grammar or in lists of words, it is usually translated as an infinitive in English: the verb *siʔal* 'to say'.

b. As is shown by the 3 M form, the basic perfect stem for this verb is *siʔal-*. In stems of this pattern (CvCvC-), the stem vowel *a* is dropped when the 3 F and 3 P suffixes are added: *siʔlat* 'she asked' and *siʔlaw* 'they asked'.

c. The 2 M and 1 S forms are always identical: *siʔálit* 'you M asked' or 'I asked'. The stress falls on the next-to-last vowel of this word and all other perfect verb forms ending in *-it*. In some verbs, like the one just cited, this results in non-automatic stress (see 9 C), and the position of stress in such words is therefore indicated by an accent mark. However, if a 2 M or 1 S verb form ending in *-it* is followed by a pronoun suffix beginning with a vowel, or by another word beginning with a (helping) vowel, the vowel *i* of the verb suffix is dropped:

siʔaltak	'I asked you M'
siʔalt ij-jaabi	'I asked the conductor'

In these new forms, the stress conforms to the automatic stress rule and need not be marked.

d. In perfect verb stems of the pattern CiCaC- or CuCaC-, the first vowel is often dropped in normal-speed speech, except in the (third-person) forms where that vowel bears the stress. This elision is particularly common when a preceding word or prefix ends in a vowel, for example *ma-sʔaltak* 'I didn't ask you M'. In this book we shall write the full forms in conjugations like that above, and the elided form where appropriate in context.

Other verbs conjugated like *siʔal* which we have had so far are (imperfect 3 M forms shown in parentheses):

difaƐ (*yidfaƐ*)	'to pay'
gidar (*yigdar*)	'to be able, can'
giƐad (*yugƐud*)	'to sit, sit down'
wuṣal (*yooṣal*)	'to arrive'
ʔaxaδ (*yaaxuδ*)	'to take'

Some verbs are conjugated like *siʔal* in the perfect except that the vowel *i* in the first syllable of the stem changes to *u* in the 3 F and 3 P forms. To illustrate this, the conjugation of *širab* (*yišrab*) 'to drink' is shown below:

3	M	*širab*	'he drank'
	F	*šurbat*	'she drank'
	P	*šurbaw*	'they drank'
2	M	*širábit*	'you M drank'
	F	*širabti*	'you F drank'
	P	*širabtu*	'you P drank'
1	S	*širábit*	'I drank'
	P	*širabna*	'we drank'

Exactly like this, of the verbs we have had so far, is:

rikab (*yirkab*)	'to ride, get on'

Iraqi verbs fall into four inflectional types. The verbs in each type share similar features in their perfect and imperfect inflections. The inflectional type of any verb may be recognized by the ending of the citation form (the perfect-tense 3 M form) of that verb. Verbs like those above which end in a single consonant preceded by the vowel *a*, for example *siʔal* 'to ask' and *širab* 'to drink', belong to the type called **sound verbs.** The other three types will be discussed later.

2. The particle *baċad* 'still, yet' plus pronoun suffixes

We have seen that pronoun suffixes may be attached to noun stems to indicate possession, and to verb and preposition stems to indicate the object. Pronoun suffixes may also be attached to a few particles (non-inflected words) other than prepositions. One of these is *šloon* 'how', which has occurred in previous lessons, for example *šloonak?* 'How are you M?'. Another is the particle *baċad* 'still, yet', for example *baċadhum ihnaak.* 'They are still there.' The stem of this particle is *baċad-* with pronoun suffixes beginning with a consonant, and *baċd-* with those beginning with a vowel. With *baċad*, the first person singular pronoun suffix has the form *-ni*. Following is a complete list of the forms:

3	M	*baċda*	'he still'
	F	*baċadha*	'she still'
	P	*baċadhum*	'they still'
2	M	*baċdak*	'you M still'
	F	*baċdič*	'you F still'
	P	*baċadkum*	'you P still'
1	S	*baċadni*	'I still'
	P	*baċadna*	'we still'

Here are a few additional examples:

baċda bid-daaʔira.	'He's still at the office.'
baċadkum gaaċdiin bil-karrada?	'Are you P still living in Karrada?'
baċadni mašġuuḷ.	'I'm still busy.'

C. DRILLS

Drill 1. In the following sentences, change the 3 M perfect verb form first to 3 F and next to 3 P, making any other necessary changes.

Cue:	*siʔal yaa paaṣ yooṣal lil-karraada.*	He asked which bus goes to Karrada.
Response 1:	*siʔlat yaa paaṣ yooṣal lil-karraada.*	She asked which bus goes to Karrada.
Response 2:	*siʔlaw yaa paaṣ yooṣal lil-karraada.*	They asked which bus goes to Karrada.

ʔaxaδ paaṣ raqam itlaaθa l-baab iš-šarji.
wuṣal ihnaak saaʕa xamsa w-nuṣṣ.
ma-gidar yiḥči wiyyaaya l-yoom.
giʕad wiyyaahum bid-daaʔira.
difaʕ l-iḥsaab bil-ʔuuteel.
w-baʕdeen širab istikaan čaay.
rikab ġeer paaṣ lil-karraada.
ma-siʔal ween il-ḅang?

Drill 2. In the following sentences, change the 2 M perfect verb form first to 2 F and next to 2 P, making any other necessary changes.

Cue:	*siʔálit yaa paaṣ laazim taaxuδ?*	Did you M ask which bus you have to take?
Response 1:	*siʔalti yaa paaṣ laazim taaxδi?*	Did you F ask which bus you have to take?
Response 2:	*siʔaltu yaa paaṣ laazim taaxδu?*	Did you P ask which bus you have to take?

ma-wṣalit lil-beet saaʕa xamsa?
širábit gahwa loo čaay?
ma-gdarit tiqra j-jaraayid?
difaʕt iḥsaabak loo laa?
giʕádit wiyyaahum bil-beet?
ʔaxáδit paaṣ raqam sitta?
yaa paaṣ rikábit baʕdeen?
ma-sʔalit fadd waaḥid bis-safaara?

Drill 3. In the following sentences, change the 1 S perfect verb form to 1 P, making any other necessary changes.

Cue:	*siʔalt il-booy.*	I asked the waiter.
Response:	*siʔalna l-booy.*	We asked the waiter.

wuṣálit lil-maṭaar saaʕa tlaaθa w-nuṣṣ.
difáʕit sittiin filis bil-gahwa.
ma-gdarit adfaʕ l-iḥsaab.
širábit biira l-yoom.
ʔaxáδit xariiṭa jdiida.
rikábit paaṣ raqam iθṇaʕaš.
siʔalt išgadd iḥsaabi.
giʕádit wiyyaahum bil-gahwa.

Drill 4. In the sentences below, change the perfect verb forms to correspond to the cue. Do not repeat the cue itself.

a. *wuṣalna lis-safaara saaʕa tisʕa.* — We arrived at the embassy at nine o'clock.

Cue:	*huwwa*	he
Response:	*wuṣal lis-safaara saaʕa tisʕa.*	He arrived at the embassy at nine o'clock.

hiyya	*ʔumm samiira*	*ʔaani*
xaalid	*ʔaani w-zuheer*	*ʔintu*
ʔiḥna	*ʔinta w-zuheer*	*humma*
ʔinta	*zuheer w-xaalid*	*ʔinti*

b. *ʔaxaðna ġeer paaṣ lil-karraada.* — We took another bus to Karrada.

c. *baʕdeen rikabna paaṣ raqam ṣiṭṭaʕaš.* — Then we got on bus number sixteen.

d. *širabna gahwa ḥilwa.* — We drank sweet coffee.

e. *ma-difaʕna l-iḥsaab.* — We didn't pay the bill.

Drill 5. In the sentences below, change the imperfect verb forms to the corresponding perfect.

Cue:	*ʔasʔal ṣadiiqi zuheer.*	I ask my friend Zuhayr.
Response:	*siʔálit ṣadiiqi zuheer.*	I asked my friend Zuhayr.

ma-ašrab biira bil-uuteel.
ʔabu xaalid yugʕud wiyyaana.
nirkab paaṣ il-baab iš-šarji.
yooṣluun lid-daaʔira saaʕa θmaanya.
ʔumm xaalid tidfaʕ l-iḥsaab.
ma-tgidriin tiḥčiin wiyyaaya?
yaa paaṣ taaxðuun minnaa?
nisʔal ṣadiiqna xaalid.

Drill 6. Change the pronoun suffix on *baʕad* to correspond to the cue. Do not repeat the cue itself.

baʕadhum bis-suug. — They're still at the market.

Cue:	*hiyya*	she
Response:	*baʕadha bis-suug.*	She's still at the market.

ʔabu xaalid	*ṣadiiqi*	*humma*
ʔaani	*zuheer w-ṣadiiqa*	*ʔinta*
ʔiḥna	*ʔintu*	*ʔaani*
ʔumm bahiija	*samiira*	*ʔinti*

UNIT 23

A. DIALOGUE

Abu Samira asks Abu Khalid about his children.

ʔabu samiira	**Abu Samira**
ʔibtidaaʔiyya	elementary F
1. *zeen abu xaalid, il-maħruusiin ween raħ-yirħuun baʕad-ma yxaḷḷṣuun il-madrasa l-ibtidaaʔiyya?*	Well, Abu Khalid, where are the children going to go after they finish elementary school?
ʔabu xaalid	**Abu Khalid**
θneenaathum	both of them, they both
θaanawiyya	secondary school, high-school
2. *xawla w-raasim iθneenaathum yirduun yxuššuun biθ-θaanawiyya.*	Khawla and Rasim both want to go to high-school.
ʔabu samiira	**Abu Samira**
ydirsuun	they study
3. *w-baʕad iθ-θaanawiyya š-raħ-ydirsuun?*	And after high-school what are they going to study?
ʔabu xaalid	**Abu Khalid**
yidrus	he studies
ħuquuq	law
miθil	like
ʔaxuu	his brother
ʔuxta	his sister
daar il-muʕallimiin il-ʕaaliya	Teachers' College
4. *raasim yriid yidrus ħuquuq miθl axuu č-čibiir, w-uxta triid itxušš ib-daar il-muʕallimiin il-ʕaaliya.*	Rasim wants to study law like his big brother, and his sister wants to enter Teachers' College.

ʔabu samiira	Abu Samira
tṣawwárit	I thought, imagined
da-yidrus	he is studying
handasa	engineering
5. *ʔoo, ʔaani ṣṣawwárit xaalid da-yidrus handasa.*	Oh, I thought Khalid was studying engineering.
ʔabu xaalid	Abu Khalid
jaayya	coming, next F
kulliyat il-Ꞓuquuq	College of Law
yqaddim ɛala	he applies for
biɛθa	scholarship, grant
ʔameerka	America, the U. S.
6. *laa, muu handasa. s-sana j-jaayya raꞒ-yxaḷḷiṣ kulliyat il-Ꞓuquuq, w-baɛdeen yriid yqaddim ɛala biɛθa l-ameerka.*	No, not engineering. Next year he'll finish law school, and then he wants to apply for a scholarship to the States.

B. GRAMMAR

1. Perfect tense: Sound verbs (2)

The perfect forms of sound verbs of the pattern CvCvC were described in 22 B 1. In this lesson we describe the perfect forms of other sound verbs, for example *xaḷḷaṣ* 'to finish' or *starxaṣ* 'to ask permission'. In the stems of all sound verbs, the stem vowel (always *a*) is dropped when the perfect 3 F and 3 P endings *-at* and *-aw* are added, unless this would result in three (different) consonants in a row, in which case the *a* is changed to either *i* or *u*. Thus *xallṣat* 'she finished' but *starxiṣat* 'she asked permission'. Following are the complete perfect conjugations of these two verbs:

3	M	*xallaṣ*	'he finished'	*starxaṣ*	'he asked permission'
	F	*xaḷḷṣat*	'she finished'	*starxiṣat*	'she asked permission'
	P	*xaḷḷṣaw*	'they finished'	*starxiṣaw*	'they asked permission'
2	M	*xaḷḷáṣit*	'you M finished'	*starxáṣit*	'you M asked permission'
	F	*xaḷḷaṣti*	'you F finished'	*starxaṣti*	'you F asked permission'
	P	*xaḷḷaṣtu*	'you P finished'	*starxaṣtu*	'you P asked permission'
1	S	*xaḷḷáṣit*	'I finished'	*starxáṣit*	'I asked permission'
	P	*xaḷḷaṣna*	'we finished'	*starxaṣna*	'we asked permission'

Following is a list of verbs thus far introduced which are conjugated in the perfect like *xallaṣ* (imperfect forms in parentheses). We have not yet had any others like *starxaṣ* (*yistarxiṣ*).

xallaṣ	(*yxalliṣ*)	'to finish'
baddal	(*ybaddil*)	'to change'
bayyan	(*ybayyin*)	'to seem'
waṣṣal	(*ywaṣṣil*)	'to convey'
sallam *ɛala*	(*ysallim*)	'to greet'
qaddam *ɛala*	(*yqaddim*)	'to apply for'
txarraj	(*yitxarraj*)	'to graduate'
tɛawwal	(*yitɛawwal*)	'to move (one's residence)'
ṭṣawwar	(*yiṭṣawwar*)	'to imagine, think'

Note the following points about these verbs and others like them:

a. The perfect stem vowel in all cases is *a*. The imperfect stem vowel is *i* or *u* (no examples of the latter yet) except for verbs which begin with *t* or *ṭ* followed by another consonant, for example *txarraj,* in which case the imperfect stem vowel is *a*: *yitxarraj*.

b. The initial *t* of verbs like the last three in the list above may assimilate (see 10 A) to the following consonant in various ways. Before an emphatic it may become *ṭ,* as in *ṭṣawwar,* or it may assimilate completely and become identical to the following consonant, for example *ṣṣawwar* (*yiṣṣawwar*). This complete assimilation is common in normal-speed speech, especially when a vowel precedes. We shall write the unassimilated or partially assimilated forms in tables and vocabularies, and the completely assimilated forms where appropriate in context.

2. Progressive prefix *da-*

The prefix *da-* is used with imperfect verb forms. It indicates progressive action; that is, action going on at the moment of speech, or action going on "these days, nowadays" as opposed to an earlier or later period. It may often be translated into English by a phrase consisting of a form of *to be* with an *-ing* form. The plain imperfect tense without any prefix, on the other hand, usually indicates habitual action not necessarily going on at the moment of speech, or facts of more or less timeless validity. Here are some examples of both:

yišrab biira.	'He drinks beer.'	*da-yišrab biira.*	'He's drinking beer.'
tiɛči hwaaya.	'She talks a lot.'	*da-tiɛči wiyyaa.*	'She's talking with him.'

kullši ma-ssawwi.	'You don't do anything.'	*š-da-ssawwi?*	'What are you doing?'
ma-yidrus ihwaaya.	'He doesn't study much.'	*da-yidrus handasa.*	'He's studying engineering.'

3. Suffixing stems of *ˀax* 'brother' and *ˀab* 'father'

The two nouns *ˀax* 'brother' and *ˀab* 'father' are unusual in that they have special stems *ˀaxuu-* and *ˀabuu-,* used with the pronoun suffixes. As these stems end in a vowel, the pronoun suffixes have the forms appropriate to such stems (see 16 B 4), as follows:

ˀaxuu	'his brother'	*ˀabuu*	'his father'
ˀaxuuha	'her brother'	*ˀabuuha*	'her father'
ˀaxuuhum	'their brother'	*ˀabuuhum*	'their father'
ˀaxuuk	'your M brother'	*ˀabuuk*	'your M father'
ˀaxuuč	'your F brother'	*ˀabuuč*	'your F father'
ˀaxuukum	'your P brother'	*ˀabuukum*	'your P father'
ˀaxuuya	'my brother'	*ˀabuuya*	'my father'
ˀaxuuna	'our brother'	*ˀabuuna*	'our father'

Note also the following points:

a. For the form *ˀaxi* see 13 Note 1.

b. Before another noun in the meaning 'father of', *ˀab* has the form *ˀabu,* as in the common forms of address like *ˀabu zuheer.*

c. The form *ˀabuuna* 'our father' is used in addressing a Christian priest.

4. Noun-adjective phrases: Agreement in definiteness (2)

In a noun-adjective phrase, if the noun is definite, the adjective is also definite (see 17 B 3). A noun is definite when it has the article prefix, and it is also definite when it has a pronoun suffix; thus a following adjective must have the article prefix in either case. Compare the following:

l-beet ič-čibiir	'the big house'	*beethum ič-čibiir*	'their big house'
s-saaƐa j-jidiida	'the new watch'	*saaƐti j-jidiida*	'my new watch'
l-yoom il-xaamis	'the fifth day'	*ˀaxuu č-čibiir*	'his big brother'
l-ibnayya l-iṣġayyra	'the little girl'	*ˀuxutha l-iṣġayyra*	'her little sister'

C. DRILLS

Drill 1. In the sentences below, change the verb forms to correspond to the cue. Do not repeat the cue itself.

a. *xaḷḷaṣ il-madrasa l-ʔibtdaaʔiyya.* He's finished elementary school.

Cue:	*hiyya*	she
Response:	*xaḷḷṣat il-madrasa l-ʔibtidaaʔiyya.*	She's finished elementary school.

huṃṃa	*ʔuxti*	*ṣadiiqna*
ʔaani	*ʔiḥna*	*ʔinta*
ʔintu	*ʔaxuuya*	*xawla*
zuheer	*ʔinti*	*muṣṭafa w-xaalid*

b. *qaddam ʕala biʕθa l-ameerka.* He's applied for a scholarship to America.

c. *has-sana txarraj imnil-xaamis.* This year he graduated from the fifth grade.

d. *baʕdeen itḥawwal minnaak il-karraadat maryam.* Afterward he moved from there to Karradat Maryam.

e. *ʔaxaδ paaṣ raqam itlaaθa w-baʕdeen baddal.* He took bus number three and then changed.

Drill 2. In the following sentences change the imperfect verb forms to the corresponding perfect forms.

Cue:	*raḥ-yitxarraj imnil-xaamis.*	He's going to graduate from the fifth grade.
Response:	*itxarraj imnil-xaamis.*	He has graduated from the fifth grade.

ysallim ʕala ʔabu xaalid.	*ma-ssallmiin ʕala ʔumm zuheer?*
yistarxiṣ imnij-jamaaʕa s-saaʕa xamsa.	*tšurbiin gahwa loo čaay?*
ʔuxti raḥ-titxarraj has-sana.	*raḥ-itḥawwluun has-sana?*
samiira raḥ-itqaddim ʕala biʕθa.	*raḥ-itxaḷḷṣuun il-madrasa has-sana?*
da-ydirsuun handasa b-bağdaad.	*ʔaṣṣawwar xaalid b-ameerka has-sana.*
raḥ-yxaḷḷṣuun kulliyyat il-ḥuquuq.	*ʔašrab biira bil-uuteel.*
yaa paaṣ raḥ-taaxuδ minnaak?	*ma-nidfaʕ l-iḥsaab.*
ma-raḥ-itqaddim ʕala biʕθa?	*nsallim ʕala ṣadiiqna.*

Drill 3. In the following sentences change the plain imperfect verb forms, or those preceded by *raħ-*, to progressive forms (*da-* plus imperfect).

Cue: *yišrab biira.* — He drinks beer.
Response: *da-yišrab biira.* — He's drinking beer.

yiqra j-jaraayid ij-jidiida.
yiħči wiyya ʔabuu bid-daaʔira.
yišrab šarbat bil-gaaziino.
samiira tiqra j-jaraayid ij-jadiida.
tiħči wiyya ʔabuuha bid-daaʔira.
tišrab gahwa bil-uuteel.
ma-tišrab biira.
ʔinta raħ-tidrus handasa?
š-raħ-issawwi hnaak?
ma-ššuuf is-sayyaara?
niqra j-jaraayid ij-jidiida.
niħči wiyya ṣadiiqna zuheer.
raħ-asʔal il-booy.
ma-ašuufhum.
ydirsuun handasa bil-kulliyya.
yiħčuun wiyya ʔaxuuhum.

Drill 4. Add the pronoun suffix *-na* 'our' to the noun, and make the necessary change in the modifying adjective, as in the example.

Cue: *haaδi sayyaara jdiida.* — This is a new car.
Response: *haaδi sayyaaratna j-jidiida.* — This is our new car.

haaδa beet jidiid.
haaδa beet čibiir.
haaδi madrasa čbiira.
haaδi madrasa jdiida.
haaδa ṣadiiq jidiid.
haay šiqqa ṣġayyra.
haay xariiṭa čbiira.
haaδa ʔuuteel iṣġayyir.
haay sayyaara zeena.
haaδa beet ʕatiig.
haaδi safaara jdiida.
haay safaara ʕatiiga.
haaδa beet iṣġayyir.
haay madrasa ṣġayyra.
haay šiqqa čbiira.
haaδi xariiṭa jdiida.

Drill 5. Replace *l-maħruusiin* with the items given, making the necessary changes in the verb forms.

l-maħruusiin ween raħ-yirħuun baʕad-ma yxaḷḷṣuun il-madrasa l-ʔibtidaaʔiyya? — Where are the children going to go after they finish elementary school?

zuheer	*ʔinta*	*ʔiħna*	*ʔaani w-uxti*
xawla	*ʔinti*	*samiira*	*ʔaxuuč l-isġayyir*
xawla w-raasim	*ʔintu*	*l-maħruusiin*	*ʔaxuu č-čibiir*
ʔaani	*ʔaxuuk*	*ʔuxtak*	*ʔinta*

Drill 6. In each of the following sentences, replace the underlined portion with the items given, making the necessary changes in the verbs and pronouns.

a. *<u>xawla w-raasim</u> yirduun yxuššuun biθ-θaanawiyya.* — Khawla and Rasim want to enter secondary school.

zuheer	*l-maCruusiin*	*ṣadiiqi*
xawla	*l-walad*	*zuheer w-muṣṭafa*
ʔaani	*l-ibnayya*	*zuheer w-muṣṭafa θneenaathum*
ʔaani w-axuuya	*ʔiCna*	*xaalid*

b. *<u>raasim</u> yriid yidrus Cuquuq miθl axuu č-čibiir.* — Rasim wants to study law like his big brother.

c. *<u>ʔuxta</u> triid itxušš ib-daar il-muCallimiin il-Caaliya.* — His sister wants to enter Teachers' College.

d. *<u>xaalid</u> xaḷḷaṣ kulliyat il-Cuquuq w-qaddam Cala biCθa l-ameerka.* — Khalid finished law school and applied for a scholarship to America.

UNIT 24

A. DIALOGUE

Abu Khalid hails a taxi and dickers with the driver about the fare.

<u>ʔabu xaalid</u>	<u>Abu Khalid</u>
š-soorja	Shorja (section of Baghdad)
1. *šgadd taaxuδ minnaa liš-šoorja, ʔaxiʔ*	How much will you charge from here to Shorja?
<u>s-saayiq</u>	<u>The driver</u>
š-ma	whatever
2. *š-ma tidfaC Cammi.*	Whatever you pay, sir.
<u>ʔabu xaalid</u>	<u>Abu Khalid</u>
Catta	so (that), in order that
ʔaCruf	I know
3. *laa, laa, guul išgadd taaxuδ Catta aCruf.*	No, no, say how much you'll charge so I'll know.

s-saayiq	The driver
tlaθ-miit-filis	three hundred fils
4. *tlaθ-miit-filis. zeen, ʕammi?*	Three hundred fils. Okay, sir?
ʔabu xaalid	Abu Khalid
miiteen	two hundred
5. *laa, haay ihwaaya.* *kull yoom adfaʕ miiteen.*	No, that's too much. I pay two hundred every day.
s-saayiq	The driver
ma-yxaalif	it doesn't matter, makes no difference
6. *zeen, ʕammi, ma-yxaalif.* *tfaḍḍal.*	All right, sir, that's all right. Hop in.

B. GRAMMAR

1. Conjunctions: Interrogatives plus suffix *-ma*

Certain conjunctions may be formed by adding the suffix *-ma* not only to prepositions (see 21 B 1), but also to interrogatives. An example occurs in the dialogue of this lesson: *š-ma,* which consists of the interrogative *š-* 'what?' and the suffix *-ma.* Depending on the context, *š-ma* might be translated 'whatever', 'anything (that)', or 'no matter what'; and other conjunctions of this type have a similar range of English equivalents. Here is a list of the most common interrogatives which may combine with *-ma* to form conjunctions. Some of these interrogatives have not appeared before, and you should learn them now.

Interrogatives		**Conjunctions**	
š-	'what?'	*š-ma*	'whatever, anything (that)'
minu	'who?'	*minu-ma*	'whoever, anyone who(m)'
ween	'where?'	*ween-ma*	'wherever, anywhere (that)'
šwakit	'when?'	*šwakit-ma*	'whenever, any time (that)'
šloon	'how?'	*šloon-ma*	'however, any way (that)'
šgadd	'how much?'	*šgadd-ma*	'however much, any amount (that)'

Here are some short illustrations of these. Sentences containing an interrogative are on the left, and sentences containing the corresponding conjunction are on the right.

š-itriid?	'What do you want?'	*ʔuxuδ iš-ma triid.*	'Take whatever you want.'
minu raꞒ-yruuꞒ?	'Who's going to go?'	*minu-ma yriid yigdar yruuꞒ.*	'Anyone who wants can go.'
ween nigdar nugɛud?	'Where can we sit?'	*nigdar nugɛud ween-ma nriid.*	'We can sit anywhere we want.'
šwakit raꞒ-tooṣal?	'When will she arrive?'	*ʔagdar ašuufha šwakit-ma tooṣal.*	'I can see her whenever she arrives.'
šloon raꞒ-itgul-la?	'How are you going to tell him?'	*šloon-ma tgul-la zeen.*	'Any way you tell him is all right.'
šgadd laazim ajiib-lak?	'How much do I have to bring you?'	*ʔajiib-lak išgadd-ma triid.*	'I'll bring you as much as you want.'

2. Noun plurals: General comments

There are two main ways of forming the plurals of Iraqi nouns. One is by adding a plural suffix to the singular stem of the noun, with relatively minor change, if any, to the stem itself. For example, *maꞒruus* '(male) child' has the plural *maꞒruusiin* 'children', and *maṭaar* 'airport' has the plural *maṭaaraat* 'airports'. This kind of plural, formed with a suffix, is called a **sound plural.** The other kind of plural is formed by a partial or complete change of the vowels in the word, somewhat like English *tooth* and *teeth.* For example, *walad* 'boy' has the plural *wulid* 'boys', and *madrasa* 'school' has the plural *madaaris* 'schools'. This kind of plural, formed by a change in the vowel pattern, is called a **broken plural**. The two types are taken up in more detail below.

3. Sound masculine plurals: Suffixes *-iin* and *-a*

A great many masculine nouns which refer to male human beings form their plural by the addition of the suffix *-iin,* and these are known as **masculine sound plurals.** We have had two so far:

Singular		**Plural**	
maꞒruus	'child'	*maꞒruusiin*	'children'
muɛallim	'teacher'	*muɛallimiin*	'teachers'

When this suffix is added to a stem, the stem vowel (short *i, u, a*) is usually dropped, unless the result would be three different consonants in a row. In certain words the dropping is optional; thus for 'teachers' one may hear either *muɛallimiin* or *muɛallmiin*. A noun ending in the suffix *-iin* refers to a group of human beings who are all males, or to a group in which there is at least one male.

Some masculine nouns referring to human beings form their plural by the addition of the suffix *-a*; these are also considered masculine sound plurals. When this suffix is added to a stem ending in *i*, the stem adds *yy* before the *-a*. We have had one example:

gahawči	'coffee-house proprietor'	*gahawčiyya*	'coffee-house proprietors'

4. Sound feminine plurals: Suffix *-aat*

A great many feminine nouns which refer to female human beings form their plural by the addition of the suffix *-aat*, and these are known as **feminine sound plurals**. This suffix is also used, however, to form the plural of a great many nouns (both masculine and feminine) which do not refer to human beings, and even of a few nouns which refer to males. Following are lists of nouns thus far introduced which form their plural with the suffix *-aat*. The first group below consists of feminine nouns whose singular ends in *a*. This vowel is dropped when the suffix *-aat* is added:

Singular		**Plural**	
maɛruusa	'(female)' child'	*maɛruusaat*	'(female) children'
ṣadiiqa	'(female) friend'	*ṣadiiqaat*	'(female) friends'
bnayya	'girl'	*bnayyaat* (or *banaat*)	'girls'
muɛallima	'(female) teacher'	*muɛallimaat*	'(female) teachers'
ṃarra	'time'	*ṃarraat*	'times'
sayyaara	'car'	*sayyaaraat*	'cars'
safaara	'embassy'	*safaaraat*	'embassies'
jamaaɛa	'group'	*jamaaɛaat*	'groups'
biṭaaqa	'ticket'	*biṭaaqaat*	'tickets'
saaɛa	'hour; watch'	*saaɛaat*	'hours; watches'
p̣anka	'fan'	*p̣ankaat*	'fans'
kulliyya	'college'	*kulliyyaat*	'colleges'
biɛθa	'scholarship'	*biɛθaat*	'scholarships'

The next group consists of masculine nouns not referring to human beings:

stikaan	'tea-glass'	*stikaanaat*	'tea-glasses'
talafoon	'telephone'	*talafoonaat*	'telephones'
gḷaaṣ	'glass'	*gḷaaṣaat*	'glasses'
ˀuuteel	'hotel'	*ˀuuteelaat*	'hotels'
maṭaar	'airport'	*maṭaaraat*	'airports'
paaṣ	'bus'	*paaṣaat*	'busses'

The last group contains nouns whose stems undergo particular changes when the suffix *-aat* is added. The first refers to a female person; the second is a feminine noun not referring to a person; and the last two are masculine nouns referring to a male person.

ˀumm	'mother'	*ˀummahaat*	'mothers'
gaaziino	'gaaziino'	*gaaziinowwaat*	'gaaziinos'
ˀab	'father'	*ˀabbahaat*	'fathers'
ˀuṣṭa	'master'	*ˀuṣṭawaat*	'masters'

The feminine noun *ˀiid* 'hand' has a plural formed by the addition of the dual suffix:

ˀiid	'hand'	*ˀiideen*	'hands'

(The dual form of this noun is usually *ˀiidteen.*)

5. Broken plurals

As we said above, a broken plural is one with a vowel pattern different from that of the singular, for example *walad* 'boy' and *wulid* 'boys'. Some broken plurals also have additional consonant material at the beginning or end or in the middle, for example *ṣadiiq* 'friend' and *ˀaṣdiqaaˀ* 'friends', or *jariida* 'newspaper' and *jaraayid* 'newspapers'. The task of learning broken plurals is not as difficult as it might seem at first, as there are only a dozen or so common broken plural patterns, and in many cases it is possible to tell from the singular pattern of a noun what kind of a broken plural it has. For example, many singulars with three consonants and a long vowel in the second syllable (*jariida* 'newspaper'), or with four consonants and all short vowels (*madrasa* 'school') have a broken plural of the pattern CaCaaCiC (*jaraayid* 'newspapers', *madaaris* 'schools'. Such clues are helpful, but in the beginning stages one must simply learn each plural along with the singular, as they occur.

Listed below are the nouns we have had up to now which have broken plurals. Those with the same or very similar plural patterns are grouped together, except for the last group, which contains a number of different patterns.

Singular		**Plural**	
šuġuḷ	'work, job'	*ˀašġaaḷ*	'jobs'
rubuƐ	'quarter'	*ˀarbaaƐ*	'quarters'
xabar	'item of news'	*ˀaxbaar*	'news'
raqam	'number'	*ˀarqaam*	'numbers'
yoom	'day'	*ˀayyaam*	'days'
šii	'thing'	*ˀašyaaˀ*	'things'
qalam	'pencil'	*qlaam*	'pencils'
Ɛamm	'(paternal) uncle'	*Ɛmaam*	'(paternal) uncles'
nuṣṣ	'half'	*nṣaaṣ*	'halves'
suug	'market'	*swaag*	'markets'
ḅang	'bank'	*bunuug*	'banks'
filis	'fils (sing.)'	*fluus*	'fils (plu.) ; money
beet	'house'	*byuut*	'houses'
šiqqa	'apartment'	*šiqaq*	'apartments'
mudda	'period of time'	*mudad*	'periods of time'
mawqif	'stop'	*mawaaqif*	'stops'
mawƐid	'appointment'	*mawaaƐid*	'appointments'
manṭiqa	'area'	*manaaṭiq*	'areas'
madrasa	'school'	*madaaris*	'schools'
šaariƐ	'street'	*šawaariƐ*	'streets'
daaˀira	'office'	*dawaaˀir*	'offices'
jariida	'newspaper'	*jaraayid*	'newspapers'
xariiṭa	'map'	*xaraayiṭ*	'maps'
gahwa	'coffee-house'	*gahaawi*	'coffee-houses'
walad	'boy'	*wulid*	'boys'
jaahil	'baby, child'	*jihaal*	'babies, children'
sayyid	'gentleman; Mr.'	*saada*	'gentlemen; Messrs.'
sana	'year'	*sniin*	'years'
ṣadiiq	'friend'	*ˀaṣdiqaaˀ*	'friends'
ˀax	'brother'	*ˀuxwa*	'brothers' (real)
		ˀixwaan	'brothers' (figurative)
ˀuxut	'sister'	*xawaat*	'sisters'

6. Numerals from 'three' to 'ten': Combining forms

The numerals from 'three' to 'ten' have two forms each. One is the independent form, listed in 18 B 5. The other, somewhat shorter, is the **combining form,** used when the counted noun follows immediately. For example, the independent form for 'three' is *tlaaaθa,* but in a phrase like 'three girls' the combining form *tlaθ-* is used: *tlaθ-banaat.* The noun following one of these numerals is in its plural form—which is not the case, as we have seen, when it follows a higher numeral. Here is a list of both the independent and the combining forms of these numerals, and some examples of numerals followed by nouns:

	Independent	**Combining**		
'three'	*tlaaθa*	*tlaθ-*	*tlaθ-wulid*	'three boys'
'four'	*ˀarbaƐa*	*ˀarbaƐ-*	*ˀarbaƐ-jaraayid*	'four newspapers'
'five'	*xamsa*	*xam(i)s-*	*xams-ifluus*	'five fils'
'six'	*sitta*	*sitt-*	*sitt-isniin*	'six years'
'seven'	*sabƐa*	*sab(i)Ɛ-*	*sabƐ-ibyuut*	'seven houses'
'eight'	*θmaanya*	*θman-*	*θman-saaƐaat*	'eight hours'
'nine'	*tisƐa*	*tis(i)Ɛ-*	*tisiƐ-ṃarraat*	'nine times'
'ten'	*Ɛašra*	*Ɛaš(i)r-*	*Ɛašir-muƐallmiin*	'ten teachers'

Note the following points about the combining forms of these numerals:

a. Four of the forms have a stem vowel *i,* shown above in parentheses. This vowel occurs whenever the following noun begins with a single consonant, as in the last two examples above, since otherwise there would be three consonants in a row. It is dropped whenever the following form begins with a vowel (including a helping vowel), as in the examples for 'five' and 'seven' above.

b. The final *θ* of *tlaθ-* and the final *tt* of *sitt-* may assimilate partially or completely to a following *t, ṭ, d, θ, δ, δ̣, s, ṣ, z, š, č, j,* for example *tlad-daqaayiq* 'three minutes', *tlas-saaƐaat* 'three hours', *siss-saaƐaat* 'six hours', *sidd-jaraayid* 'six newspapers'.

c. A few nouns have special plurals called **counting forms,** used only after one of the combining forms above. Among these are *tarbaaƐ* 'quarters', as in *tlat-tarbaaƐ* 'three quarters', and *tiyyaam* 'days', as in *sabiƐ-tiyyaam* 'seven days'.

7. Numerals: The hundreds

The independent form for 'one hundred' is *miyya,* and the combining form *miit-.* The independent form for 'two hundred' is *miiteen,* with the usual dual ending; there is no special combining form. The independent forms for 'three hundred' to 'nine hundred' consist of the combining forms of the numerals from 'three' to 'ten' (see 2 above) with the form *miyya,* for example *tlaθ-miyya* 'three hundred'. When a counted noun follows immediately, the word for hundred also occurs in its combining form, for example *tlaθ-miit-sana* 'three hundred years'. The noun following any numeral higher than 'ten' is in the *singular* form, not the plural as in English. Here is a list of the independent and combining forms, with examples.

	Independent	**Combining**	
'100'	*miyya*	*miit-ṃarra*	'a hundred times'
'200'	*miiteen*	*miiteen sana*	'two hundred years'
'300'	*tlaθ-miyya*	*tlaθ-miit-filis*	'three hundred fils'
'400'	*ˀarbaƐ-miyya*	*ˀarbaƐ-miit-yoom*	'four hundred days'
'500'	*xamis-miyya*	*xamis-miit-walad*	'five hundred boys'
'600'	*sitt-miyya*	*sitt-miit-ibnayya*	'six hundred girls'
'700'	*sabiƐ-miyya*	*sabiƐ-miit-saaƐa*	'seven hundred hours'
'800'	*θman-miyya*	*θman-miit-beet*	'eight hundred houses'
'900'	*tisiƐ-miyya*	*tisiƐ-miit-biṭaaqa*	'nine hundred tickets'

Numbers between the multiples of a hundred, from 'one hundred one' to 'nine hundred ninety-nine', are expressed by phrases consisting of one of the even hundreds as above, then the prefix *w-* 'and', then the appropriate lower numeral or numeral phrase (20 B 2), for example:

miyya w-waaƐid	'one hundred one'
miyya w-iθneen	'one hundred two'
miiteen w-itlaaθa	'two hundred three'
ˀarbaƐ-miyya-w-sabƐa	'four hundred seven'
xamis-miyya w-ṣiṭṭaƐaš	'five hundred sixteen'
sitt-miyya w-Ɛišriin	'six hundred twenty'
sabiƐ-miyya w-tisƐa w-xamsiin	'seven hundred fifty-nine'

With a counted noun, the following constructions occur:

a. If the final number involved is 'one', several constructions are possible; a common one is:

tlaθ-miit-yoom w-yoom	'three hundred one days'
sitt-miit-sana w-sana	'three hundred one years'

b. If the final number involved is 'two', one of the possible constructions is:

tlaθ-miit-yoom w-yoomeen	'three hundred two days'
tlaθ-miit-sana w-santeen	'three hundred two years'

c. If the final numeral involved is one of those between 'three' and 'ten', the numeral is in its combining form, and the noun is plural:

tlaθ-miyya w-itlaθ-wulid	'three hundred three boys'
sabiε-miyya w-xamis saaεaat	'seven hundred five hours'

d. If the final numeral is a teen or a multiple of ten, no combining forms are involved, and the following noun is singular:

ʔarbaε-miyya w-daεaš walad	'four hundred eleven boys'
xamis-miyya w-iθṇaεaš ibnayya	'five hundred twelve girls'
θman-miyya w-waaħid w-εišriin yoom	'eight hundred twenty-one days'
tisiε-miyya w-xamsa w-sittiin saaεa	'nine hundred sixty-five hours'

C. DRILLS

Drill 1. In the following sentences, replace the portions underlined with the items given, and make any other necessary changes.

a. *<u>ʔuxuδ</u> š-ma triid.* — <u>Take M</u> whatever you M want.

ʔuxδi	*jiib*	*ʔidfaε*	*ʔišrab*
ʔuxδu	*jiibi*	*difεi*	*šurbi*
ʔuxuδ	*jiibu*	*difεu*	*šurbu*

b. *minu-ma yriid yigdar <u>yruuħ</u>.* — Anyone who wants can <u>go</u>.

yugεud	*yiqra j-jaraayid*	*ysallim εalee*
yguum	*yjiib sayyaarta*	*yqaddim εaleeha*
yirkab	*yidrus handasa*	*yruuħ lil-beet*

c. *nigdar <u>nugεud</u> ween-ma nriid.* — We can <u>sit</u> wherever we want.

nruuħ	*nšuufhum*	*nxalliihum*
nirkab	*niħči wiyyaahum*	*nqaddim εala biεθa*
nidrus	*nišrab gahwa*	*nugεud*

Drill 2. In the following sentences, change the pronoun suffixes to correspond to the cue, and make any other necessary changes. Do not repeat the cue.

a. *ˀagdar ašuufha šwakit-ma tooṣal.* I can see her whenever she arrives.

Cue:	*zuheer*	Zuhayr
Response:	*ˀagdar ašuufa šwakit-ma yooṣal.*	I can see him whenever he arrives.

ˀinta	*l-wulid*	*huwwa*	*raasim w-xawla*
huṃṃa	*ˀinti*	*ˀintu*	*ˀabuuya*
ˀumm xaalid	*ˀinti-w-axuuč*	*hiyya*	*ˀinta w-axuuk*

b. *šloon-ma tgul-la zeen.* Any way you M tell him is all right.
c. *ˀajiib-lak išgadd-ma triid.* I'll bring you M as much as you M want.

Drill 3. In the following sentences change the numeral to correspond to the cue.

a. *ʕidhum itlaθ-wulid.* They have three boys.

Cue:	*ˀarbaʕa*	four
Response:	*ʕidhum ˀarbaʕ-wulid.*	They have four boys.

xamsa	*θmaanya*	*tlaaθa*
sitta	*tisʕa*	*ˀarbaʕa*
sabʕa	*ʕašra*	

b. *txarrájit baʕad itlaθ-isniin.* I graduated after three years.
c. *raʕ-nooṣal baʕad itlaθ-saaʕaat.* We'll arrive in three hours.
d. *sˀalta tlaθ-ṃarraat.* I've asked him three times.

Drill 4. Change the numeral to the next higher.

Cue:	*ʕidhum itlaθ-wulid.*	They have three boys.
Response:	*ʕidhum ˀarbaʕ-wulid.*	They have four boys.

laazim inšuuf xams-ibyuut il-yoom.	*ʕidna waladeen biθ-θaanawiyya.*
zuheer yiqra tlaθ-jaraayid kull yoom.	*ˀaxuuya yidrus sitt-saaʕaat kull yoom.*
nṭiini ˀarbaʕ-ifluus rajaaˀan.	*txarrajna gabuḷ iθman-isniin.*
laazim nisˀal tisiʕ-muʕallmiin.	*raʕ-niʕči wiyya sabiʕ-banaat.*

Drill 5. Change the hundreds numeral to correspond to the cue.

a. *kull yoom adfaʕ miit-filis.* Every day I pay a hundred fils.

Cue:	*θneen*	two
Response:	*kull yoom adfaʕ miiteen filis.*	Every day I pay two hundred fils.

sitta	*tlaaθa*	*θmaanya*
ˀarbaʕa	*xamsa*	*waaḥid*
tisʕa	*sabʕa*	*xamsa*
waaḥid	*θneen*	*tisʕa*

b. *ˀaku miit-walad bil-madrasa θ-θaanawiyya.* — There are a hundred boys in the high school.

c. *ˀaku miit-muʕallim bil-madaaris wil-kulliyyaat.* — There are a hundred teachers in the schools and colleges.

Drill 6. Change the singular noun to the plural, preceded by the appropriate form of *xamsa* 'five'.

Cue:	*jiib-li gḷaaṣ*	Bring me a glass.
Response:	*jiib-li xams igḷaaṣaat.*	Bring me five glasses.

ˀaku maṭaar ihnaa.	*haaδa ma-yiswa filis.*
ˀaku ˀuuteel ib-hal-manṭiqa.	*raḥ-atxarraj baʕad sana.*
ma-ariid aqra jariida.	*laazim adrus saaʕa l-yoom.*
šloon il-maḥruus?	*ma-tḥibb tiḥči wiyya l-muʕallim?*

UNIT 25

A. NARRATIVE

yibquun — they stay

1. *ˀabu samiira w-abu xaalid yibquun nuṣṣ saaʕa bil-gahwa,* — Abu Samira and Abu Khalid stay half an hour at the coffee-house,

ʕala — about, concerning

2. *w-yiḥčuun ʕala wulidhum w-banaathum.* — and talk about their sons and daughters.

3. *w-baʕdeen waaḥid minhum yruuḥ yjiib bitta mnil-madrasa.* — Then one of them goes to get his daughter from school.

θaani — second, other
ˀabu t-taksi — the taxi driver

4. *wiθ-θaani yisˀal abu t-taksi šgadd yaaxuδ liš-šoorja.* — The other asks the taxi driver how much he charges to Shorja.

5. *w-ygul-la šgadd yidfaƐ kull yoom,*	He tells him how much he pays every day,
6. *w-yaaxuδ taksi w-yruuC.*	and takes a taxi and goes off.

B. GRAMMAR

1. Perfect tense: Hollow verbs

In 22 B 1 and 23 B 1 we described the perfect tense of sound verbs like *siʔal* 'to ask' and *txarraj* 'to graduate'. Now we begin to take up the perfect tense of the three other inflectional types. One of these is known as **hollow verbs,** and includes all those verbs whose citation forms end in a single consonant preceded by the long vowel *aa,* for example *raaC* 'to go' and *jaab* 'to bring'. Hollow verbs with the pattern CaaC, like the two just mentioned, have two perfect stems. One stem is CaaC-, which is used with the third-person endings; and the other is either CiC- or, in only a few verbs, CuC-, which is used with the endings of the other persons. For example: *raaCat* 'she went', but *riCna* 'we went'. Given below is the full perfect conjugation of *raaC* 'to go' (stems *raaC* and *riC-*) and *gaam* 'to get up' (stems *gaam* and *gum-*):

3	M	*raaC*	'he went'	*gaam*	'he got up'
	F	*raaCat*	'she went'	*gaamat*	'she got up'
	P	*raaCaw*	'they went'	*gaamaw*	'they got up'
2	M	*riCit*	'you M went'	*gumit*	'you M got up'
	F	*riCti*	'you F went'	*gumti*	'you F got up'
	P	*riCtu*	'you P went'	*gumtu*	'you P got up'
1	S	*riCit*	'I went'	*gumit*	'I got up'
	P	*riCna*	'we went'	*gumna*	'we got up'

Following is a list of all the hollow verbs of the pattern CaaC which have occurred thus far. Of these, only *gaam* has the vowel *u* in its shorter stem; all the others are conjugated in the perfect exactly like *raaC*. In the list below, two forms appear within parentheses after each verb. The first of these is the perfect 2 M (or 1 S) form, to show whether the shorter stem has the vowel *i* or *u,* and the second is the imperfect 3 M form, to show the vowel of the imperfect.

baas (*bisit ybuus*)	'to kiss'	*gaam* (*gumit yguum*)	'to get up'
raaC (*riCit yruuC*)	'to go'	*jaab* (*jibit yjiib*)	'to bring'
šaaf (*šifit yšuuf*)	'to see'	*raad* (*ridit yriid*)	'to want'
gaal (*gilit yguul*)	'to say'	*ṣaar* (*ṣirit yṣiir*)	'to become'

Note that some hollow verbs of the pattern CaaC have the long vowel *uu* in the imperfect and others the long vowel *ii*. A few others, which we have not yet had, have the long vowel *aa* in the imperfect. These are facts which must be learned for each verb.

2. Perfect-tense verbs with pronoun suffixes

When a pronoun suffix (or the preposition suffix -(*i*)*l*- 'to, for' plus a pronoun suffix) is added to a verb in the perfect tense, the verb form as a whole functions as a stem and may undergo certain stem changes, as follows:

a. A 3 M verb form ending in -*aC* (a consonant preceded by a short *a*) with a pronoun suffix beginning with a vowel has the stress on the last vowel of the verb stem, for example *siˀal* 'he asked' but *siˀála* 'he asked him'. This is one of the important exceptions to the automatic stress rule (see 3 F and 9 C). With a pronoun suffix beginning with a consonant, such verbs also have stress on the last vowel of the verb stem, but this is a regular shift in accordance with the automatic stress rule, and thus need not be marked: *siˀalha* 'he asked her'. Further examples:

siˀal	'he asked'	*siˀálak*	'he asked you M'
waṣṣal	'he took, conveyed'	*waṣṣálič*	'he took you F'

b. The same facts about stress are also true of 3 F verb forms, all of which end in -*at*. Examples:

siˀlat	'she asked'	*siˀláta*	'she asked him'
šurbat	'she drank'	*šurbáta*	'she drank it M'
šaafat	'she saw'	*šaafátak*	'she saw you M'
waṣṣlat	'she took, conveyed'	*waṣṣlátič*	'she took you F'

c. 2 M and 1 S forms, all of which end in -*it*, drop the vowel of the ending when a pronoun suffix beginning with a vowel is added, for example *siˀálit* 'you M asked, I asked' but *siˀalta* 'you M asked him, I asked him'. (For the stress in such verbs see 22 B 1 c.) Further examples:

siˀálit	'you M, I asked'	*siˀaltak*	'I asked you M'
šifit	'you M, I saw'	*šiftič*	'I saw you F'
xaḷḷáṣit	'you M, I finished'	*xaḷḷaṣta*	'you M, I finished it M'

d. The 2 F, 2 P, and 1 P forms all end in a vowel, for example *šifna* 'we saw'. When a pronoun suffix is added to one of these, the final vowel becomes long, for example *šifnaaha* 'we saw her'. The stem of such verb forms is thus a vowel stem, and the pronoun suffixes themselves have the forms which go with vowel stems (see 16 B 4 and 5). Further examples:

*si*ˀ*alti*	'you F asked'	*si*ˀ*altii*	'you F asked him'
*si*ˀ*altu*	'you P asked'	*si*ˀ*altuuna*	'you P asked us'
šifna	'we saw'	*šifnaak*	'we saw you M'
jibna	'we brought'	*jibnaa-lak*	'we brought to you M'

e. The 3 P forms all end in *-aw,* for example *si*ˀ*law* 'they asked'. When a pronoun suffix is added, this ending changes to *-oo,* and the form thus becomes a vowel stem like those above. Examples:

*si*ˀ*law*	'they asked'	*si*ˀ*loo*	'they asked him'
jaabaw	'they brought'	*jaaboo-la*	'they brought to him'
šaafaw	'they saw'	*šaafooč*	'they saw you F'

3. Special forms of *gaal* 'to say' used with preposition suffix *-l-* 'to, for' (2)

In 21 B 3 we saw that the imperfect and imperative forms of the verb 'to say' have some special stems used when the preposition suffix *-l-* 'to, for' is added. The same is true of the perfect forms, for example *gaal* 'he said' but *gal-la* 'he said to him'. These forms are illustrated below, with the ending *-la* 'to him' serving as a model for *-l-* plus any pronoun suffix beginning with a vowel, and *-(i)lha* 'to her' as a model for *-l-* plus any pronoun suffix beginning with a consonant. Note that in most cases there are two possible forms for each verb.

		With *-l-* and vowel suffix	With *-l-* and consonant suffix
3 M	*gaal*	*gal-la*	*gal-lha* *gall-ilha*
F	*gaalat*	*gaalat-la* *gallat-la*	*gaalat-ilha* *gallat-ilha*
P	*gaalaw*	*gaaloo-la* *galloo-la*	*gaaloo-lha* *galloo-lha*

2 M	*gilit*	*gilit-la* *gitt-la*	*gilt-ilha* *gitt-ilha*
F	*gilti*	*giltii-la* *gittii-la*	*giltii-lha* *gittii-lha*
P	*giltu*	*giltuu-la* *gittuu-la*	*giltuu-lha* *gittuu-lha*
1 S	*gilit*	*gilit-la* *gitt-la*	*gilt-ilha* *gitt-ilha*
P	*gilna*	*gilnaa-la*	*gilnaa-lha*

The 1 P forms are commonly pronounced *ginna, ginnaa-la, ginnaa-lha* (see 10 A).

C. DRILLS

Drill 1. In the sentences below, change the verb forms from 3 M to 1 S, and make any other necessary changes.

Cue:	*raaȻ lil-beet is-saaƐa xamsa.*	He went home at five o'clock.
Response:	*riȻit lil-beet is-saaƐa xamsa.*	I went home at five o'clock.

ma-raaȻ wiyyaahum lil-gahwa.
šaaf il-wulid bil-madrasa.
jaab ij-jihaal wiyyaa.
ṣaar muƐallim miθil abuu.
jaabhum imnil-kulliyya.
šaafak wiyya l-muƐallimiin.
ma-gaal haaδa.
gaam is-saaƐa sitta w-nuṣṣ.

Drill 2. Change the verb forms to correspond to the cue, and make any other necessary changes.

a. *jaab axuu lil-kulliyya.* He brought his brother to the college.

Cue:	*samiira*	Samira
Response:	*jaabat axuuha lil-kulliyya.*	She brought her brother to the college.

xaalid	*l-muƐallim*	*l-wulid*	*l-banaat*
ˀaani	*ˀiȻna*	*ˀintu*	*ˀinta*
ˀinti	*hiyya*	*huwwa*	*ˀumm muṣṭafa*

b. *raaȻ liš-soorja wiyya ˀuxta.* He went to Shorja with his sister.

c. *ma-raad yaaxuδ taksi lil-uuteel.* He didn't want to take a taxi to the hotel.

d. *šaaf sayyaara ṣġayyra yamm beeta.* He saw a little car by his house.

Drill 3. Change each imperfect verb form to the corresponding perfect.

Cue: *yriid sayyaara jdiida.* He wants a new car.
Response: *raad sayyaara jdiida.* He wanted a new car.

ˀašuuf il-wulid bil-madrasa.
samiira ma-tguul haaδa.
baƐad arbaƐ-isniin inṣiir muƐallimiin.
ma-yguumuun is-saaƐa sitta?
tirƐiin wiyyaahum?
zuheer yjiib axuu wiyyaa.
ˀinta ma-tšuuf ij-jaraayid?
ˀintu ma-tbuusuun ij-jihaal?

Drill 4. Repeat each sentence, changing the noun object first to the 3 M pronoun suffix, then the 3 F, then the 3 P.

Cue: *šifit xaalid bil-madrasa.* I saw Khalid at school.
Response 1: *šifta bil-madrasa.* I saw him at school.
Response 2: *šifitha bil-madrasa.* I saw her at school.
Response 3: *šifithum bil-madrasa.* I saw them at school.

jibit zuheer wiyyaaya.
jibti zuheer wiyyaač?
jibtu zuheer wiyyaakum?
jibna zuheer wiyyaana?
šaaf il-muƐallim bil-kulliyya.
šaafat il-muƐallim bil-kulliyya.
šaafaw il-muƐallim bil-kulliyya.
šifna l-muƐallim bil-kulliyya.

Drill 5. Change the noun object to the pronoun suffix corresponding to the cue.

a. *siˀal il-muƐallim.* He asked the teacher.

Cue: *ˀaani* I.
Response: *siˀalni.* He asked me.

ˀinta	*ˀaani*	*ˀinti*	*l-muƐaalimiin*
ˀinti	*ˀiƐna*	*ˀabu xaalid*	*ˀinta*
ˀintu	*huwwa*	*ˀumm xaalid*	*ˀaani*

b. *ˀaxδaw il-walad wiyyaahum?* Did they take the boy with them?
c. *šaafat ij-jaahil biš-saariƐ.* She saw the child in the street.

Drill 6. To the verb form add first *-li* 'to me' and then *-lhum* 'to them'.

Cue: *ma-gaal ihwaaya.* He didn't say much.
Response 1: *ma-gal-li hwaaya.* He didn't tell me much.
Response 2: *ma-gall-ilhum ihwaaya.* He didn't tell them much.

ma-gaalat ihwaaya.
ma-gaalaw ihwaaya.
ma-gilt ihwaaya.
ma-gilti hwaaya.
ma-giltu hwaaya.
ma-ginna hwaaya.
ma-gilt ihwaaya.
ma-gaal ihwaaya.

UNIT 26

A. DIALOGUE

Abu Khalid and his wife visit Abu Mustafa and his wife to discuss a family matter. Umm Khalid and Umm Mustafa are sisters; the latter has a daughter, Zahda.

ʔabu xaalid — Abu Khalid

1. *ʔinšaaḷḷa mawδuuɛ iz-zawaaj xiḷaṣ, ʔumm muṣṭafa.* — I hope the matter of the marriage has been settled, Umm Mustafa.

ʔumm muṣṭafa — Umm Mustafa

2. *laa, waḷḷa, baɛadna da-nfakkir bii.* — No, actually we're still thinking about it.

ʔumm xaalid — Umm Khalid

3. *šgadd raḥ-iδδilluun itfakkruun bii, šahar, šahreen?* — How long are you going to go on thinking about it, a month, two months?

ʔumm muṣṭafa — Umm Mustafa

4. *walla ma-nuɛruf š-raḥ-insawwi.* — Really we don't know what we're going to do.

ʔabu xaalid — Abu Khalid

5. *leeš? ʔaku šii jdiid?* — Why? Is there something new?

ʔabu muṣṭafa — Abu Mustafa

6. *bali, zaahda hassa da-yirduuha θneen, w-ma-da-nuɛruf il-man ninṭiiha.* — Yes, now there are two who want Zahda, and we don't know whom to give her to.

VOCABULARY

(New vocabulary items from the dialogue are listed above the dotted line. Additional items, for use in drills, appear below the line. The plural of nouns is shown in parentheses after the singular. Verbs are listed in the perfect-tense 3 M form, followed by the imperfect-tense 3 M form in parentheses. In the case of hollow verbs, the perfect 2 M form is also given, preceding the imperfect 3 M form. If a verb in a certain meaning is always followed by a particular preposition, the latter is given as the last item of the entry, without parentheses, for example *sallam* (*ysallim*) *Ɛala* 'to greet'; if a verb can occur, depending on context, with or without a particular preposition, the latter is given in parentheses, as in *fakkar* below.)

mawδ̣uuƐ (*mawaaδ̣iiƐ*)	matter, subject
xiḷaṣ (*yixḷaṣ*)	to be settled, finished
fakkar (*yfakkir*) (*b-*)	to think (about), consider
δ̣all (*yδ̣ill*)	(with imperfect verb) to continue, go on (doing something)
šahar (*ˀašhur*; counting form *tušhur*)	month
Ɛiraf (*yuƐruf*)	to know
leeš	why?
ˀil-man	to whom; whom
niṭa (*yinṭi*)	to give

---

dazz (*ydizz*)	to send
sadd (*ysidd*)	to close
f̣akk (*yf̣ukk*)	to open
Ɛaṭṭ (*yƐuṭṭ*)	to put
baġdaad	Baghdad
l-Ɛiraaq	Iraq

Note on dialogue

Family and marriage in Iraq. Family ties are very strong in Iraq, as generally throughout the Middle East, and the family unit includes not just the parents and children but the uncles, aunts, and cousins as well. All the older family members frequently participate in decisions which are thought to be of importance to the family as a whole. One such matter would be the marriage of a daughter. Marriages are still "arranged" to a certain extent by the two families involved, but the feelings of the young people themselves are a prime consideration, and very few parents nowadays would force their daughter into a match which she opposed.

B. GRAMMAR

1. Annexions

Note the following constructions from this and previous units:

(a)	*stikaan čaay*	'a glass of tea'
(b)	*gḷaaṣ liban baarid*	'a glass of cold yoghurt'
(c)	*mawqif il-paaṣ*	'the bus stop'
(d)	*mawδ̣uuƐ iz-zawaaj*	'the matter of the marriage'
(e)	*kulliyyat il-Ɛuquuq*	'the Law College'
(f)	*daar il-muƐallimiin il-Ɛaaliya*	'the Teachers' College' ("the high institution of the teachers")
(g)	*ʔabu t-taksi*	'the taxi driver'
(h)	*ʔabu zuheer*	'Zuhayr's father'
(i)	*ʔaxbaar samiira*	'the news of Samira'

These are all examples of a kind of construction called an **annexion.** We have already seen how a noun may be modified by an adjective in a noun-adjective phrase, for example *gḷaaṣ čibiir* 'a big glass'. In an annexion, on the other hand, a noun is modified by another noun, for example *gḷaaṣ liban* 'a glass of yoghurt', or *mawδ̣uuƐ iz-zawaaj* 'the matter of the marriage'. Thus an annexion, in its most basic form, is a phrase consisting of two nouns, the first being modified in some way by the second. An annexion almost always corresponds to one of three types of English constructions. The first is a phrase in which the first noun has the possessive ending *'s* or *s',* as in (f) and (h) above. Other examples:

ʔumm muṣṭafa	'Mustafa's mother'
ʔuxut bahiija	'Bahija's sister'
ʔiid il-jaahil	'the child's hand'
šuğuḷ il-banaat	'the girls' work'

The second is a construction in which the second noun is the object of the preposition *of,* as in (a), (b), (d), and (i) above. Other examples:

muddat yoomeen	'a period of two days'
kulliyyat il-handasa	'the college of engineering'

The third is a construction of two nouns immediately juxtaposed, the first modifying the second, as in (c), (e), and (g) above. Some combinations of this sort are written as single compound words in English, with or without a hyphen; others are written as separate words. Other examples:

saaɛat ʔiid	'a wristwatch'
maṭaar baġdaad	'the Baghdad airport'

Note that in the three types of English constructions the order of modifying noun and modified noun varies: in the first and third types the modified noun follows the modifier, while in the second type it precedes. In the Arabic annexion, however, regardless of how it may be translated into English, the modified noun always precedes the modifier. Below are several other points to be noted about annexions:

a. Definiteness. The first noun in an annexion may be definite or indefinite, but it never has the article prefix or a pronoun suffix. It is definite if the second noun is definite. The second noun is definite when:

(1) it has the article prefix:

saaɛt il-iid	'the wristwatch'

(2) it has a pronoun suffix:

mawḏuuɛ zawaajha	'the matter of her marriage'
madrasat wulidhum	'their children's school'

(3) it is a proper name:

ʔuxut xaalid	'Khalid's sister'
maṭaar baġdaad	'the Baghdad airport'

Otherwise the second noun is indefinite, and so therefore is the first:

saaɛat ʔiid	'a wristwatch'
glaaṣ liban	'a glass of yoghurt'

b. Adjective agreement. Either noun in an annexion may be modified by an adjective, which agrees in the usual way with its noun as to gender and definiteness (see 17 B 3 and 23 B 4). An annexion, however, is a tightly knit construction, and cannot be divided by an adjective. Therefore, if the first noun is modified by an adjective, the latter comes after the whole annexion, for example:

saaCat ˀiid jidiida	'a new wristwatch'
maṭaar baġdaad ij-jidiid	'the new Baghdad airport'
ˀuxut xaalid l-iṣġayyra	'Khalid's little sister'

If the second noun is modified by an adjective, the latter comes immediately after it in the usual way. This is the same position as for an adjective modifying the first noun, and occasionally there is some ambiguity, but usually the gender of the adjective or the context will show which noun the adjective modifies. Examples:

gḷaaṣ liban baarid	'a glass of cold yoghurt'
sayyaarat ˀaxuuya č-čibiir	'my big brother's car'

c. Annexing forms. Certain words, or classes of words, have special **annexing forms** used when they are the first noun of an annexion. All feminine nouns ending in *-a* have an annexing form ending in *-at;* for example *sayyaara* 'car' becomes *sayyaarat*:

sayyaarat zuheer	'Zuhayr's car'

The vowel in the *-at* ending is usually dropped if the following word begins with a (helping) vowel, as long as that would not result in a cluster of more than two consonants:

sayyaart is-safaara	'the embassy car'

The two words *ˀab* 'father' and *ˀab* 'brother' have annexing forms *ˀabu* and *ˀaxu* respectively:

ˀabu zuheer	'Zuhayr's father'
ˀaxu mCammad	'Muhammad's brother'

Notice the similarity of these annexing forms to the suffixing stems described in 19 B 3 and 23 B 3.

2. Preposition *b-* 'in' with pronoun suffixes

The preposition *b-* (see 15 B 1), which often corresponds to English 'in' but in some contexts is translated by various other English prepositions, has a special stem *bii-* for use with pronoun suffixes. This stem changes to *biy-* before the 1 S suffix *-ya*. Here are the forms:

3	M	*bii*	'in him'
	F	*biiha*	'in her'
	P	*biihum*	'in them'
2	M	*biik*	'in you M'
	F	*biič*	'in you F'
	P	*biikum*	'in you P'
1	S	*biyya*	'in me'
	P	*biina*	'in us'

3. Perfect tense: Doubled verbs

Verbs like *dazz* 'to send' (see vocabulary above), which end in a double consonant, are known as **doubled verbs.** In the perfect tense, the stem of doubled verbs remains unchanged before the 3 F and 3 P endings *-at* and *-aw,* for example *dazzat* 'she sent' and *dazzaw* 'they sent'. Before the other endings, however, the stem adds *-ee-,* for example *dazzeet* 'you M sent' or 'I sent', and *dazzeena* 'we sent'. Here is the full conjugation:

3	M	*dazz*	'he sent'
	F	*dazzat*	'she sent'
	P	*dazzaw*	'they sent'
2	M	*dazzeet*	'you M sent'
	F	*dazzeeti*	'you F sent'
	P	*dazzeetu*	'you P sent'
1	S	*dazzeet*	'I sent'
	P	*dazzeena*	'we sent'

In doubled verbs of the pattern CaCC (like *dazz*), the vowel before the double consonant is always *a* in the perfect tense, but in the imperfect it is *i* in some verbs, *u* in others, and *a* in only one. Given below is a list of all such doubled verbs which we have had thus far, with the 3 M imperfect form given in parentheses with each:

dazz	(*ydizz*)	'to send'
cabb	(*ycibb*)	'to like, love'
ḍall	(*yḍill*)	'to continue'
sadd	(*ysidd*)	'to close'

f̣akk	*(yf̣ukk)*	'to open'
ḥaṭṭ	*(yḥuṭṭ)*	'to put'
gaṣṣ	*(yguṣṣ)*	'to cut'
xašš	*(yxušš) b-*	'to enter'

C. DRILLS

Drill 1. Replace the noun after *mawδ̣uuʕ* with the items given.

ʔinšaaḷḷa mawδ̣uuʕ iz-zawaaj xiḷaṣ. I hope the matter of the marriage has been settled.

il-kulliyya	the college
il-biʕθa	the scholarship
is-sayyaara	the car
it-talafoon	the telephone
il-biṭaaqa	the ticket
l-iḥsaab	the bill
is-saaʕa	the watch
ij-jariida	the newspaper
il-madrasa	the school
iz-zawaaj	the marriage

Drill 2. Change the following sentences to contain an annexion, as in the example:

Cue: *zuheer ʕinda sayyaara.* Zuhayr has a car.
Response: *haay sayyaarat zuheer.* This is Zuhayr's car.

xaalid ʕinda šiqqa.
bahiija ʕidha šuğuḷ.
ʔaxuuya ʕinda biṭaaqa.
ʔuxti ʕidha kulliyya.
l-ibnayya ʕidha xariiṭa.
j-jihaal ʕidhum iqlaam.
ʔumm xaalid ʕidha ʔaxbaar.
ʔabu muṣṭafa ʕinda sayyaara.

Drill 3. Change the following sentences so that the adjective modifies the first noun in the annexion, as in the example:

Cue: *maṭaar bağdaad jidiid.* The Baghdad airport is new.
Response: *haaδa maṭaar bağdaad ij-jidiid.* This is the new Baghdad airport.

kulliyyat bağdaad ʕatiiga.
ʔuxut xaalid iṣğayyra.
beet axuuya jdiid.
šiqqat axuuya jdiida.
safaarat ameerka čbiira.
xariiṭat ameerka jdiida.
mawδ̣uuʕ iz-zawaaj ʕatiig.
ʔuuteel bağdaad čibiir.

Drill 4. Change the pronoun suffix on *baƐad-* and the verb form to correspond to the cue.

baƐadna da-nfakkir bii. We're still thinking about it.

Cue: *bahiija* Bahija
Response: *baƐadha da-tfakkir bii.* She's still thinking about it.

zuheer	*ˀinta*	*ˀiCna*	*Ɛammi*
ˀaani	*ˀinti*	*l-muƐallimiin*	*hiyya*
j-jihaal	*ˀintu*	*ˀumm xaalid*	*ˀabuuha*

Drill 5. Change the verb form to correspond to the cue.

a. *dazz il-wulid lil-kulliyya.* He sent the boys to the college.

Cue: *ˀaani* I
Response: *dazzeet il-wulid lil-kulliyya.* I sent the boys to the college.

ˀiCna	*ˀaani*	*ˀinta*
ˀumm musṭafa	*ˀinti*	*ˀabuuhum*
ˀintu	*humma*	*l-muƐallimiin*

b. *ween Caṭṭ il-jariida?* Where did he put the newspaper?
c. *leeš ma-sadd il-baab?* Why didn't he close the door?
d. *ḍall yfakkir bii šahreen.* He went on thinking about it for two months.

Drill 6. Change each perfect verb form to *raC-* with the corresponding imperfect.

Cue: *dazz banaata liθ-θaanawiyya.* He sent his daughters to high school.

Response: *raC-ydizz banaata liθ-θaanawiyya.* He's going to send his daughters to high school.

saddat baab is-sayyaara.
gaṣṣeet biṭaaqa maal manṭiqteen?
šwakit xaššeeti biθ-θaanawiyya?
ḍalleet asawwi šuġli.
Caṭṭaw xariiṭa čbiira b-daaˀirathum.
leeš ma-fakkeetu l-baab?
ḍalleena nfakkir bil-mawḍuuƐ.
dazz-li saaƐat ˀiid jidiida.

UNIT 27

A. DIALOGUE

The discussion about Zahda's engagement continues. Umm Khalid asks about the young men who have asked for Zahda's hand.

ʔumm xaalid	Umm Khalid
1. *minu ðoola l-wulid?*	Who are these boys?
ʔumm muṣṭafa	Umm Mustafa
2. *saami w-hišaam, w-inti tεurfiihum ṭabεan.*	Sami and Hisham, and you know them, of course.
ʔumm xaalid	Umm Khalid
3. *bali, ʔaεrufhum, bass zaahda š-itguul?*	Yes, I know them, but what does Zahda say?
ʔumm muṣṭafa	Umm Mustafa
4. *zaahda hamm caayra, εeeni, w-ma-da-tuεruf š-issawwi.*	Zahda's undecided too, my dear. She doesn't know what to do.
ʔumm xaalid	Umm Khalid
5. *šinu caayra? ṣiicuuha, w-xal-da-niccči wiyyaaha kullatna w-inšuuf raʔiiha bil-mawðuuε.*	What do you mean undecided? Call her, and let's all talk with her and see what her opinion is on the matter.
ʔumm muṣṭafa	Umm Mustafa
6. *xooš fikra. yaa faaṭma! ruuci ṣiiciiha l-uxtič w-gullii-lha tiji hnaa fadd daqiiqa.*	Good idea. Oh, Fatma! Go call your sister and tell her to come here a minute.

VOCABULARY

minu	who?
δoola	these, those
ṭabƐan	of course, naturally
bass	but
hamm	too, also
Ɛaayir	undecided, perplexed
Ɛeen (*Ɛyuun*)	eye
Ɛeeni	(term of endearment) my dear, old friend
sawwa (*ysawwi*)	to do
ṣaaƐ (*ṣiƐit yṣiiƐ*)	to call (someone); to shout
Ɛiča (*yiƐči*)	to speak, talk
kullatna	all of us, we all, us all
raʔi (*ʔaaraaʔ*)	opinion
xooš	(preceding a noun) good
fikra	idea
ʔija (*yiji*)	to come
daqiiqa (*daqaayiq*)	minute

---

nisa (*yinsa*)	to forget
liga (*yilgi*)	to find
bina (*yibni*)	to build
štira (*yištiri*)	to buy

B. GRAMMAR

1. Perfect tense: Defective verbs

Verbs which end in a vowel, for example *nisa* 'to forget' (see vocabulary above), are known as **defective verbs.** In the perfect tense, the final vowel (always *a*) is dropped in all forms other than 3 M. Thus the stem of *nisa* is *nis-* before the 3 F and 3 P endings, for example *nisat* 'she forgot' and *nisaw* 'they forgot'. Before the other endings, the stem adds *-ee-*, like that of doubled verbs (see 26 B 3), for example *niseet* 'you M forgot' or 'I forgot'. Here is the full conjugation:

3 M	*nisa*	'he forgot'
F	*nisat*	'she forgot'
P	*nisaw*	'they forgot'

2	M	*niseet*	'you M forgot'
	F	*niseeti*	'you F forgot'
	P	*niseetu*	'you P forgot'
1	S	*niseet*	'I forgot'
	P	*niseena*	'we forgot'

In most defective verbs of the pattern CvCa, the short vowel in the first syllable is *i*, as in *nisa* above; but in a few it is *u*, as in *buqa* 'to stay'. In all such verbs, whenever the stress falls on the following syllable, the short vowel of the first syllable is commonly dropped in normal-speed speech. Thus *nisa* 'he forgot', but either *nisaaha* or *nsaaha* 'he forgot her'; and either *niseet* or *nseet* 'you M forgot', either *buqeeti* or *bqeeti* 'you F stayed', and so on.

In the imperfect, some defective verbs of the pattern CvCa end in *i* and others in *a*; the facts must be learned for each verb. Here is a list of all the defective verbs of this pattern which have occurred so far, with the 3 M imperfect form indicated in parentheses (see 15 B 3 for conjugation of defective verbs in the imperfect):

ɛiča	(*yiɛči*)	'to speak, talk'
niṭa	(*yinṭi*)	'to give'
liga	(*yilgi*)	'to find'
bina	(*yibni*)	'to build'
ˀija	(*yiji*)	'to come' (see 2 below)
qira	(*yiqra*)	'to read'
nisa	(*yinsa*)	'to forget'
siwa	(*yiswa*)	'to be worth' (used mainly in imperfect)
buqa	(*yibqa*)	'to stay'

Defective verbs of other patterns end in either *i* or *a* in the imperfect, according to the pattern. Those we have had so far all end in *i*; they are:

sawwa	(*ysawwi*)	'to do'
xalla	(*yxalli*)	'to let'
štira	(*yištiri*)	'to buy'

2. The verb *ˀija* or *jaa* 'to come'

The verb 'to come' has two sets of forms in the perfect. One set, beginning with the 3 M form *ˀija*, is exactly like any defective verb of this pattern. The other, beginning with the 3 M form *jaa*, shows some unique irregularities.

You will hear forms from both sets, and should be familiar with all of them; here they are:

3	M	*ˀija*	*jaa*	'he came'
	F	*ˀijat*	*jatti*	'she came'
	P	*ˀijaw*	*jaw*	'they came'
2	M	*ˀijeet*	*jeet*	'you M came'
	F	*ˀijeeti*	*jeeti*	'you F came'
	P	*ˀijeetu*	*jeetu*	'you P came'
1	S	*ˀijeet*	*jeet*	'I came'
	P	*ˀijeena*	*jeena*	'we came'

The imperfect 3 M form is *yiji,* and the other imperfect forms proceed from that, as shown on the left below. The imperative forms, however, are based on a totally different stem *taʕaal-*; these are shown on the right below.

3	M	*yiji*	'he comes'		
	F	*tiji*	'she comes'		
	P	*yijuun*	'they come'		
2	M	*tiji*	'you M come'	*taʕaal*	'come M'
	F	*tijiin*	'you F come'	*taʕaali*	'come F'
	P	*tijuun*	'you P come'	*taʕaalu*	'come P'
1	S	*ˀaji*	'I come'		
	P	*niji*	'we come'		

The imperative form *taʕaay* 'come F' is often used instead of *taʕaali.*

3. The post-stated object

Note the two following sentences, the second taken from the dialogue above:

(1) *ṣiiʕi ˀuxtič* 'Call your sister.'
(2) *ṣiiʕiiha l-uxtič.* 'Call your sister.'

The construction in (1) is simply a verb followed by a noun object. In (2), however, we see illustrated a slightly more complex but quite common Iraqi construction, which may be termed the **post-stated object.** In this kind of construction there is a verb with an attached pronoun suffix, followed by the preposition prefix *l-* with a noun. The pronoun suffix functions grammatically as the direct object of the verb, while the noun following is the post-stated object. The pronoun suffix refers in anticipatory fashion to the noun following, and agrees with it as to gender and number in the usual way. The two kinds of constructions, (1) and (2), are both translated into English in the same way. In many cases either may be used. There is one restriction on the post-stated object construction, however, which is that the noun must be definite: it must have the article prefix, or have an attached pronoun suffix, or be a proper name, or be the first noun of an annexion in which the last noun is definite. Here are some additional examples:

leeš ma-sʔalta lil-muCallim?	'Why didn't you ask the teacher?'
ma-aCibbhum il-hal-wulid.	'I don't like those boys.'
šaafoo l-axuuya hnaak.	'They saw my brother there.'
ligeenaaha s-sayyaarat zuheer.	'We found Zuhayr's car.'

4. The particle *xooš* 'good'

The word *xooš* is equivalent in meaning to the English adjective 'good', but it is unlike Iraqi adjectives in that it precedes the noun it modifies and is invariable in form (that is, it is not inflected for gender and number). Examples:

xooš walad	'good boy'
xooš wulid	'good boys'
xooš ibnayya	'good girl'
xooš fikra	'good idea'

C. DRILLS

Drill 1. Change each 3 M verb to the corresponding 1 S form.

Cue:	*qira kull ij-jaraayid.*	He read all the newspapers.
Response:	*qireet kull ij-jaraayid.*	I read all the newspapers.

Ciča wiyya l-banaat.
bina beet jidiid ib-hal manṭiqa.
liga saaCat ʔiid biš-šaariC.
nisa l-mawCid wiyya l-muCallim.
qira l-axbaar bil-jariida.
buqa šahreen ib-baġdaad.
kullši ma-sawwa b-hal-mawðuuC.
nṭaaha miiteen filis.
ma-xallaahum yirCuun lil-madrasa.
štiraa-lak xariiṭa ṣġayyra.

Drill 2. Using the sentences in Drill 1 above, change each 3 M verb form to the corresponding 3 P form.

Cue:	*qira kull ij-jaraayid.*	He read all the newspapers.
Response:	*qiraw kull ij-jaraayid.*	They read all the newspapers.

Drill 3. Change the verb form to correspond to the cue.

a. *qira kull ij-jaraayid* — He read all the newspapers.

Cue:	*bahiija*	Bahija
Response:	*qirat kull ij-jaraayid.*	She read all the newspapers.

ʔaani	*ʔuxti*	*ʔinta*
ʔinti	*ʔiḥna*	*ʔintu*
ʔaxuuya	*l-wulid*	*hiyya*

b. *štira sayyaara kulliš ḥilwa.* — He bought a very pretty car.
c. *leeš ma-xallaaha tibqa hnaaʔ* — Why didn't he let her stay here?
d. *nšaaḷḷa ma-nisa l-biṭaaqaat.* — I hope he didn't forget the tickets.

Drill 4. Replace *xallooha* with the items given, and make the necessary change in the following imperfect verb.

leeš ma-xallooha tibqa bil-beetʔ — Why didn't they let her stay at home?

xalloohum	*xalloona*	*xallookum*
xalloo	*xallook*	*xalloo*
xallooni	*xallooč*	*xallooha*

Drill 5. Change each perfect verb form to *raḥ-* with the corresponding imperfect.

Cue:	*qira jariidt il-yoom.*	He read today's newspaper.
Response:	*raḥ-yiqra jariidt il-yoom.*	He's going to read today's newspaper.

jeena lil-beet saaɛa xamsa.	*nṭeetak itlaθ-miit-filis.*
jeetu lid-daaʔira wiyyaahumʔ	*nṭooni biɛθa l-ameerka.*
štireet xooš xariiṭa bis-suug.	*leeš ma-sawweeti šuġḷič il-yoomʔ*
štiraw sittiin qalam il-wulidhum.	*kullši ma-sawwa bid-daaʔira l-yoom.*
bneena xooš ʔuuteel ihnaa.	*ligeet-lak xooš šiqqa yamm is-safaara.*
leeš ibneetu madrasa b-hal-manṭiqaʔ	*ligat ij-jaahil biš-šaariɛ.*

Drill 6. Replace *l-muċallimiin* with the items indicated, and make the necessary change in the preceding pronoun suffix.

laazim issiˀluuhum lil-muċallimiin. You have to ask the teachers.

l-muċallim
s-sayyid ihnaak
ˀabuukum
j-jihaal
ˀumm samiira
ˀabu t-taksi.
ˀummkum
l-wulid
ˀabu xaalid
l-muċallimiin

UNIT 28

A. DIALOGUE

Zahda's aunt tries to get her to say how she really feels about her two suitors.

ˀumm xaalid	Umm Khalid
1. *binti, ˀinti tċurfiin il-wulid δoola θneenhum, muu hiič?*	Child, you know both those boys, don't you?
zaahda	Zahda
2. *bali, xaaḷa, ˀaċrufhum.*	Yes, aunt, I know them.
ˀumm xaalid	Umm Khalid
3. *zeen, ma-tfaδδliin waaċid minhum ċaθ-θaani?*	All right, don't you prefer one of them over the other?
zaahda	Zahda
4. *waḷḷa ma-aċruf, xaaḷa. haaδa suˀaal ṣaċub.*	Really, I don't know, aunt. That's a hard question.
ˀumm xaalid	Umm Khalid
5. *zeen, xalliini ˀasiˀlič ġeer šikil. ma-tċibbiin waaċid minhum išwayya ˀakθar imnil-laax?*	Well, let me ask you another way. Don't you like one of them a little bit more than the other?

zaahda	Zahda
6. *walla, tirdiin iṣ-ṣudug, xaaḷa, ˀaani ˀafaḏḏla s-saami ʕala hišaam.*	Well, actually, if you want the truth, aunt, I prefer Sami to Hisham.
ˀumm xaalid	**Umm Khalid**
7. *baarak aḷḷaa biič, zaahda binti! haaδa huwwa, nḥallat il-muškila.*	God bless you, Zahda my child! That's it, the problem's been solved.

VOCABULARY

binti	(used as form of address by older persons to younger females) my daughter, my child
θneenhum	both of them, the two of them
hiič	thus, so
muu hiič	isn't it so? (used at end of a statement to invite agreement, like French *n'est-ce pas* or English *don't you, hasn't he, aren't they,* etc.)
xaaḷa	maternal aunt
faḏḏal (yfaḏḏil) (ʕala)	to prefer (to)
suˀaal (ˀasˀila)	question
ṣaʕub	difficult, hard
šikil (ˀaškaal)	manner, way
šwayya	a little, a little bit
ˀakθar	more
min	than
laax (feminine lux)	other
ṣudug	truth
baarak (ybaarik) (b-)	to bless
nḥall (yinḥall)	to be solved
muškila (mašaakil)	problem

---

sahil	easy
ṭuwiil	long; tall
gṣayyir	short
xafiif	light (in weight)
θigiil	heavy

rixiiṣ	cheap
ġaali	expensive
niðiif	clean
waṣix	dirty
ṭayyib	good, tasty (of food)

B. GRAMMAR

1. Roots and patterns

Most Iraqi words can be analysed as containing a root and a pattern; for example the word *diras* 'to study' is made up of the root *d r s* and a pattern consisting of the vowel *i* after the first root consonant and the vowel *a* after the second. A **root** is a set of consonants in a certain order; most roots consist of three consonants, but quite a few have four consonants, and a handful have two or five. The individual consonants of a root are known as **radicals.** Each root has a general sort of meaning, and different words which share the same root usually have meanings related in some way to that broad concept. For example, the root *d r s* is associated with the general idea of "studying"; and the words *diras* 'to study', *diraasa* 'study, studies', and *madrasa* 'school'—all of which have that root—do indeed have meanings related to that idea. A **pattern** consists of one or more vowels disposed among and around the consonants of the root (as in *diras* and *diraasa*), and may also include additional consonants as part of an affix (as in *madrasa,* where the pattern is ma--a-a). A particular pattern can often be seen to have a kind of grammatical meaning; for example the pattern -i-a-, found not only in *diras* but also in *širab* 'to drink', *siʔal* 'to ask', and many other verbs, might be said to have the meaning "perfect-tense verb stem" of that class of verbs. Thus the root, with its broad lexical meaning, and the pattern, with its grammatical meaning, intersect to form a particular stem with its particular meaning. To this stem there may be added one or more inflectional or other affixes. For example, the root *ʕ r s* and the mattern ma--uu- intersect to form the stem *maʕruus.* This stem happens to occur itself as an independent word 'guarded one; child', or it may have various affixes attached: *l-maʕruus* 'the child', *maʕruusiin* 'children', *l-maʕruusiin* 'the children', and so on. The kernel, or core, of all these words is the stem, which consists of an interlocked root and pattern.

Roots are classified in two main ways. The first, already mentioned, is according to the number of radicals. A few roots are **biliteral,** with only two radicals; examples of these are *ʔab* 'father' and *ʔax* 'brother', with the roots *ʔ b* and *ʔ x* respectively. A few are **multiliteral,** with more than four radicals; an example is *barnaamaj* 'program', with the root *b r n m j.* Many are **quadriliteral,** with four radicals; one which has occurred so far is *handasa* 'engineering', with the root *h n d s*. But the great majority of all roots are **triliteral,** with three radicals, as in *diras* 'to study' and *madrasa* 'school' (root *d r s*), *šuġuḷ* 'work' and *mašġuuḷ* 'busy' (root *š ġ ḷ*), and *fikra* 'idea' and *fakkar* 'to think' (root *f k r*).

The other way of classifying roots applies mainly to triliterals and quadriliterals; the discussion here will be limited to the former. According to this classification, which has to do with the nature of the radicals and their stability, roots are called **strong** or **weak.** Strong roots are further divided into sound and double. A **sound** root is one in which the second and third radicals are different consonants, for example *d r s* and *f k r*; while a **double** root is one in which the second and third radicals are the same, for example the root *d z z* as in *dazz* 'to send' and the root *j-d-d* as in *jidiid* 'new'. Weak roots are those in which one of the radicals is unstable; that is, in the various words having the same root, one of the radicals may appear in one word as a consonant, in another as a long vowel, and in still another not at all. For example, consider the words *raayiC* 'going', *raaC* 'he went', *yruuC* 'he goes', and *riCit* 'I went', all of which have the same root. In the first, the middle radical occurs as the consonant *y*; in the second and third, the middle radical merges with the vowel of the pattern and appears as a long vowel; and in the third (stem *riC-*), there is no trace of the middle radical at all. When a weak radical does occur as a consonant, as in *raayiC,* it is almost always *y, w,* or *ʔ*. Weak roots are further subdivided into **weak-first, weak-middle,** and **weak-last** roots, according to the position of the weak radical. A weak radical is symbolized by a capital V; thus the root of the examples just cited may be written *r V C*.

A convenient way to symbolize patterns, which we shall adopt from here on, is within a framework of the capital letters F M L, representing the first, middle, and last radicals of any triliteral root. In this way the pattern of *diras* 'to study', *širab* 'to drink', and many others (the pattern consisting of a short *i* after the first radical and a short *a* after the second) may be referred to as the pattern FiMaL; the pattern of *madrasa* 'school', and many others, may be referred to as the pattern maFMaLa; and so on. For double roots we shall use the letters F D D; thus the pattern of *dazz* 'to send' can be symbolized as FaDD. For quadriliteral roots we shall use the letters F S T L, representing the first, second, third, and last radicals; thus the pattern of *handasa* 'engineering' is referred to as the pattern FaSTaLa.

2. Feminine form of adjectives

In 11 B 3 we noted that the feminine singular of an adjective is formed by adding *-a* to the masculine stem, and in 13 B 6 we mentioned two types of change that occur in the stem when the feminine ending is added. We can now summarize the types of stem-change that occur in all the adjectives we have had thus far.

a. No change. If the masculine stem ends in a consonant preceded by a long vowel, or in a double consonant, or in a sequence -CCvC (with a stem vowel *i* or *u* preceded by two different consonants), there is no change:

Masculine	**Feminine**	
zeen	*zeena*	'good'
jidiid	*jidiida*	'new'
rixiiṣ	*rixiiṣa*	'cheap'
mirtaaꞒ	*mirtaaꞒa*	'satisfied'
jaayy	*jaayya*	'coming'
Ꞓaarr	*Ꞓaarra*	'hot'
mistaɛjil	*mistaɛjila*	'in a hurry'

b. Stem vowel drops. If the masculine stem has a stem vowel *i* or *u* preceded by a single consonant or a double consonant, the vowel drops:

sahil	*sahla*	'easy'
ṣaɛub	*ṣaɛba*	'difficult'
laazim	*laazma*	'necessary'
baarid	*baarda*	'cold'
gaaɛid	*gaaɛda*	'sitting; residing'
raayiꞒ	*raayꞒa*	'going'
Ꞓaamuð̣	*Ꞓaamð̣a*	'sour'
ṭayyib	*ṭayyba*	'tasty'
ṣġayyir	*ṣġayyra*	'little'
gṣayyir	*gṣayyra*	'short'

c. Final *u* changes to *w*:

Ꞓilu	*Ꞓilwa*	'sweet; pretty, handsome'

d. Final *i* changes to *y* in some cases:

maaši	*maašya*	'walking'
ɛaali	*ɛaalya*	'high'
ġaali	*ġaalya*	'expensive'
θaani	*θaanya*	'second; other'

e. Final *i* adds *yy* in the other cases:

ʔibtidaaʔi	*ʔibtidaaʔiyya*	'elementary'
θaanawi	*θaanawiyya*	'secondary'

3. The comparative

Iraqi comparatives, often corresponding to English forms such as ***bigger, newer,*** and so on, have the pattern ʔaFMaL, with two variations for certain root-types. A comparative is generally associated in meaning with some adjective and, with a few exceptions, has the same root. Here are examples. Note that the pattern of the comparatives is the same in all cases, even though the associated adjectives may have quite diverse patterns.

Adjectives		Comparatives	
ɛatiig	'old'	*ʔaɛtag*	'older'
niδiif	'clean'	*ʔanδaf*	'cleaner'
θigiil	'heavy'	*ʔaθgal*	'heavier'
rixiiṣ	'cheap'	*ʔarxaṣ*	'cheaper'
jidiid	'new'	*ʔajdad*	'newer'
ṭuwiil	'long; tall'	*ʔaṭwal*	'longer; taller'
baarid	'cold'	*ʔabrad*	'colder'
ɔaamuδ	'sour'	*ʔaɔmaδ̣*	'sourer'
ṭayyib	'tasty'	*ʔaṭyab*	'tastier'
waṣix	'dirty'	*ʔawṣax*	'dirtier'
sahil	'easy'	*ʔashal*	'easier'
ṣaɛub	'difficult'	*ʔaṣɛab*	'more difficult'
gṣayyir	'short'	*ʔagṣar*	'shorter'
ṣġayyir	'small'	*ʔaṣġar*	'smaller'

A few very common comparatives have roots which are slightly or completely different from the root of the associated word. Here are three of these. (The third word on the left is not an adjective, but a particle.)

čibiir	'big'	*ʔakbar*	'bigger'
zeen	'good'	*ʔaɔsan*	'better'
hwaaya	'much'	*ʔakθar*	'more'

In the case of double roots, the comparative pattern is ʔaFaDD in most cases. (The comparative *ʔajdad* 'newer' in the list above is a notable exception.) Examples:

ɔaarr	'hot'	*ʔaɔarr*	'hotter'
xafiif	'light' (in weight)	*ʔaxaff*	'lighter'

In the case of weak-last roots, the comparative pattern is ʔaFMa. Examples:

ɔilu	'sweet; pretty, handsome'	*ʔaɔla*	'sweeter; prettier, handsomer'
ɛaali	'high'	*ʔaɛla*	'higher'
ġaali	'expensive'	*ʔaġla*	'more expensive'

Comparatives in Iraqi, unlike adjectives, are invariable in form: they are not inflected for gender or number. For example:

zuheer ʔakbar min muṣṭafa.	Zuhayr is bigger than Mustafa.
samiira ʔakbar min zaahda.	Samira is bigger than Zahda.
hal-wulid ʔakbar min xaalid.	These boys are bigger than Khalid.

Iraqi comparatives correspond to English comparatives in two major constructions:

a. When serving as the (indefinite) predicate of an equational sentence:

haaδa ʔashal.	'This is easier.'
sayyaartak ʔaḥsan.	'Your car is better.'

b. When serving as the modifier of an indefinite noun, the latter preceding:

laazim nilgi beet ʔakbar.	'We have to find a bigger house.'
leeš ma-štireet xariiṭa ʔaḥsan?	'Why didn't you buy a better map?'

In either of the two constructions illustrated above, the comparative may be followed by the preposition *min* with a noun object or a pronoun suffix. Here *min* corresponds to English 'than'. Examples:

a. *sayyaartak ʔaḥsan min sayyaarti.*	'Your car is better than my car.'
zuhayr ʔakbar minnak.	'Zuhayr is bigger than you.'
b. *leeš ma-štireet xariiṭa ʔaḥsan min haay?*	'Why didn't you buy a better map than this?'

Iraqi comparative forms may also correspond to English superlatives such as 'biggest,' 'newest', 'most difficult', and so on. There are two major constructions in which this is the case:

a. When the form has the article prefix:

huwwa l-ʔakbar.	'He's the biggest.'
hiyya l-ʔaḥla.	'She's the prettiest.'

b. In a noun phrase preceding the noun. If the noun is singular, it has no article prefix:

huwwa ʔakbar walad bil-madrasa.	'He's the biggest boy in the school.'
hiyya ʔaḥla binit bil-kulliyya.	'She's the prettiest girl in the college.'

If the noun is plural, it usually has the article prefix. In such a construction, the reference may be either to one or to more than one individual, as is shown by the translations below:

huwwa ˀakbar il-wulid.	'He's the biggest boy.' 'He's the biggest of the boys.'
humma ˀakbar il-wulid	'They're the biggest boys.' 'They're the biggest of the boys.'
zaahda ˀaCla l-banaat.	'Zahda's the prettiest girl.' 'Zahda's the prettiest of the girls.'
banaathum ˀaCla l-banaat.	'Their daughters are the prettiest girls.' 'Their daughters are the prettiest of the girls.'

There is no distinction in Iraqi, as there is in English, between *the bigger* (of two) and *the biggest* (of more than two). Thus 'the bigger boy' and 'the biggest boy' both correspond to *ˀakbar walad*. However, 'a bigger boy' would be *walad ˀakbar*.

Certain adjectives, including most of those which have patterns with a prefix (for example *mistaCjil* 'in a hurry' and *mirtaaC* 'happy, contented'), do not have associated comparative forms. In these cases, the comparative idea is expressed instead by the appropriate form of the adjective followed by the comparative *ˀakθar* 'more'. For example, *ˀaani mistaCjil ˀakθar minnak* 'I am more in a hurry than you', or *hiyya mirtaaCa ˀakθar hassa* 'She's happier now'.

C. DRILLS

Drill 1. In the following sentences, change *zuheer* to *samiira,* and make the appropriate change in the adjective.

Cue:	*zuheer mistaCjil.*	Zuhayr's in a hurry.
Response:	*samiira mistaCjila.*	Samira's in a hurry.

zuheer mašǵuul̩ il-yoom.
zuheer muu mirtaaC ihnaa.
zuheer raayiC lil-beet.
zuheer gaaCid bil-uuteel.
zuheer jaay lid-daaˀira.
zuheer Caayir b-hal-mawðuuC.
zuheer maaši wiyya j-jihaal.
zuheer ṣǵayyir.
zuheer čibiir.
zuheer Cilu.

Drill 2. Replace *Ɛatiiga* with the appropriate form of the adjectives given.

hal-xariiṭa Ɛatiiga.		This map is old.
jidiid	*niðiif*	
zeen	*rixiiṣ*	
θigiil	*ġaali*	
xafiif	*ṣġayyir*	
waṣix	*Ɛilu*	

Drill 3. Progressive substitution. In the following sentences, replace first the adjective and then the noun, alternately, from the two lists given, as in the example. Use the appropriate form of each adjective.

a. *šifna xariiṭa Ɛatiiga.* — We saw an old map.

Cue: *jidiid* — new
Response: *šifna xariiṭa jdiida.* — We saw a new map.

Cue: *beet* — house
Response: *šifna beet jidiid.* — We saw a new house.

beet	*jidiid*
šiqqa	*rixiiṣ*
saaƐa	*ġaali*
ˀuuteel	*waṣix*
sayyaara	*θaani*
madrasa	*ṣġayyir*

b. *ma-triid taaxuð il-xariiṭa l-Ɛatiiga?* — Don't you want to take the old map?

paaṣ	*waṣix*
biṭaaqa	*θaani*
qalam	*rixiiṣ*
sayyaara	*ṭuwiil*
beet	*ġaali*
xariiṭa	*Ɛatiig*

Drill 4. Change the adjective to the corresponding comparative.

Cue: *haš-šuġuḷ ṣaƐub.* — This work is hard.
Response: *haš-šuġul ˀaṣƐab.* — This work is harder.

has-sayyaara ġaalya.	*hač-čaay Ɛaarr.*	*beet zuheer čibiir.*
ˀiidak waṣxa.	*l-gahwa baarda.*	*daaˀirt abuuk Ɛilwa.*

ʔiidi niδ̣iifa.
ʔumm samiira ɛilwa.
hal-istikaan xafiif.

hal-uuteel rixiiṣ.
hal-qalam ṭuwiil.
mawδ̣uuɛ iz-zawaaj ṣaɛub.

sayyaaratna waṣxa.
has-suʔaal sahil.
hal-manṭiqa jdiida.

Drill 5. Change the sentences to include a comparative with *min,* as in the example:

Cue:	*l-walad čibiir wil-ibnayya čbiira.*	The boy is big and the girl is big.
Response:	*l-walad ʔakbar imnil-ibnayya.*	The boy is bigger than the girl.

l-iglaaṣ waṣix wil-istikaan waṣix.
l-uuteel iṣġayyir wis-safaara ṣġayyra.
l-ṃaay baarid wil-ɛaliib baarid.
l-maṭaar jidiid wil-kulliyya jdiida.
s-saaɛa ġaalya wis-sayyaara ġaalya.
d-daaʔira niδ̣iifa wil-beet niδ̣iif.
samiira ɛilwa w-zaahda ɛilwa.
xaalid ṭuwiil w-zuheer ṭuwiil.
t-taksi zeen wil-paaṣ zeen.
l-biira ṭayyba wiš-šarbat ṭayyib.
ʔaani mašġuuḷ w-inta mašguuḷ.

ʔaani čbiir w-inta čbiir.
hiyya ṭwiila w-aani ṭwiil.
hiyya ṣġayyra w-inti ṣġayyra.
ʔaani ɛilwa w-hiyya ɛilwa.
ʔinta čbiir w-huwwa čbiir.
haaδa zeen w-haaδa zeen.
sayyaarti θgiila w-sayyaarathum θigiila.
l-muškila sahla wiš-šuġuḷ sahil.
ʔaku hwaaya hnaa w-ihwaaya hnaak.
ʔaani ʔariid ihwaaya w-inta triid ihwaaya.
hiyya mistaɛjila w-aani mistaɛjil.

Drill 6. Change the sentences to include a comparative form followed by a noun, with superlative meaning, as in the example.

Cue:	*zuheer walad čibiir.*	Zuhayr's a big boy.
Response:	*zuheer ʔakbar walad ib-baġdaad.*	Zuhayr's the biggest boy in Baghdad.

haay madrasa zeena.
haaδa ʔuuteel waṣix.
zaahda bnayya ɛilwa.
štiraw sayyaara ġaalya.
štireena beet rixiiṣ.
riɛna l-gaaziino niδ̣iifa.
da-ydirsuun ib-kulliyya jdiida.
ɛindi šuġuḷ sahil.
ma-raɛ-asawwi šuġuḷ ṣaɛub.
haaδa šaariɛ ṭuwiil.

haay sayyaara xafiifa.
haay sayyaara θigiila.
dazzeenaahum il-madrasa zeena.
haaδa ḅang ɛatiig.
huwwa xooš walad.
ɛidna šarbat ṭayyib.
ɛindi šiqqa ṣġayyra.
ɛinda daaʔira čbiira.
haaδa čaay ɛaarr.
haaδa qalam igṣayyir.

UNIT 29

A. DIALOGUE

The members of the family express general satisfaction at Zahda's choice, and congratulate her.

ˀabu muṣṭafa	Abu Mustafa
1. *lḥamdilla, hamm zeen il-qaḍiyya nḥallat ib-haš-šikil.*	Thank heaven. It's a good thing the matter was solved this way.
ˀabu xaalid	Abu Khalid
2. *ybayyin čaan ʕindak šakk, ˀabu muṣṭafa.*	It seems you had doubts, Abu Mustafa.
ˀabu muṣṭafa	Abu Mustafa
3. *laa waḷḷa, ma-čaan ʕindi šakk, bass čint atmanna zaahda tguul hiiči.*	No, no, I didn't have doubts. I was just hoping Zahda would say that.
ˀabu xaalid	Abu Khalid
4. *zeen laʕad, hassa kullši giʕad ib-mukaana.*	Well, then, now everything's been straightened out.
ˀumm xaalid	Umm Khalid
5. *ˀii waḷḷa, kulliš zeen. mabruuk, ʕeeni zaahda, w-nitmannaa-lič kull il-xeer ib-zawaajič.*	Yes indeed, very well. Congratulations, Zahda my dear, and we wish you all happiness in your marriage.
zaahda	Zahda
6. *šukran, xaaḷa, šukran.*	Thank you, aunt, thank you.

VOCABULARY

hamm zeen	it's a good thing (that) . . .
qaḍiyya (qaḍaaya)	matter, affair, problem
b-haš-šikil	in this manner, this way
čaan (činit ykuun)	to be
čaan ʕindak	there was with you, you had
šakk (šukuuk)	doubt(s), misgiving(s)
tmanna (yitmanna)	to hope
tmanna (yitmanna) l-	to wish (someone something)
hiiči	thus, this way
mukaan (mukaanaat)	place, position
giʕad (yugʕud) ib-mukaana	to fall into (its) place, get straightened out
mabruuk	congratulations (see Note)
xeer	good things, happiness

Note on dialogue

Polite formula . The word *mabruuk* is said to someone (male or female) who has acquired a new possession or to whom some other pleasant thing has happened. The literal meaning is 'blessed, fortunate', and it often corresponds to English 'Congratulations!'.

B. GRAMMAR

1. The verb *čaan* 'to be'

This verb is unusual in that it has the root *č V n* in the perfect tense but *k V n* in the imperfect. Otherwise, it is a hollow verb like *šaaf* 'to see' (15 B 3, 25 B 1), and is conjugated exactly the same way. The forms are as follows:

		Perfect		Imperfect	
3	M	*čaan*	'he was'	*ykuun*	'he is'
	F	*čaanat*	'she was'	*tkuun*	'she is'
	P	*čaanaw*	'they were'	*ykuunuun*	'they are'
2	M	*činit*	'you M were'	*tkuun*	'you M are'
	F	*činti*	'you F were'	*tkuuniin*	'you F are'
	P	*čintu*	'you P were'	*tkuunuun*	'you P are'
1	S	*činit*	'I was'	*ʔakuun*	'I am'
	P	*činna*	'we were'	*nkuun*	'we are'

The imperfect forms of this verb are *not* used to express the simple present tense, as *is, are,* and *am* are used in English. For this, Iraqi uses the equational sentence (14 B 2), in which there is no verb between the subject and predicate. The Iraqi imperfect forms are used, however, after the future prefix *raC-* (14 B 7), the negative prefix *la-* in negative commands (16 B 3), *laazim* 'must' (16 B 1), or any verb in a string (15 B 6). Examples:

raC-itkuun bid-daaˀira l-yoom?	'Are you M going to be in the office today?
la-tkuuniin hiiči.	'Don't F be that way.'
laazim inkuun bis-safaara saaCa xamsa.	'We have to be at the embassy at five o'clock.'
ˀariid akuun ihnaak baačir.	'I want to be there tomorrow.'
tgidruun itkuunuun ihnaa kull il-yoom?	'Can you P be here all day?'

The perfect forms of *čaan* are used to form the past-tense equivalent of equational sentences; they usually correspond closely to English *was* and *were:*

zaahda Caayra.	'Zahda is undecided.'
zaahda čaanat Caayra.	'Zahda was undecided.'
huṃṃa mirtaaCiin ib-zawaajhum.	'They are happy in their marriage.'
čaanaw mirtaaCiin ib-zawaajhum.	'They were happy in their marriage.'
l-igḷaaṣ waṣix.	'The glass is dirty.'
l-igḷaaṣ čaan waṣix.	'The glass was dirty.'
ˀaani gaaCid yammha.	'I'm sitting beside her.'
činit gaaCid yammha.	'I was sitting next to her.'

2. The verb *čaan* as an auxiliary

In addition to its uses as an independent verb as described above, *čaan* is used as an auxiliary verb, that is, preceding other words and modifying their time reference. Some of these uses are described below; others will come up later.

a. With imperfect verb. A phrase consisting of a perfect form of *čaan* followed by an imperfect form of another verb in the same person refers to habitual action in the past. It often corresponds to English *used to* plus verb. Examples:

čaan yidrus saaCteen kull yoom.	'He used to study two hours every day.'
čaanat tidrus saaCa kull yoom.	'She used to study an hour every day.'

čaanaw yšurbuun ihwaaya.	'They used to drink a lot.'
ma-čint iddizz-ilhum ifluus?	'Didn't you M use to send them money?'
činna nirkab il-paaṣ lil-madrasa.	'We used to ride the bus to school.'
čint atmanna zaahda tguul hiiči.	'I was hoping Zahda would say that.'

As the translation of the last example shows, it may in some contexts be appropriate to translate this kind of Iraqi phrase with an English verb construction other than *used to*. The choice frequently depends on the particular verb involved.

b. With *da-* and an imperfect verb. A phrase consisting of a perfect form of *čaan* followed by *da-* with the imperfect of another verb in the same person refers to action continuing over a specified period of time in the past. It is often used to describe action which was going on at the time when something else occurred, and it usually corresponds to English phrases like *was reading* or *were studying*.

čaan da-yidrus min wuṣálit.	'He was studying when I arrived.'
čaanat da-tidrus min šifnaaha.	'She was studying when we saw her.'
š-čaanaw da-ysawwuun?	'What were they doing?'
činti da-tiʕčiin wiyyaahum?	'Were you F talking with them?'
činit da-aqra j-jariida min ṣiʕitni.	'I was reading the newspaper when you M called me.'

c. With *ʔaku* and *ʕind*. The 3 M perfect form *čaan* preceding *ʔaku* 'there is, there are' indicates the corresponding past time: *čaan ʔaku* 'there was, there were'. For example:

ʔaku xooš madrasa ib-hal manṭiqa.	'There's a good school in this area.'
čaan ʔaku xooš madrasa b-hal-manṭiqa.	'There was a good school in this area.'
ʔaku ʕašir-muʕallimiin bil-kulliyya.	'There are ten teachers in the college.'
čaan ʔaku muʕallimeen bil-kulliyya.	'There were two teachers in the college.'

The same form *čaan* preceding the preposition *ʕind* with a pronoun suffix (usually translated 'I have, you have, he has' and so on; see 12 B 2) indicates the corresponding past time of that idea: *čaan ʕindi* 'I had'. Further examples:

ʕindi saaʕa jdiida.	'I have a new watch.'
čaan ʕindi saaʕa jdiida.	'I had a new watch.'
ʕidna mawʕid wiyya ṣadiiq.	'We have an appointment with a friend.'
čaan ʕidna mawʕid wiyya ṣadiiq.	'We had an appointment with a friend.'

C. DRILLS

Drill 1. In the following sentences, change the verb to correspond to the cue, and make any other necessary changes.

a. *čaan bid-daaʔira l-yoom.* — He was in the office today.

Cue: *hiyya* — she
Response: *čaanat bid-daaʔira l-yoom.* — She was in the office today.

huṃṃa	*ʔinta*	*huwwa*	*l-banaat*
ʔaani	*ʔinti*	*ʔummič*	*xaaḷti*
ʔiεna	*ʔintu*	*ʔabuukum*	*ʔaani*

b. *čaan mašġuuḷ išwayya.* — He was a little busy.
c. *čaan wiyya xaaḷta.* — He was with his aunt.
d. *ma-čaan mirtaaε ib-sayyaarta.* — He wasn't satisfied with his car.

Drill 2. Change each of the following equational sentences to past time by using the appropriate form of *čaan*. If the equational sentence has an independent personal pronoun (e.g. *huwwa*) as subject, leave it out in the new sentence.

Cue: *huwwa bil-beet.* — He's at home.
Response: *čaan bil-beet.* — He was at home.

huwwa bil-gahwa.
hiyya bis-suug.
huṃṃa wiyya ʔaṣdiqaahum.
ween ʔinta?
ʔinti mašġuuḷa?
ʔintu gaaεdiin bil-karraada?
ʔaani muu εaayir.
ʔiεna muu mirtaaεiin.
ʔabuuhum bis-suug.
ʔumm xaalid mirtaaεa biz-zawaaj.
samiira bil-beet wiyya ʔummha.
l-muεallimiin muu mirtaaεiin.
saami bid-daaʔira wiyya ʔaxuu.
l-uuteel rixiiṣ.
s-sayyaara muu ġaalya.
ʔaṣdiqaaʔi bis-safaara.

Drill 3. Change the following sentences to past time by using the word *čaan*.

Cue: *ʔaku εaliib ihwaaya bil-beet.* — There's plenty of milk in the house.
Response: *čaan ʔaku εaliib ihwaaya bil-beet.* — There was plenty of milk in the house.

ʔaku xooš uuteel ihnaak.
ma-aku xariiṭa bid-daaʔira?
kullši ma-aku bid-daaʔira.
leeš ma-aku gahwa hnaa?
ʔaku walad iṣġayyir bis-safaara.
ʔaku gaaziino b-hal-manṭiqa?
εindi mawεid bil-maṭaar.
ma-εindak ifluus?
εidhum šuġuḷ ihwaaya.
εidna beet jidiid.
εidkum beet ib-baġdaad?
εidha jaahil iṣġayyir.

Drill 4. Change the following sentences to past time by using the appropriate form of *čaan*.

Cue:	*yidrus saaεteen kull yoom.*	He studies two hours every day.
Response:	*čaan yidrus saaεteen kull yoom.*	He used to study two hours every day.

yruuε lil-gahwa wiyya ʔaṣdiqaaʔa.
ddizz ifluus ihwaaya l-axuuha.
yguεduun bil-beet wiyya j-jihaal.
ma-tiqra j-jaraayid?
yaa paaṣ itrukbiin lis-safaara?
leeš ma-tiεčuun wiyyaa?

ʔašuufhum bil-gaaziino.
naakul bid-daaʔira.
ʔaṣdiqaaʔi yijuun lil-beet.
ʔumm xaalid ma-truuε lis-suug.
ʔaxuuya yištiri kull il-ašyaaʔ.
ʔabuu yišrab ihwaaya.

Drill 5. Change the following sentences by using the appropriate form of *čaan* before the verb, and adding the phrase *min wuṣlaw* 'when they arrived' at the end.

Cue:	*da-yišrab biira.*	He's drinking beer.
Response:	*čaan da-yišrab biira min wuṣlaw.*	He was drinking beer when they arrived.

da-tiεči wiyya ʔuxutha.
da-yaakluun.
ʔinta š-da-ssawwi?
š-da-tiqriin?
š-da-ddirsuun?
ʔaxuuk š-da-ysawwi?

da-abuusha.
da-nfakkir bii.
xaalid da-yidfaε l-iεsaab.
l-wulid da-yxuššuun bil-madrasa.
ʔummi da-ssidd il-baab.
da-yiεčuun wiyyaaha.

Drill 6. In the two sentences below, replace *zawaajič* by the items given, and make the necessary changes in the pronoun suffix on the verb.

a. *nitmannaa-lič kull il-xeer ib-zawaajič.*	We wish you F all happiness in your F marriage.
zawaajak	your M marriage
zawaajkum	your P marriage
zawaaja	his marriage
zawaajha	her marriage
zawaajhum	their marriage

b. *ʔatmannaa-lič kull il-xeer ib-zawaajič.* I wish you F all happiness in your F marriage.

UNIT 30

A. NARRATIVE

1. *ʔabu xaalid siʔal ʔabu musṭafa ʕala xuṭbat binta zaahda.*	Abu Khalid asked Abu Mustafa about the engagement of his daughter Zahda.
2. *w-abu musṭafa gal-la l-mawḏuuʕ baʕda ma-nḥall liʔann ʔaku wuld iθneen w-zaahda baʕadha ḥaayra . . .*	Abu Mustafa told him that the matter hadn't been solved yet, because there were *two* boys, and Zahda was still undecided . . .
3. *w-umm xaalid siʔlat zaahda yaa waaḥid itḥibb ʔakθar.*	Umm Khalid asked Zahda which one she liked more.
4. *w-zaahda bil-ʔawwal ma-raadat idjaawub, bass baʕd išwayya gaalat saami.*	At first Zahda didn't want to answer, but after a while she said Sami.
5. *w-abu zaahda w-ummha w-xaalatha w-zooj xaalatha kullhum hannooha,*	And Zahda's father, her mother, her aunt and her uncle all congratulated her,
6. *w-itmannoo-lha čull il-xeer ib-zawaajha.*	and wished her all happiness in her marriage.

VOCABULARY

xuṭba	engagement
binit (*banaat*)	daughter; girl
liʔann	because
ʔawwal	first
bil-ʔawwal	at first
jaawab (*yjaawub*)	to answer
zooj (*ʔazwaaj*)	husband
hanna (*yhanni*)	to congratulate

ʔibin (*wulid*)	son
zawja (*zawjaat*)	wife

ɛamm	uncle (father's brother)
ɛamma	aunt (father's sister)
xaaḷ	uncle (mother's brother)
xaaḷa	aunt (mother's sister)
zawjat ɛamm	aunt (wife of father's brother)
zooj ɛamma	uncle (husband of father's sister)
zawjat xaaḷ	aunt (wife of mother's brother)
zooj xaaḷa	uncle (husband of mother's sister)
ˀibin ɛamm	cousin (son of father's brother)
bint ɛamm	cousin (daughter of father's brother)
ˀibin ɛamma	cousin (son of father's sister)
bint ɛamma	cousin (daughter of father's sister)
ˀibin xaaḷ	cousin (son of mother's brother)
bint xaaḷ	cousin (daughter of mother's brother)
ˀibin xaaḷa	cousin (son of mother's sister)
bint xaaḷa	cousin (daughter of mother's sister)
ˀibin ˀax	nephew (brother's son)
ˀibin ˀuxut	nephew (sister's son)
bint ˀax	niece (brother's daughter)
bint ˀuxut	niece (sister's daughter)

NOTE

Kinship terms. As you can see from the vocabulary list above, certain family relationships are expressed by much more exact terms than in English. Our word *uncle* is used to refer not only to the brother of either parent, but also to the husband of the sister of either parent; whereas the Iraqi word or phrase expresses the precise nature of the relationship. The same is true of the various terms for *aunt, cousin, nephew,* and *niece*. Grammatically, all the two-word phrases shown above are annexions (26 B 1); thus the article prefix or a pronoun suffix may be attached to the last noun only:

zawjat xaaḷ	'an aunt'
zawjat il-xaaḷ	'the aunt'
zawjat xaaḷi	'my aunt'

B. DRILLS

Drill 1. In each of the following sentences, replace *ɛamm* with the items given and make any other necessary changes.

a. *<u>εammha</u> hannaaha b-xuṭbatha.* — Her <u>uncle</u> congratulated her on her engagement.

εamma	*ʔibin εamma*	aunt	cousin
xaaḷ	*ʔibin ʔax*	uncle	nephew
xaaḷa	*ʔibin ʔuxut*	aunt	nephew
ʔibin εamm		cousin	

b. *<u>εammi</u> baεda ḥaayir b-hal-mawð̣uuε.* — My <u>uncle</u> is still undecided in this matter.

εamma	*ʔibin xaaḷ*	aunt	cousin
ʔumm	*bint ʔax*	mother	niece
xaaḷ	*bint ʔuxut*	uncle	niece
ʔab		father	

c. *laazim tiḥči wiyya <u>εammak</u>.* — You have to talk with your <u>uncle</u>.

ʔibin	*ʔibin xaaḷa*	son	cousin
binit	*ʔibin ʔax*	daughter	nephew
bint xaaḷ	*bint ʔax*	cousin	niece
bint xaaḷa		cousin	

d. *<u>εamma</u> čaan da-yiqra min wuṣal.* — His <u>uncle</u> was reading when he arrived.

ʔibin εamm	*ʔibin xaaḷ*	cousin	cousin
bint εamm	*ʔibin xaaḷa*	cousin	cousin
zawjat εamm	*ʔibin ʔuxut*	aunt	nephew
zawjat xaaḷ	*bint ʔuxut*	aunt	niece

Drill 2. Change the verb form and the pronoun suffix to correspond to the cue.

laazim tisʔal ʔibin xaaḷtak. — You M have to ask your M cousin.

Cue: *ʔaani* — I

Response: *laazim ʔasʔal ʔibin xaaḷti.* — I have to ask my cousin.

huṃṃa	*ʔinti*	*ʔaani*	*l-wulid*
ʔiḥna	*ʔintu*	*ʔinta*	*ṣadiiqi*
hiyya	*huwwa*	*samiira*	*ṣadiiqti*

Drill 3. Change the verb forms and the pronoun suffix to correspond to the cue. Use the cues given in Drill 2 above.

hanna bint εamma w-itmannaa-lha kull il-xeer.	He congratulated his cousin and wished her all happiness.

Cue: *ʔaani*
Response: *hanneet bint εammi w-itmanneet-ilha kull il-xeer.* — I congratulated my cousin and wished her all happiness.

Drill 4. Replace the post-stated object with the items given, and make the necessary changes in the preceding pronoun suffix.

ṣiεta l-axuuya. — I called my brother.

Cue: *ʔumm* — mother
Response: *ṣiεitha l-ʔummi.* — I called my mother.

ʔab	*xaaḷ*	*l-banaat*	*bint ʔuxut*
ʔuxut	*xaaḷa*	*bint xaaḷa*	*l-aṣdiqaaʔ*
ṣadiiq	*j-jihaal*	*ʔabu zuheer*	*ʔibin ʔax*
zaahda	*zawjat εamm*	*εamma*	*bahiija*

Drill 5. Form a question, beginning with *š-* 'what', for which each of the following sentences would be an appropriate answer.

Cue: *jibna l-xaraayiṭ wiyyaana.* — We brought the maps with us.
Response: *š-jibtu wiyyaakum?* — What did you P bring with you P?

širábit liban bil-gahwa.	*ligeena saaεat ʔiid biš-šaariε.*
ʔaεibb ašrab čaay.	*štirat stikaaneen.*
gall-ilhum il-mawδ̣uuε inεall.	*kullši ma-da-asawwi.*
dazzaw ifluus lil-wulid.	*raε-yaaxuδ is-sayyaara l-yoom.*

Drill 6. Form a question, beginning with *minu* 'who', for which each of the following sentences would be an appropriate answer.

Cue: *samiira raε-taaxuδ l-igḷaaṣaat.*
Response: *minu raε-yaaxuδ l-igḷaaṣaat?*

ʔaani ʔagdar asawwi haay.	*j-jihaal ʔaṣğar minni.*
j-jihaal yirduun yirεuun wiyyaana.	*ʔinta waṣṣalitha lil-uuteel.*
ʔiεna raε-nibqa hnaa bil-beet.	*ʔiεna dazzeenaa-lhum l-ifluus.*
ʔinti nseeti l-aqlaam.	*ʔaṣdiqaaʔak yigidruun yjiibuun ič-čaay.*

UNIT 31

A. DIALOGUE

Zahda and her mother begin to shop for household furnishings.

ʔumm muṣṭafa	Umm Mustafa
1. *ʔisimħi, zaahda, ʔiħna xoo ma-raħ-nigdar inxaḷḷiṣ kull miswaagna hal-yoom.*	Listen, Zahda, we're not going to be able to finish all our shopping today, you know.
zaahda	Zahda
2. *ṭabʕan laa. yirraad-inna ʕal-ʔaqall fadd isbuuʕ isbuuʕeen ib-hal-masaaʔil, ṃaaṃa.*	Of course not. It'll take us at least a week or two for these matters, mama.
ʔumm muṣṭafa	Umm Mustafa
3. *zeen, ma-daam hiič, xal-da-ništiri bass il-pardaat w-ħaajaat l-ifraaš il-yoom.*	Well, in that case, let's buy just the curtains and the bed things today.
zaahda	Zahda
4. *zeen, w-masaaʔil il-muṭbax inxalliiha l-ġeer yoom.*	All right, and the kitchen matters we'll leave for another day.
ʔumm muṣṭafa	Umm Mustafa
5. *laazim. haay yirraad-ilha rooħa liš-šoorja, w-aani taʕbaana šwayya l-yoom.*	Have to. That requires a trip to the Shorja, and I'm a little tired today.
zaahda	Zahda
6. *w-hamm ariid asʔal nabiiha mneen štirat ġaraað̣ha gabuḷ-ma aštiri šii.*	And also I want to ask Nabiha where she bought her things before I buy anything.

VOCABULARY

simaƐ (yismaƐ)	to hear, listen
xoo	(particle expressing apprehension or hope and inviting reassurance)
miswaag	shopping
hal-yoom	this day; today
ṭabƐan	naturally, of course
nraad (yinraad)	to be needed, necessary, required
yinraad-ilna, yirraad-inna	it is required for us, we need
ˀaqall	less; least
Ɛal-ˀaqall	at least
sbuuƐ (ˀasaabiiƐ)	week
masˀala (masaaˀil)	matter, affair, question
ma-daam	inasmuch as, since, as
ma-daam hiič	since it's this way, in this/that case
parda (pardaat)	curtain
Caaja (Caajaat)	necessity, requirement
fraaš (fraašaat)	bed
muṭbax, maṭbax (maṭaabix)	kitchen
rooCa	(an act of) going, trip
taƐbaan	tired
mneen	from where?
garaḍ (ġaraaḍ)	(usually in plural) things, belongings

GRAMMAR

1. Sentence types: Equational, verbal, and topical

There are three main types of sentences in Iraqi. One type, the **equational sentence,** was discussed in 14 B 2; it consists of a subject and a predicate, with no linking verb, and usually corresponds to an English sentence containing a present-tense form of the verb *to be*. Examples:

haaδa beeti.	'This is my house.'
ˀaani taƐbaana šwayya l-yoom.	'I'm a little tired today.'
ˀinta raayiC lid-daaˀira?	'Are you M going to the office?'

A second type is the **verbal sentence,** which differs from the equational sentence in that it contains a verb. It may consist of a verb alone (the form of the verb indicating the subject), or it may consist of an expressed subject and a verb, and in either case it may also contain an object of the verb and various modifiers. Most of the sentences presented thus far have been of this type. Examples:

wuṣlat.	'She has arrived.'
ma-šifta.	'I didn't see him.'
mawδ̣uuε iz-zawaaj xiḷaṣ.	'The matter of the marriage has been settled.'
raasim yriid yidrus εuquuq.	'Rasim wants to study law.'

The third type is the **topical sentence.** This consists of a **topic** and a **comment.** The topic, which comes first, is usually a noun, a pronoun, or some form of the demonstrative *haaδa.* The comment is itself a full sentence of either the equational or the verbal type, and always includes a pronoun form (independent or pronoun suffix) referring to the topic. First some examples; in these, the topic and comment are separated by a vertical line, and the pronoun form referring to the topic is underlined.

zaahda | *hassa da-yirduu<u>ha</u> θneen.*	'Two (suitors) now want Zahda.'
masaaʔil il-muṭbax | *inxallii<u>ha</u> l-ġeer yoom.*	'The kitchen matters we'll leave for another day.'
l-wulid | *laazim itwaṣṣil<u>hum</u> lil-madrasa.*	'You M have to take the boys to school.'
haaδa | *ma-ariid ašuuf<u>a</u> l-yoom.*	'I don't want to see this man today.'

The difference between a topical sentence and an ordinary verbal sentence is mainly one of focus. In a topical sentence the speaker first mentions the person or thing on which he wishes attention concentrated—the topic—and then says what he has to say about it—the comment. Often the topic is something which has already been in the conversation, or something which the speaker and the hearer already have in mind. The difference in focus indicated by a topical sentence is not always easily translated into English. Occasionally a good English equivalent involves a construction in which the object comes before the verb, as in the second example above. Sometimes the English equivalent involves extra loudness on one element in the sentence; thus the last example above might be rendered: 'I don't want to see HIM today.' In most instances, however, an Iraqi topical sentence would probably be best translated into English in the same way as one of the other types.

2. Plural forms of adjectives

As we saw in 11 B 3, certain adjectives have masculine plural forms ending in *-iin,* and feminine plural forms ending in *-aat.* These are the same endings as those which form the sound plurals of certain nouns, and thus these forms are also called sound masculine plural and sound feminine plural forms. Here are further examples:

MS	FS	MP	FP	
mirtaaḥ	*mirtaaḥa*	*mirtaaḥiin*	*mirtaaḥaat*	'happy'
mistaεjil	*mistaεjila*	*mistaεjiliin*	*mistaεjilaat*	'in a hurry'
ḥaayir	*ḥaayra*	*ḥaayriin*	*ḥaayraat*	'undecided'
waṣix	*waṣxa*	*waṣxiin*	*waṣxaat*	'dirty'
ḥilu	*ḥilwa*	*ḥilwiin*	*ḥilwaat*	'pretty, handsome'
maaši	*maašya*	*maašiin*	*maašyaat*	'walking'

Note that the changes which occur in the adjective stem when the sound feminine plural ending *-aat* is added are the same as for the feminine singular ending *-a.* The changes which occur when the masculine sound plural ending *-iin* is added are also the same, except that (see the last example above) when the stem ends in *i* and this is changed to *y* before *-a,* it is dropped altogether before *-iin.*

Only adjectives which may be applied to human beings (and not all of those) have a sound masculine plural form. Many common adjectives, including some which are normally applied to human beings and some which are not, have a broken plural form instead of a masculine sound plural. The patterns of these adjective broken plurals are generally the same as those of noun broken plurals, but there are fewer different ones in common use. Here is a list of the adjectives we have had thus far which have broken plural forms; note that the only two patterns involved here are FMaaL and FiMMaL. Note also (first example) the change from *č* to *k* in the broken plural of *čibiir.*

čibiir	*čibiira*	*kbaar*	*čibiiraat*	'big'
ṣġayyir	*ṣġayyra*	*ṣġaar*	*ṣġayyraat*	'small'
ṭuwiil	*ṭuwiila*	*ṭwaal*	*ṭuwiilaat*	'long, tall'
gṣayyir	*gṣayyra*	*gṣaar*	*gṣayyraat*	'short'
xafiif	*xafiifa*	*xfaaf*	*xafiifaat*	'light'
θigiil	*θigiila*	*θgaal*	*θigiilaat*	'heavy'
rixiiṣ	*rixiiṣa*	*rxaaṣ*	*rixiiṣaat*	'cheap'
nið̣iif	*nið̣iifa*	*nð̣aaf*	*nið̣iifaat*	'clean'
jidiid	*jidiida*	*jiddad*	*jidiidaat*	'new'
εatiig	*εatiiga*	*εittag*	*εatiigaat*	'old'
taεbaan	*taεbaana*	*tεaaba*	*taεbaanaat*	'tired'

Some adjectives have both a sound masculine plural and a broken plural form, for example the last adjective above also has the sound masculine plural *taᶜbaaniin*.

3. Adjective agreement in gender and number

As the preceding section illustrates, adjectives may have four forms: MS, FS, MP, and FP. The form used in a given context depends on the number and gender of the noun to which the adjective refers, and also in some cases on whether the noun refers to human beings or not. All this is true regardless of whether the adjective follows the noun immediately in a noun-adjective phrase, or occurs as the predicate of an equational sentence referring to a noun subject, or refers to a noun which has already been mentioned in another sentence, or refers to a pronoun which in turn refers to some noun. The relationship between the form of an adjective and the noun it refers to is called agreement. The major facts[1] of adjective agreement are as follows:

a. Singular noun

(1) If the noun is masculine singular, the adjective is also masculine singular:

walad čibiir	'big boy'
beet ᶜatiig	'old house'
ˀaani taᶜbaan.	'I'm tired.' (male speaker)

(2) If the noun is feminine singular, the adjective is also feminine singular:

bnayya čbiira	'big girl'
madrasa ᶜatiiga	'old school'
ˀaani taᶜbaana.	'I'm tired.' (female speaker)

b. Dual noun

(1) If the noun is masculine dual and refers to human beings, the adjective is masculine plural (sound or broken as the case may be):

waladeen ikbaar	'two big boys'
l-muᶜallimeen mašǧuuliin.	'The two teachers are busy.'

[1] In the case of dual and plural nouns there are some variant usages not listed here.

(2) If the noun is feminine dual and refers to human beings, the adjective is in the broken plural form if it has one; otherwise it is feminine plural:

bnayyteen iṣġaar	'two little girls'
muʕallimteen mašġuulaat	'two busy teachers F'

(3) If the noun is dual and does not refer to human beings, the adjective is in the broken plural form if it has one; otherwise it is feminine singular:

beeteen jiddad	'two new houses'
sayyaarteen iṣġaar	'two little cars'
suˀaaleen ṣaʕba	'two hard questions'
madrasteen ˀibtidaaˀiyya	'two elementary schools'

c. Plural noun

(1) If the noun is masculine plural and refers to human beings, the adjective is also masculine plural (sound or broken as the case may be):

wulid ikbaar	'big boys'
ˀaṣdiqaaˀi mašġuuliin.	'My friends are busy.'

(2) If the noun is feminine plural and refers to human beings, the adjective is in the broken plural form if it has one; otherwise it is feminine plural:

banaat iṣġaar	'little girls'
ṣadiiqaat jiddad	'new friends F'
l-muʕallimaat mašġuulaat.	'The teachers F are busy.'

However, in the case of adjectives which do not have a broken plural form, the masculine sound plural is sometimes used instead of the feminine. This form is most common when the adjective is in the predicate of an equational sentence, and is usual in the case of those adjectives which indicate physical position or motion, such as *gaaʕid* 'sitting' or *raayiḥ* 'going':

l-banaat kulliš maṣġuuliin.	'The girls are very busy.'
ṣadiiqaatha raayḥiin lil-beet.	'Her friends F are going home.'

(3) If the noun is plural and does not refer to human beings, the adjective may be either feminine singular or, if it has one, in the broken plural form:

madaaris ˀibtidaaˀiyya	'elementary schools'
byuut jidiida *byuut jiddad*	'new houses'
sayyaaraat čibiira *sayyaaraat ikbaar*	'big cars'

4. Agreement of pronouns and verbs

Like adjectives, third-person pronouns (independent or suffixed) agree in certain ways with the noun to which they refer, and verb forms with the noun which is their subject. The main facts are as follows. (The statements on pronouns also apply to demonstratives.)

a. Singular noun

(1) If the noun is masculine singular, the pronoun or verb is masculine singular:

haaδa xooš ˀuuteel.	'This is a good hotel.'
laa, ˀaani ma-aḥibba.	'No, I don't like it.'
čaan ˀaḥsan gabuḷ santeen.	'It was better two years ago.'

(2) If the noun is feminine singular, the pronoun or verb is feminine singular:

haay xooš sayyaara.	'This is a fine car.'
hiyya ˀaḥsan min sayyaarti.	'It's better than my car.'

b. Dual noun

(1) If the noun is dual and refers to human beings, the pronoun or verb is plural:

wil-muʕallimeen ween nigdar nilgiihum?	'And where can we find the two teachers?'
čaanaw ysiˀluun ʕaleek.	'They were asking about you.'

(2) If the noun is dual and does not refer to human beings, the pronoun or verb is usually plural but may also be feminine singular:

(*laazim ništiri xariiṭteen jiddad lid-daaˀira.*)	('We have to buy two new maps for the office.')
štireethum (*štireetha*) *ḷ-yoom biš-šoorja.*	'I bought them today at the Shorja.'

c. Plural

(1) If the noun is plural and refers to human beings, the pronoun or verb is plural:

j-jihaal ma-čaanaw bil-madrasa.	'The children weren't at school.
weenhum hassa?	Where are they now?'
da-ydirsuun bil-beet.	'They're studying at home.'

(2) If the noun is plural and does not refer to human beings, the pronoun or verb is usually feminine singular but may also be plural:

mneen jibt haay l-iqlaam?	'Where did you get these pencils?
ma-aCibbha (ma-aCibbhum).	I don't like them.'

C. DRILLS

Drill 1. Change each of the following into topical sentences, as in the example.

Cue:	*nxalli masaaʔil il-muṭbax il-ġeer yoom.*	We'll leave the kitchen matters for another day.
Response:	*masaaʔil il-muṭbax inxalliiha l-ġeer yoom.*	The kitchen matters we'll leave for another day.

laazim ništiri l-paardaat il-yoom.
ma-ariid ašuuf hal-wulid bil-beet.
ma-agdar aqra haj-jariida.
ma-tigdar tišrab hal-biira.
laazim tiCčiin wiyya l-banaat.
laazim inxalliṣ haš-šuġuḷ il-yoom.
ma-ariid arkab ib-has-sayyaaraat il-Catiiga.
samiira raC-tištiri Caajaat l-ifraaš.
ʔabuuk laazim yidfaC l-iCsaab.
laazim injiib il-wulid wiyyaana.

Drill 2. In each of the following sentences, change the singular noun to plural, and make the appropriate change in the adjective form.

Cue:	*l-uuteel ihnaa kulliš ġaali.*	The hotel here is very expensive.
Response:	*l-uuteelaat ihnaa kulliš ġaalya.*	The hotels here are very expensive.

hal-istikaan waṣix išwayya.
ʔinta tCibb hal-beet il-Catiig?
ween qalami j-jidiid?
laazim nilgi šiqqa rxiiṣa.
hal-xariiṭa kulliš iṣġayyra.
tigdar idjiib l-iglaaṣ ič-čibiir wiyyaak?
l-paaṣ ihnaak kulliš niðiif.
l-madrasa θ-θaanawiyya kulliš zeena.
samiira Cidha jaahil iṣġayyir.
leeš tisʔal suʔaal ṣaCub?
hal-muškila kulliš sahla.
l-ibnayya Caayra b-hal-mawðuuC.

Drill 3. Change the verb to *laazim* plus the imperfect tense.

Cue:	*Ččeet wiyya ðoola l-wulid?*	Did you M talk with these boys?
Response:	*laazim tiČči wiyya ðoola l-wulid.*	You M must talk with these boys.

simáČit l-axbaar?
xaḷḷáṣit šuġḷak?
gaṣṣeet biṭaaqa maal manṭiqteen?
nseet l-muškila ṣ-ṣaČba?
simaČti l-axbaar?
xaḷḷaṣti šuġḷič?
gaṣṣeeti biṭaaqa maal manṭiqteen?
nseeti l-muškila ṣ-ṣaČba?
simaČtu l-axbaar?
xaḷḷaṣtu šuġuḷkum?
gaṣṣeetu biṭaaqa maal manṭiqteen?
nseetu l-muškila ṣ-ṣaČba?

Drill 4. Change the verb form (*raČ-* plus the imperfect) to the perfect tense.

Cue:	*raČ-tištiruun il-pardaat il-yoom?*	Are you P going to buy the curtains today?
Response:	*štireetu l-pardaat il-yoom?*	Did you P buy the curtains today?

raČ-tismaČ il-axbaar?
raČ-titxarraj has-sana?
raČ-titČawwal lil-karraada?
raČ-issawwi kull iš-šuġuḷ?
raČ-issimČiin il-axbaar?
raČ-titxarrjiin has-sana?
raČ-titČawwliin lil-karraada?
raČ-issawwiin kull iš-šuġuḷ?
raČ-issimČuun il-axbaar?
raČ-titxarrjuun has-sana?
raČ-titČawwluun lil-karraada?
raČ-issawwuun kull iš-šuġuḷ?

Drill 5. Change the numeral from *Čišriin* to *Čaš(i)r-*, and make the appropriate changes in the noun and adjective.

Cue:	*Čindi Čišriin iktaab jidiid.*
Response:	*Čindi Čašir-kutub jiddad.*

laazim idjiibiin Čišriin igḷaaṣ niðiif.
kull yoom Čidna Čišriin muškila ṣaČba.
šifit Čišriin walad iṣġayyir bil-beet.
yirraad-inna Čišriin maṭaar čibiir.
jiib-li Čišriin qalam ṭuwiil.
triid tištiri Čišriin sayyaara ġaalya?
yirraad-inna Čišriin madrasa θaanawiyya.
jiibuu-nna Čišriin panka xafiifa.
šifna Čišriin ibnayya mašġuuḷa hnaak.
yirraad-li Čišriin xariiṭa jdiida.

Drill 6. Replace the topic noun by the items given, and make the appropriate change in the pronoun suffix.

l-pardaat inxaḷḷiiha l-ġeer yoom. The curtains we'll leave for another day.

Cue:	*l-muṭbax*	the kitchen
Response:	*l-muṭbax inxallii l-ġeer yoom.*	The kitchen we'll leave for another day.

mawðuuƐ iz-zawaaj	*kull hal-qaðaaya*
l-pardaat	*j-jihaal*
l-ifraaš	*l-masaaʔil il-lux*
garaaði	*Ɛaajaat il-beet*
miswaagna	*zuheer w-muṣṭafa*

UNIT 32

A. DIALOGUE

Zahda and Sami discuss some furniture they are going to have made.

zaahda	Zahda
1. *šifta lin-najjaar w-waṣṣeeta Ɛal-aθaaθ il-gitt-lak Ɛalee?*	Did you see the carpenter and order the furniture I told you about?
saami	Sami
2. *bali, šifta l-baarƐa w-waṣṣeeta Ɛala meez ʔakil w-sitt-iskamliyyaat.*	Yes, I saw him yesterday and ordered a dining-room table and six chairs.
zaahda	Zahda
3. *nšaaḷḷa ma-nseet itgul-la Ɛala meez il-kitaaba maalak.*	I hope you didn't forget to tell him about your desk.
saami	Sami
4. *laa, ma-nseet. git-la Ɛala hal-ašyaaʔ kullha. ʔaku šii ʔaaxar Ɛindič?*	No, I didn't forget. I told him about all these things. Is there anything else you have in mind?

zaahda	Zahda
5. *bali, yirraad-inna baƐad zuuliyya čbiira l-ġurfat il-xuṭṭaar w-izwaali ṣġayyra l-ġurfat in-noom wil-hooḷ.*	Yes, we still need a big rug for the parlor, and small rugs for the bedroom and the living-room.

saami	Sami
6. *ṭayyib, baačir irruuƐ suwa l-abu z-zuwaali w-inšuuf hal-ašyaaʔ kullha.*	All right, tomorrow we'll go together to the rug man and see about all these things.

VOCABULARY

najjaar (*najjaariin*)	carpenter
waṣṣa (*ywaṣṣi*) *Ɛala*	to give (someone) an order for, order (something) from (someone) (e.g. *waṣṣeet in-najjaar Ɛala meez* 'I ordered a table from the carpenter')
ʔaθaaθ	furniture
l-baarƐa	yesterday
meez (*myuuza*)	table
ʔakil	eating; food
meez ʔakil	table for eating, dining-room table
skamli (*skamliyyaat*)	chair
kitaaba	writing
meez kitaaba	writing-table, desk
maalak	your M, yours M
šii (*ʔašyaaʔ*)	thing
ʔaaxar (fem. *ʔuxra*)	other
šii ʔaaxar	something else, anything else
zuuliyya (*zwaali*)	rug
ġurfa (*ġuraf*)	room
xuṭṭaar (*xṭaaṭiir*)	guest(s), company
ġurfat xuṭṭaar	parlor (room where guests are received)
noom	sleep, sleeping
ġurfat noom	bedroom
hooḷ	living-room (room used by family)
baačir	tomorrow
ʔabu zwaali	rug merchant, rug man

B. GRAMMAR

1. Relative clauses

Note the three following sentences, each of which contains a relative clause:

a. *huwwa l-walad il-wuṣal il-baarḥa.*	'He's the boy who arrived yesterday.'
b. *huwwa l-walad iš-šifta l-baarḥa.*	'He's the boy whom I saw yesterday.'
c. *huwwa l-walad il-gitt-lak ʕalee.*	'He's the boy that I told you about.'

In all these sentences the **antecedent** of the relative clause—that is, the noun which the relative clause describes or modifies—is definite, in this case by virtue of the fact that it has the article prefix: *l-walad* 'the boy'. When the antecedent of a relative clause is definite, the clause is introduced by a form of the **relative particle.** Sometimes this particle has a longer form *ʔilli,* or *illi,* or *lli,* for example *l-walad illi wuṣal* 'the boy who arrived' and *l-ibnayya lli wuṣlat* 'the girl who arrived'. Much more commonly, however, the relative particle has a set of shorter forms, which are identical to the various forms of the article prefix (see 12 B 5), for example:

l-walad il-wuṣal	'the boy who arrived'
l-walad id-diras	'the boy who studied'
l-walad is-siʔal	'the boy who asked'
l-walad l-ištira	'the boy who bought'

The relative particle corresponds to the English relative pronouns *who, whom, which,* or *that.*

The three examples shown at the beginning of this section illustrate the three most common types of relative clause: one in which the subject of the verb is the same as (refers to the same entity as) the antecedent, one in which the object of the verb is the same as the antecedent, and one in which the object of a preposition is the same as the antecedent. In general it may be said that in any type of relative clause there must be some form which refers to the antecedent and serves to tie the clause to the antecedent grammatically. Here are some further details on the three types just mentioned, in which we shall see how this statement applies to each of them:

a. *Subject same as antecedent.* In this type of relative clause it is the form of the verb itself which refers to the antecedent. This is because a verb form like *wuṣal* does not correspond exactly to a subjectless form like English *arrived,* but rather means specifically 'he arrived'; *wuṣlat* means specifically 'she arrived', and so on. Thus one can say that the verb form itself expresses a pronoun subject, and it is this which refers to the antecedent. Another point to note—and this is true for all types of Iraqi relative clauses—is that the clause itself (everything after the relative particle) could serve as an independent sentence, which is not true of English. This is illustrated in the following examples:

wuṣal il-baarḥa.	'He arrived yesterday.'
huwwa l-walad il-wuṣal il-baarḥa.	'He's the boy who arrived yesterday.'
wuṣlat il-yoom.	'She arrived today.'
hiyya l-ibnayya l-wuṣlat il-yoom.	'She's the girl that arrived today.'
wuṣlaw gabuḷ saaεa.	'They arrived an hour ago.'
huṃṃa l-wulid il-wuṣlaw gabuḷ saaεa.	'They're the boys that arrived an hour ago.'

b. *Object of verb same as antecedent.* If the object of the verb in the relative clause refers to the same entity as the antecedent, then the verb always has attached to it a pronoun suffix referring to the antecedent and agreeing with it in the usual ways. Note again that the relative clause is capable of acting as a complete sentence:

šifta l-baarḥa.	'I saw him yesterday.'
huwwa-l-walad iš-šifta l-baarḥa.	'He's the boy (that) I saw yesterday.'
šifitha l-baarḥa.	'I saw her yesterday.'
hiyya l-ibnayya š-šifitha l-baarḥa.	'She's the girl (that) I saw yesterday.'
šifithum il-baarḥa.	'I saw them yesterday.'
huṃṃa l-wulid iš-šifithum il-baarḥa.	'They're the boys (that) I saw yesterday.'

c. *Object of preposition same as antecedent.* In this case the preposition in the relative clause has attached to it a pronoun suffix referring to the antecedent, and agreeing with it in the usual ways. Examples:

gitt-lak εalee.	'I told you about him.'
huwwa l-walad il-gitt-lak εalee.	'He's the boy (that) I told you about.'
ḥčeet wiyyaaha.	'I talked with her.'
hiyya l-ibnayya l-iḥčeet wiyyaaha.	'She's the girl (that) I talked with.'
dazzeet-ilhum l-ifluus.	'I sent the money to them.'
huṃṃa l-ixwaan id-dazzeet-ilhum l-ifluus.	'They're the gentlemen (that) I sent the money to.'

Note that in types **b** and **c** the relative pronoun may be omitted in English, but not in Iraqi.

The discussion and examples above have been limited to cases in which the antecedent is definite. When the antecedent is **indefinite,** everything thus far noted still applies, with one exception: there is no relative particle at all. Here are examples of the three types of relative clauses again, but this time with an indefinite antecedent:

a. *haaδa walad ma-yidrus ihwaaya.*	'This is a boy who doesn't study much.'
b. *štireet zuuliyya ma-aCibbha.*	'I bought a rug I don't like.'
c. *ʔaku muCallimiin ihnaak laazim aCči wiyyaahum.*	'There are teachers there that I have to talk with.'

2. Constructions with *maal*

As we saw in an early lesson, one way of indicating possession is by the use of a pronoun suffix attached to the possessed noun: *beetak* 'your M house'. Another way involves the use of the particle *maal-,* which may be translated as 'property of' or 'belonging to'. This construction consists of a definite noun (either bearing the article prefix or in an annexion with a noun bearing the article prefix) followed by *maal-* with the appropriate pronoun suffix indicating the possessor. Examples:

l-beet maalak	'your M house'
meez il-kitaaba maalak	'your M desk'
l-iskamli maali	'my chair'

There are three forms of *maal-* which are used in such constructions. One is the form *maal-* itself, which is used when the noun possessed is masculine singular, as in the foregoing examples. Another is the form *maalat-* (before suffixes beginning with a consonant) or *maalt-* (before suffixes beginning with a vowel), which is used when the possessed noun is feminine singular, or any dual or plural not referring to human beings:

ġurfat in-noom maalatna	'our bedroom'
l-iskamliyyaat maaltič	'your F chairs'

The third is the form *maalaat-,* which is used when the noun possessed is a feminine dual or plural referring to human beings:

l-muCallimaat maalaatna	'our teachers F'

When the noun possessed is a masculine dual or plural referring to human beings, the form *maal-* is occasionally used, but in this case the construction is generally avoided. If an adjective modifies the possessed noun, it follows the latter immediately, and is in turn followed by *maal-*:

l-imyuuza j-jidiida maalatkum	'your P new tables'

In meaning, the *maal-* construction is equivalent to a noun with a pronoun suffix, and in many cases either can be used: *zuuliyyatha* or *z-zuuliyya maalatha* 'her rug'. The general tendency, however, is to use the pronoun suffix with nouns which indicate a close or permanent possession or relationship, such as parts of the body or kinship terms, for example *ˀiidi* 'my hand' and *xaaḷta* 'his aunt', and to use the *maal-* construction with nouns borrowed from other languages, with dual nouns, and with nouns in an annexion, for example *t-talafoon maalna* 'our telephone', *l-ibnayyteen maalaathum* 'their two girls', and *meez il-akil maali* 'my dining-table'.

Another kind of construction involving *maal* is also common. This consists of a noun or noun phrase, then the word *maal* without a suffix, then another noun or noun phrase, for example:

madrasa maal banaat	'a school for girls, a girls' school'
meez il-kitaaba maal saami	'Sami's writing-desk'

This kind of construction is equivalent in meaning to an annexion (see 26 B 1), and in many cases either might be used. The *maal* construction, however, is often used instead of an annexion when the first noun is one borrowed from another language, when the first noun is modified by an adjective, or when either noun is itself part of an annexion. Here are some other examples:

gḷaaṣaat maal ṃaay	'water glasses'
l-ġuraf maal beetna	'the rooms of our house'
l-pardaat maal ġurfat il-xuṭṭaar	'the parlor curtains'
l-aθaaθ ij-jidiid maal bint axuuya	'my niece's new furniture'

C. DRILLS

Drill 1. Form sentences beginning with *tuCruf,* and containing relative clauses, as in the model.

Cue:	*l-wulid wuṣlaw il-baarCa.*	The boys arrived yesterday.
Response:	*tuCruf il-wulid il-wuṣlaw il-baarCa?*	Do you M know the boys who arrived yesterday?

s-sayyid da-yiqra j-jariida.
l-ibnayya da-tugƐud bil-muṭbax.
l-ʔax waṣṣalni lil-uuteel.
l-ixwaan yšurbuun gahwa kull yoom.
l-ibnayya jatti wiyya ʔummha.
l-walad ištira l-iskamliyyaat.
l-wulid dirsaw handasa.
l-muƐallimiin raḤ-yibquun ihnaa.

Drill 2. Form sentences beginning with *ween,* and containing relative clauses, as in the model.

Cue:	*štireet il-pardaat il-baarḤa.*	I bought the curtains yesterday.
Response:	*ween il-pardaat l-ištireetha l-baarḤa?*	Where are the curtains I bought yesterday?

šift iz-zuuliyya bil-hooḷ.
činti da-tiqriin ij-jariida.
jibtu j-jihaal wiyyaakum.
jibna l-ġaraaḍ wiyyaana.
štireet saaƐat ʔiid biš-šoorja.
Ḥaṭṭeet gḷaaṣ ṃaay Ɛal-meez.
tƐurfuun il-muƐallimiin ihnaa.
ʔaxáḍit l-ifluus minni.

Drill 3. Form sentences beginning with *ma-tḤibb,* and containing relative clauses, as in the model.

Cue:	*gitt-lak Ɛal-aθaaθ.*	I told you M about the furniture.
Response:	*ma-tḤibb il-aθaaθ il-gitt-lak Ɛalee?*	Don't you like the furniture I told you M about?

gitt-lak Ɛal-fikra j-jidiida.
da-tugƐud bil-iskamli.
Ḥčeet wiyya l-ibnayya.
činit gaaƐid bil-manṭiqa.
gitt-lak Ɛal-pardaat il-Ḥilwa.
jeet wiyya l-ixwaan.
štireetha mnin-najjaar.
da-tiḤči wiyya l-banaat.

Drill 4. Form sentences beginning with *ma-aku,* and containing relative clauses, as in the model.

Cue:	*ma-agdar aḤči wiyya hal-muƐallim.*	I can't talk with that teacher.
Response:	*ma-aku muƐallim agdar aḤči wiyyaa?*	Isn't there a teacher I can talk with?

ma-agdar ašrab hal-biira.
ma-agdar aqra haj-jariida.
ma-agdar asawwi haš-šuġuḷ.
ma-agdar abqa b-hal-uuteel.
ma-agdar agul-lak Ɛala hal-qaḍiyya.
ma-agdar ašrab min hal-igḷaaṣ.
ma-agdar ansa hal-banaat.
ma-agdar adfaƐ hal-iḤsaab.
ma-agdar arkab ib-has-sayyaaraat.
m-agdar adrus hal-mawḍuuƐ.

Drill 5. Form sentences beginning with *ween,* and containing *maal-* with a suffix, as in the model.

Cue:	*εindak meez kitaaba.*	You M have a writing-desk.
Response:	*ween meez il-kitaaba maalak?*	Where is your M writing-desk?

εindi meez ʔakil čibiir.
εindič pardaat jidiida.
εidhum maṭaareen.
εidna ġurfat xuṭṭaar.
εidha talafoon.
εinda skamliyyaat iṣġayyra.
εidna madrasteen θaanawiyya.
εidhum izwaali.
εindak saaεat ʔiid.
εidkum xaraayiṭ jidiida.

Drill 6. Form sentences beginning with *laazim inšuuf,* and containing a *maal* construction, as in the model.

Cue:	*bint axuuya εidha pardaat jidiida.*	My niece has new curtains.
Response:	*laazim inšuuf il-pardaat ij-jidiida maal bint axuuya.*	We must see my niece's new curtains.

zuheer εinda šiqqa jidiida.
saami w-zaahda εidhum ʔaθaaθ jidiid.
ʔibin xaaḷi εinda sayyaara čbiira.
zooj εammti εinda meez kitaaba.
ʔibn axuuya εinda ġurfat noom čibiira.
ʔumm xaalid εidha saaεat ʔiid ġaalya.
xaaḷti εidha skamli εatiig.
l-wulid εidhum ʔašyaaʔ ġaalya.

UNIT 33

A. DIALOGUE

Sami telephones the railroad station for reservations to Basra, where he and Zahda are going on their honeymoon.

l-muwaδδaf	The employee
1. *maħaṭṭat il-baṣra, ṣabaaħ il-xeer.*	Basra Station, good morning.
saami	Sami
2. *ṣabaaħ il-xeer. ʔariid asawwi ħajiz ʔili wil-ṃarti lil-baṣra bid-daraja θ-θaanya yoom sitta biš-šahar.*	Good morning. I want to make a reservation for me and my wife to Basra, second class, on the sixth.

l-muwað̣ð̣af	The employee
3. *tḥibb ib-qiṭaar il-leel loo b-qiṭaar in-nahaar?*	Would you like it on the night train or the day train?
saami	Sami
4. *bil-qiṭaar is-sariiʕ. haaða yiṭlaʕ il-miġrib, muu?*	On the fast train. That leaves at sunset, doesn't it?
l-muwað̣ð̣af	The employee
5. *bali, saaʕa sitta w-θiliθ. zeen, raḥ-aḥjiz-lak qamaara raqam sabʕa. b-isim-man ʔaḥjizha?*	Yes, at six-twenty. All right, I'll reserve compartment number seven for you. In whose name shall I reserve it?
saami	Sami
6. *ʔismi saami maḥmuud.*	My name is Sami Mahmoud.
l-muwað̣ð̣af	The employee
7. *l-biṭaaqa maaltak itkuun ḥaað̣ra baačir iṣ-ṣubuḥ. laakin l-ifluus laazim tindifiʕ gabuḷ yoom il-xamiis, ḥatta ma-yinliġi l-ḥajiz maalak.*	Your ticket will be ready tomorrow morning. But the money must be paid before Thursday, so your reservation won't be cancelled.

VOCABULARY

muwað̣ð̣af (*muwað̣ð̣afiin*)	employee (especially of government), civil servant, official
maḥaṭṭa (*maḥaṭṭaat*)	station
l-baṣra	Basra (city in southern Iraq)
ṣabaaḥ il-xeer	good morning
ḥajiz	reservation
ʔil-	(with pronoun suffix) to, for
ṃara	wife
daraja (*darajaat*)	class (on trains etc.); degree (of heat)

qiṭaar (*qiṭaaraat*)	train
leel	night, nighttime
nahaar	day, daytime
sariiɛ	fast, rapid
ṭilaɛ (*yiṭlaɛ*)	to leave, depart; to come out, go out
miġrib	sunset, sundown
ɛijaz (*yiɛjiz*)	to reserve
qamaara (*qamaaraat*)	compartment
ˀisim (*ˀasaami*)	name
-man	(suffixed to noun) whose? (suffixed to preposition) whom?
ɛaaḏir (*ɛaaḏriin*)	ready; present
ṣubuɛ	morning
baačir iṣ-ṣubuɛ	tomorrow morning
laakin	but
ndifaɛ (*yindifiɛ*)	to be paid
yoom il-xamiis	Thursday
nliġa (*yinliġi*)	to be cancelled

(For additional vocabulary items see B below.)

B. GRAMMAR

1. Verb classes

The great majority of Iraqi verbs are based on triliteral roots (see 28 B 1). These verbs fall into ten **derivational classes,** each one characterized by a particular feature in its pattern (the pattern of the 3 M perfect-tense stem). For example, Class II verbs all have a doubled middle radical, as in *xallaṣ* 'to finish'; and Class III verbs all have a long *aa* after the first radical, as in *jaawab* 'to answer'. The verbs within a given derivational class may include several, or all, of the inflectional types previously discussed: sound verbs (22 B 1), doubled verbs (26 B 3), hollow verbs (25 B 1), and defective verbs (27 B 1). Some of the derivational classes are associated with a particular kind of grammatical meaning; for example, Class VII verbs are mostly passive: *ndifaɛ* 'to be paid'. These various points are described below for each class. (With each example below, the corresponding 3 M imperfect-tense form is shown in parentheses.)

Class I

Class I verbs are characterized in a negative way: by their lack of any of the characteristics of the other nine classes. Their stem patterns are thus simpler than those of the others. In Class I there are sound, doubled, hollow, and defective verbs.

Sound verbs: Patterns FaMaL, FiMaL, FuMaL

FaMaL	*ʔaxaδ*	(*yaaxuδ*)	'to take'
	ʔakal	(*yaakul*)	'to eat'
FiMaL	*simaɛ*	(*yismaɛ*)	'to hear'
	kitab	(*yiktib*)	'to write'
	diras	(*yidrus*)	'to study'
	giɛad	(*yugɛud*)	'to sit'
	yibas	(*yeebas*)	'to get dry'
FuMaL	*ṭubax*	(*yuṭbux*)	'to cook'
	wuṣal	(*yooṣal*)	'to arrive'

Note: (1) There are only two verbs with the pattern FaMaL, but they are very common, and are both shown above. Notice that their imperfect stem has no *ʔ*, but has the pattern -aaMuL.

(2) FiMaL and FuMaL verbs have imperfect forms with various different vowels, and these must generally be learned in each case. The most common combinations are shown above.

(3) FiMaL verbs beginning with *y* have imperfect stems beginning with *ee*; FuMaL verbs beginning with *w* have imperfect stems beginning with *oo*.

Doubled verbs: Pattern FaDD

ɛaδ̣δ̣	(*yɛaδ̣δ̣*)	'to bite'
dazz	(*ydizz*)	'to send'
gaṣṣ	(*yguṣṣ*)	'to cut'

Note: The vowel of the imperfect may be *a*, *i*, or *u*, as illustrated above, but the first is very rare.

Hollow verbs: Pattern FaaL

naam	(*ynaam*)	'to sleep'
jaab	(*yjiib*)	'to bring'
šaaf	(*yšuuf*)	'to see'

Note: Hollow verbs with *aa* in the imperfect are much less common than the other two types.

Defective verbs: Patterns FiMa, FuMa

FiMa	*qira*	(*yiqra*)	'to read'
	liga	(*yilgi*)	'to find'
FuMa	*buqa*	(*yibqa*)	'to stay'

Class II

Class II verbs are characterized by a doubled middle radical. They include sound and defective verbs only.

Sound verbs: Pattern FaMMal

xaḷḷaṣ	(*yxaḷḷiṣ*)	'to finish'
naδ̣δ̣af	(*ynaδ̣δ̣uf*)	'to clean'

Note: The stem vowel of the imperfect may be *i* or *u*, as illustrated above.

Defective verbs: Pattern FaMMa

sawwa	(*ysawwi*)	'to do'

Note: The final vowel of the imperfect is *i* in all cases.

Most Class II verbs are transitive. Many of them are the transitive equivalents of intransitive Class I verbs, for example Class I *xiḷaṣ* 'to be settled, finished' and Class II *xaḷḷaṣ* 'to finish' (something), or Class I *wuṣal* 'to arrive' and Class II *waṣṣal* 'to convey' (someone to a destination). Some are similarly associated with words other than verbs, for example the adjective *niδ̣iif* 'clean' and Class II *naδ̣δ̣af* 'to clean' (something).

Class III

Class III verbs are characterized by a long vowel *aa* after the first radical. They include sound and defective verbs only.

Sound verbs: Pattern FaaMaL

saaƐad	(*ysaaƐid*)	'to help'
jaawab	(*yjaawub*)	'to answer'

Note: The stem vowel of the imperfect may be *i* or *u,* as illustrated above.

Defective verbs: Pattern FaaMa

daara	(*ydaari*)	'to take care of'

Note: The final vowel of the imperfect is *i* in all cases.

Most Class III verbs are transitive.

Class IV

Class IV verbs are characterized, in their perfect-tense forms, by a prefix *ˀa-* before the first radical. The imperfect-tense forms, however, have no *ˀa-,* and are indistinguishable from Class I forms. Class IV contains sound, doubled, hollow, and defective verbs. However, very few verbs of this class are in common use.

Sound verbs: Pattern ˀaFMaL

ˀaƐlan	(*yiƐlin*)	'to announce'

Note: The stem vowel of the imperfect may be *i,* as above, or in a few cases *u.*

Doubled verbs: Pattern ˀaFaDD

ˀaṣarr	(*yṣirr*)	'to insist'

Note: The stem vowel of the imperfect is generally *i,* as above.

Hollow verbs: Pattern ˀaFaaL

ˀaδaaƐ	(*yδiiƐ*)	'to broadcast'

Note: The vowel of the imperfect is *ii* in all cases.

Defective verbs: Pattern ʔaFMa

ʔalqa (*yilqi*) 'to deliver' (speech)

Note: The final vowel of the imperfect is *i* in all cases.

Class IV verbs are generally transitive. As noted above, they are rare, and their use in most cases is limited to a somewhat formal style of speaking. In many cases, even where a Class IV verb exists, the corresponding Class I verb is used instead, with the same meaning; for example, instead of Class IV *ʔaεlan* (*yiεlin*, the Class I verb *εilan* (*yiεlin*) 'to announce' is used. The imperfect forms of the two classes are identical in any case.

Class V

Class V verbs are characterized by a prefix *t-* before the first radical, and a doubled middle radical. The prefix *t-* is subject to assimilation in some contexts (see 23 B 1 b). Class V includes sound and defective verbs only.

Sound verbs: Pattern tFaMMaL

txarraj (*yitxarraj*) 'to graduate'

Note: The stem vowel of the imperfect is *a* in all cases.

Defective verbs: Pattern tFaMMa

tmanna (*yitmanna*) 'to wish'

Note: The final vowel of the imperfect is *a* in all cases.

Class V verbs are generally intransitive, and many have a passive meaning or the meaning of an action performed on oneself. Often there is a relationship between a Class II verb, with a transitive and active meaning, and a Class V verb of the same root, with the corresponding intransitive or passive meaning. For example Class II *ċawwal* 'to transfer' (someone) and Class V *tċawwal* 'to be transferred, to transfer oneself, to move', or Class II *ṣawwar* 'to depict, picture' (something) and Class V *tṣawwar* 'to picture to oneself, to imagine, to suppose'.

Class VI

Class VI verbs are characterized by a prefix *t-* before the first radical, and a long vowel *aa* after the first radical. The prefix *t-* is subject to the same assimilations as in Class V verbs (see 23 B 1 b). They include sound and defective verbs only.

Sound verbs: Pattern tFaaMaL

tƐaaraf (*yitƐaaraf*) 'to become acquainted'

Note: The stem vowel of the imperfect is *a* in all cases.

Defective verbs: Pattern tFaaMa

tɛaača (*yitɛaača*) 'to talk to each other, converse'

Note: The final vowel of the imperfect is *a* in all cases.

Class VI verbs are generally intransitive. They often indicate a reciprocal action involving more than one person; this kind of meaning is implicit when the form is plural, for example *tƐaarafna* 'we became acquainted (with each other'. The form may be singular, but in that case a preposition with its object is generally required *tƐaaráfit wiyyaa* 'I became acquainted with him'. In some cases there is a relationship between a verb of Class I or III, with a transitive meaning, and a Class VI verb of the same root, with an intransitive or reciprocal meaning. For example Class I *Ɛiraf* 'to know' and Class VI *tƐaaraf* 'to become acquainted (with each other)', or Class III *xaabar* 'to telephone' (someone) and Class VI *txaabar* 'to talk (with each other) by phone'.

Class VII

Class VII verbs are characterized by a prefix *n-* before the first radical. They include sound, doubled, hollow, and defective verbs.

Sound verbs: Patterns nFiMaL, nFuMaL

nFiMaL	*ndifaƐ* (*yindifiƐ*)	'to be paid'
nFuMaL	*njubar* (*yinjubur*)	'to be forced'

Note: In the imperfect-tense conjugation of these verbs, when a suffix (*-iin* or *-uun*) is added, the stem vowel is dropped, and the preceding vowel is changed to *a*. Thus *yindifiƐ* 'he is paid' but *yindafƐuun* 'they are paid'; *ninjubur* 'we are forced' but *tinjabriin* 'you F are forced' (see **2** below).

Doubled verbs: Pattern nFaDD

ndazz	(*yindazz*)	'to be sent'

Note: The vowel of the imperfect is *a* in all cases.

Hollow verbs: Pattern nFaaL

nraad	(*yinraad*)	'to be needed'

Note: The vowel of the imperfect is *aa* in all cases.

Defective verbs: Patterns nFiMa, nFuMa

nFiMa	*nliga*	(*yinligi*)	'to be found'
nFuMa	*nṭuwa*	(*yinṭuwi*)	'to be folded'

Note: The final vowel of the imperfect is *i* in all cases.

Class VII verbs are almost all intransitive, with passive meaning. In most cases there is an association between a Class I verb, with active meaning, and the corresponding Class VII verb of the same root, with passive meaning. For example Class I *simaƐ* 'to hear' and Class VII *nsimaƐ* 'to be heard', or Class I *Ɔall* 'to solve' and Class VII *nƆall* 'to be solved', or Class I *nisa* 'to forget' and Class VII *nnisa* 'to be forgotten'. Class VII also has a passive potential meaning, indicating that something can (or, more commonly, cannot) be done. For example *l-baab ma-yinsadd* 'The door cannot be closed', or *hal-ṃaay ma-yinširib* 'This water is undrinkable'.

Class VIII

Class VIII verbs are characterized by an infix *-t-* after the first radical. This *-t-* is subject to certain assimilatory changes, the most common of which are that after an emphatic it becomes *ṭ*, for example *ṣṭubar* 'to be patient', and after *d* or *z* it becomes *d*, for example *zdiƆam* 'to be crowded'. Class VIII verbs include sound, doubled, hollow, and defective verbs.

Sound verbs: Patterns FtiMaL, FtuMaL

FtiMaL	*ftiham*	(*yiftihim*)	'to understand'
	štiġaḷ	(*yištuġuḷ*)	'to work'
FtuMaL	*ṣṭubar*	(*yiṣṭubur*)	'to be patient'

Note: The stem vowel of the imperfect may be *i* or *u*. Also see **2** below.

Doubled verbs: Pattern FtaDD

htamm (*yihtamm*) 'to be concerned'

Note: The vowel of the imperfect is *a* in all cases.

Hollow verbs: Pattern FtaaL

ctaaj (*yictaaj*) 'to need'

Note: The vowel of the imperfect is *aa* in all cases.

Defective verbs: Patterns FtiMa, FtuMa

FtiMa	*štira*	(*yištiri*)	'to buy'
FtuMa	*stuwa*	(*yistuwi*)	'to ripen'

Note: The final vowel of the imperfect is *i* in all cases.

Class VIII contains both transitive and intransitive verbs, and cannot be said to have any particular meaning as a class.

Class IX

Class IX verbs are characterized by a doubled third radical, and thus include only doubled verbs. The pattern is FMaLL, and the vowel of the imperfect is *a* in all cases.

cmarr (*yicmarr*) 'to turn red, blush'

Class IX verbs are primarily associated with adjectives of the patttern ʔaFMaL which indicate a color or a defect, and the verbs have the meaning 'to become (that color)' or 'to come to have (that defect)'. Here are the most important ones:

ʔaεmar	'red'	*εmarr*	'to turn red, to blush'
ʔaxδ̣ar	'green'	*xδ̣arr*	'to turn green'
ʔazrag	'blue'	*zragg*	'to turn blue'
ʔaṣfar	'yellow'	*ṣfarr*	'to turn yellow; to turn pale'
ʔaswad	'black'	*swadd*	'to turn black'
ʔabyaδ̣	'white'	*byaδ̣δ̣*	'to turn white'
ʔaṭraš	'deaf'	*ṭrašš*	'to grow deaf'
ʔaṣḷaε	'bald'	*ṣḷaεε*	'to grow bald'
ʔaεwal	'cross-eyed'	*εwall*	'to become cross-eyed'

Class X

Class X verbs are characterized by a prefix *sta-* or *sti-* before the first radical. They include sound, doubled, hollow, and defective verbs. The prefix is *sta-* when two consonants follow (which is the case in sound and defective verbs). It may be *sta-* or *sti-* when a single consonant follows (as in doubled and hollow verbs), and the facts must be learned for each verb. In some verbs either form of the prefix may occur interchangeably. In all verb types, if the first radical is an emphatic, the consonants of the prefix may assimilate, becoming *ṣṭa-* or *ṣṭi-*.

Sound verbs: Pattern staFMaL

staεmal	(*yistaεmil*)	'to use'
stajwab	(*yistajwub*)	'to question'

Note: The stem vowel of the imperfect may be *i* or *u*.

Doubled verbs: Patterns staFaDD, stiFaDD

staFaDD	*staεaqq*	(*yistiεiqq*)	'to deserve'
stiFaDD	*stimarr*	(*yistimirr*)	'to continue'

Note: The last vowel of the imperfect is *i* in all cases.

Hollow verbs: Patterns staFaaL, stiFaaL

staFaaL	*staqaal*	(*yistiqiil*)	'to resign'
stiFaaL	*stifaad*	(*yistifiid*)	'to benefit'

Note: The last vowel of the imperfect is normally *ii,* but some verbs have a variant form with *aa*: *yistifaad.*

Defective verbs: Pattern staFMa

stanga	(*yistangi*)	'to choose'

Note: The final vowel of the imperfect is *i* in all cases.

Class X includes both transitive and intransitive verbs. Some are associated in meaning with adjectives, and have the meaning 'to consider (something) to be (the quality indicated by the adjective)', for example *ġaali* 'expensive' and Class X verb *staġla* 'to consider expensive', *ṭayyib* 'tasty, delicious' and Class X verb *sṭaṭyab* 'to find delicious'. Some are associated with other verbs, or nouns, and have the meaning 'to ask for, try to obtain', for example *jawaab* 'answer' and Class X verb *stajwab* 'to question, interrogate'.

Quadriliteral verbs

Besides the verbs based on triliteral roots, which fall into the ten classes described above, Iraqi has a sizable number of verbs which are based on quadriliteral roots, for example *tarjam* 'to translate', which has the root **t r j m** and the pattern FaSTaL. Quadriliteral verbs fall into two main derivational classes, **simple** and **derived.** (A third, much less common, class with the pattern FSaTaLL will not be treated here.) Simple and derived quadriliteral verbs include verbs of the sound and defective inflectional types only; the latter is of minor importance and will not be illustrated below.

Simple quadriliterals

Sound verbs: Patterns FaSTaL, FaDFaD, FooTaL, FeeTal

FaSTaL	*barhan*	(*ybarhin*)	'to prove'
	tarjam	(*ytarjum*)	'to translate'
FaDFaD	*dagdag*	(*ydagdig*)	'to pound'
	baqbaq	(*ybaqbuq*)	'to bubble'
FooTaL	*ṣoogar*	(*yṣoogir*)	'to insure'
FeeTaL	*neešan*	(*yneešin*)	'to aim'

Note: The stem vowel of the imperfect may be *i* or *u*.

Quadriliteral verbs of the FaDFaD pattern are said to have **reduplicated** roots; that is, the third and last radicals are repetitions of the first and second respectively. Many of these verbs are onomatopoetic, as in the examples above. Others are associated with Class I verbs, and have the meaning 'to perform repetitively or intensively (the action indicated by the Class I verb)', for example Class I *gaṣṣ* 'to cut' and Quadriliteral *gaṣgaṣ* 'to cut up, cut into pieces'. Quadriliterals of the FooTaL and FeeTaL patterns have a weak-second root, the second radical being *w* and *y* respectively.

Derived quadriliterals

Derived quadriliteral verbs are characterized by a prefix *t-* before the first radical. This *t-* is subject to the same assimilatory variations as those described for Class V and VI verbs.

Sound verbs: Patterns tFaSTaL, tFaDFaD, tFooTaL, tFeeTaL

tFaSTaL	*tbarhan*	(*yitbarhan*)	'to be proved'
	ttarjam	(*yittarjam*)	'to be translated'
tFaDFaD	*tgaṣgaṣ*	(*yitgaṣgaṣ*)	'to be cut up'
tFooTaL	*tṣoogar*	(*yitṣoogar*)	'to be insured'
tFeeTaL	*ddeewar*	(*yiddeewar*)	'to be turned'

Note: The stem vowel of the imperfect is *a* in all cases.

Most derived quadriliteral verbs are associated with simple quadriliterals of the same root, and have the corresponding passive meaning, for example *barhan* 'to prove' and *tbarhan* 'to be proved'.

2. Inflection of derived and quadriliteral verbs

Among the derivational classes described above are representatives of the four inflectional types of verbs: sound, doubled, hollow, and defective. Generally speaking, verbs of the same inflectional type are conjugated similarly —have the same prefixes and/or suffixes—regardless of the derivational class to which they belong. (For the conjugation of sound verbs, see 15 B 3, 18 B 1, 22 B 1, and 23 B 1; for doubled verbs, 15 B 3 and 26 B 3; for hollow verbs,

15 B 3 and 25 B 1; for defective verbs, 15 B 3, 27 B 1, and 27 B 2.) There are some differences, however, and these are described below, together with a few other reminders on points to be specially noted.

Sound verbs

In the imperfect of Class VII and VIII verbs, when the stem vowel (*i* or *u*) is dropped before the suffixes *-uun* and *-iin*, the *preceding* vowel *i* or *u* is changed to *a*:

Class and verb			Perfect	Imperfect
VIII *ftiham* 'to understand'	3	M	*ftiham*	*yiftihim*
		F	*ftihmat*	*tiftihim*
		P	*ftihmaw*	*yiftahmuun*
	2	M	*ftihámit*	*tiftihim*
		F	*ftihamti*	*tiftahmiin*
		P	*ftihamtu*	*tiftahmuun*
	1	S	*ftihámit*	*ʔaftihim*
		P	*ftihamna*	*niftihim*

The same kind of change occurs when a pronoun suffix beginning with a vowel is added: *yiftahma* 'he understands it M'.

In the perfect of Class X and Quadriliteral verbs, the stem vowel *a* is changed to *i* or *u* (whichever occurs in the imperfect) before the suffixes *-at* and *-aw*:

X *staEmal* 'to use'	3	M	*staEmal*	*yistaEmil*
		F	*staEmilat*	*tistaEmil*
		P	*staEmilaw*	*yistaEmiluun*
	2	M	*staEmálit*	*tistaEmil*
		F	*staEmalti*	*tistaEmiliin*
		P	*staEmaltu*	*tistaEmiluun*
	1	S	*staEmálit*	*ʔastaEmil*
		P	*staEmalna*	*nistaEmil*

Alternatively, in both the perfect and the imperfect, the stem vowel may be shifted before a suffix beginning with a vowel: *staEilmat, yistaEimluun.*

Doubled verbs

All doubled verbs are conjugated similarly, though of course the vowel of the imperfect may differ from verb to verb:

I *Cabb* 'to like'	3 M	*Cabb*	*yCibb*
	F	*Cabbat*	*tCibb*
	P	*Cabbaw*	*yCibbuun*
	2 M	*Cabbeet*	*tCibb*
	F	*Cabbeeti*	*tCibbiin*
	P	*Cabbeetu*	*tCibbuun*
	1 S	*Cabbeet*	*ʔaCibb*
	P	*Cabbeena*	*nCibb*
VIII *htamm* 'to be concerned'	3 M	*htamm*	*yihtamm*
	F	*htammat*	*tihtamm*
	P	*htammaw*	*yihtammuun*
	2 M	*htammeet*	*tihtamm*
	F	*htammeeti*	*tihtammiin*
	P	*htammeetu*	*tihtammuun*
	1 S	*htammeet*	*ʔahtamm*
	P	*htammeena*	*nihtamm*

Hollow verbs

Unlike hollow verbs of Class I, hollow verbs of the other classes are conjugated in the perfect tense like doubled verbs, adding *-eet-* to the stem in the second and first persons:

VIII *Ctaaj* 'to need'	3 M	*Ctaaj*	*yiCtaaj*
	F	*Ctaajat*	*tiCtaaj*
	P	*Ctaajaw*	*yiCtaajuun*
	2 M	*Ctaajeet*	*tiCtaaj*
	F	*Ctaajeeti*	*tiCtaajiin*
	P	*Ctaajeetu*	*tiCtaajuun*
	1 S	*Ctaajeet*	*ʔaCtaaj*
	P	*Ctaajeena*	*niCtaaj*

Defective verbs

Defective verbs of all classes are conjugated similarly, though the final vowel may differ from verb to verb:

I *qira* 'to read'	3	M	*qira*	*yiqra*
		F	*qirat*	*tiqra*
		P	*qiraw*	*yiqruun*
	2	M	*qireet*	*tiqra*
		F	*qireeti*	*tiqriin*
		P	*qireetu*	*tiqruun*
	1	S	*qireet*	*ʔaqra*
		P	*qireena*	*niqra*
VIII *štira* 'to buy'	3	M	*štira*	*yištiri*
		F	*štirat*	*tištiri*
		P	*štiraw*	*yištiruun*
	2	M	*štireet*	*tištiri*
		F	*štireeti*	*tištiriin*
		P	*štireetu*	*tištiruun*
	1	S	*štireet*	*ʔaštiri*
		P	*štireena*	*ništiri*

3. Ordinal numerals

The Iraqi ordinal numerals from 'first' to 'tenth' are as follows (the corresponding cardinal numerals are shown on the left in parentheses, for convenience of comparison):

	Masculine	**Feminine**	
(*waaCid*)	*ʔawwal*	*ʔuula*	'first'
(*θneen*)	*θaani*	*θaanya*	'second'
(*tlaaθa*)	*θaaliθ*	*θaalθa*	'third'
(*ʔarbaCa*)	*raabiC*	*raabCa*	'fourth'
(*xamsa*)	*xaamis*	*xaamsa*	'fifth'
(*sitta*)	*saadis*	*saadsa*	'sixth'
(*sabCa*)	*saabiC*	*saabCa*	'seventh'
(*θmaanya*)	*θaamin*	*θaamna*	'eighth'
(*tisCa*)	*taasiC*	*taasCa*	'ninth'
(*Cašra*)	*Caašir*	*Caašra*	'tenth'

Note the following points about these forms:

a. Except for *ˀawwal* 'first', all the (masculine) forms have the pattern FaaMiL (or, in the case of *θaani* 'second', FaaMi).

b. Again except for *ˀawwal,* the roots of the ordinals are generally the same as those of the corresponding cardinals. In several cases, however, there are slight differences, and these should be noted carefully.

These ordinal numerals usually serve to modify nouns, and they can do so in two different kinds of constructions, both translated the same in English. In one kind, the ordinal functions like an adjective in a noun-adjective phrase, following the noun and agreeing with it in definiteness and in gender:

l-beet iθ-θaaliθ	'the third house'
l-bint iθ-θaalθa	'the third daughter'

In the other kind, the ordinal serves as the first term of an annexion, preceding the noun it modifies. In this case the ordinal does not agree in gender but always has the masculine form; and neither it nor the following noun has the article prefix:

ˀawwal yoom	'the first day'
ˀawwal sana	'the first year'

We may also note here that the word *ˀaaxir* 'last' functions like an ordinal in such constructions:

ˀaaxir yoom	'the last day'
ˀaaxir ṃarra	'the last time'

For ordinals higher than 'tenth' there are no special forms; the cardinal numerals are used instead. The numeral follows the noun and has the article prefix; the noun itself may but need not have the article prefix:

(l-) yoom il-arḅaaṭaƐaš	'the fourteenth day'

4. Numerals: The thousands and millions

The word for 'thousand' is a noun *ˀalif* or *ˀalf,* with a dual form *ˀalfeen* 'two thousand', and a broken plural form *ˀluuf* 'thousands'. The latter is used only to indicate an unspecified number of thousands, as in *šifna ˀluuf imnil-wulid ihnaak* 'We saw thousands of boys there'. In the counting of thousands, *ʔalif* behaves like other nouns: after the numerals from 'three' to 'ten' a plural form is used, and after higher numerals the singular. The plural form used in the former case is a special counting form *taalaaf,* used only after one of the numerals from 'three' to 'ten'. Here are examples:

ʔalif (or *ʔalf*)	'one thousand'
ʔalfeen	'two thousand'
tlat-taalaaf	'three thousand'
ʔarbaɛ-taalaaf	'four thousand'
xamis-taalaaf	'five thousand'
sitt-taalaaf	'six thousand'
sabiɛ-taalaaf	'seven thousand'
θman-taalaaf	'eight thousand'
tisiɛ-taalaaf	'nine thousand'
ɛašir-taalaaf	'ten thousand'
daɛaš ʔalif	'eleven thousand'
ṣiṭṭaɛaš ʔalif	'sixteen thousand'
ɛišriin ʔalif	'twenty thousand'
sabɛa w-xamsiin ʔalif	'fifty-seven thousand'
miit-ʔalif	'100,000'
miiteen ʔalif	'200,000'
ʔarbaɛ-miit-ʔalif	'400,000'
sitt-miyya w-itlaaθiin ʔalif	'630,000'
θman-miyya w-iθneen w-tisɛiin ʔalif	'892,000'

The word for 'million' is also a noun, *milyoon,* with a dual form *milyooneen* 'two million', and a plural form *malaayiin* 'millions'. Examples:

sitt-malaayiin	'six million'
xamsiin milyoon	'fifty million'
miit-milyoon	'one hundred million'

The counted noun following any of these numerals is in the singular, for example *tlat-taalaaf walad* 'three thousand boys'; *milyoon sana* 'a million years'.

5. Days of the week, months, and dates

The days of the week have names with considerable similarity to numerals. They are:

yoom il-ˀaCCad	'Sunday'
yoom il-iθneen	'Monday'
yoom iθ-θilaaθaa	'Tuesday'
yoom il-arbiCaa	'Wednesday'
yoom il-xamiis	'Thursday'
yoom il-jumCa	'Friday'
yoom is-sabit	'Saturday'

The word *yoom* may be omitted from the names:

wuṣalna yoom is-sabit.
wuṣalna s-sabit. 'We arrived Saturday.'

The names of the twelve months of the solar calendar are:

kaanuun iθ-θaani	'January'	*tammuuz*	'July'
šbaaṭ	'February'	*ˀaab*	'August'
ˀaaδaar	'March'	*ˀayluul*	'September'
niisaan	'April'	*tišriin il-ˀawwal*	'October'
ˀayyaar	'May'	*tišriin iθ-θaani*	'November'
Czeeraan	'June'	*kaanuun il-ˀawwal*	'December'

Days of the month are usually given as ordinal numerals, rather than cardinals as in English, with or without the word *yoom,* as follows:

wuṣalna yoom sabCa biš-šahar.	'We arrived on the seventh (of the month).'
raC-tooṣal Cišriin tammuuz.	'She'll arrive the twentieth of July.'

Years are cited as cardinal numbers, usually preceded by the word for 'year' in its annexing form *san(a)t,* as follows:

ˀabuuya jaa l-baġdaad sant alf w-iθman-miyya w-tisCiin.	'My father came to Baghdad in 1890.'
raC-adrus b-ameerka min sant alf w-tisiC-miyya w-tisCa w-sittiin Catta sant alf w-tisiC-miyya w-iθneen w-sabCiin.	'I'm going to study in America from 1969 to 1972.'

C. DRILLS

Drill 1. Change the Class I verb to the corresponding Class VII verb, making the object of the former into the subject of the latter, as in the model.

Cue:	*dazz il-ifluus il-baarḉa.*	He sent the money yesterday.
Response:	*l-ifluus indazzat il-baarḉa.*	The money was sent yesterday.

difaḉ l-iḉsaab gabuḷ yoomeen.
šaaf aṣdiqaaᵓa yamm is-safaara.
nisa l-qaδiyya.
sadd il-baab saaḉa sitta.
simaḉ il-wulid bil-ġurfa θ-θaanya.
siᵓal kull il-ᵓasᵓila.
ḉiraf haaδa gabuḷ isbuuḉ.
liga l-wulid l-iṣġaar biš-šaariḉ.

Drill 2. Change the Class I imperative to the corresponding Class VII verb, making the object of the former into the subject of the latter, as in the example:

Cue:	*sidd il-baab.*	Close the door.
Response:	*il-baab ma-yinsadd.*	The door can't be closed.

ᵓidfaḉ l-iḉsaab.
ᵓidrus il-muškila.
ᵓisᵓal is-suᵓaal.
ᵓismaḉ il-muḉallima.
guṣṣ iz-zuuliyya.
ḟukk il-baab.
šuuf il-ġurfa.
ᵓiqra l-jariida.

Drill 3. In this drill the cue will be the name of a month. Form sentences using an ordinal numeral where possible, as in the model.

Cue:	*kaanuun iθ-θaani*	January
Response:	*kaanuun iθ-θaani ᵓawwal šahar bis-sana.*	January is the first month in the year.

šbaaṭ
ᵓaaδaar
niisaan
ᵓayyaar
ḉzeeraan
tammuuz
ᵓaab
ᵓayluul
tišriin il-ᵓawwal
tišriin iθ-θaani
kaanuun il-ᵓawwal
kaanuun iθ-θaani

Drill 4. Make progressive substitutions in the following sentence, making any other necessary changes each time.

haaða ʔibinhum il-ʔawwal.	This is their first son.
bitthum	daughter
iθ-θaanya	second
ʔibinhum	son
iθ-θaaliθ	third
bitthum	daughter
ir-raabεa	fourth
ʔibinhum	son
il-xaamis	fifth

Drill 5. Answer each question negatively, using in your answer the name of the day of the week after the day mentioned in the question.

Cue:	*raħ-tiji yoom il-ʔaħħad?*	Are you coming on Sunday?
Response:	*laa, raħ-aji yoom il-iθneen.*	No, I'm coming on Monday.

triid εajiz bil-qiṭaar yoom il-arbiεaa?
raħ-iššuufhum bil-baṣra yoom is-sabit?
l-ifluus laazim tindifiε gabuḷ yoom il-jumεa?
raħ-tiħči wiyya l-muwað̣ð̣af yoom il-xamiis?
l-qiṭaar is-sariiε yiṭlaε yoom il-iθneen?
l-εajiz raħ-yinliği yoom il-ʔaħħad?
ma-raħ-yxaḷḷiṣ iš-šuğuḷ yoom iθ-θilaaθaa?
ma-raħ-itnað̣ð̣uf il-beet il-yoom?

Drill 6. Repeat the sentence, making the date later each time by the number of years given in the cue.

txarrájit min kulliyyat il-handasa sant alf w-tisiε-miyya w-xamsiin.	I graduated from the College of Engineering in 1950.

Cue:	*wi-itlaθ-isniin*	and three years
Response:	*txarrájit min kulliyyat il-handasa sant alf w-tisiε-miyya w-itlaaθa w-xamsiin.*	I graduated from the College of Engineering in 1953.

w-xams-isniin	*w-arbaε-isniin*	*w-santeen*
w-santeen	*w-sana wiħda*	*w-sana wiħda*

UNIT 34

A. DIALOGUE

Sami and Zahda are talking about their impending honeymoon trip to Basra.

zaahda	Zahda
1. *sawweet il-ħajiz bil-qiṭaar, saamiʔ*	Did you make the reservation on the train, Sami?
saami	Sami
2. *ʔii, xaabarithum ʔawwal il-baarħa, w-raħ-aaxuδ il-biṭaaqa baačir loo εugba.*	Yes, I called them day before yesterday, and I'm going to get the ticket tomorrow or the day after.
zaahda	Zahda
3. *kulliš zeen. ʔinta šaayif il-baṣra gabuḷ, muuʔ*	Very good. You've seen Basra before, haven't you?
saami	Sami
4. *laa, ma-šaayifha, bass saamiε εanha ħilwa hwaaya.*	No, I haven't seen it, but I've heard (about it) that it's very pretty.
zaahda	Zahda
5. *ʔaani hamm ma-šaayfatha. l-uuteelaat laazim ʔarxaṣ min bağdaad.*	I haven't seen it either. The hotels must be cheaper than Baghdad.
saami	Sami
6. *wil-ʔakil hamm ʔarxaṣ. w-ma-aku ʔaḷṭaf min manaaδ̣ir šaṭṭ il-εarab.*	And the food's cheaper too. And there's nothing nicer than the views of the Shatt al-Arab.

zaahda	Zahda
7. *yguuluun ˀaḥla šii manḍar in-naxaḷ wakt il-ġuruub.*	They say the prettiest thing is the view of the palm trees at sunset.
saami	Sami
8. *ˀaani hamm saamiʕ haaδa, laakin ˀaḥsan šii l-waaḥid yšuuf ib-nafsa.*	I've heard that too, but the best thing is that one sees for oneself.

VOCABULARY

xaabar (yxaabur)	(Class III) to telephone
ˀawwal il-baarḥa	day before yesterday
ʕugba	day after tomorrow
šaayif	having seen
saamiʕ	having heard
ʕan	about, concerning
baġdaad	Baghdad
hamm	also, too; (with negative) (not) either
ḷaṭiif (ḷaṭiifiin)	nice, pleasant, agreeable
manḍar (manaaḍir)	view, sight, scene
šaṭṭ (šṭuuṭ)	river
šaṭṭ il-ʕarab	Shatt al-Arab (river in southern Iraq, formed by confluence of Tigris and Euphrates)
naxaḷ	(date) palm trees
ġuruub	setting of the sun
wakt il-ġuruub	sunset
l-waaḥid	one, you (impersonal), French *on*, German *man*
naf(i)s	(in annexion with following noun, e.g. *nafs il-yoom*) the same; (with pronoun suffix, e.g. *nafsa, nafisha*) himself, herself, etc.

B. GRAMMAR

1. Suffix *-man* 'whose, whom'

The interrogative particle *-man* is a suffix which may be attached to a noun or to a preposition. With a noun, it corresponds to the English interrogative 'whose?'. The noun is in its annexing form if it has one (see 26 B 1 c). Examples:

ˀisim-man	'whose name?'
beet-man	'whose house?'
ˀabu-man	'whose father?'
sayyaarat-man	'whose car?'
ġurfat-man	'whose room?'

With a preposition, *-man* corresponds to the English objective form 'whom?', serving as the object of the preposition. With *-man,* certain prepositions have the same form as with an attached pronoun suffix beginning with a consonant, and others may have their independent form. Here is a list of the most common:

ˀil-man	'to whom, for whom?'
bii-man	'in whom; with whom?'
ɛala-man	'on whom; about whom?'
ɛan-man	'about whom?'
ɛid-man	'in the possession of whom (who has)?'
miθil-man	'like whom?'
min-man	'from whom?'
wiyya-man	'with whom?'
yamm-man	'beside whom?'

The form *ˀil-man* is also used as the direct object of a verb, for example:

ˀil-man šifit bil-gahwa?	'Whom did you see in the coffee-house?'

The particle *-man* may also be attached to *maal-* (see 32 B 2), the whole form serving as the subject or predicate of an equational sentence. If the noun referred to is feminine, *maalat-* may optionally be used instead of *maal-*). Examples:

haaδa maal-man?	'Whose is this?'
hal-qalam maal-man?	'Whose is this pencil?'
had-daaˀira maal(at)-man?	'Whose is this office?'

2. Active participles: Class I

Besides the various inflectional forms of the perfect and the imperfect tense, Iraqi verbs have forms called active and passive participles. The latter will be discussed later. An **active participle** is like an adjective in some ways and like a verb in others. It is like an adjective in that it is inflected for gender and number (but not for person, like a verb); but it is like a verb in that it is usually negated by *ma-* and in that it can have a direct object, either a noun or a pronoun suffix. For example, in the sentence

ˀinta šaayif il-baṣraˀ	'Have you M seen Basra?'

there is an active participle *šaayif,* in its masculine singular form to agree with the pronoun *ˀinta* to which it refers; and this active participle has the direct object *l-baṣra.* In the following paragraphs we will first show the forms of active participles associated with Class I verbs, and then discuss the use and meaning of active participles in general.

The forms of Class I active participles differ slightly according to the inflectional type of the verb with which they are associated (sound, doubled, hollow, or defective). Following is a chart showing the patterns. The chart shows, for each type, first the verb, and then the masculine singular, feminine singular, and masculine plural forms of the active participle. (The feminine plural form is not given here, because it is less commonly used in most active participle constructions, and because it is in any case easily derived from the feminine singular form by changing the *-a* ending of the latter to *-aat.*)

Sound verbs: AP patterns FaaMiL, FaaMuL

Verb		*AP: MS*	*FS*	*MP*	
diras	'to study'	*daaris*	*daarsa*	*daarsiin*	'having studied'
širab	'to drink'	*šaarub*	*šaarba*	*šaarbiin*	'having drunk'

Doubled verbs: AP pattern FaaDD

dazz	'to send'	*daazz*	*daazza*	*daazziin*	'having sent'
Cuṭṭ	'to put'	*Caaṭṭ*	*Caaṭṭa*	*Caaṭṭiin*	'having put'

Hollow verbs: AP pattern FaayiL

šaaf	'to see'	*šaayif*	*šaayfa*	*šaayfiin*	'having seen'
raaC	'to go'	*raayiC*	*raayCa*	*raayCiin*	'having gone; going

Defective verbs: AP pattern FaaMi

qira	'to read'	*qaari*	*qaarya*	*qaariin*	'having read'
buqa	'to stay'	*baaqi*	*baaqya*	*baaqiin*	'having stayed; remaining'

Three important verbs have somewhat irregular AP forms:

ʔaxaδ	'to take'	*maaxiδ*	*maaxδa*	*maaxδiin*	'having taken'
ʔakal	'to eat'	*maakil*	*maakla*	*maakliin*	'having eaten'
jaa	'to come'	*jaayy*	*jaayya*	*jaayyiin*	'having come; coming

As this chart shows, an active participle has the inflectional forms of an adjective; and it can also function as an adjective, for example serving to modify a noun in a noun-adjective phrase:

l-ifluus il-baaqya 'the remaining money'

Also, however, an active participle may play a verb-like role in a sentence, sometimes taking a direct object, and indicating a tense-meaning somewhat different from that of the perfect or the imperfect. The imperfect tense alone usually indicates habitual action, for example:

zuheer ydizz ifluus l-axuu. 'Zuhayr sends money to his brother.'

The perfect tense alone indicates that the action was performed at some past time, without further implications:

zuheer dazz ifluus l-axuu. 'Zuhayr sent money to his brother.'

The active participle, however, indicates that the action was performed at some past time and that the results of the action are still apparent or existent; in English a similar implication is usually expressed by *have* or *has* with a past participle:

zuheer daazz ifluus l-axuu. 'Zuhayr has sent money to his brother.' (and the money is still on its way, or still in the brother's possession)

ʔaani šaayif il-baṣra. 'I've seen Basra.' (and the memory is still with me)

ma-qaari l-jariida. 'I haven't read the newspaper.' (so I don't know what's in it)

Note that, even though active participles may have a verb-like function and meaning in certain contexts, as in the sentences just cited, the sentences themselves are of the equational type; that is, they consist basically of a subject (noun or pronoun) and a predicate (the active participle). Thus, from the point of view of sentence structure, the two following Arabic sentences are both equational sentences:

ʔaani taƐbaan.	'I am tired.'
ʔaani šaayif il-baṣra.	'I have seen Basra.'

Sometimes, when the predicate is an active participle, the pronoun subject is omitted, as the previous context of the conversation will make the reference clear. Thus *ma-qaari l-jariida* could refer to any masculine singular subject, and could thus be translated as 'I (male speaker) haven't read the newspaper', or 'You M haven't . . .', or 'He hasn't . . .'

In the case of certain verbs, the active participle may indicate present or even future action. These are notably verbs indicating a change of bodily position such as those meaning 'to go, come, sit, stand' and so on. For example:

ʔaani raayiC lil-beet.	'I'm going home.'
humṃa gaaƐdiin bil-gahwa.	'They're sitting in the coffee-house.'

The stems of active participles may undergo certain changes when pronoun suffixes are attached, depending on the ending of the stem and on whether the suffix begins with a consonant or a vowel. (Attached to active participles one may find not only simple pronoun suffixes, but also the prepositional suffix *-l-* 'to, for' plus pronoun suffix, for example *huwwa daazz-li l-ifluus* 'He has sent the money to me'.) Following are the main points to be noted:

a. *Masculine singular stems ending in a single consonant*

Example: *šaayif* 'having seen'

With consonant suffixes, no change:

ʔaani šaayifha.	'I have seen her.'

With vowel suffixes, the stem vowel is dropped, as long as the result would be no more than two consonants in a row:

ʔaani šaayfa.	'I have seen him.'

b. *Masculine singular stems ending in a double consonant*

Example: *daazz* 'having sent'

With consonant or vowel suffixes, no change:

ˀaani daazzhum.	'I have sent them.'
ˀaani daazz-ilhum l-ifluus.	'I have sent (to) them the money.'

c. *Masculine singular stems ending in -i:*

Example: *naasi* 'having forgotten'

With all suffixes, the final *-i* lengthens to *-ii*. This is thus a vowel stem, and the pronoun suffixes have the forms appropriate to that kind of stem (see 16 B 4).

ˀaani naasiiha.	'I have forgotten her.'
ˀaani naasii.	'I have forgotten him.'

d. *Feminine singular stems ending in -a preceded by two different consonants (except -Cy-)*

Examples: *šaayfa* 'having seen F'
šaarba 'having drunk F'

These (and all feminine singular active participles ending in *-a*) have suffixing stems ending in *-t-*. With consonant suffixes this *-t-* is simply added:

hiyya šaayfathum.	'She has seen them.'

With vowel suffixes, either of two stem forms may be used.[1] In one, the *-t-* is simply added, as above, but there is non-automatic stress on the preceding *-a-*:

hiyya šaayfáta.	'She has seen him.'
hiyya šaarbáta.	'She has drunk it M.'

In the other, which is more common, the preceding *-a-* is shifted (see 15 B 2) to a position between the two consonants preceding it, and changed to either *i* or *u*, whichever appears in the corresponding masculine singular form. Thus *šaayfat-* becomes *šaayift-*, and *šaarbat-* becomes *šaarubt-*:

hiyya šaayifta.	'She has seen him.'
hiyya šaarubta.	'She has drunk it M.'

[1] Here, and in f. and g. below, both of two variant stem forms are given for your information. For drilling purposes, however, you should learn and use only the one which in each case is said to be the more common.

e. *Feminine singular stems ending in -a preceded by a double consonant*

Example: *daazza* 'having sent F'

With consonant and vowel suffixes, *-t-* is added, but with vowel suffixes there is non-automatic stress on the preceding *-a-*:

hiyya daazzatha.	'She has sent it F.'
hiyya daazzáta.	'She has sent it M.'

f. *Feminine singular stems ending -a preceded by -y-*

Example: *naasya* 'having forgotten F'

With consonant suffixes, *-t-* is added:

hiyya naasyatna.	'She has forgotten us.'

With vowel suffixes, either of two stem forms may be used. In one, the *-t-* is simply added, as above, but there is non-automatic stress on the preceding *-a-*:

hiyya naasyátak.	'She has forgotten you M.'

In the other, which is more common, the final sequence *-Cyat* is changed to *-Ciit-*:

hiyya naasiitak.	'She has forgotten you M.'

g. *Masculine plural stems ending in -iin*

Example: *šaayfiin* 'having seen P'

With both consonant and vowel suffixes, there are two possible stem forms. In one, there is no change:

ʔiCna šaayfiinhum.	'We have seen them.'
ʔiCna šaayfiina.	'We have seen him.'

In the other, which is more common, the final *-n* is dropped, and the result is a vowel stem. Thus *šaayfiin* becomes *šaayfii-*.

ʔiCna šaayfiihum.	'We have seen them.'
ʔiCna šaayfii.	'We have seen him.'

3. The word *nafis* 'soul; same; self'

The word *nafis* (plural *nfuus, ˀanfus*) has several useful functions. First, it is a noun meaning 'soul, spirit, personality'. Second, in the form *nafs,* it occurs before another noun in an annexion (the latter noun always with the article prefix), with the meaning 'the same', for example:

nafs il-yoom	'the same day'
nafs iš-šii	'the same thing'
nafs il-muškila	'the same problem'
nafs il-wulid	'the same boys'
nafs il-madaaris	'the same schools'

Third, it serves as a stem for the pronoun suffixes, in the form *nafis-* with consonant suffixes and *nafs-* with vowel suffixes. These forms correspond in meaning to English 'myself, ourselves' and so on.

nafsa	'himself'
nafisha	'herself'
nafishum	'themselves'
nafsak	'yourself M'
nafsič	'yourself F'
nafiskum	'yourselves'
nafsi	'myself'
nafisna	'ourselves'

Some speakers occasionally use the plural form with the plural suffixes: *ˀanfushum* 'themselves', *ˀanfuskum* 'yourselves', *ˀanfusna* 'ourselves'.

C. DRILLS

Drill 1. In this drill, the cues are statements which might serve as answers to a question involving the interrogative *whose.* You are to form the question, using a noun and the suffix *-man,* which would produce each answer.

Cue:	*haay sayyaarat zuheer.*	This is Zuhayr's car.
Response:	*sayyaarat-man haay?*	Whose car is this?

haaδa beetna.	*raaCaw b-sayyaarat ṣadiiqhum.*
haay qamaaratkum.	*Cičaw wiyya ˀabu l-walad.*
haaδa qalam il-muCallim.	*ˀaxδaw biṭaaqathum.*
haay zuuliyyat samiira.	*jaabaw meez ˀumm bahiija.*

Drill 2. In this drill, the cues are statements which might serve as answers to a question involving the interrogative *whom*. You are to form the question, using a preposition and the suffix *-man*, which would produce each answer.

Cue:	*ċiča wiyya ʔabu zuheer.*	He spoke with Abu Zuhayr.
Response:	*wiyya-man ċiča?*	With whom did he speak?

štira myuuza l-binta.
sallam ʕala ṣadiiqa bil-gahwa.
sawwa l-ʕajiz b-isim saami.
kull il-ġaraaδ ʕid xaalid.
štira l-iskamliyyaat minni.
huwwa raayiħ lil-baṣra wiyya zawujta.
šaaf ʔabu xaalid bil-madrasa.
laazim yisʔal ʔabuu.

Drill 3. Change the verbs in the following sentences to the appropriate form of the active participle. Where no subject is mentioned, supply the proper pronoun subject.

Cue:	*qireena kull ij-jaraayid.*	We read all the newspapers.
Response:	*ʔiħna qaariin kull ij-jaraayid.*	We've read all the newspapers.

xaalid ṭilaʕ wiyya ʔaṣdiqaaʔa.
simaʕt il-axbaar?
minu ʔaxaδ l-ifluus?
saami ʔakal kull il-ʔakil.
zaahda ʔaklat kull il-ʔakil.
ween raħ-itruuħiin?
ma-šifti baġdaad?
ʔumm samiira dazzat kull il-ġaraaδ.
qiraw kull ij-jaraayid.
nseetu ʔaṣdiqaakum?
gaṣṣeena biṭaaqteen.
raħ-tijuun il-beetna?

Drill 4. Change the verbs plus pronoun suffixes in the following sentences to the appropriate form of the active participle plus pronoun suffixes. Where no subject is mentioned, supply the proper pronoun subject.

Cue:	*šiftiiha?*	Did you F see her?
Response:	*ʔinti šaayfatha?*	Have you F seen her?

difaʕtii?
širabtii?
ʔakaltii?
ċijaztiiha?
ʔakaltiiha?
ween ċaṭṭeetii?
ʔil-man dazzeetiiha?
ma-šiftii?
ma-jibtiiha?
nseetiihum?
ligeetii?

difaʕtuu?
širabtuu?
ʔakaltuu?
ċijaztuuha?
ʔakaltuuha?
ween ċaṭṭeetuu?
ʔil-man dazzeetuuha?
ma-šiftuu?
ma-jibtuuha?
nseetuuhum?
ligeetuu?

difaʕta?
širabta?
ʔakalta?
ċijazitha?
ʔakalitha?
ween ċaṭṭeeta?
ʔil-man dazzeetha?
ma-šifta?
ma-jibitha?
nseethum?
ligeeta?

Drill 5. Repeat the following sentences, inserting *nafs* 'the same' before the noun.

Cue: *ʕidna ḥajiz bil-qiṭaar.* We have a reservation on the train.
Response: *ʕidna ḥajiz ib-nafs il-qiṭaar.* We have a reservation on the same train.

tigdar issawwi š-šuġuḷ?
raḥ-noosal il-yoom.
ma-ariid ašrab imnil-istikaan.
ʔiḥna gaaʕdiin bil-uuteel.
čaan yištuġuḷ bid-daaʔira.
činna nirkab il-paaṣ.
raḥ-adrus il-mawḍuuʕ.
tigidruun tirḥuun bit-taksi.
laazim aḥči wiyya l-muʕallim.
ʔaani saamiʕ l-axbaar.
huṃṃa raayḥiin lil-gahwa.
hiyya šaayfa l-manaaḍir.

Drill 6. Change the verb to correspond with the cues, and make the necessary change in the word *nafsa*. Do not repeat the cues themselves.

ʔaḥsan šii tšuuf ib-nafsak. The best thing is that you M see for yourself.

Cue: *ʔinti* you F
Response: *ʔaḥsan šii tšuufiin ib-nafsič.* The best thing is that you F see for yourself.

ʔintu	*ʔaani*	*ʔinti*	*samiira*
huwwa	*huṃṃa*	*ʔinta*	*ʔaṣdiqaaʔak*
ʔiḥna	*hiyya*	*xaalid*	*ʔaani*

UNIT 35

A. NARRATIVE

1. *saami w-zaahda nxubṣaw ib-tartiib safrat šahr il-ʕasal min giraḅ mawʕid zawaajhum.* Sami and Zahda became very busy with arranging the honeymoon trip when the date of their wedding drew near.

2. *saami sawwa l-ḥajiz bil-qiṭaar w-bil-uuteel, w-ḥatta ḍṭarr yxaabur il-baṣra min itʔaxxar jawaab il-uuteel.* Sami made the reservation on the train and at the hotel, and he even had to telephone Basra when the hotel's reply was delayed.

3. *θaani yoom il-ʕiris zaahda ḥaδδrat ij-junaṭ wil-ġaraaδ. bayynat farḥaana hwaaya.* — The day after the wedding Zaahda got the suitcases and things ready. She seemed very happy.

4. *zuheer waddaahum lil-maḥaṭṭa b-sayyaarta laakin ij-junaṭ inḥaṭṭat ib-sayyaarat ˀahal zaahda liˀann ˀakbar.* — Zuheer took them to the station in his car, but the bags were put in Zaahda's family's car because it's bigger.

5. *baqiit il-aṣdiqaaˀ wil-ˀahal raaḥaw lil-maḥaṭṭa fadd raas.* — The rest of the friends and the family went straight to the station.

VOCABULARY

nxubaṣ (yinxubuṣ) (b-)	(Class VII) to become busy, rushed, wholly tied up (with)
tartiib	arranging, arrangement(s)
safra (safraat)	trip
ʕasal	honey
šahr il-ʕasal	the honeymoon
girab̧ (yigrab̧)	(Class I) to approach, draw near
ḥatta	even
δṭarr (yiδṭarr)	(Class VIII) to be forced, have to
tˀaxxar (yitˀaxxar)	(Class V) to be delayed, be late
jawaab (ˀajwiba)	answer
ʕiris	wedding
ḥaδδar (yḥaδδir)	to prepare, get (something) ready
junṭa (junaṭ)	suitcase
farḥaan (farḥaaniin)	happy
laakin	but
nḥaṭṭ (yinḥaṭṭ)	(Class VII) to be put, placed
ˀahal (ˀahaali)	family, relatives; people
baqiyya	remainder, rest (of)
raas (ruus)	head
fadd raas	straight, directly

B. GRAMMAR

1. Active participles: Classes II to X and Quadriliterals

The forms of these active participles are easy to learn. They all consist of a prefix *m-*, *mi-*, or *mu-*, and a stem. If the stem begins with a single consonant, the prefix is *m-;* if it begins with two consonants, the prefix is *mi-* or, less commonly, *mu-*. The stem (in the masculine singular form of the participle) is the same as the stem of the 3 M imperfect tense stem, unless that stem ends in *-aC* (in which case the participle stem ends in *-iC* or *-uC*) or in *-a* (in which case the participle stem ends in *-i*). Thus *xaḷḷaṣ* (*yxaḷḷiṣ*) 'to finish', AP *mxaḷḷiṣ* 'having finished M'; *sawwa* (*ysawwi*) 'to do', AP *msawwi* 'having done M'; *xaabar* (*yxaabur*) 'to telephone', AP *mxaabur* 'having telephoned M'; *txarraj* (*yitxarraj*) 'to graduate', AP *mitxarrij* 'having graduated M'; *tmanna* (*yitmanna*) 'to wish', *mitmanni* 'having wished M'.

Class II

Sound verbs: AP patterns mFaMMiL, mFaMMuL

Verb		*AP: MS*	*FS*	*MP*
xaḷḷaṣ (*yxaḷḷiṣ*)	'to finish'	*mxaḷḷiṣ*	*mxaḷḷṣa*	*mxaḷḷṣiin*
naδ̣δ̣af (*ynaδ̣δ̣uf*)	'to clean'	*mnaδ̣δ̣uf*	*mnaδ̣δ̣fa*	*mnaδ̣δ̣fiin*

Defective verbs: AP pattern mFaMMi

sawwa (*ysawwi*)	'to do'	*msawwi*	*msawwya*	*msawwiin*

Class III

Sound verbs: AP patterns mFaaMil, mFaaMuL

saaεad (*ysaaεid*)	'to help'	*msaaεid*	*msaaεda*	*msaaεdiin*
xaabar (*yxaabur*)	'to phone'	*mxaabur*	*mxaabra*	*mxaabriin*

Defective verbs: AP pattern mFaaMi

daara (*ydaari*)	'to take care of'	*mdaari*	*mdaarya*	*mdaariin*

Class IV

Class IV verbs are rare, and the use of Class IV participles in a verb-like meaning is also very rare; we will therefore not list examples of these. There are, however, quite a few adjectives and nouns which have the form of

Class IV participles, and correspond to Class IV verbs some of which are no longer used. These generally begin with *mu-* rather than with *mi-* or *m-*, for example *muxliṣ* 'sincere', *muhimm* 'important', *mudiir* 'director'. Such words are best learned as individual vocabulary items, each with its own specialized meaning.

Class V

Sound verbs: AP patterns mitFaMMiL, mitFaMMuL

txarraj (*yitxarraj*)	'to graduate'	*mitxarrij*	*mitxarrja*	*mitxarrjiin*

Defective verbs: AP patterns mitFaMMi

tmanna (*yitmanna*)	'to wish'	*mitmanni*	*mitmannya*	*mitmanniin*

Class VI

Sound verbs: AP patterns mitFaaMiL, mitFaaMuL

ddaayan (*yiddaayan*)	'to borrow'	*middaayin*	*middaayna*	*middaayniin*

Defective verbs: AP pattern mitFaaMi

tƈaača (*yitƈaača*)	'to converse'	*mitƈaači*	*mitƈaačya*	*mitƈaačiin*

Class VII

Sound verbs: AP patterns: minFiMiL, minFuMuL

nziƈaj (*yinziƈij*)	'to be annoyed'	*minziƈij*	*minzaƈja*	*minzaƈjiin*
nxubaṣ (*yinxubuṣ*)	'to be rushed'	*minxubuṣ*	*minxabṣa*	*minxabṣiin*

Doubled verbs: AP pattern minFaDD

nƈall (*yinƈall*)	'to be solved'	*minƈall*	*minƈalla*	*minƈalliin*

Hollow verbs: AP pattern minFaaL

nraad (*yinraad*)	'to be wanted'	*minraad*	*minraada*	*minraadiin*

Defective verbs: AP patterns minFiMi, minFuMi

nƐina (yinƐini)	'to be bent over'	*minƐini*	*minƐanya*	*minƐiniin*
nṭuwa (yinṭuwi)	'to be folded'	*mintuwi*	*minṭawya*	*minṭuwiin*

Class VIII

Sound verbs: AP patterns miFtiMiL, miFtuMuL

ftiham (yiftihim)	'to understand'	*miftihim*	*miftahma*	*miftahmiin*
štiġaḷ (yištuġuḷ)	'to work'	*mištuġuḷ*	*mištaġḷa*	*mištaġḷiin*

Doubled verbs: AP pattern miFtaDD

htamm (yihtamm)	'to be concerned'	*mihtamm*	*mihtamma*	*mihtammiin*

Hollow verbs: AP pattern miFtaaL

Ɛtaaj (yiƐtaaj)	'to need'	*miƐtaaj*	*miƐtaaja*	*miƐtaajiin*

Defective verbs: AP patterns miFtiMi, miFtuMi

štira (yištiri)	'to buy'	*mištiri*	*mištarya*	*mištiriin*
stuwa (yistuwi)	'to ripen'	*mistuwi*	*mistawya*	*mistuwiin*

Class IX

These are all doubled verbs. The AP pattern is miFMaLL.

Ɛmarr (yiƐmarr)	'to turn red'	*miƐmarr*	*miƐmarra*	*miƐmarriin*

Class X

Sound verbs: AP patterns mistaFMiL, mistaFMuL

staƐmal (yistaƐmil)	'to use'	*mistaƐmil*	*mistaƐmila*	*mistaƐmiliin*

Doubled verbs: AP pattern mistiFiDD

staƐaqq (yistiƐiqq)	'to deserve'	*mistiƐiqq*	*mistiƐiqqa*	*mistiƐiqqiin*

Hollow verbs: AP pattern mistiFiiL

staqaal (yistiqiil)	'to resign'	*mistiqiil*	*mistiqiila*	*mistiqiiliin*

Defective verbs: AP pattern mistaFMi

stanga (yistangi)	'to choose'	*mistangi*	*mistangiya*	*mistangiin*

Simple Quadriliterals

Sound verbs: AP patterns mFaSTiL, mFaSTuL, mFaDFiD, mFaDFuD, mFooTiL, mFooTuL, mFeeTiL, mFeeTuL

barhan (ybarhin)	'to prove'	*mbarhin*	*mbarhina*	*mbarhiniin*
tarjam (ytarjum)	'to translate'	*mtarjum*	*mtarjuma*	*mtarjumiin*

Derived Quadriliterals

Sound verbs: AP patterns mitFaSTiL, mitFaSTuL, mitFaDFiD, mitFaDFuD, mitFooTiL, mitFooTuL, mitFeeTiL, mitFeeTuL

ṭṣoogar (yiṭṣoogar)	'to be insured'	*miṭṣoogir*	*miṭṣoogra*	*miṭṣoogriin*

The remarks made in 34 B 2 on the stem changes undergone by Class I active participles when pronoun suffixes are added also apply to the active participles of the other classes described above, with the addition of the following points.

a. *Class VII and VIII masculine singular stems ending in a single consonant*

Example: *miftihim* 'having understood M'

With vowel suffixes, the stem vowel is dropped *and* the preceding vowel is changed to *a*. (This is in accordance with a feature that applies to all Class VII and VIII imperfect and imperative verb forms as well as active participles: the vowel before the middle radical is *i* or *u* unless that radical is followed immediately by another consonant, in which case the preceding vowel is *a*.) Thus *miftihim* becomes *miftahm-*:

huwwa miftahmak.	'He has understood you M.'

b. *Class VII and VIII feminine singular stems ending in -a preceded by two different consonants (except -Cy-)*

Example: *miftahma* 'having understood F'

With consonant suffixes, the stem adds *-t-*: *miftahmat-*. With vowel suffixes, the stem adds *-t-*, the preceding *a* is shifted to a position before the last radical and changed to *i* or *u* (whichever occurs in the masculine form), *and* the *a* before the middle radical is changed to *i* or *u* (whichever occurs in the masculine form). Thus the stem (for consonant suffixes) *miftahmat-* becomes (for vowel suffixes) *miftihimt-*. The latter stem is the same as the masculine singular active participle with an added *t*.

hiyya miftihimta.	'She has understood you M.'

c. *Class VII and VIII feminine singular stems ending in -a preceded by -y-*

Example: *mištarya* 'having bought F'

With consonant suffixes, the stem adds *-t-*: *mištaryat-*. With vowel suffixes, the final sequence *-yat-* is changed to *-iit*, *and* the preceding *a* is changed to *i* or *u* (whichever occurs in the masculine form). Thus *mištaryat-* becomes *mištiriit-*. The latter stem is the same as the masculine singular active participle with a long *ii* and an added *t*.

hiyya mištiriita.	'She has bought it M'.

2. The auxiliary *čaan* with active participle

As we saw in 34 B 2, the active participle alone may have a verb-like meaning expressing the idea of an action which was done at some time in the past, with results still existing or of interest at the time of speaking, for example:

hiyya mnaṣṣfa kull il-ġuraf.	'She has cleaned all the rooms.'

The implication in the sentence above is that, as a result of her action, the rooms are still clean at the time this sentence is spoken. It is also possible to express the idea of an action which was done at some time in the past, with results which were still existing or of interest at another, less remote, time in the past. This idea is expressed by a verb phrase consisting of a perfect-tense form of the verb *čaan* and an active participle; the usual English equivalent is *had* and a past participle. Examples:

min wuṣálit lil-beet, čaanat imnaḍḍfa kull il-ġuraf.	'When I arrived at the house, she had cleaned all the rooms.'
čint imxaḷḷiṣ iš-šuġuḷ min xaabaritni.	'I (male speaker) had finished the work when you phoned me.'
čint imxaḷḷsa š-šuġul min xaabaritni.	'I (female speaker) had finished the work when you phoned me.'
ma-čaanaw saamƐiin il-axbaar min šifnaahum.	'They hadn't heard the news when we saw them.'
ma-činna šaayfiihum gabuḷ.	'We hadn't seen them before.'

As these examples show, the auxiliary verb *čaan,* like any verb, agrees with the subject in person, gender, and number, while the participle form agrees in gender and number, just as it does when not preceded by *čaan.*

3. Adjectives of color and defect

A number of adjectives indicating a color, like *ʔaƐmar* 'red', or a physical defect, like *ʔaṭraš* 'deaf', have similar forms, and can conveniently be treated together. A list of the most common was given in the discussion of Class IX verbs (33 B 1). Shown below are the masculine, feminine, and plural forms of these. Note that the colors all have broken plurals; the adjectives of defect may also have the same kind of broken plural, or a sound plural (the latter shown in parentheses).

Masculine	Feminine	Plural	
ʔaƐmar	*Ɛamra*	*Ɛumur*	'red'
ʔaxḍar	*xaḍra*	*xuḍur*	'green'
ʔazrag	*zarga*	*zurug*	'blue'
ʔaṣfar	*ṣafra*	*ṣufur*	'yellow'
ʔaswad	*sooda*	*suud*	'black'
ʔabyaḍ	*beeḍa*	*biiḍ*	'white'
ʔaṭraš	*ṭarša*	*ṭuruš (ṭaršiin)*	'deaf'
ʔaṣlaƐ	*ṣalƐa*	*ṣuluƐ (ṣalƐiin)*	'bald'
ʔaƐwal	*Ɛoola*	*Ɛuul (Ɛooliin)*	'cross-eyed'

Plural nouns, referring to human beings or not, are usually modified by the broken plural forms of the color adjectives (see 31 B 3 c):

zwaali zurug	'red rugs'
pardaat biiḍ	'white curtains'

C. DRILLS

Drill 1. Change the verbs in the following sentences to the appropriate form of the active participle. Where no subject is mentioned, supply the proper pronoun subject.

Cue:	*naḏḏfat kull il-ġuraf.*	She cleaned all the rooms.
Response:	*hiyya mnaḏḏfa kull il-ġuraf.*	She has cleaned all the rooms.

ma-xaḷḷaṣ šuġḷa.
saami sawwa l-ʕajiz bil-qiṭaar.
leeš ma-jaawbat?
ʔinta txarrájit?
ʔinti txarrajti?
ʔasdiqaaʔi ddaaynaw ifluus minni.
ʔintu ma-tʕaačeetu gabuḷ?
ʔabuuya ftiham il-qaḏiyya.
ʔummi ftihmat il-qaḏiyya.
ftihmaw il-qaḏiyya.
zaahda ʕmarrat išwayya.
ma-staʕmálit hal-aθaaθ gabuḷ.

Drill 2. In the following sentences, change each active participle first to active participle plus 3 MS pronoun suffix 'him' or 'it M', and next to active particple plus 3 FS pronoun suffix 'her' or 'it F'.

Cue:	*huwwa mxaḷḷiṣ.*	He has finished.
Response:	*huwwa mxaḷḷṣa.*	He has finished it M.
	huwwa mxaḷḷiṣha.	He has finished it F.

huwwa mbaddil.	*hiyya mbaddla.*	*humma mbaddliin.*
huwwa mʕawwil.	*hiyya mʕawwla.*	*humma mʕawwliin.*
huwwa mnaḏḏuf.	*hiyya mnaḏḏfa.*	*humma mnaḏḏfiin*
huwwa msaaʕid.	*hiyya msaaʕda.*	*humma msaaʕdiin.*
huwwa mxaabur.	*hiyya mxaabra.*	*humma mxaabriin.*
huwwa miṣṣawwir.	*hiyya miṣṣawwra.*	*humma miṣṣawwriin.*
huwwa middaayin.	*hiyya middaayna.*	*humma middaayniin.*
huwwa miftihim.	*hiyya miftahma.*	*humma miftahmiin.*
huwwa mistaʕmil.	*hiyya mistaʕmila.*	*humma mistaʕmiliin.*
huwwa mtarjum.	*hiyya mtarjuma.*	*humma mtarjumiin.*
huwwa msawwi.	*hiyya msawwya.*	*humma msawwiin.*
huwwa mdaari.	*hiyya mdaarya.*	*humma mdaariin.*
huwwa mištiri.	*hiyya mištarya.*	*humma mištiriin.*
huwwa mistangi	*hiyya mistangiya.*	*humma mistangiin.*

Drill 3. Change each of the following sentences by inserting the appropriate perfect-tense form of *čaan* before the active participle. If the cue sentence contains a pronoun subject, leave it out in the response.

Cue:	*hiyya ma-mistaɛmila s-sayyaara.*	
Response:	*ma-čaanat mistaɛmila s-sayyaara.*	

ʔinti saamɛa l-axbaar?	*ʔintu mxaabriiha?*
l-banaat ṭaabxiin ihwaaya ʔakil.	*ʔaani ma-miftihim il-muškila.*
ʔaani saadd kull il-ibwaab.	*l-ibnayya ma-mnaδ̣δ̣fa gurfat in-noom.*
ʔiḥna naaṭiihum l-ifluus.	*ʔaṣdiqaaʔi mitxarrjiin imnil-kulliyya.*
samiira ma-qaarya j-jariida.	*zaahda ma-mištarya šii z-zawaajha.*
ʔintu daafɛiiha?	*xaalid ma-mištuġuḷ ihnaa gabuḷ.*

Drill 4. Repeat the sentence, replacing the color adjective with those given.

a. *laazim tistaɛmil qalam ʔaḥmar.*	You M have to use a red pencil.
ʔaṣfar	yellow
ʔaswad	black
ʔabyaδ̣	white
ʔaxδ̣ar	green
ʔazrag	blue
ʔaḥmar	red
b. *šaayif sayyaarathum il-ḥamra?*	Have you M seen their red car?
ṣafra	yellow
sooda	black
beeδ̣a	white
xaδ̣ra	green
zarga	blue
ḥamra	red
c. *čaanaw mištiriin pardaat ḥumur.*	They had bought red curtains.
ṣufur	yellow
suud	black
biiδ̣	white
xuδ̣ur	green
zurug	blue
ḥumur	red

Drill 5. Repeat each sentence, adding the appropriate form of *ʔazrag* 'blue' to modify the noun.

Cue:	*šaayif is-sayyaara?*	Have you M seen the car?
Response:	*šaayif is-sayyaara z-zarga?*	Have you M seen the blue car?

ween qalami?	*ma-tḥibb hal-izwaali?*
laazim taaxuδ il-paaṣ.	*yiraad-inna fadd iskamli.*
raḥ-yistanguun iz-zuuliyya.	*ɛidha ɛyuun ḥilwa.*
štireena pardaat il-ġurfat in-noom.	*ma-agdar arkab ib-sayyaara.*

Drill 6. Repeat each sentence, adding the appropriate form of *ˀabyaδ̣* 'white' to modify the noun.

Cue:	*buqa bil-beet.*	He stayed in the house.
Response:	*buqa bil-beet il-abyaδ̣.*	He stayed in the white house.

ċinda talafoon ib-daaˀirta.
ma-tgidruun tistaċmiluun pardaat ihnaa.
ruuċ lil-baab w-ˀisˀal.
laa, la-tištiriin zuuliyya.
ma-aku qalam ihnaak.
ma-tċibbuun il-xaraayiṭ?
šaayfiin sayyaarathum?
stangat izwaali.

UNIT 36

A. DIALOGUE

Abu Mustafa goes to the grocer for fruit and vegetables.

ˀabu muṣṭafa	Abu Mustafa
1. *gul-li, ċindak ˀaċsan min hal-mooz wil-purtaqaal?*	Tell me, have you got any better than these bananas and oranges?
l-baggaaḷ	The grocer
2. *ṭabċan, ċammi, ċindi kullši. š-itċibb aṭalliċ-lak?*	Certainly, sir, I've got everything. What would you like me to bring out for you?
ˀabu muṣṭafa	Abu Mustafa
3. *nṭiina fadd sitt-purtaqaalaat w-itlaθ-moozaat.*	Give us about six oranges and three bananas.
l-baggaaḷ	The grocer
4. *ṭayyib, ċammi. ˀaku šii laax itċibb? ċindi xyaar kulliš mumtaaz il-yoom.*	All right, sir. Is there anything else you'd like? I have very fine cucumbers today.

ˀabu muṣṭafa	Abu Mustafa
5. *laa, nṭiina keelu beetinjaan w-keeluween ṭamaaṭa.*	No, give us a kilo of eggplant and two kilos of tomatoes.
l-baggaaḷ	The grocer
6. *ma-triid ʕinab, raggi . . .ˀ*	Don't you want any grapes, watermelon . . .?
ˀabu muṣṭafa	Abu Mustafa
7. *bali, ˀoozin-li fadd raggiyya waṣṭaaniyya w-baṭṭiixteen.*	Yes, weigh me out a medium-sized watermelon and two cantaloupes.
l-baggaaḷ	The grocer
8. *tuˀmur, ʕammi.*	Yes, sir.

VOCABULARY

baggaaḷ (bgaagiil)	grocer (seller of fruit and vegetables)
mooz	(collective) bananas
mooza (moozaat)	banana
purtaqaal	(collective) oranges
purtaqaala (purtaqaalaat)	orange
ṭallaʕ (yṭalliʕ)	(Class II) to take out, bring out
fadd	(before a numeral) about, approximately
xyaar	(collective) cucumbers
xyaara (xyaaraat)	cucumber
mumtaaz (mumtaaziin)	fine, excellent
keelu (keeluwaat)	kilo(gram)
beetinjaan	(collective) eggplant
beetinjaana (beetinjaanaat)	an eggplant
ṭamaaṭa	(collective) tomatoes
ṭamaaṭaaya	tomato
ʕinab	(collective) grapes
ʕinbaaya (ʕinbaayaat)	grape
wuzan (yoozin)	(Class I) to weigh
raggi	(collective) watermelon

raggiyya (*raggiyyaat*)	a watermelon
waṣṭaani	medium-sized
baṭṭiix	(collective) cantaloupe
baṭṭiixa (*baṭṭiixaat*)	a cantaloupe
tuˀmur	yes, sir ("you command")

---

namil	(collective) ants
namla	ant
tamur	(collective) dates
tamra	date
simač	(collective) fish
simča	a fish
laƹma	(collective) meat
laƹma	piece of meat
liilu	(collective) pearls
liiluwwa	a pearl
xoox	(collective) peaches
xooxa, xooxaaya	peach
tiffaaƹ	(collective) apples
tiffaaƹa, tiffaaƹaaya	apple
čaayči (*čaayčiyya*)	tea vendor
saaƹači (*saaƹačiyya*)	watch dealer, watch repairman
gahawči (*gahawčiyya*)	coffee-house proprietor
qundara (*qanaadir*)	shoe
qundarči (*qundarčiyya*)	shoemaker, shoe repairman
ˀuuti (*ˀuutiyyaat*)	iron (for pressing)
ˀuutači (*ˀuutačiyya*)	presser

B. GRAMMAR

1. Collectives and unit nouns

Certain Iraqi nouns have not only a singular, a dual, and a plural form, but also a **collective** form. The collective form expresses the concept of a substance or material in the mass, or a collection of objects viewed as a whole, without regard to the individual objects included in it. Thus *mooz* means 'bananas' in general, viewed as a group or a type of food, and does not refer to a certain number of individual bananas. The singular form associated with a collective is a feminine noun ending in *-a*; this form is known as a **unit noun,** and is used to refer to one individual object or item. Thus *mooza* means 'banana', that is, a single individual banana. A unit noun such as this one normally has a dual form (for example *moozteen* 'two bananas'), and a plural form ending in *-aat* (for example *moozaat* 'bananas'). The difference between the collective form and the plural form is that the latter refers to a number of specific individual items of the material in question, and is thus used mainly after numerals. Thus, using a collective, one might say *ween Ꞩaṭṭeet il-mooz?* 'Where did you put the bananas?', or *ma-aꞨibb il-mooz* 'I don't like bananas'; whereas one would use the plural to say *jiib-li ʔarbaꞨ-moozaat* 'Bring me four bananas'.

Collectives (and the unit nouns associated with them) are typically found among words referring to fruits, vegetables, and other kinds of food; those referring to material substances such as stone or wood; those referring to trees and plants; and those referring to lower life forms such as fish or insects.

Most collectives are masculine nouns, and end in a consonant, *-i,* or *-u.* The corresponding unit noun in each case is feminine, and is formed by adding *-a* to the collective, with appropriate stem changes in the latter: if it ends in a consonant, the stem vowel is dropped (unless that would result in a cluster of three consonants); if it ends in *-i, -yy-* is added; if it ends in *-u, -ww-* is added. Examples:

Collective		**Unit noun**	
mooz	'bananas'	*mooza*	'banana'
beetinjaan	'eggplant'	*beetinjaana*	'an eggplant'
namil	'ants'	*namla*	'ant'
tamur	'dates'	*tamra*	'date'
simač	'fish'	*simča*	'a fish'
laꞨam	'meat'	*laꞨma*	'piece of meat'
naxaḷ	'palm trees'	*naxḷa*	'a palm tree'
raggi	'watermelon'	*raggiyya*	'a watermelon'
liilu	'pearls'	*liiluwwa*	'a pearl'

A few collectives, however, are feminine nouns, and end in *-a.* In such cases the corresponding unit noun is formed by changing the *-a* to *-aaya.* Also, several unit nouns may end in either *-a* or *-aaya* even when the corresponding collective does not end in *-a.* Examples:

ṭamaaṭa	'tomatoes'	*ṭamaaṭaaya*	'tomato'
xoox	'peaches'	*xooxa(aya)*	'peach'
tiffaaꞨ	'apples'	*tiffaaꞨa(aya)*	'apple'

In the case of those unit nouns which may end in either *-a* or *-aaya,* the dual and plural forms are usually based on the shorter stem: *xooxteen* 'two peaches', *tlat-tiffaaꞨaat* 'three apples'.

As we have seen above, collectives have the form of masculine singular or feminine singular nouns; and they also follow the same rules of agreement (for adjectives, pronouns, and verbs) as do such nouns (see 31 B 3 and 4):

xyaar mumtaaz	'fine cucumbers'
ṭamaaṭa mumtaaza	'fine tomatoes'

Occasionally, however, plural forms may be used to refer to collective nouns, as for example in *hat-tiffaaƈ iṣġaar* 'These apples are little'.

Unit nouns are all feminine singular, and follow the rule of agreement for such nouns:

xyaara čbiira	'a big cucumber'

2. Passive participles

In addition to the active participles described in 34 B 2 and 35 B 1, most transitive verbs have associated forms known as **passive participles.** These forms function as adjectives, and indicate a state or condition resulting from having undergone the action named by the verb. They usually correspond to English past participles. For example *kitab* 'to write' has the passive participle *maktuub* 'written', and *sadd* 'to close' has the passive participle *masduud* 'closed'. Being adjectives, passive participles are inflected for gender and number: most have sound rather than broken plurals. Details are given below. (Plural forms are shown in all cases as models, but they would be used only for those which might apply to human beings.)

Class I

Sound, doubled, hollow verbs: PP pattern maFMuuL

Verb		PP: *MS*	*FS*	*MP*
ƈiraf (yuƈruf)	'to know'	*maƈruuf*	*maƈruufa*	*maƈruufiin* 'known'
sadd (ysidd)	'to close'	*masduud*	*masduuda*	*masduudiin* 'closed'
šaaf (yšuuf)	'to see'	*mašyuuf*	*mašyuufa*	*mašyuufiin* 'seen'

Defective verbs: PP pattern maFMi

nisa (yinsa)	'to forget'	*mansi*	*mansiyya*	*mansiyyiin* 'forgotten'

In Classes II to X and the Quadriliterals, the passive participle consists of a prefix and a stem. If the stem begins with one consonant, the prefix is *m-*; if it begins with two consonants, the prefix *mi* or *mu-*. The stem (masculine singular form) is the same as the stem of the 3 M imperfect verb form, except that the stem vowel or final vowel is always *a*. Here are some selected examples:

Class II

Sound verbs: PP pattern mFaMMaL

baddal (*ybaddil*)	'to change'	*mbaddal*	*mbaddla*	*mbaddliin* 'changed'
naṣṣaf (*ynaṣṣuf*)	'to clean'	*mnaṣṣaf*	*mnaṣṣfa*	*mnaṣṣfiin* 'cleaned'

Defective verbs: PP pattern mFaMMa

sawwa (*ysawwi*)	'to do'	*msawwa*	*msawwaaya*	*msawwaayiin* 'done'

Class III

Sound verbs: PP pattern mFaaMaL

saaεad (*ysaaεid*)	'to help'	*msaaεad*	*msaaεda*	*msaaεdiin* 'helped'

Defective verbs: PP pattern mFaaMa

daara (*ydaari*)	'to care for'	*mdaara*	*mdaaraaya*	*mdaaraayiin* 'cared for'

Class X

Sound verbs: PP pattern mustaFMaL

staεmal (*yistaεmil*)	'to use'	*mustaεmal*	(*mustaεmala* / *mustaεmila*)	(*mustaεmaliin* / *mustaεmiliin*) 'used'

Defective verbs: PP pattern mustaFMa

stanga (*yistangi*)	'to choose'	*mistanga*	*mistangaaya*	*mistangaayiin* 'chosen'

Quadriliterals

Sound verbs: PP pattern mFaSTaL

barhan (*ybarhin*)	'to prove'	*mbarhan*	(*mbarhana* / *mbarhina*)	(*mbarhaniin* / *mbarhiniin*) 'proved'
tarjam (*ytarjum*)	'to translate'	*mtarjam*	(*mtarjama* / *mtarjuma*)	(*mtarjamiin* / *mtarjumiin*) 'translated'

Note that where the masculine form of the passive particple ends in *-a,* the feminine and plural forms end in *-aaya* and *-aayiin* respectively. Note also that where the masculine form ends in *-aC,* and the stem vowel cannot be dropped in the feminine and plural forms because that would result in three consonants together, the stem vowel may be changed to *i* or *u* (whichever occurs in the imperfect). The latter point is illustrated in *staƐmal, barhan,* and *tarjam* above.

Passive participles, like other adjectives, are most commonly found modifying a noun in a noun-adjective phrase, or as the predicate of an equational sentence:

štireena sayyaara mustaƐmila.	'We bought a used car.'
l-baab masduud.	'The door is closed.'

3. Nouns ending in *-či*

Nouns ending in the suffix *-či* generally refer to persons engaged in certain trades or occupations. Such nouns are formed by adding *-či* to another noun, sometimes with minor stem changes in the latter. Here are some useful nouns of this type:

čaay	'tea'	*čaayči*	'tea vendor'
saaƐa	'watch'	*saaƐači*	'watch dealer'
gahwa	'coffee-house'	*gahawči*	'coffee-house proprietor'

qundara	'shoe'	*qundarči*	'shoemaker'
ˀuuti	'iron' (for pressing)	*ˀuutači*	'presser'

The plural of such nouns is formed by adding *-yya* to the singular:

čaayčiyya	'tea vendors'
gahawčiyya	'coffee-house proprietors'

For the annexing form of such plurals, a *-t-* is added:

gahawčiyyat baġdaad	'the coffee-house proprietors of Baghdad'

C. DRILLS

Drill 1. Repeat the sentence, replacing the word *mooz* with each of the other collectives given.

gul-li, ʕindak ˀaḥsan min hal-mooz? — Tell me, have you got any better than these bananas?

purtaqaal	oranges
ṭamaaṭa	tomatoes
beetinjaan	eggplants
baṭṭiix	cantaloupes
tamur	dates
raggi	watermelons
simač	fish
laḥam	meat
xoox	peaches
tiffaaḥ	apples

Drill 2. Respond to each statement as in the example.

Cue:	*ʕidna xyaar mumtaaz il-yoom.*	We have fine cucumbers today.
Response:	*ṭayyib, inṭiini xyaara wiḥda.*	All right, give me one cucumber.

ʕidna beetinjaan mumtaaz il-yoom.
ʕidna baṭṭiix mumtaaz il-yoom.
ʕidna tamur mumtaaz il-yoom.
ʕidna simač mumtaaz il-yoom.
ʕidna mooz mumtaaz il-yoom.
ʕidna tiffaaḥ mumtaaz il-yoom.
ʕidna raggi mumtaaz il-yoom.
ʕidna xoox mumtaaz il-yoom.
ʕidna purtaqaal mumtaaz il-yoom.
ʕidna xyaar mumtaaz il-yoom.

Drill 3. Repeat each sentence, changing the noun to the dual form, as in the example.

Cue:	*laazim ništiri mooz.*	We have to buy bananas.
Response:	*laazim ništiri moozteen.*	We have to buy two bananas.

laazim njiib tiffaaʕ.
laazim taaxuð baṭṭiix.
laazim taakul ṭamaaṭa.
laazim astangi raggi.
laazim astaʕmil ixyaar.
laazim toozin-li l-beetinjaan.
laazim tistangii-li l-purtaqaal.
laazim idjiib-li l-xoox.
laazim itxallii-li s-simač.
laazim taaxuð-li t-tamur.

Drill 4. Repeat the sentence, replacing the numeral and the noun alternately, using the appropriate forms of the items given.

ʔaku sitt-purtaqaalat ʕal-meez.	There are six oranges on the table.
tlaaθa	three
baṭṭiix	cantaloupes
ʕašra	ten
tamur	dates
xamsa	five
raggi	watermelons
sabʕa	seven
tiffaaʕ	apples
ʔarbaʕa	four
ṭamaaṭa	tomatoes

Drill 5. Respond to each statement using a passive participle, as in the example.

Cue:	*sidd il-baab.*	Close the door.
Response:	*l-baab masduud.*	The door is closed.

fukk il-baab.
ʔišrab il-biira.
ʔidfaʕ l-iʕsaab.
ʔiʕjiz il-ġurfa.
ʔiktib il-isim ihnaak.
ʔuṭbux il-ʔakil.
guṣṣ il-laʕma.
naððuf il-ġurfa.
xalliṣ iš-šuġuḷ.
daari l-wulid zeen.

Drill 6. Repeat the sentence, changing two words each time.

ʔabu samiira da-yiʕči ʕan is-saaʕa wiyya s-saaʕači.	Abu Samira is talking about the watch with the watchmaker.

Cue:	*gahwa*	coffee-house
Response:	*ˀabu samiira da-yiḥči ʕan il-gahwa wiyya l-gahawči.*	Abu Samira is talking about the coffee-house with the coffee-house proprietor.

čaay *ˀuuti*
qanaadir *saaʕa*
gahwa

UNIT 37

A. DIALOGUE

Abu Jalal would like to get his son a job in a bank. His friend Abu Khalid offers to recommend him.

ˀabu jalaal	**Abu Jalal**
1. *ṣaar-li sbuuʕ ˀadawwur ʕala ˀaḥḥad yuʕruf mudiir il-ḅang.*	For a week I've been looking for someone who knows the bank director.
ˀabu xaalid	**Abu Khalid**
2. *š-aku ʕindak wiyyaa?*	What business do you have with him?
ˀabu jalaal	**Abu Jalal**
3. *qaḍiyyat taʕyiin ˀibni yammi.*	The matter of my son's appointment (to a position) with him.
ˀabu xaalid	**Abu Khalid**
4. *ˀaani ˀagraḅ-la. loo gaayil-li čaan ḥičeet wiyyaa. baʕadha l-waḍiifa?*	I'm related to him. If you had told me I would have talked with him. Is the position still open?
ˀabu jalaal	**Abu Jalal**
5. *laazim baʕadha. loo mʕayyniin ˀaḥḥad čaan simaʕna. tsawwiini mamnuun ˀiδaa txaabra.*	It must still be. If they had appointed someone we would have heard. I'll be grateful if you call him.

ˀabu xaalid	Abu Khalid
6. *ma-tiƐtiqid loo ˀaruuƇ-la b-nafsi ˀaƇsanˀ xalliiha yammi.*	Don't you think it would be better if I went to see him myself? Leave it to me.

VOCABULARY

dawwar (ydawwur) Ɛala	(Class II) to look for
ˀaƇƇad	someone
mudiir (mudaraaˀ)	director
taƐyiin	appointing, appointment (to a position)
girab̧ (yigrab̧) (l-)	(Class I) to be related (to)
loo	if
waδ̧iifa (waδ̧aayif)	position, job
Ɛayyan (yƐayyin)	(Class II) to appoint, nominate
ˀíδaa	if
Ɛtiqad (yiƐtiqid)	(Class VIII) to think, consider
δaak	that M, that one M
δiič, δiiča	that F, that one F
δoolaak	those

B. GRAMMAR

1. Conditional sentences

The typical conditional sentence consists of two clauses, an if-clause, beginning with a word meaning 'if' or the equivalent, and a result clause, stating what would happen or would have happened under the circumstances set forth in the if-clause. Thus in *loo gaayil-li čaan Ƈičeet wiyyaa* 'If you had told me I would have talked with him' the if-clause begins with *loo,* and the result clause with *čaan.* In Iraqi there are two words for 'if', *loo* and *ˀíδaa.* Generally speaking, *loo* means 'if' in the sense 'if it were the case that (but it is not)'; while *ˀíδaa* means 'if' in the sense 'assuming that' or 'since it seems to be the case that'. Following is a description of the main kinds of conditional sentences in which these two words are used.

a. *If-clause introduced by loo*

(1) *Past unreal conditions.* An if-clause introduced by *loo* and containing an active participle form generally refers to past time, and indicates a

condition contrary to the facts as they actually occurred in the past. Thus the if-clause *loo gaayil-li* means 'if you had told me', the fact being that you did not tell me. The accompanying result clause usually contains the auxiliary *čaan* (invariable here) and the appropriate form of a perfect-tense verb, for example *čaan Ꜫičeet wiyyaa* 'I would have talked with him'. Further examples:

loo mƐayyniin ˀaꜪꜪad čaan simaƐna.	'If they had appointed someone we would have heard.'
loo šaayfak čaan inṭeetak l-ifluus.	'If I had seen you I would have given you the money.'
loo-ma-msawwya l-Ꜫajiz ma-čaan gidarna nruuꜪ.	'If you F hadn't made the reservation we wouldn't have been able to go.'

(2) *General unreal conditions.* An if-clause introduced by *loo* and containing a form other than an active participle expresses a condition contrary to fact, but the forms used do not necessarily indicate whether the reference is to past or present time; for this one must depend on the overall context of the sentence. However, if-clauses containing the auxiliary *čaan* more commonly indicate past than present time. The accompanying result clause, as above, usually (but not always) contains the auxiliary *čaan* and the appropriate form of a perfect-tense verb. Examples:

loo ˀaƐruf ir-raqam čaan xaabarta.	'If I knew the number I'd phone him.'
ˀaani loo b-mukaanak ma-asawwiiha.	'If I were in your place I wouldn't do it.'
loo ˀaani l-mudiir ma-čaan Ɛayyanta.	'If I were (had been) the director I wouldn't appoint (have appointed) him.'
loo Ɛidna fluus čaan riꜪna lil-baṣra.	'If we had (had had) money we'd go (would have gone) to Basra.'
loo čaan Ɛidna fluus čaan riꜪna lil-baṣra.	'If we had had money we would have gone to Basra.

(3) *Conditions referring to the future.* An if-clause introduced by *loo* may refer to a future possibility rather than express a condition contrary to fact; it then generally includes an imperfect-tense verb. This corresponds in most cases to an English if-clause with a verb in the past tense, or a verbal construction with *should* or *were to*. For example *loo ˀaruuꜪ-la b-nafsi* 'if I went (*or* should go, *or* were to go) to him myself'. The accompanying result clauses have various types of structures. Further examples:

loo tiktib-la čaan yjaawbak.	'If you wrote to him he'd answer you.'

loo tijuun saaʕa xamsa ʔaḥsan.	'If you came at five o'clock it would be better.'
loo nšuufa ngul-la l-ʔaxbaar.	'If we should see him we'll tell him the news.'

b. *If-clause introduced by ʔiδaa*

An if-clause introduced by *ʔíδaa* expresses an assumption that certain facts are actually or possibly so. Examples:

ʔíδaa triid itruuḥ hassa ʔawaṣṣlak ib-sayyaarti.	'If you want to go now I'll take you in my car.'
ʔíδaa šifta leeš ma-sallámit ʕalee?	'If you saw him, why didn't you greet him?'
ʔíδaa da-yiḥči bit-talafoon laazim yiṣṭabruun.	'If he's talking on the telephone they'll have to wait.'

An if-clause introduced by *ʔíδaa* may also refer to a future possibility. The verb may be either perfect or imperfect, but is usually best translated by a present-tense English verb, for example *ʔíδaa šifta* (or *tšuufa*) *gul-la yxaaburni*) 'If you see him tell him to phone me.' Further examples:

ʔíδaa tooṣal baʕd is-saaʕa θinteen ma-agdar ašuufha.	'If she arives after two o'clock I can't see her.'
xaaburni ʔíδaa simáʕit šii.	'Phone me if you hear anything.'
ʔíδaa ma-tilgii bil-beet dawwur ʕalee bil-gahwa.	'If you don't find him at home look for him at the coffee-house.'

In some cases of the sort just described, *ʔíδaa* and *loo* are interchangeable.

2. Imperatives: Summary; prefixes *di-* and *xal-*

Imperatives are verb forms used in making affirmative requests or commands (for negative commands see 16 B 3 and 38 B 2). There is a masculine, a feminine, and a plural imperative form, used respectively in addressing a command to one male, to one female, and to more than one person. Three verbs have irregular imperative forms; these are listed on the right below, and the corresponding second-person imperfect forms are also shown for the sake of comparison.

		Imperfect		Imperative	
ʔaxaδ	2 M	*taaxuδ*	'you M take'	*ʔuxuδ*	'take M'
(*yaaxuδ*)	F	*taaxδiin*	'you F take'	*ʔuxδi*	'take F'
'to take'	P	*taaxδuun*	'you P take'	*ʔuxδu*	'take P'
ʔakal	2 M	*taakul*	'you M eat'	*ʔukul*	'eat M'
(*yaakul*)	F	*taakliin*	'you F eat'	*ʔukli*	'eat F'
'to eat'	P	*taakluun*	'you P eat'	*ʔuklu*	'eat P'
ʔija or *jaa*	2 M	*tiji*	'you M come'	*taɛaal*	'come M'
(*yiji*)	F	*tijiin*	'you F come'	*taɛaali* or *taɛaay*	'come F'
'to come'	P	*tijuun*	'you P come'	*taɛaalu*	'come P'

All other imperatives may be formed from the corresponding imperfect forms by the following process: Remove the inflectional prefix *t-*, *ti-*, or *tu-*; change the 2 F ending *-iin* to *-i*, and the 2 P ending *-uun* to *-u*; and prefix *ʔ-*, *ʔi-*, *ʔu-*, or nothing, as follows:

a. If the remainder (after removal of the inflectional prefix) begins with a long vowel, prefix *ʔ-*:

		Imperfect		Imperative	
wuzan	2 M	*toozin*	'you M weigh'	*ʔoozin*	'weigh M'
(*yoozin*)	F	*toozniin*	'you F weigh'	*ʔoozni*	'weigh F'
'to weigh'	P	*tooznuun*	'you P weigh'	*ʔooznu*	'weigh P'

b. In verbs of Class I and IV, if the remainder begins with two consonants, prefix *ʔi-* or *ʔu-* (same vowel as in the imperfect prefix). In the feminine and plural forms of sound Class I and IV verbs (stem pattern -CvCC-), either prefix *ʔi-* or *ʔu-* (as above) or prefix nothing, optionally.

kitab	2 M	*tiktib*	'you M write'	*ʔiktib*	'write M'
(*yiktib*)	F	*tkitbiin*	'you F write'	(*ʔi*)*kitbi*	'write F'
'to write'	P	*tkitbuun*	'you P write'	(*ʔi*)*kitbu*	'write P'
simaɛ	2 M	*tismaɛ*	'you M hear'	*ʔismaɛ*	'listen M'
(*yismaɛ*)	F	*tsimɛiin*	'you F hear'	(*ʔi*)*simɛi*	'listen F'
'to hear, listen'	P	*tsimɛuun*	'you P hear'	(*ʔi*)*simɛu*	'listen P'
širab	2 M	*tišrab*	'you M drink'	*ʔišrab*	'drink M'
(*yišrab*)	F	*tšurbiin*	'you F drink'	(*ʔi*)*šurbi*	'drink F'
'to drink'	P	*tšurbuun*	'you P drink'	(*ʔi*)*šurbu*	'drink P'

giεad	2	M	*tugεud*	'you M sit'	*ʔugεud*	'sit M'
(*yugεud*)		F	*tguεdiin*	'you F sit'	(*ʔu*)*guεdi*	'sit F'
'to sit'		P	*tguεduun*	'you P sit'	(*ʔu*)*guεdu*	'sit P'
ḥiča	2	M	*tiḥči*	'you M speak'	*ʔiḥči*	'speak M'
(*yiḥči*)		F	*tiḥčiin*	'you F speak'	*ʔiḥči*	'speak F'
'to speak'		P	*tiḥčuun*	'you P speak'	*ʔiḥču*	'speak P'
qira	2	M	*tiqra*	'you M read'	*ʔiqra*	'read M'
(*yiqra*)		F	*tiqriin*	'you F read'	*ʔiqri*	'read F'
'to read'		P	*tiqruun*	'you P read'	*ʔiqru*	'read P'

c. In all other cases, prefix nothing.

sadd	2	M	*tsidd*	'you M close'	*sidd*	'close M'
(*ysidd*)		F	*tsiddiin*	'you F close'	*siddi*	'close F'
'to close'		P	*tsidduun*	'you P close'	*siddu*	'close P'
šaaf	2	M	*tšuuf*	'you M see'	*šuuf*	'look M'
(*yšuuf*)		F	*tšuufiin*	'you F see'	*šuufi*	'look F'
'to see, look'		P	*tšuufuun*	'you P see'	*šuufu*	'look P'
baddal	2	M	*tbaddil*	'you M change'	*baddil*	'change M'
(*ybaddil*)		F	*tbaddliin*	'you F change'	*baddli*	'change F'
'to change'		P	*tbaddluun*	'you P change'	*baddlu*	'change P'
xalla	2	M	*txalli*	'you M let'	*xalli*	'let M'
(*yxalli*)		F	*txalliin*	'you F let'	*xalli*	'let F'
'to leave, let'		P	*txalluun*	'you P let'	*xallu*	'let P'
ddaayan	2	M	*tiddaayan*	'you M borrow'	*ddaayan*	'borrow M'
(*yiddaayan*)		F	*tiddaayniin*	'you F borrow'	*ddaayni*	'borrow F'
'to borrow'		P	*tiddaaynuun*	'you P borrow'	*ddaaynu*	'borrow P'
štiġaḷ	2	M	*tištuġuḷ*	'you M work'	*štuġuḷ*	'work M'
(*yištuġuḷ*)		F	*tištaġḷiin*	'you F work'	*štaġḷi*	'work F'
'to work'		P	*tištaġḷuun*	'you P work'	*štaġḷu*	'work P'
štira	2	M	*tištiri*	'you M buy'	*štiri*	'buy M'
(*yištiri*)		F	*tištiriin*	'you F buy'	*štiri*	'buy F'
'to buy		P	*tištiruun*	'you P buy'	*štiru*	'buy P'
staεmal	2	M	*tistaεmil*	'you M use'	*staεmil*	'use M'
(*yistaεmil*)		F	*tistaεmiliin*	'you F use'	*staεmili*	'use F'
'to use'		P	*tistaεmiluun*	'you P use'	*staεmilu*	'use P'
stanga	2	M	*tistangi*	'you M choose'	*stangi*	'choose M'
(*yistangi*)		F	*tistangiin*	'you F choose'	*stangi*	'choose F'
'to choose'		P	*tistanguun*	'you P choose'	*stangu*	'choose P'

The prefix di-. The prefix *di-* is used with an imperative form to add a note of emphasis, impatience, or cajolery. There is no one English equivalent for this prefix, but the examples below will give some idea of the tone it conveys. Before an imperative beginning with *ˀi-* or *ˀu-*, the prefix has the form *d-*, and the *ˀ* of the imperative is dropped; elsewhere the prefix has the form *di-*. Here are some examples:

di-guum!	'Come on, get up!'
di-stangi!	'Go on, go on, choose!'
d-ukul!	'Eat, eat!'
d-ismaع!	'Listen, will you!'

The prefix xal-. This prefix is used with a first-person plural imperfect verb form to express a command or suggestion of the type expressed in English by *let's* plus a verb:

xal-inruuح.	'Let's go.'
xal-nirkab.	'Let's ride.'
xal-ništiri.	'Let's buy.'

The prefix *xal-* also occurs before the progressive prefix *da-* with the imperfect (see 23 B 2):

xal-da-nruuح.	'Let's go.'
xal-da-ništiri.	'Let's buy.'

3. Far demonstratives and summary

There are two sets of demonstratives in Iraqi, each with a masculine (singular), a feminine (singular), and a plural form. One is the **general demonstratives,** of which the masculine and feminine forms were introduced in Unit 14 and the plural form in Unit 27. These are shown in the first table below. The second set is the **far demonstratives,** shown in the second table below. Most of these demonstratives have three or more different forms, but the ones shown in the tables below are probably the most common.

General demonstratives

haaδa	'this (one) M, that (one) M'
haaδi, haay	'this (one) F, that (one) F'
δool, δoola	'these, those'

Far demonstratives

δaak, δaaka	'that (one) M'
δiič, δiiča	'that (one) F'
δoolaak	'those'

As the translations indicate, the general demonstratives are often used not only in situations where English *this* or *these* would be appropriate, but also where English *that* or *those* would fit. The far demonstratives, on the other hand, are used in referring to people and things at a greater distance, either in space or time, and are also used for contrast when a nearer person or thing is also mentioned. Both the general and the far demonstratives may function as pronouns, serving independently as the subject or predicate of a sentence, or as the object of a verb or preposition. They agree in gender and number with the person or thing to which they refer in the ways described for pronouns in 31 B 4.

haaδa ʔarxaṣ min δaak.	'This one M is cheaper than that M.'
haay ibnayya kulliš ɛilwa laakin δiiča ʔaɛla.	'That's a very pretty girl but that (other) one is prettier.'
ʔaani ʔaɛibb δoola ʔakθar min δoolaak.	'I like these (people) more than those.'

Sometimes the demonstratives, especially the general ones, have a meaning more like that of third-person personal pronouns, and are then best translated as 'he, him, she, her, it, they, them':

haaδa xooš walad.	'He's a good boy.'
ma-aɛibba l-haaδa.	'I don't like him.'
haaδi ma-tiqra zeen.	'She doesn't read well.'
ʔaani loo b-mukaanak ma-aɛči wiyya δoola.	'If I were in your place I wouldn't talk with them.'

The demonstratives also occur as the first element in demonstrative phrases, always followed by a noun with the article prefix:

haaδa l-walad	'this, that boy'
haaδi l-ibnayya	'this, that girl'
δool il-wulid	'these, those boys'
δaak il-walad	'that boy'
δiič l-ibnayya	'that girl'
δoolaak il-wulid	'those boys'

Demonstrative phrases consisting of a general demonstrative plus a noun, like the first three examples above, are equivalent in meaning to a noun with the demonstrative prefix (see 12 B 6): *hal-walad* 'this boy', *hal-ibnayya* 'this girl', *hal-wulid* 'these boys', *hal-beet* 'this house', *has-safra* 'this trip', and so on.

C. DRILLS

Drill 1. In the following sentences, change the active participle in the if-clause, and the verb in the result clause, to agree with the cue.

a. *loo msawwi l-Ċajiz čaan raaĊ.* — If he had made the reservation he would have gone.

Cue: *hiyya* — she
Response: *loo msawwya l-Ċajiz čaan raaĊat.* — If she had made the reservation she would have gone.

hum̩m̩a	*ˀinta*	*ˀinti*
ˀiĊna	*hiyya*	*ˀintu*
huwwa	*ˀaani*	*hum̩m̩a*

b. *loo msawwi l-Ċajiz čaan gidar yruuĊ.* — If he had made the reservation he would have been able to go.

c. *loo šaayfa čaan inṭaa l-ifluus.* — If he had seen him he would have given him the money.

Drill 2. Change the result clause, using the appropriate form of the verb in the cue.

loo gaayil-li čaan Ċičeet wiyyaa. — If you had told me I would have spoken with him.

Cue: *raĊ-ajiib iṭ-ṭamaata.* — I'll bring the tomatoes.
Response: *loo gaayil-li čaan jibt iṭ-ṭamaaṭa.* — If you had told me I would have brought the tomatoes.

raĊ-adizz-lak il-aθaaθ.	*raĊ-astangi ġeer šii.*
ma-raĊ-aaxuδ il-laĊam.	*ma-raĊ-axaaburhum.*
raĊ-asˀal il-poosṭači.	*ma-raĊ-atˀaxxar.*
raĊ-anaδδuf id-daaˀira.	*raĊ-addaayan išwayya fluus.*
raĊ-aštiri l-beetinjaan.	*ma-raĊ-astaĊmil it-tamur.*

Drill 3. Change the if-clause, using the appropriate active participle form of the verb in the cue.

loo maaxiδ il-ˀuuti čaan galloo-li. — If you M had taken the iron they would have told me.

Cue:	*štirat il-pardaat.*	She bought the curtains.
Response:	*loo mištarya l-pardaat čaan galloo-li.*	If she had bought the curtains they would have told me.

buqeeti bil-madrasa.	*ddaaynat ifluus minhum.*
staʕmilaw is-sayyaara.	*txarraj imnil-kulliyya.*
ṣoograw beethum.	*ma-daarat ij-jihaal zeen.*
štireetu l-aθaaθ.	*ma-sawwaw iš-šuġuḷ.*
štiġálit kull il-yoom.	*ʔaklaw it-tiffaaḥ.*

Drill 4. Change the if-clause, using the appropriate imperfect form of the verb in the cue.

loo ʔaruuḥ-la b-nafsi ʔaḥsan. If I went to him myself it would be better.

Cue:	*štireena sayyaara mustaʕmila.*	We bought a used car.
Response:	*loo ništiri sayyaara mustaʕmila ʔaḥsan.*	If we bought a used car it would be better.

ḥijazna qamaarteen.	*ʔaxaδti l-pardaat il-ḥumur.*
ṭubaxti ġeer šii.	*štiġaḷna bid-daaʔira θ-θaanya.*
buqeetu bil-beet.	*saaʕadithum išwayya.*
ḥičeet wiyya l-mudiir.	*waṣṣalnaaha lil-beet.*
nisa l-qaδ̣iyya.	*riḥit-la b-nafsi.*

Drill 5. Change the verbs to the masculine, feminine, and plural imperative forms, as in the model.

Cue:	*raḥ-tiqra haaδa?*	Are you M going to read this?
Response:	(1) *ʔiqra haaδa.*	Read M this.
	(2) *ʔiqri haaδa.*	Read F this.
	(3) *ʔiqru haaδa.*	Read P this.

raḥ-tišrab il-ṃaay?	*raḥ-tirkab il-p̣aaṣ?*	*raḥ-itgul-li l-axbaar?*
raḥ-tidfaʕ l-iḥsaab?	*raḥ-itsidd il-baab?*	*raḥ-tinṭiini l-qalam?*
raḥ-tuṭbux il-akil?	*raḥ-iddizz-ilha l-ifluus?*	*raḥ-tiji saaʕa xamsa?*
raḥ-tisʔal il-mudiir?	*raḥ-itḥuṭṭ il-mooz ʕal-meez?*	*raḥ-taakul il-ʕinab?*
raḥ-issallim ʕalee?	*raḥ-ithanniihum?*	*raḥ-itnaδ̣δ̣uf il-beet?*
raḥ-issaaʕidna?	*raḥ-itxaaburhum il-yoom?*	*raḥ-tiddaayan ifluus minna?*
raḥ-tištuġuḷ ihnaa?	*raḥ-tištiri haay?*	*raḥ-tistaʕmil δiič iz-zuuliyya?*

Drill 6. Change the general demonstrative to the corresponding far demonstrative.

Cue: *ma-tḥibb haaḏa l-beet?*
Response: *ma-tḥibb ḏaak il-beet?*

haay is-sayyaara ʔaḥsan.
laakin haaḏi ʔarxaṣ.
ma-ariid aḥči wiyya ḏool il-wulid.
simáʕit ʕan haay il-qaḏiyya?
min ween ḏoola?
š-gaal haaḏa l-muʕallim?
haaḏa xooš walad.
ʔaḥibb haaḏi šwayya ʔakθar.
ḏoola yirḥuun kull yoom lil-gahwa.
ma-tiʕtiqid haaḏa l-beet ʔaḥsan?

UNIT 38

A. DIALOGUE

Khalid has spent all his money and is trying to get a temporary loan.

xaalid	Khalid
1. *loo ʕindi fluus čaan riḥit lis-siinama.*	If I had some money I'd go to the movies.
ʕali	**Ali**
2. *loo ma-ṣaaruf kull ifluusak ʕal-kutub, ma-čaan itnaddámit.*	If you hadn't spent all your money on the books, you wouldn't be sorry.
xaalid	**Khalid**
3. *kullha mn-iidak. loo ma-gaayil-li l-kutub zeena ma-čaan ištireetha.*	It's all your fault. If you hadn't told me the books were good I wouldn't have bought them.
ʕali	**Ali**
4. *ʔaani loo ʔabu l-maktaba? huwwa ḏ̣-ḏ̣all yraawiik kutub w-yraġġbak biiha.*	Me or the book-seller? He's the one who kept showing you books and getting you interested in them.

xaalid	Khalid
5. *hassa ma-ʕleena. ʕindak iddaayinni?*	We can't do anything about it now. Have you got some you'll lend me?
ʕali	Ali
6. *ʕala šarṭ itrajjiʕ-li-yyaaha baačir.*	On condition you return it to me tomorrow.
xaalid	Khalid
7. *ṣaar. ʔanṭiik-iyyaaha ṣ-ṣubuʕ.*	Done. I'll give it to you in the morning.

VOCABULARY

siinama (siinamaat)	movie theatre, movies
ṣiraf (yuṣruf)	(Class I) to spend
ktaab (kutub)	book
tnaddam (yitnaddam)	(Class V) to be sorry
kullha mn-iidak	it's all your fault, your doing
maktaba (maktabaat)	bookstore; library
ʔabu maktaba	book-seller
raawa (yraawi)	(Class III) to show
raġġab (yraġġub) (b-)	(Class II) to interest (in)
ma-ʕleena	it's not up to us, we can't do anything about it
daayan (ydaayin)	(Class III) to lend
šariṭ (šuruuṭ)	condition
ʕala šariṭ	on condition (that)
rajjaʕ (yrajjiʕ)	(Class II) to give back, return
-yyaa-	(stem for second pronoun suffix; see 38 B 1)
šubuʕ	morning
ṣ-ṣubuʕ	in the morning

---

wala	and not, nor (see 38 B 2)

B. GRAMMAR

1. The stem *-yyaa-*

Certain Iraqi verbs may have two objects, the first corresponding to what in English would be called the indirect object, and the second to the direct object. Often the first (indirect) object is a pronoun suffix, and the second (direct) object is a noun. Below are two examples of this kind of construction; note that in English there are usually two ways of expressing it, but in Iraqi only one:

raawaani l-iktaab.	'He showed me the book.' 'He showed the book to me.'
raħ-yinṭiini l-ifluus.	'He'll give me the money.' 'He'll give the money to me.'

However, the second object as well as the first may be a pronoun suffix. When both objects are pronoun suffixes, the second is attached to the stem *-yyaa-* (or, after a consonant, *-iyyaa-*), which in turn is attached to the first. The form *-yyaa-* has no meaning of its own; it simply serves as a stem for a second suffix. It is a vowel stem, and the pronoun suffixes attached to it have the forms which go with any vowel stem. Here are examples; note that in these there is only one common English version, and that the order of the pronouns in Iraqi is the reverse of that in English.

raawaani-yyaa.	'He showed it M (*or* him) to me.'
raawaani-yyaaha.	'He showed it F (*or* her) to me.'
raawaani-yyaahum.	'He showed them to me.'
raħ-yinṭiini-yyaa.	'He'll give it M to me.'
raħ-yinṭiini-yyaaha.	'He'll give it F to me.'
raħ-yinṭiini-yyaahum.	'He'll give them to me.'
ʔanṭiik-iyyaa.	'I'll give it M to you M.'
ʔanṭiik-iyyaaha.	'I'll give it F to you M.'
ʔanṭiik-iyyaahum.	'I'll give them to you M.'

Some verbs require the use of the preposition suffix *-l-* 'to, for', for example:

dazz-li l-iktaab.	'He sent me the book.' 'He sent the book to me.'
rajjaʕ-ilhum l-ifluus.	'He returned the money to them.'

In such cases also, when the second object is a pronoun suffix, it is attached to *-iyyaa-*:

dazz-li-yyaa.	'He sent it M to me.'
dazz-li-yyaaha.	'He sent it F to me.'
dazz-li-yyaahum.	'He sent them to me.'

rajjaε-ilhum-iyyaa.	'He returned it M to them.'
rajjaε-ilhum-iyyaaha.	'He returned it F to them.'
rajjaε-ilhum-iyyaahum.	'He returned them to them.'

The third-person masculine pronoun suffix (which elsewhere has the form *-a* after a consonant and zero after a long vowel) and the third-person feminine pronoun suffix (which elsewhere has the form *-ha*) both have the special form *-h-* when followed immediately by *-iyyaa-*. In that case, moreover, both *-iyyaa-* plus the 3 M pronoun suffix and *-iyyaa-* plus the 3 F pronoun suffix have the form *-iyyaa*. Examples:

nṭeeta l-iktaab.	'I gave him the book.'	*nṭeeth-iyyaa.*	'I gave it M to him.'
nṭeetha l-iktaab.	'I gave her the book.'		'I gave it M to her.'
nṭeeta l-ifluus.	'I gave him the money.'		'I gave it F to him.'
nṭeetha l-ifluus.	'I gave her the money.'		'I gave it F to her.'

ʔanṭii l-iktaab.	'I'll give him the book.'	*ʔanṭiih-iyyaa.*	'I'll give it M to him.'
ʔanṭiiha l-iktaab.	'I'll give her the book.'		'I'll give it M to her.'
ʔanṭii l-ifluus.	'I'll give him the money.'		'I'll give it F to him.'
ʔanṭiiha l-ifluus.	'I'll give her the money.'		'I'll give it F to her.'

dazz-la l-iktaab.	'He sent him the book.'	*dazz-ilh-iyyaa.*	'He sent it M to him.'
dazz-ilha l-iktaab.	'He sent her the book.'		'He sent it M to her'
dazz-la l-ifluus.	'He sent him the money.'		'He sent it F to him.'
dazz-ilha l-ifluus.	'He sent her the money.'		'He sent it F to her.'

Finally, the combinations *-lak* 'to you M' and *-lič* 'to you F', also usually have special forms before *-iyyaa*. They are *-(i)lk-* and *-(i)lč,* the initial vowel occurring when a consonant precedes. Examples:

dazz-lak l-iktaab.	'He sent you M the book.'	*dazz-ilk-iyyaa.*	'He sent it M to you M.'
dazz-lič l-iktaab.	'He sent you F the book.'	*dazz-ilč-iyyaa.*	'He sent it M to you F.'
dazz-lak l-ifluus.	'He sent you M the money.'	*dazz-ilk-iyyaaha.*	'He sent it F to you M.'
dazz-lič l-ifluus.	'He sent you F the money.'	*dazz-ilč-iyyaaha.*	'He sent it F to you F.'
štiraa-lak qalam.	'He bought you M a pencil.'	*štiraa-lk-iyyaa.*	'He bought it M for you M.'
štiraa-lič qalam.	'He bought you F a pencil.'	*štiraa-lč-iyyaa.*	'He bought it M for you F.'
štiraa-lak xooxa.	'He bought you M a peach.'	*štiraa-lk-iyyaaha.*	'He bought it F for you M.'
štiraa-lič xooxa.	'He bought you F a peach.'	*štiraa-lč-iyyaaha.*	'He bought it F for you F.'

2. Summary of negatives

Following is a summary of forms used in negative constructions. A few new items are included.

a. *laa* is the negative reply to a question, corresponding to English 'no'.

ˀinta šaayif il-baṣra gabuḷ?	'Have you seen Basra before?'
laa, ma-šaayifha.	'No, I haven't seen it.'

b. *la-* 'not' is prefixed to second-person imperfect verbs to form a negative command. It may also be used with third-person imperfect verbs to form a negative indirect command, and after *xal-* to form a negative first-person command (*ma-* may also be used in these cases).

la-tf̣ukk il-baab.	'Don't open the door.'
gul-la la-yruuḥ.	'Tell him not to go.'
xal-la-nugʕud ihnaa.	'Let's not sit here.'

c. *ma-* 'not' is used to form the negative of verbs other than negative commands, of active participles functioning as verbs (see 34 B 2), of *ˀaku* 'there is, there are', of *ʕi(n)d-* with an attached pronoun suffix indicating possession, and of certain other prepositions with attached pronoun suffixes when these have the meaning 'there is/are (something) in it', 'there is/are (something) on it', and the like. It is also commonly used to form the negative of active or passive participles functioning as adjectives; and it may be used to negate some other adjectives, and certain participles such as *hwaaya* 'much (*muu* may also be used in these cases). In negating verbs with the prefixes *da-* and *raC-*, the negative *ma-* precedes.

ma-šifta.	'I didn't see him.'
ma-yaakluun laCam.	'They don't eat meat.'
ma-da-yaakluun hassa.	'They're not eating now.'
ma-raC-aštiri haaδa.	'I'm not going to buy this.'
ma-saamƐiin il-axbaar.	'They haven't heard the news.'
leeš ma-aku xaraayiṭ ihnaa?	'Why aren't there any maps here?'
ma-Ɛidna fluus.	'We haven't any money.'
hal-ġurfa ma-biiha ˀaθaaθ.	'There's no furniture in this room.'
ˀaani ma-mašġuul il-yoom.	'I'm not busy today.'
laa, huwwa ma-taƐbaan.	'No, he's not tired.'
haaδa ma-hwaaya.	'That's not much.'

d. *muu* 'not' is used (except in the cases mentioned above) to negate nouns, pronouns, adjectives, demonstratives, prepositions and other particles, phrases, and clauses.

ˀabu xaalid muu muƐallim.	'Abu Khalid is not a teacher.'
hal-ašyaaˀ muu ġaalya.	'These things are not expensive.'
l-mudiir muu hnaak.	'The director is not there.'
laazim issawwiiha l-yoom, muu baačir.	'You have to do it today, not tomorrow.
laa, muu Ɛal-meez!	'No, not on the table!'
ˀinta-l-laazim issawwiiha, muu ˀaani.	'You're the one who has to do it, not I.'
laa, muu haaδa.	'No, not this one.'

When *muu* is used to negate a whole clause, it generally indicates a rhetorical question, something like 'Isn't it a fact that . . .' or 'You know that . . ., don't you?'

muu šifta l-yoom bil-gahwa?	'Didn't I see him in the coffee-house today?' (meaning 'I certainly did . . .')
muu ˀaani taƐbaan?	'You know I'm tired, don't you?'

e. *wala* 'and not, nor, or' is used to negate the second of two items being negated. The first of two such items may be negated by *la-*, *ma-*, or *muu*, as described above; or it may be negated by *la-* or *laa* in all cases. There are several English equivalents of such constructions, as may be seen in the translations below.

la-taakul wala tišrab.	'Don't eat or drink.'
ma-naḏḏfat il-beet wala ṭubxat il-ˀakil.	'She neither cleaned the house nor cooked the food.'
ma-ʕinda ktaab wala qalam.	'He has neither a book nor a pencil.'
haay muu madrasa wala daaˀira.	'This is not a school or an office.'

After a form negated by *la-* or *ma-*, the first of two items may be preceded by *la-* or *laa*, for greater emphasis.

ma-yuʕruf la-yiqra wala yiktib.	'He doesn't know how to read or write.'
ma-ʕidhum laa ˀakil wala fluus.	'They have neither food nor money.'

After a form negated by *la-* or *ma-*, a single item may be preceded by *wala*. This corresponds to English 'not a single', 'not even one', and the like.

la-tinṭii wala filis.	'Don't give him a single fils.'
ma-ariid abqa hnaa wala yoom.	'I don't want to stay here even one day.'

C. DRILLS

Drill 1. Change the second object from noun (or noun phrase) to the corresponding pronoun suffix attached to -(*i*)*yyaa-*.

Cue:	*raawaani l-iktaab.*	He showed me the book.
Response:	*raawaani-yyaa.*	He showed it M to me.

raawaani s-simča	*dazz-li l-meez.*
raawaani l-wulid.	*dazz-li-l-ifluus.*
daayanni l-ˀuuti.	*dazz-li l-banaat.*
daayanni saaʕta.	*rajjaʕ-li l-ˀaθaaθ maali.*
daayanni l-kutub.	*rajjaʕ-li l-biṭaaqa.*
nṭaani l-iskamli.	*štiraa-li ktaab.*
nṭaani l-iskamliyyaat.	*štiraa-li tiffaaʕa.*
nṭaani z-zuuliyya maalta.	*štiraa-li meez ˀakil.*

Drill 2. Change the first pronoun suffix object to correspond to the cue.

a. *raawaani-yyaa.* He showed it to me.

Cue: *huwwa* he
Response: *raawaah-iyyaa* He showed it to him.

hiyya	*xaalid*	*l-banaat*	*ˀabu zuheer*
humma	*ˀaani*	*ˀiḥna*	*wulidhum*
ˀinta	*samiira*	*ˀinti*	*ˀintu*

b. *daayanni-yyaa.* He lent it to me.
c. *dazz-li-yyaa.* He sent it to me.
d. *štiraa-li-yyaa.* He bought it for me.

Drill 3. Change the verb form to correspond to the cue.

a. *raawaah-iyyaa.* He showed it to him.

Cue: *hiyya* She
Response: *raawath-iyyaa.* She showed it to him.

ˀinti	*ˀaani*	*ˀiḥna*	*huwwa*
ˀummi	*ˀintu*	*ˀinta*	*ˀaani*
ˀaṣdiqaaˀi	*l-muɛallimiin*	*hiyya*	*l-mudiir*

b. *raḥ-yinṭiih-iyyaa.* He's going to give it to him.
c. *ma-yriid ydaayinh-iyyaa.* He doesn't want to lend it to him.
d. *raḥ-ydizz-ilh-iyyaa baačir.* He's going to send it to him tomorrow.
e. *leeš ma-yoozin-ilh-iyyaa hassaˀ?* Why doesn't he weigh it out for him now?
f. *ma-yigdar yištirii-lh-iyyaa l-yoom.* He can't buy it for him today.

Drill 4. In the if-clause, change the verb form and the noun object as indicated in the cue, and make any necessary changes in the result clause.

ˀíδaa triid l-iktaab ydizz-ilk-iyyaa baačir. If you M want the book he'll send it M to you M tomorrow.

Cue: *tirdiin iz-zuuliyya.* You F want the rug
Response: *ˀíδaa tirdiin iz-zuuliyya ydizz-ilč-iyyaaha baačir.* If you F want the rug he'll send it F to you F tomorrow.

yriid il-ˀuuti	*tirduun is-simač*
(hiyya) triid meez il-ˀakil	*ˀariid il-qanaadir*
yirduun l-ifraaš	*nriid ij-jaraayid*
(ˀinta) triid il-biṭaaqa	*yriid l-imyuuza*
tirdiin il-pardaat	*tirdiin iṭ-ṭamaata*

Drill 5. Change to the negative, using the appropriate negative particle.

Cue:	*ˀariid aĉĉi wiyya l-mudiir.*	I want to talk with the director.
Response:	*ma-ariid aĉĉi wiyya l-mudiir.*	I don't want to talk with the director.

raḥ-nigdar inxalliṣ kull miswaagna l-yoom.
xal-ništiri l-baṭṭiix il-yoom.
ˀaani taʕbaan il-yoom.
hal-iktaab ˀaġla min ðaak.
ˀariid ˀasˀal nabiiha.
waṣṣeet in-najjaar ʕal-aθaaθ?
ˀaku šii ˀaaxar?
taʕaal baačir.
huwwa mudiir il-ḅang.
ˀukul hal-mooza.
šaayfa baġdaad gabuḷ?
msawwiin il-ḥajiz.

Drill 6. Change to the negative, using the particle *wala*.

Cue:	*yaakul w-yišrab.*	He eats and drinks.
Response:	*ma-yaakul wala yišrab.*	He doesn't eat or drink.

yiktib w-yiqra.
saaʕadni w-ḥiča wiyyaaya.
ˀukul tiffaaḥa.
huwwa muʕallim w-mudiir ḅang.
mištiri l-laḥam wis-simač.
raḥ-aštiri šii.

UNIT 39

A. DIALOGUE

Hussein has just arrived in Baghdad, where he has applied for a job. He has found a hotel and checked in, and now he rings for service.

l-booy	The boy
1. *daggeet jaraṣ, ʕammi?*	You rang, sir?
ḥseen	Hussein
2. *ʕindi θyaab w-malaabis taḥtaaniyya waṣxa, w-hamm ariid hal-qaaṭ yitnaððaf.*	I have some dirty shirts and underwear and also I want this suit cleaned.

l-booy	The boy
3. *zeen, ʕammi, l-iθyaab wil-malaabis it-taḥtaaniyya niġsilha bil-uuteel, wil-qaaṭ awaddii-lk-iyyaa lil-mukawwi.*	Very well, sir, the shirts and the underwear we'll wash in the hotel, and the suit I'll send to the cleaner's for you.
ḥseen	Hussein
4. *ʔiδaa ninṭii l-qaaṭ il-yoom, šwakit yrajjiʕ-inna-yyaa?*	If we give him the suit today, when will he return it to us?
l-booy	The boy
5. *baʕad yoomeen. tḥibb ʔaaxδa hassa?*	In two days. Would you like me to take it now?
ḥseen	Hussein
6. *ʔii baḷḷa, liʔann ʔaani msaafir baʕad tlat-tiyyaam.*	Yes please, because I'm leaving in three days.

VOCABULARY

dagg (ydugg)	(Class I) to ring; to knock on
jaraṣ (jraaṣ)	bell
θoob (θyaab)	shirt
malaabis (plural only)	clothes
taḥtaani	lower, under-
qaaṭ (quuṭ)	suit
tnaδδaf (yitnaδδaf)	(Class V) to be cleaned
ġisal (yiġsil)	(Class I) to wash
wadda (ywaddi)	(Class II) to take, send (something somewhere)
mukawwi (mukawwiin)	cleaner, presser
saafar (ysaafir)	(Class III) to travel, take a trip; to leave (on a trip)

---

nafnuuf (nafaaniif)	dress
tannuura (tannuuraat)	skirt

panṭaruun (*panṭaruunaat, panaaṭiir*)	trousers
qappuuṭ (*qpaapiiṭ*)	overcoat
sitra (*sitar*)	jacket
booyinbaaġ (*booyinbaaġaat*)	tie
jooraab (*jwaariib*)	(pair of) socks
libas (*yilbas*)	(Class I) to put on, to wear

(For list of place-names and corresponding nisba adjectives, see B 1 below.)

B. GRAMMAR

1. Nisba adjectives

Nisba adjectives are adjectives formed by the addition of the ending *-i* to another form, usually a noun, with stem changes in some cases. In general, a nisba adjective means 'pertaining to' or 'having the characteristics of' the corresponding noun. Some examples:

l-Ciraaq	'Iraq'	*Ciraaqi*	'Iraq'
ˀameerka	'America'	*ˀameerkaani*	'American'
baġdaad	'Baghdad'	*baġdaadi*	'Baghdadi, from Baghdad'
l-baṣra	'Basra'	*baṣraawi*	'from, of Basra'
yoom	'day'	*yawmi*	'daily'
šahar	'month'	*šahri*	'monthly'
sana	'year'	*sanawi*	'yearly, annual'
ṭibb	'medical science'	*ṭibbi*	'medical'
θaani	'second'	*θaanawi*	'secondary'
taCat	'under'	*taCtaani*	'lower, under-'
waṣaṭ	'center, middle'	*waṣṭaani*	'middle, medium-sized'

The nisba adjectives in the examples above are shown in their masculine singular form. The feminine singular, masculine sound plural, and feminine sound plural are formed by the addition of *-yy-* to the stem and the endings *-a, -iin,* and *-aat* respectively, for example:

Ciraaqi	'Iraqi M'	*Ciraaqiyyiin*	'Iraqi MP'
Ciraaqiyya	'Iraqi F'	*Ciraaqiyyaat*	'Iraqi FP'

Most nisba adjectives, if they have plural forms at all (which is to say, if they can be used to refer to human beings) have sound plurals. However, one important group of nisbas, the adjectives derived from place-names, include a number which have broken plural forms instead of (or in some cases in addition to) sound plurals. Following is a list of some useful place-names, with the corresponding nisba adjectives. Those in the first group have sound plurals, those in the second group have broken masculine plurals identical with the masculine singular minus the *-i* ending, and those in the last group have other broken plural patterns. Where two plural types are possible, one is shown in parentheses. The feminine singular and plural forms are predictable in all cases, and are not shown here.

		MS	MP	
ʔooruṗṗa	'Europe'	*ʔooruṗṗi*	*ʔooruṗṗiyyiin*	'European'
l-ʔardun	'Jordan'	*ʔarduni*	*ʔarduniyyiin*	'Jordanian'
suurya	'Syria'	*suuri*	*suuriyyiin*	'Syrian'
l-εiraaq	'Iraq'	*εiraaqi*	*εiraaqiyyiin*	'Iraqi'
fransa	'France'	*fransaawi*	*fransaawiiyyiin*	'French'
l-ikweet	'Kuwait'	*kweeti*	*kweetiyyiin*	'Kuwaiti'
lubnaan	'Lebanon'	*lubnaani*	*lubnaaniyyiin*	'Lebanese'
miṣir	'Egypt'	*miṣri*	*miṣriyyiin*	'Egyptian'
ʔaḷmaanya	'Germany'	*ʔaḷmaani*	*ʔaḷmaan*	'German'
ʔameerka	'America'	*ʔameerkaani* or *ʔameerki*	(*ʔameerkaan* *ʔameerkaaniyyiin*, *ʔameerkiyyiin*)	'American'
ʔingiltara	'England'	*ʔingiliizi*	*ʔingiliiz*	'English'
ruusya	'Russia'	*ruusi*	*ruus*	'Russian'
l-yuunaan	'Greece'	*yuunaani*	(*yuunaan* *yuunaaniyyiin*)	'Greek'
l-baṣra	'Basra'	*baṣraawi*	(*bṣaarwa* *baṣraawiyyiin*)	'from Basra'
baġdaad	'Baghdad'	*baġdaadi*	(*bġaadda* *baġdaadiyyiin*)	'Baghdadi, from Baghdad'
l-muuṣil	'Mosul'	*maṣlaawi*	*mṣaalwa*	'from Mosul'
turkiya	'Turkey'	*turki*	*ʔatraak*	'Turkish'
l-hind	'India'	*hindi*	*hnuud*	'Indian'

The word *εarabi* (plural *εarab*) 'Arab, Arabic', although not based on a particular place name, is a nisba like those in the second group above. Similarly *kurdi* (plural *kraad*) 'Kurdish' is a nisba like those in the third group.

All the nisba forms referring to human beings are commonly used as nouns as well as adjectives:

ʔingiliizi	'an Englishman'
ʔameerkaaniyya	'an American woman'
l-ɛarab	'the Arabs'

The masculine singular form of these nisbas are used as nouns to mean the language:

yiɛči ʔingiliizi zeen.	'He speaks English well.'
ma-yiɛčuun ɛarabi wala turki.	'They don't speak Arabic or Turkish.'

2. Feminine *-t-* stems of the pattern FvMLat-

The general matter of feminine *-t-* stems was presented in 19 B 3, but one feature remains to be discussed. This concerns feminine nouns whose independent form ends in *-a* preceded by two consonants (of which the second is not *w* or *y*). The great majority of such nouns have the pattern FiMLa, FuMLa, or FaMLa, for example *fikra* 'idea, opinion', *ġurfa* 'room', and *safra* 'trip'. The consonant-suffixing stem of such nouns, like that of other feminine nouns ending in *-a,* is formed by adding *-t-,* for example:

fikratha	'her idea'
ġurfatna	'our room'
safrathum	'their trip'

For the vowel-suffixing stem, however, the stem vowel *a* cannot be simply dropped as in the case of other nouns, since that would result in a cluster of more than three consonants. Instead the vowel is shifted to a position between the two preceding consonants, and is changed to *i* or *u*. It is changed to *i* if the vowel in the first syllable is *i*; to *u* if the vowel in the first syllable is *u*; and to either *i* or *u* (depending on the adjacent consonants) if the vowel in the first syllable is *a*. Thus:

Independent		**Consonant-suffixing stem**	**Vowel-suffixing stem**
fikra	'idea'	*fikrat-*	*fikirt-*
ġurfa	'room'	*ġurfat-*	*ġuruft-*
safra	'trip'	*safrat-*	*safirt-*
raġba	'wish'	*raġbat-*	*raġubt-*

The consonant-suffixing stem, as we have seen, is used with pronoun suffixes beginning with a consonant; and the vowel-suffixing stem is used with pronoun suffixes beginning with a vowel, and with the dual suffix *-een*. All these forms are shown below with *fikra* and *ġurfa,* as models.

fikra	'idea'	*ġurfa*	'room'
fikirta	'his idea'	*ġurufta*	'his room'
fikratha	'her idea'	*ġurfatha*	'her room'
fikrathum	'their idea'	*ġurfathum*	'their room'
fikirtak	'your M idea'	*ġuruftak*	'your M room'
fikirtič	'your F idea'	*ġuruftič*	'your F room'
fikratkum	'your P idea'	*ġurfatkum*	'your P room'
fikirti	'my idea'	*ġurufti*	'my room'
fikratna	'our idea'	*ġurfatna*	'our room'
fikirteen	'two ideas'	*ġurufteen*	'two rooms'

C. DRILLS

Drill 1. Change the prepositional phrase to a nisba, as in the example.

Cue:	*l-mudiir imnil-ʕiraaq.*	The director is from Iraq.
Response:	*l-mudiir ʕiraaqi.*	The director is (an) Iraqi.

zawjat saami mnil-ʕiraaq.
kullhum imnil-ʕiraaq.
l-banaat imnil-ʕiraaq.
zawjat ˀibni min ˀingiltara.
mudiir il-bang min ˀameerka.
ˀabuuya min ˀaḷmaanya.
ˀummi mnil-baṣra.
ˀibin xaaḷti min baġdaad.
ˀaani mnil-muuṣil.
ˀinti mnil-muuṣil?
ˀiḥna min lubnaan.
l-muʕallmiin min suurya.
ˀummi w-abuuya min miṣir.
l-uutači min turkiya.
ˀabu t-taksi mnil-baṣra.
ˀaṣdiqaaˀi mnil-baṣra.

Drill 2. Repeat the sentences, replacing the nisba adjective with the appropriate form of the items given.

a. *štireet ˀaθaaθ ˀingiliizi.* — I bought English furniture.

ˀooruppi
ˀaḷmaani
fransaawi
yuunaani
ˀameerkaani
turki
suuri
lubnaani
ruusi
hindi
ʕiraaqi
miṣri

b. *da-yiḥčuun wiyya fadd ibnayya miṣriyya* — They're talking with an Egyptian girl.'

yuunaani
hindi
kweeti
ˀalmaani
ˀarduni
ɛiraaqi

c. *l-muɛallmiin il-ɛiraaqiyyiin wuslaw il-yoom.* — The Iraqi teachers arrived today.

ˀameerkaani
baṣraawi
ˀingiliizi
ˀarduni
suuri
ˀalmaani

Drill 3. Repeat the sentences, replacing the noun with the items given, and making any other necessary changes.

a. *ˀariid hal-qaaṭ yitnaẓẓaf.* — I want this suit cleaned.

nafnuuf	dress
tannuura	skirt
panṭaruun	trousers
qappuuṭ	overcoat
sitra	jacket
booyinbaaġ	tie

b. *raḥ-albas il-qaaṭ ij-jidiid.* — I'm going to wear the new suit.

booyinbaaġ	tie
jooraab	socks
qanaadir	shoes
sitra	jacket
panṭaruun	trousers
qappuuṭ	overcoat
tannuura	skirt

Drill 4. Change the sentence, using a pronoun suffix as in the example.

Cue:	*ʕinda xooš fikra.*	He has a good idea.
Response:	*laa, fikirta ma-tiswa šii.*	No, his idea isn't worth anything.

ʕidha xooš fikra.	*ʕidna xooš fikra.*
ʕindič xooš fikra.	*ʕindak xooš fikra.*
ʕidhum xooš fikra.	*ʕinda xooš fikra.*
ʕindi xooš fikra.	*ʕidkum xooš fikra.*

Drill 5. Change the verb form to correspond to the cue, and make the necessary changes in the pronoun suffix(es).

a. *laazim anaḍḍuf ġurufti l-yoom.* I have to clean my room today.

Cue:	*ʔinta*	you M
Response:	*laazim itnaḍḍuf ġuruftak il-yoom.*	You M have to clean your M room today.

hiyya	*ʔaani*	*ʔiḥna*	*ʔuxtič*
ʔaani	*l-wulid*	*ʔintu*	*ʔinta*
humma	*samiira*	*huwwa*	*ʔinti*

b. *baʕda da-yiḥči ʕala safirta.* He's still talking about his trip.

Drill 6. Replace the first verb form with the items given, and make the necessary changes in the second verb and/or its attached suffixes.

ʔiðaa ʔanṭii l-qappuuṭ il-yoom, šwakit yrajjiʕ-li-yyaa? If I give him the overcoat today, when will he return it to me?

ʔanṭiiha	*yinṭii*	*yinṭiiha*
ʔanṭiik	*tinṭii*	*yinṭuuhum*
ʔanṭiihum	*yinṭuu*	*tinṭiič*
ʔanṭiič	*ninṭii*	*ninṭiikum*
ʔanṭiikum	*tinṭuu*	*ʔanṭiik*
ʔanṭii	*ʔanṭii*	*tinṭuu*

UNIT 40

A. NARRATIVE

Hussein is describing his arrival in Baghdad and how he got settled.

1. *baƐad-ma wṣalit baġdaad gumit ˀadawwur Ɛal-uuteel il-gitt-li Ɛalee.*	After I arrived in Baghdad I began to look for the hotel that you told me about.
2. *siˀálit fadd waaƇid yuƐruf mukaana w-dallaani Ɛalee.*	I asked someone who knew where it was, and he directed me to it.
3. *min wuṣalt il-uuteel ligeet Ɛidhum ġurfa w-Ƈammaam miθil-ma ridit.*	When I got to the hotel I found they had a room and bath as I wanted.
4. *l-booy ˀaxaδ ihduumi l-waṣxa Ƈatta tinġisil, w-wadda qaaṭi lil-mukawwi.*	The boy took my dirty clothes to be washed, and sent my suit to the cleaner's.
5. *baƐdeen baddálit w-riƇit zayyánit,*	Then I changed, and went and had a haircut.
6. *liˀann čaan Ɛindi mawƐid bid-daaˀira lli qaddámit Ɛala waδ̣iifa biiha.*	Because I had an appointment at the office where I had applied for a job.

VOCABULARY

dalla (*ydalli*) (*Ɛala*)	(Class II) to direct, show the way (to)
fadd waaƇid	someone
Ƈammaam (*Ƈammaamaat*)	bath
hduum (plural only)	clothes
nġisal (*yinġisil*)	(Class VII) to be washed
baddal (*ybaddil*)	(Class II) to change (one's clothes)
zayyan (*yzayyin*)	(Class II) to have a haircut or shave; to give a haircut or shave to (someone)

tƈaaša (yitƈaaša)	(Class VI) to avoid
ntiha (yintihi)	(Class VIII) to end
handas (yhandis)	(Quadriliteral) to design, engineer
mzayyin (mzaayna)	barber

B. GRAMMAR

1. Verbal nouns

Associated with verbs of all classes are forms known as **verbal nouns.** These are nouns which generally have the meaning 'act of performing (the action indicated by the verb)'. For example, with the verb *ƈayyan* 'to appoint' is associated the verbal noun *taƈyiin* 'appointment'; with *saaƈad* 'to help', the verbal noun *musaaƈada* 'aid, assistance'; with *staƈmal* 'to use', the verbal noun *stiƈmaal* 'use' (noun). Verbal nouns of Class I verbs differ widely in their patterns, and must be learned as they occur. The other verbal nouns have only one or two patterns in each class, and thus in most cases can be predicted from the form of the verb. Following are examples of the forms in common use:

Class I (*Various verbal noun patterns, not restricted to those illustrated here*)

Verb		*Verbal noun*	
si⁹al (yis⁹al)	'to ask'	*su⁹aal*	'question'
širab (yišrab)	'to drink'	*šurub*	'drinking'
wuṣal (yooṣal)	'to arrive'	*wuṣuul*	'arrival'
kitab (yiktib)	'to write'	*kitaaba*	'writing'
gaṣṣ (yguṣṣ)	'to cut'	*gaṣṣ*	'cutting'
baas (ybuus)	'to kiss'	*boos*	'kissing'
ƈiča (yiƈči)	'to talk'	*ƈači*	'talking'

Class II

Sound verbs: VN pattern taFMiiL

ƈawwal (yƈawwil)	'to transfer'	*taƈwiil*	'transferring, transfer'
naḍḍaf (ynaḍḍuf)	'to clean'	*tanḍiif*	'cleaning'

Defective verbs: VN pattern taFMiya

hanna (*yhanni*)	'to congratulate'	*tahniya*	'congratulation'

Class III

Sound verbs: VN patterns muFaaMaLa, FiMaaL

saaƐad (*ysaaƐid*)	'to help'	*musaaƐada*	'aid, assistance'
xaalaf (*yxaalif*)	'to differ'	*xilaaf*	'difference, disagreement'

Defective verbs: VN pattern mFaaMaa

daara (*ydaari*)	'to take care of'	*mdaaraa*	'care, attention'

Class IV

As Class IV verbs are relatively rare, there is not the same kind of direct association between them and verbal nouns as in the other classes. Class IV verbal nouns themselves are not uncommon, but they are best learned as individual nouns. The patterns are ʔiFMaaL, ʔiiMaaL, and ʔiFaaLa.

Class V

Sound verbs: VN pattern taFaMMuL (or *tFiMMiL, tFuMMuL*)

ṭṣawwar (*yiṭṣawwar*)	'to imagine'	*taṣawwur*	'imagining, imagination'

Defective verbs: VN pattern taFaMMi (or tFiMMi)

tmanna (*titmanna*)	'to wish'	*tamanni*	'wish, wishing'

Class VI

Sound verbs: VN pattern taFaaMuL

tƐaaraf (*yitƐaaraf*)	'to get acquainted'	*taƐaaruf*	'getting acquainted'

Defective verbs: VN pattern taFaaMi

tčaaša (yitčaaša)	'to avoid'	*tačaaši*	'avoiding'

Class VII

All verbs: VN pattern nFiMaaL (in the verbal noun of hollow verbs, the consonant in the M position is *y*; in that of defective verbs, the consonant in the L position is ˀ. These are not very common.)

nzičaj (yinzičij)	'to be annoyed'	*nzičaaj*	'being annoyed'
nčall (yinčall)	'to be solved, dissolved'	*nčilaal*	'dissolution'

Class VIII

All verbs: VN pattern FtiMaaL (in the verbal noun of hollow verbs, the consonant in the M position is *y*; in that of defective verbs, the consonant in the L position is ˀ)

čtiqad (yičtiqid)	'to believe'	*čtiqaad*	'belief'
htamm (yihtamm)	'to be concerned'	*htimaam*	'concern, interest'
čtaaj (yičtaaj)	'to need'	*čtiyaaj*	'need'
ntiha (yintihi)	'to end'	*ntihaaˀ*	'end'

Class IX

All verbs: VN pattern FMiLaaL (these are not very common)

čmarr (yičmarr)	'to turn red'	*čmiraar*	'turning red'

Class X

Sound, doubled and defective verbs: VN pattern stiFMaaL (in the verbal noun of defective verbs, the consonant in the L position is ˀ)

stačmal (yistačmil)	'to use'	*stičmaal*	'use'
stimarr (yistimirr)	'to continue'	*stimraar*	'continuing'
stanga (yistangi)	'to choose'	*stingaaˀ*	'choosing'

Hollow verbs: VN pattern stiFaaLa

staqaal (yistiqiil)	'to resign'	*stiqaala*	'resignation'

Simple quadriliterals

Patterns FaSTaL and FaDFaD: VN pattern FaSTaLa

handas (yhandis)	'to design, engineer'	*handasa*	'engineering'
tarjam (ytarjum)	'to translate'	*tarjama*	'translating, translation'
baqbaq (ybaqbuq)	'to bubble'	*baqbaqa*	'bubbling'

C. DRILLS

Drill 1. Change each sentence to one using a verbal noun, as in the example.

Cue:	*raC-yƐayyin ˀibni.*	He's going to appoint my son.
Response:	*ˀariid aCči wiyyaa Ɛala qaṣiyyat taƐyiin ˀibni.*	I want to talk with him about the matter of appointing my son (or, the appointment of my son)

raC-yCawwil ˀaxuuya.	*raC-ynaṣṣuf qaaṭi.*
raC-ybaddil ihduuma.	*raC-yistaƐmil is-sayyaara.*
raC-yqaddim Ɛala waṣiifa.	*raC-ytarjum l-iktaab.*

Drill 2. Change the following sentences so that the subject corresponds to the cue, and make any other necessary or logical changes.

a. *baƐad-ma wṣalit baġdaad gumit ˀadawwur Ɛal-uuteel.* After I arrived in Baghdad I began to look for the hotel.

Cue:	*hiyya*	she
Response:	*baƐad-ma wuṣlat baġdaad gaamat iddawwur Ɛal-uuteel.*	After she arrived in Baghdad she began to look for the hotel.

huṃṃa	*ˀinti*	*hiyya*
ˀiCna	*ˀintu*	*ˀaani*
ˀinta	*huwwa*	

b. *siˀálit fadd waaCid yuƐruf mukaana w-dallaani Ɛalee.* I asked someone who knew where it was and he directed me there.

c. *min wuṣalt il-uuteel ligeet ɛidhum ġurfa w-ḥammaam miθil-ma ridit.* — When I arrived at the hotel I found they had a room and bath as I wanted.

d. *čaan ɛindi mawɛid bid-daa'ira lli qaddámit ɛala waḏiifa biiha.* — I had an appointment at the office where I had applied for a job.

Drill 3. Replace *l-uuteel* with the items given, and make any other necessary changes.

baɛad-ma wṣálit baġdaad gumit adawwur ɛal-uuteel il-gitt-li ɛalee. — After I arrived in Baghdad I began to look for the hotel you told me about.

l-gahwa	*d-daa'ira*	*l-imzayyin*
l-bang	*l-muɛallim*	*l-aṣdiqaa'*
l-ibyuut	*l-madrasa*	*l-maktaba*
l-ixwaan	*l-baggaal*	*l-muwaḏḏafiin*

Drill 4. Answer the following questions, based on the narrative in Unit 30.

binit-man zaahda?
minu 'abu xaalid?
ɛala-weeš si'al 'abu xaalid?
'il-man si'al?
zaahda leeš čaanat ḥaayra?
minu 'umm xaalid?
š-gaalat hiyya?
yaa walad itḥibb zaahda 'akθar?
š-ism il-walad iθ-θaani?
šwakit hannooha z-zaahda?

Drill 5. Answer the following questions, based on the narrative in Unit 35.

saami w-zaahda leeš inxubṣaw?
šwakit mawɛid zawaajhum?
ween raayḥiin baɛdeen?
ɛidhum ḥajiz bil-paaṣ?
leeš xaabar saami l-uuteel?
minu waddaahum lil-maḥaṭṭa?
leeš ma-waddaahum lil-maṭaar?
b-sayyaarat-man waddaahum?
ween inḥaṭṭat junaṭhum?
ma-raaḥ 'abu zaahda lil-maḥaṭṭa?

Drill 6. Answer the following questions, based on the narrative in Unit 40.

mneen jaa ḥseen il-baġdaad?
leeš čaan ydawwur ɛala 'uuteel?
šloon liga l-uuteel?
čaan msawwi ḥajiz bil-uuteel?
l-booy leeš 'axaḏ ihduuma l-waṣxa?
'il-man wadda qaaṭa?
ḥseen ween raaḥ baɛdeen?
štira qaaṭ jidiid?
ween čaan ɛinda mawɛid?
raḥ-yištuġuḷ ib-baġdaad?

IRAQI-ENGLISH GLOSSARY

These glossaries generally include all the words given in the vocabularies of Units 11 to 40, and most of those given as examples in the Grammar sections. Not included, however, are active participles, passive participles, and verbal nouns, where these have meanings predictable from the meanings of the associated verbs. Also not included are certain place names and associated nisba adjectives (for a list of these see 39 B 1), most comparative forms (see 28 B 3), and most Class IX verbs (see 33 B 1).

Iraqi verbs are listed in the citation form (third-person masculine singular form of the perfect tense), with the third-person masculine singular form of the imperfect tense following in parentheses; the English equivalents are listed as infinitives. Iraqi nouns and adjectives (and other word-types with gender distinctions) are listed in the masculine singular form, with the plural form indicated in parentheses. If the latter is a regularly formed sound masculine or sound feminine plural, that fact is indicated by (*-iin*) or (*-aat*) respectively. If there is some irregularity in these plurals, and in all cases of the broken plural, the full plural form is given. In some cases the feminine singular form is also given in parentheses; it is then preceded by the abbreviation *F*, and the following plural form by the abbreviation *P*. After each Iraqi entry is a number indicating the unit in which that item first appears or is explained.

Iraqi entries are alphabetized in the following order: *aa a ee ii i oo o uu u ᵽ b p t θ j č ɛ x d δ r z s š ṣ δ̣ ṭ ɛ̣ ġ f q g k l m n h w y*. Emphatics other than *ṣ δ̣ ṭ* are alphabetized as though non-emphatic. A hyphen after a form indicates that it is a prefix; before a form, a suffix. Abbreviations used are as follows:

coll.	collective	neg.	negative
conj.	conjunction	P	plural
dem.	demonstrative	perf.	perfect
F	feminine	pref.	prefix
impf.	imperfect	prep.	preposition
interrog.	interrogative	PS	pronoun suffix
M	masculine	rel.	relative

-a (or lengthened final vowel) (suffixed to noun) 15 his, its M
-a (or lengthened final vowel) (suffixed to verb or prep.) 15 him, it M (objective)
-ak, -k (suffixed to noun) 11 your M
-ak, -k (suffixed to verb or prep.) 11 you M (objective)
-i (suffixed to noun) 12 my
-i (suffixed to prep.) 12 me
-ič, -č (suffixed to noun) 11 your F
-ič, -č (suffixed to verb or prep.) 11 you F (objective)

ʔ

ʔaab 33 August
ʔaaxar (F *ʔuxra*) 32 other
ʔaaδaar 33 March
ʔaani 13 I
ʔab (*ʔaabaaʔ*) 23 father
ʔabu taksi 25 taxi driver
ʔabu zwaali 32 rug merchant, rug man
ʔabu maktaba 38 book-seller
ʔabyaḍ (F *beeḍa*, P *biiḍ*) 35 white
ʔaθaaθ 32 furniture
ʔaḥḥad 37 someone
(*yoom*) *il-ʔaḥḥad* 33 Sunday
ʔaḥmar (F *ḥamra*, P *ḥumur*) 35 red
ʔaḥwal (F *ḥoola*, P *ḥuul*, *ḥooliin*) 35 cross-eyed
ʔax (*ʔuxwa*, *ʔixwaan*) 13 brother
ʔaxaδ (*yaaxuδ*) 18 to take
ʔaxbaar (P) 22 news
ʔaxḍar (F *xaḍra*, P *xuḍur*) 35 green
ʔaδaaʕ (*yδiiʕ*) 33 to broadcast
ʔarbaaṭaʕaš 19 fourteen
ʔarbaʕa 18 four
ʔarbaʕiin 20 forty
(*yoom*) *il-ʔarbiʕaa* 33 Wednesday
ʔazrag (F *zarga*, P *zurug*) 35 blue
ʔaswad (F *sooda*, P *suud*) 35 black
ʔaṣarr (*yṣirr*) 33 to insist
ʔaṣfar (F *ṣafra*, P *ṣufur*) 35 yellow
ʔaṣlaʕ (F *ṣalʕa*, P *ṣuluʕ*, *ṣalʕiin*) 35 bald
ʔaṭraš (F *ṭarša*, P *ṭuruš*, *taršiin*) 35 deaf
ʔaʕlan (*yiʕlin*) 33 to announce
ʔaqall 31 less; least
ʕal-ʔaqall 31 at least

ʔakal (*yaakul*) 33 to eat
ʔakil 32 eating; food
ʔaku 12 there is, there are
ʔakθar 28 more
ʔal(i)f (*ʔluuf*, *taalaaf*) 33 thousand
ʔalqa (*yilqi*) 33 to deliver (speech)
ʔaḷḷa(a) 16 God
ʔaḷḷa wiyyaak, -č, -kum 16 God be with you, good-bye
ʔameerka 23 America, the U.S.
ʔahal (*ʔahaali*) 35 family, relatives; people
ʔawwal (F *ʔuula*) 30 first
ʔawwal il-baarḥa 34 day before yesterday
bil-ʔawwal 30 at first
ʔayluul 33 September
ʔayyaar 33 May
ʔii 12 yes
ʔiid (F) (*ʔiideen*) 11 hand
ʔibin (*wulid*) 30 son
ʔibin ʔax 30 nephew (brother's son)
ʔibin ʔuxut 30 nephew (sister's son)
ʔibin xaaḷ 30 cousin (son of mother's brother)
ʔibin xaaḷa 30 cousin (son of mother's sister)
ʔibin ʕamm 30 cousin (son of father's brother)
ʔibin ʕamma 30 cousin (son of father's sister)
ʔibtidaaʔi 23 elementary
ʔija, jaa (*yiji*) 27 to come
ʔiḥna 13 we
ʔiδaa 37 if
ʔisim (*ʔasaami*) 33 name
ʔil- (with PS) 33 to, for
ʔilla 20 except
(*ʔi*)*lli* 32 who(m), which, that (rels.)
ʔil-man 26 to whom; whom
ʔinta 11 you M
ʔinti 11 you F
ʔintu 11 you P
ʔinšaḷḷa 21 if God wills
ʔuutači (*ʔuutačiyya*) 36 presser
ʔuuteel (*-aat*) 14 hotel
ʔuuti (*ʔuutiyyaat*) 36 iron (for pressing)
ʔuxut (*xawaat*) 23 sister
ʔusṭa (*ʔusṭawaat*) 17 master
ʔumm (*ʔummahaat*) 11 mother

b

b- 15 in
baab iš-šarji 18 Bab ish-Sharji (area in Baghdad)
baačir 32 tomorrow
baačir iṣ-ṣubuḥ 33 tomorrow morning
baarak (*ybaarik*) 28 to bless
baarid 13 cold
l-baarḥa 32 yesterday
baas (*ybuus*) 11 to kiss
baddal (*ybaddil*) 18 to change
barhan (*ybarhin*) 33 to prove
bass 27 but
l-baṣra 33 Basra (city in southern Iraq)
baṭṭiix (coll.) 36 cantaloupe
baṭṭiixa (*-aat*) 36 a cantaloupe
baʕad still, yet 16, after, since (preps.) 22
baʕad-ma 15 after (conj.)
baʕdeen 15 then, afterward
baġdaad 39 Baghdad
baqiyya 35 remainder, rest (of)
baqbaq (*ybaqbuq*) 33 to bubble
baggaal̥ (*bgaagiil*) 36 grocer (seller of fruits and vegetables)
bali 13 yes
bang (*bunuug*) 12 bank
bayyan (*ybayyin*) 22 to seem
beet (*byuut*) 12 house, home
beetinjaan (coll.) 36 eggplant
beetinjaana (*-aat*) 36 an eggplant
b-eeš 19 for what, how much
biira 13 beer
biṭaaqa (*-aat*) 19 ticket
biʕθa 23 scholarship, grant
bina (*yibni*) 27 to build
bin(i)t (*banaat*) 30 daughter, girl
bint ʔax 30 niece (brother's daughter)
bint ʔuxut 30 niece (sister's daughter)
bint xaal̥ 30 cousin (daughter of mother's brother)
bint xaal̥a 30 cousin (daughter of mother's sister)
bint ʕamm 30 cousin (daughter of father's brother)
bint ʕamma 30 cousin (daughter of father's sister)
booy 13 waiter
booyinbaaġ (*-aat*) 39 tie
buqa (*yibqa*) 25 to stay
bnayya (*-aat, banaat*) 22 girl

p

paaṣ (*-aat*) 18 bus
parda (*-aat*) 31 curtain
panṭaruun (*-aat, panaaṭiir*) 39 trousers
p̥anka (*-aat*) 17 fan
pooṣṭa (*-aat*) 36 post office; mail
pooṣṭači (*pooṣṭačiyya*) 36 postman
purtaqaal (coll.) 36 oranges
purtaqaala 36 an orange

t

taasiʕ 33 ninth
taḥat 39 under
taḥtaani 39 lower, under-
tartiib 35 arranging, arrangement(s)
tarjam (*ytarjum*) 33 to translate
taʕbaan (*-iin, tʕaaba*) 31 tired
taʕyiin 37 appointing, appointment (to a position)
talafoon (*-aat*) 12 telephone
tamur (coll.) 36 dates
tamra 36 date
tammuuz 33 July
tannuura (*-aat*) 39 skirt
tisʕa 18 nine
tisʕiin 20 ninety
tišriin iθ-θaani 33 November
tišriin il-ʔawwal 33 October
tiffaaḥ (coll.) 36 apples
tiffaaḥa, tiffaaḥaaya (*-aat*) 36 apple
tʔaxxar (*yitʔaxxar*) 35 to be delayed, be late
tḥaača (*yitḥaača*) 33 to converse
tḥaaša (*yitḥaaša*) 40 to avoid
tḥawwal (*yitḥawwal*) 22 to move
txarraj (*yitxarraj*) 21 to graduate
tʕaaraf (*yitʕaaraf*) 33 to get acquainted
tfaḍḍal (M), *tfaḍḍali* (F), *tfaḍḍalu* (P) 14 please
tlaaθa 18 three
tlaaθiin 20 thirty
tmanna (*yitmanna*) 29 to hope, wish
tnaddam (*yitnaddam*) 38 to be sorry
tnaḍḍaf (*yitnaḍḍaf*) 39 to be cleaned

θ

θaaliθ 33 third
θaamin 33 eighth

θaanawi 39 secondary
θaanawiyya 23 secondary school, high-school
θaani 25 second, other
θigiil (*θgaal*) 28 heavy
(*yoom*) *iθ-θilaaθaa* 33 Tuesday
θiliθ 20 (one) third
θoob (*θyaab*) 39 shirt
θmaaniin 20 eighty
θmaanya 18 eight
θṃuntaʕaš 19 eighteen
θṇaʕaš 19 twelve
θneen (F *θinteen*) 17 two
θneen-, *θneenaat-* (with PS) 23 both of us, you, them
(*yoom*) *il-iθneen* 33 Monday

j

jaa, *ʔija* (*yiji*) 27 to come
jaab (*yjiib*) 13 to bring
jaahil (*jihaal*) 22 child
jaawab (*yjaawub*) 30 to answer
jaayy 23 next, coming
jaraṣ (*jraaṣ*) 39 bell
jariida (*jaraayid*) 15 newspaper
jamaaʕa (*-aat*) 16 group (of people)
jawaab (*ʔajwiba*) 35 answer
jawwa 17 under
jidiid (*jiddad*) 17 new
jooraab (*jwaariib*) 39 (pair of) socks
(*yoom*) *il-jumʕa* 33 Friday
junṭa (*junaṭ*) 35 suitcase

č

čaan (*ykuun*) 29 to be
čaay 12 tea
čaayči (*čaayčiyya*) 36 tea vendor
čam (with S noun) 17 how many
čam waaḥid 17 how many (persons, things)
čibiir (*kbaar*) 17 big

ḥ

ḥaaja (*-aat*) 31 necessity, requirement
ḥaarr 13 hot
ḥaaδ̣ir (*ḥaaδ̣riin*) 33 ready; present
ḥaamuδ̣ 13 sour; lemon-tea
ḥaayir (*ḥaayriin*) 27 undecided, perplexed
ḥabb (*yḥibb*) 13 to like, love
ḥatta so (that), in order that 24, even 35
ḥajiz 33 reservation
ḥači 16 talk
ḥaδ̣δ̣ar (*yḥaδ̣δ̣ir*) 35 to prepare (something)
ḥaṭṭ (*yḥuṭṭ*) 26 to put
ḥaliib 13 milk
ḥammaam (*-aat*) 40 bath
ḥawwal (*yḥawwil*) 33 to transfer
ḥijaz (*yiḥjiz*) 33 to reserve
ḥiča (*yiḥči*) 15 to speak, talk
ḥilu (F *ḥilwa*, P *ḥilwiin*) 13 sweet; pretty, handsome
ḥuquuq (P) 23 law
ḥtaaj (*yiḥtaaj*) 33 to need
ḥzeeraan 33 June
ḥsaab (*-aat*) 16 bill, check, account
ḥmarr (*yiḥmarr*) 33 to turn red

x

xaabar (*yxaabur*) 34 to telephone
xaaḷ 30 uncle (mother's brother)
xaaḷa 28 aunt (mother's sister)
xaalaf (*yxaalif*) 40 to differ
xaamis 21 fifth
xariiṭa (*xaraayiṭ*) 12 map
xašš (*yxušš*) 21 to enter
xafiif (*xfaaf*) 28 light (in weight)
xal- (with impf. verb) 12 let's
xalla (*yxalli*) 22 to leave; to let
xaḷḷaṣ (*yxaḷḷiṣ*) 21 to finish
(*yoom*) *il-xamiis* 33 Thursday
xamsa 16 five
xamsiin 20 fifty
xeer 29 good things, happiness
xiḷaṣ (*yixḷaṣ*) 26 to be settled, finished
xoo 31 (particle expressing apprehension or hope and inviting reassurance)
xoox (coll.) 36 peaches
xooxa, *xooxaaya* (*-aat*) 36 peach
xooš (preceding a noun) 27 good
xuṭba 30 engagement
xuṭṭaar (*xṭaaṭiir*) 32 guest(s), company
xṃuṣtaʕaš 19 fifteen
xyaar (coll.) 36 cucumbers
xyaara (*-aat*) 36 cucumber

d

daaʔira (*dawaaʔir*) 14 office
daar il-muʕallimiin il-ʕaaliya 23 Teachers' College
daara (*ydaari*) 33 to take care of
daayan (*ydaayin*) 38 to lend
da- 23 (progressive prefix)
daraja (*-aat*) 33 class (on trains, etc.); degree (of heat)
dazz (*ydizz*) 26 to send
daʕaš 19 eleven
daqiiqa (*daqaayiq*) 27 minute
dagdag (*ydagdig*) 33 to pound
dagg (*ydugg*) 39 to ring; to knock on
dalla (*ydalli*) (*ʕala*) 40 to direct, show the way (to)
dawwar (*ydawwur*) *ʕala* 37 to look for
diinaar (*dnaaniir*) dinar (Iraqi unit of currency)
diraasa 21 study, studies
diras (*yidrus*) 23 to study
difaʕ (*yidfaʕ*) 16 to pay
ddaayan (*yiddaayan*) 35 to borrow

δ

δaak (M), *δiič*(*a*) (F) 37 that, that one
δoolaak 37 those
δoola 27 these, those

r

raabiʕ 33 fourth
raaḥ (*yruuḥ*) 16 to go
raad (*yriid*) 14 to want
raas (*ruus*) 35 head
raawa (*yraawi*) 38 to show
raʔi (*ʔaaraaʔ*) 27 opinion
rajaaʔan 13 please
rajjaʕ (*yrajjiʕ*) 38 to give back, return
raḥ- (with impf.) 14 going to, will (do something)
raġba (*-aat*) 39 wish
raġġab (*yraġġub*) (*b-*) 38 to interest (in)
raqam (*ʔarqaam*) 18 number
raggi (coll.) 36 watermelon
raggiyya (*-aat*) 36 a watermelon
rixiiṣ (*rxaaṣ*) 28 cheap
rikab (*yirkab*) 18 to ride, get on
rooḥa 31 (an act of) going, trip
rubuʕ 20 (one-)fourth, quarter

z

zawaaj 22 marriage
zawja (*-aat*) 30 wife
zawjat xaal 30 aunt (wife of mother's brother)
zawjat ʕamm 30 aunt (wife of father's brother)
zayyan (*yzayyin*) 40 to have a haircut or shave; to give a haircut or shave to (someone)
zeen (*-iin*) 11 good, well
zooj (*ʔazwaaj*) 30 husband
zooj xaala 30 uncle (husband of mother's sister)
zooj ʕamma 30 uncle (husband of father's sister)
zuuliyya (*zwaali*) 32 rug

s

saabiʕ 33 seventh
saadis 33 sixth
saaʕa (*-aat*) 16 hour; clock, watch
saaʕači (*saaʕačiyya*) 36 watch dealer, watch repairman
saaʕad (*ysaaʕid*) 33 to help
saafar (*ysaafir*) 39 to travel, take a trip; to leave (on a trip)
(*yoom*) *is-sabit* 33 Saturday
sabʕa 18 seven
sabʕiin seventy
sariiʕ 33 fast, rapid
safaara (*-aat*) 14 embassy
safra (*-aat*) 35 trip
s-salaamu ʕalaykum 14 the peace upon you
sallam (*ysallim*) *ʕala* 15 to greet
sana (*sniin*) 21 year
sanawi 39 yearly, annual
sahil 28 easy
sawwa (*ysawwi*) 17 to do, make
sayyaara (*-aat*) 12 car
sayyid 17 sir, mister
siinama (*-aat*) 38 movie theatre, movies
siʔal (*yisʔal*) 15 to ask
sitta 18 six
sittiin 17 sixty
sitra (*sitar*) 39 jacket
simač (coll.) 36 fish
simaʕ (*yismaʕ*) 31 to hear, listen

simča (*-aat*) 36 a fish
suug (*swaag*) 14 market
suʔaal (*ʔasʔila*) 28 question
suwa 12 together
sbuuε (*ʔasaabiiε*) 31 week
stajwab (*yistajwub*) 33 to question
staɛaqq (*yistiɛiqq*) 33 to deserve
staraaɛ (*yistiriiɛ*) 14 to rest
starxaṣ (*yistarxiṣ*) 16 to ask permission
staεmal (*yistaεmil*) 33 to use
staqaal (*yistiqiil*) 33 to resign
stanga (*yistangi*) 33 to choose
stifaad (*yistifiid*) 33 to benefit
stikaan (*-aat*) 12 glass (small, for tea)
stimarr (*yistimirr*) 33 to continue
stuwa (*yistuwi*) 33 to ripen
skamli (*skamliyyaat*) 32 chair

š

š- 13 what
šaariε (*šawaariε*) 15 street
šaaf (*yšuuf*) 11 to see
šariṭ (*šuruuṭ*) 38 condition
εala šariṭ 38 on condition (that)
šarbat 13 sherbet (flavored liquid drink)
šaṭṭ (*šṭuuṭ*) 34 river
šaṭṭ il-εarab 34 Shatt al-Arab (river in southern Iraq)
šakk 29 doubt(s), misgiving(s)
šahar (*ʔašhur, tušhur*) 26 month
šahr il-εasal 35 (the) honeymoon
šahri 39 monthly
šii (*ʔašyaaʔ*) 13 thing, something
šii ʔaaxar 32 something else, anything else
širab (*yišrab*) 12 to drink
šiqqa (*šiqaq*) 12 apartment
šikil (*ʔaškaal*) 28 manner, way
šiniina 13 diluted yoghurt
šinu 14 what
š-šoorja 24 Shorja (section of Baghdad)
šuġuḷ (*ʔašġaaḷ*) 11 work, business
šukran 14 thanks, thank you
šbaaṭ 33 February
štira (*yištiri*) 27 to buy
štiġaḷ (*yištuġuḷ*) 33 to work
šgadd 14 how much, how long
šgadd-ma 24 however much
šloon 11 how
šloonak (M), *-ic* (F), *-kum* (P) 11 how are you
šloon-ma 24 however (conj.)
š-ma 24 whatever
šwakit 24 when
šwakit-ma 24 whenever
šwayya 28 a little, a little bit

ṣ

ṣaaɛ (*yṣiiɛ*) 27 to call (someone); to shout
ṣaar (*yṣiir*) 14 to become
ṣabaaɛ il-xeer 33 good morning
ṣadiiq (*ʔaṣdiqaaʔ*) 15 friend
ṣaεub 28 difficult, hard
ṣawwar (*yṣawwur*) 33 to depict, picture
ṣiraf (*yuṣruf*) 38 to spend
ṣiṭṭaεaš 19 sixteen
ṣoogar (*yṣoogir*) 33 to insure
ṣubuɛ 33 morning
ṣ-ṣubuɛ 38 in the morning
ṣudug 28 truth
ṣbaaṭaεaš 19 seventeen
ṣṭubar (*yiṣṭubur*) 33 to be patient
ṣġayyir (*ṣġaar*) 17 small, little

ð̣

ð̣all (*yð̣ill*) (with imperfect verb) 26 to continue, go on (doing something)

ṭ

ṭabεan 27 of course, naturally
ṭallaε (*yṭalliε*) 36 to take out, bring out
ṭamaaṭa (coll.) 36 tomatoes
ṭamaaṭaaya (*-aat*) 36 tomato
ṭayyib 13 good, tasty; all right
ṭibbi 39 medical
ṭibbiyya 21 medical science, (study of) medicine
ṭilaε (*yiṭlaε*) 33 to leave, depart; to come out, go out
ṭubax (*yuṭbux*) 33 to cook
ṭuwiil (*ṭwaal*) 28 long; tall
ṭṣaaṭaεaš 19 nineteen
ṭṣawwar (*yiṭṣawwar*) 23 to think, imagine
ṭṣoogar (*yiṭṣoogar*) 33 to be insured
ṭlaṭṭaεaš 19 thirteen

ع

ʕaašir 33 tenth
ʕaal 12 fine, excellent
ʕatiig (*ʕittag*) 17 old
ʕajab 12 wonder
ʕasal 35 honey
ʕašra 18 ten
ʕaḍḍ (*yʕaḍḍ*) 33 to bite
ʕala 16 on; about
ʕalaykum is-salaam 14 upon you the peace
ʕamm 17 uncle (father's brother)
ʕamma 30 aunt (father's sister)
ʕan 34 about, concerning
ʕayyan (*yʕayyin*) 37 to appoint, nominate
ʕeen (F) (*ʕyuun*) 27 eye
ʕeeni 27 (term of endearment) my dear, old friend
l-ʕiraaq 39 Iraq
ʕiraf (*yuʕruf*) 24 to know
ʕiris 35 wedding
ʕišriin 20 twenty
ʕilan (*yiʕlin*) 33 to announce
ʕinab (coll.) 36 grapes
ʕinbaaya (*-aat*) 36 grape
ʕi(n)d 12 on, with, in the possession of, at the residence or place of business of
ʕugba 34 day after tomorrow
ʕtiqad (*yiʕtiqid*) 37 to think, consider

ġ

ġaali 28 expensive
ġaraḍ (*ġaraaḍ*) (usually in plural) 31 things, belongings
ġeer 20 other, different
ġisal (*yiġsil*) 39 to wash
ġuruub 34 setting of the sun
ġurfa (*ġuraf*) 32 room
ġurfat xuṭṭaar 32 parlor (room where guests are received)
ġurfat noom 32 bedroom

f

fadd 12 a, an; about, approximately
fadd raas 35 straight, directly
fadd šii 20 something
fadd waaḥid 20 someone
farḥaan (*-iin*) 35 happy
faḍḍal (*yfaḍḍil*) 28 to prefer
fakk (*yfukk*) 26 to open
fakkar (*yfakkir*) (*b-*) 26 to think (about), consider
fiimaanillaa 16 good-bye (in the protection of God)
fikra (*-aat, fikar*) 27 idea
filis (*fluus*) 17 fils (Iraqi penny; one-thousandth of a dinar)
ftiham (*yiftihim*) 33 to understand
fraaš (*fraašaat*) 31 bed
fluus (F) 17 money

q

qaaṭ (*quuṭ*) 39 suit
qappuuṭ (*qpaapiiṭ*) 39 overcoat
qaddam (*yqaddim*) *ʕala* 23 to apply
qaḍiyya (*qaḍaaya*) 29 matter, affair, problem
qalam (*qlaam*) 12 pencil
qamaara (*-aat*) 33 compartment
qira (*yiqra*) 15 to read
qiṭaar (*-aat*) 33 train
qundara (*qanaadir*) 36 shoe
qundarči (*qundarčiyya*) 36 shoemaker, shoe repairman

g

gaaziino (F) 14 (see 14 C, Drill 1)
gaal (*yguul*) 11 to say, tell
gaam (*yguum*) 15 to get up; (with impf. verb) to begin
gabuḷ 21 before (prep.)
gabuḷ-ma 21 before (conj.)
gaṣṣ (*yguṣṣ*) 19 to cut; to buy (ticket)
gahawči (*gahawčiyya*) 36 coffee-house proprietor
gahwa 13 coffee
gahwa (*gahaawi*) 12 coffee-house
gidar (*yigdar*) 18 to be able, can
girab (*yigrab*) 35 to approach, draw near
girab (*yigrab*) (*l-*) 37 to be related (to)
giʕad (*yugʕud*) 14 to sit
giʕad (*yugʕud*) *ib-mukaana* 29 to fall into (its) place
gubaḷ 16 straight ahead
gṣayyir (*gṣaar*) 28 short
glaaṣ (*-aat*) 13 glass

k

kaanuun iθ-θaani 33 January
kaanuun il-ˀawwal 33 December
l-karraada 18 Karrada (section of Baghdad)
karradat maryam 22 Karradat Maryam (section of Baghdad)
keef 16 wish, feeling
keelu (*keeluwaat*) 36 kilo(gram)
kitaaba 32 writing
kitab (*yiktib*) 33 to write
kull 16 all, every, any
kullat- (with PS) 27 all of us, you, them
kulliš 22 very
kulliyat il-ɕuquuq 23 College of Law
kullši 12 everything; anything; (with neg.) nothing
-kum (suffixed to noun) 11 your P
-kum (suffixed to verb or prep.) 11 you P (objective)
ktaab (*kutub*) 38 book

l

l- 12 the
l- 13 to, for
l- 32 who(m), which, that (rels.)
laa 12 no
laax (F *lux*) 28 other
laazim 16 necessary; (with impf. verb) must, have to
laakin 33 but
la- 38 not
laɕam (coll.) 36 meat
laɕma (*-aat*) 36 piece of meat
ḷaṭiif (*ḷaṭiifiin*) 34 nice, pleasant, agreeable
laƹad 12 then, in that case
leeš 26 why
leel 33 night, nighttime
liilu (coll.) 36 pearls
liiluwwa (*-aat*) 36 a pearl
liˀann 30 because
libas (*yilbas*) 39 to put on, to wear
liban 13 yoghurt
liga (*yilgi*) 27 to find
loo 13 or
loo 37 if
lɕamdilla 11 praise to God

m

maašaaḷḷaa 21 whatever God wills (expression of admiration)
maal 19 of, belonging to, for
maal-, *maal*(*a*)*t-* (with PS) 32 my, mine; your, yours; his; her, hers; our, ours; their, theirs
ṃaay 13 water
ma- 38 not
mabruuk 29 congratulations
ma-tiswa 16 it isn't worth (it)
maɕaṭṭa (*-aat*) 33 station
maɕruusiin 11 children
ma-daam 31 inasmuch as, since, as
madrasa (*madaaris*) 21 school
marɕaba 11 hello
ṃarra (*-aat*) 11 a time; sometimes
masˀala (*masaaˀil*) 31 matter, affair, question
mašġuuḷ (*-iin*) 11 busy
maṭaar (*-aat*) 14 airport
maƹa s-salaama 17 good-bye (with the safety)
maktaba (*-aat*) 38 bookstore; library
malaabis (P) 39 clothes
mamnuun (*-iin*) 17 grateful
-man (suffixed to prep.) 33 whom
-man (suffixed to noun) 33 whose
manḍ̣ar (*manaaḍ̣ir*) 34 view, sight, scene
manṭiqa (*manaaṭiq*) 12 area
mawḍ̣uuƹ (*mawaaḍ̣iiƹ*) 26 matter, subject
mawƹid (*mawaaƹid*) 16 appointment, engagement
mawqif (*mawaaqif*) 20 stopping place, bus stop
ma-yxaalif 24 it doesn't matter, makes no difference
meez (*myuuza*) 32 table
meez ˀakil 32 table for eating, dining-room table
meez kitaaba 32 writing-table, desk
miiteen 24 two hundred
miθil 21 like
miθil-ma 21 as (conj.)
mirtaaɕ (*-iin*) 22 happy, contented
mistaƹjil (*-iin*) 16 urgent; in a hurry
miswaag 31 shopping
miša (*yimši*) 11 to walk

miġrib 33 sunset, sundown
milyoon (*malaayiin*) 33 million
min from, of 20; than 28
minu 27 who
minu-ma 24 whoever
minnaa 18 from here
minnaak 18 from there
miyya 24 hundred
mooz (coll.) 36 bananas
mooza (*-aat*) 36 banana
muu 11 not
mudiir (*mudaraaʔ*) 37 director
mudda 15 period of time, (a) while
muškila (*mašaakil*) 28 problem
muṭbax (*maṭaabix*) 31 kitchen
mukaan (*-aat*) 29 place, position
mukawwi (*-iin*) 39 cleaner, presser
mumtaaz (*-iin*) 36 fine, excellent
muwað̣ð̣af (*-iin*) 33 employee (especially of government), civil servant, official
mzayyin (*mzaayna*) 40 barber
mneen 31 from where?

n

-na (suffixed to noun) 12 our
-na (suffixed to verb or prep.) 12 us
najjaar (*-iin*) 32 carpenter
naxaḷ (coll.) 34 (date) palm trees
nað̣ð̣af (*ynað̣ð̣uf*) 33 to clean
naf(*i*)*s* (with noun) 34 same
naf(*i*)*s-* (with PS) 34 myself, yourself, etc.
nafnuuf (*nafaaniif*) 39 dress
namil (coll.) 36 ants
namla (*-aat*) 36 ant
nahaar 33 day, daytime
neešan (*yneešin*) 33 to aim
niisaan 33 April
-ni (suffixed to verb) 12 me
nisa (*yinsa*) 27 to forget
niðiif (*nðaaf*) 28 clean
niṭa (*yinṭi*) 26 to give
noom 32 sleep, sleeping
nuṣṣ 20 half
ntiha (*yintihi*) 40 to end
njubar (*yinjubur*) 33 to be forced
nʕaṭṭ (*yinʕaṭṭ*) 35 to be put, placed
nʕall (*yinʕall*) 28 to be solved
nʕina (*yinʕini*) 35 to be bent over
nxubaṣ (*yinxubuṣ*) (*b-*) 35 to become busy, rushed, wholly tied up (with)
ndazz (*yindazz*) 33 to be sent
ndifaʕ (*yindifiʕ*) 33 to be paid
nraad (*yinraad*) 31 to be needed, necessary, required
nziʕaj (*yinziʕij*) 40 to be annoyed
nṭuwa (*yinṭuwi*) 33 to be folded
nġisal (*yinġisil*) 40 to be washed
nliġa (*yinliġi*) 33 to be cancelled
nliga (*yinligi*) 33 to be found

h

haaða (M); *haaði, haay* (F) 11 this, this one
-ha (suffixed to noun) 15 her (possessive), its F
-ha (suffixed to verb or prep.) 15 her, it F (objective)
hassa 21 now
hal- 12 this, these
hamm 27 too, also; (with neg.) (not) either
hamm zeen 29 it's a good thing (that) ...
handas (*yhandis*) 40 to design, engineer
handasa 23 engineering
hanna (*yhanni*) 30 to congratulate
hiič(*i*) 28 thus, so
hiyya 18 she, it F
hooḷ 32 living-room (room used by family)
-hum (suffixed to noun) 15 their
-hum (suffixed to verb or prep.) 15 them
humṃa 18 they
huwwa 18 he, it M
htamm (*yihtamm*) 33 to be concerned
hduum (P) 40 clothes
hnaa 14 here
hnaak 15 there
hwaaya 14 much, a lot

w

w- 13 and
waaʕid (F *wiʕda*) 17 one
l-waaʕid 34 one, you (impersonal), French *on*, German *man*
wadda (*ywaddi*) 39 to take, send (something somewhere)
waṣaṭ 39 center, middle

waṣix (*waṣxiin*) 28 dirty
waṣṣa (*ywaṣṣi*) *ʕala* 32 to give (someone) an order for, order (something) from (someone)
waṣṣal (*ywaṣṣil*) 18 to convey, take (someone somewhere)
waṣṭaani 36 medium-sized
waðiifa (*waðaayif*) 37 position, job
wakit 16 time
wakt il-ġuruub 34 sunset
wala 38 and not, nor
walad (*wulid*) 22 boy
walḷa 11 really, honestly
ween 12 where
ween-ma 24 wherever
wiyya 15 with
wuzan (*yoozin*) 36 to weigh
wuṣal (*yooṣal*) 18 to arrive

y

yaa 18 which (interrog.)
yaa 16 (vocative particle)
-ya (suffixed to noun) 12 my
-ya (suffixed to prep.) 12 me
yamm 12 by, next to
yawmi 39 daily
yibas (*yeebas*) 33 to get dry
yoom (*ʔayyaam, tiyyaam*) 11 day
l-yoom 13 the day; today
hal-yoom 31 this day; today
-yyaa- 38 (stem for second pronoun suffix)

ENGLISH-IRAQI GLOSSARY

In the glossary below, certain complex English verb phrases are alphabetized according to the last, or most important, word; for example, "to be settled" is found under "settled," and "to turn red" under "red." For other comments, and abbreviations, see the Iraqi-English glossary above.

A

a *fadd* 12
to be able *gidar (yigdar)* 18
about *ɛala* 25, *ɛan* 34, *fadd* 36
account *ħsaab* 16
to get acquainted *tɛaaraf (yitɛaaraf)* 33
affair *qað̣iyya (qað̣aaya)* 29, *masʔala (masaaʔil)* 31
after (conj.) *baɛad-ma* 15
after (prep.) *baɛad* 22
afterward *baɛdeen* 15
agreeable *ḷaṭiif (-iin)* 34
airport *maṭaar (-aat)* 14
to aim *neešan (yneešin)* 33
all *kull* 16
all of us, you, them *kullatna, kullatkum, kullathum* 27
all right *zeen* 11, *ṭayyib* 13
also *hamm* 27
America *ʔameerka* 23
an *fadd* 12
and *w-* 13
to announce *ɛilan (yiɛlin), ʔaɛlan (yiɛlin)* 33
to be annoyed *nziɛaj (yinziɛij)* 40
annual *sanawi* 39
answer *jawaab (ʔajwiba)* 35
to answer *jaawab (yjaawub)* 30
ant *namla (-aat)* 36
ants *namil* (coll.) 36
(not) any *kull* (with neg.) 16
(not) anything *kullši* (with neg.) 12
anything else *šii ʔaaxar* 32
apartment *šiqqa (šiqaq)* 12
apple *tiffaaħa, (-aat), tiffaaħaaya* 36
apples *tiffaaħ* (coll.) 36
to apply for *qaddam (yqaddim) ɛala* 23
to appoint *ɛayyan (yɛayyin)* 37
appointing, appointment (to a position) *taɛyiin* 37
appointment (for a meeting) *mawɛid (mawaaɛid)* 16
to approach *giraḅ (yigraḅ)* 35
approximately *fadd* (before a numeral) 36
April *niisaan* 33
area *manṭiqa (manaaṭiq)* 12
arrangement(s), arranging *tartiib* 35
to arrive *wuṣal (yooṣal)* 18
as (conj.) *miθil-ma* 21, *ma-daam* 31
to ask *siʔal (yisʔal)* 15
to ask permission *starxaṣ (yistarxiṣ)* 16
August *ʔaab* 33
aunt (mother's sister) *xaaḷa* 28
aunt (father's sister) *ɛamma* 30
aunt (wife of father's brother) *zawjat ɛamm* 30
aunt (wife of mother's brother) *zawjat xaaḷ* 30
to avoid *tħaaša (yitħaaša)* 40

B

Bab ish-Sharji (area in Baghdad) *baab iš-šarji* 18
bad *muu zeen (zeeniin)* 11
Baghdad *baġdaad* 39
bald *ʔaṣlaɛ* (F *ṣalɛa*, P *ṣuluɛ, ṣalɛiin*) 35
banana *mooza (-aat)* 36
bananas *mooz* (coll.) 36
bank *ḅang (bunuug)* 12

barber *mzayyin* (*mzaayna*) 40
Basra (city in southern Iraq) *l-başra* 33
bath *ḥammaam* (*-aat*) 40
to be *čaan* (*ykuun*) 29
because *li?ann* 30
to become *şaar* (*yşiir*) 14
bed *fraaš* (*-aat*) 31
bedroom *ġurfat noom* 32
beer *biira* 13
before (conj.) *gabuḷ-ma* 21
before (prep.) *gabuḷ* 21
to begin (to do something) *gaam* (*yguum*) (with impf.) 15
bell *jaraş* (*jraaş*) 39
belonging to *maal* 19
belongings *garað̣* (*ġaraað̣*) (usually in plural) 31
to benefit *stifaad* (*yistifiid*) 33
to be bent over *nḥina* (*yinḥini*) 35
big *čibiir* (*kbaar*) 17
bill *ḥsaab* (*-aat*) 16
to bite *ʕað̣ð̣* (*yʕað̣ð̣*) 33
black *?aswad* (F *sooda*, P *suud*) 35
to bless *baarak* (*ybaarik*) 28
blue *?azrag* (F *zarga*, P *zurug*) 35
book *ktaab* (*kutub*) 38
book-seller *?abu maktaba* 38
bookstore *maktaba* (*-aat*) 38
to borrow *ddaayan* (*yiddaayan*) 35
both of us, you, them *θneen-*, *θneenaat-* (with PS) 23
boy *walad* (*wulid*) 22
to bring *jaab* (*yjiib*) 13
to broadcast *?aðaaʕ* (*yðiiʕ*) 33
brother *?ax* (*?uxwa*, *?ixwaan*) 13
to bubble *baqbaq* (*ybaqbuq*) 33
to build *bina* (*yibni*) 27
business *šuġuḷ* (*?ašġaaḷ*) 11
busy *mašġuuḷ* (*-iin*) 11
to become busy *nxubaş* (*yinxubuş*) 35
but *bass* 27, *laakin* 33
to buy *štira* (*yištiri*) 27
to buy (tickets) *gaşş* (*yguşş*) 19
by, beside *yamm* 12

C

to call (someone) *şaaḥ* (*yşiiḥ*) 27
can, to be able *gidar* (*yigdar*) 18
to be cancelled *nliġa* (*yinliġi*) 33
cantaloupe *baṭṭiix* (coll.) 36
a cantaloupe *baṭṭiixa* (*aat*) 36
car *sayyaara* (*-aat*) 12
carpenter *najjaar* (*-iin*) 32
center *waşaṭ* 39
chair *skamli* (*skamliyyaat*) 32
to change *baddal* (*ybaddil*) 18
cheap *rixiiş* (*rxaaş*) 28
check, bill *ḥsaab* (*-aat*) 16
child *jaahil* (*jihaal*) 22
children *maḥruusiin* 11
to choose *stanga* (*yistangi*) 33
civil servant *muwað̣ð̣af* (*-iin*) 33
class (on trains etc.) *daraja* (*-aat*) 33
clean *nið̣iif* (*nð̣aaf*) 28
to clean *nað̣ð̣af* (*ynað̣ð̣uf*) 33
to be cleaned *tnað̣ð̣af* (*yitnað̣ð̣af*) 39
cleaner *mukawwi* (*mukawwiin*) 39
clock *saaʕa* (*-aat*) 16
clothes *malaabis* (P) 39, *hduum* (P) 40
coffee *gahwa* 13
coffee-house *gahwa* (*gahaawi*) 12
coffee-house proprietor *gahawči* (*gahawčiyya*) 36
cold *baarid* 13
College of Law *kulliyat il-ḥuquuq* 23
to come *jaa*, *?ija* (*yiji*) 14
to come out *ṭiḷaʕ* (*yiṭḷaʕ*) 33
coming, next *jaayy* 23
company, guest(s) *xuṭṭaar* (*xṭaaṭiir*) 32
compartment *qamaara* (*-aat*) 33
to be concerned *htamm* (*yihtamm*) 33
concerning *ʕala* 25, *ʕan* 34
condition *šariṭ* (*šuruuṭ*) 38
on condition (that) *ʕala šariṭ* 38
to congratulate *hanna* (*yhanni*) 30
congratulations *mabruuk* 29
to consider *fakkar* (*yfakkir*) (*b-*) 26
contented *mirtaaḥ* (*-iin*) 22
to continue *stimarr* (*yistimirr*) 33
to continue (doing something) *ð̣all* (*yð̣ill*) (with impf.) 26
to converse *tḥaača* (*yitḥaača*) 33
to convey *waşşal* (*ywaşşil*) 18
to cook *ṭubax* (*yuṭbux*) 33
cousin (daughter of father's brother) *bint ʕamm* 30
cousin (daughter of father's sister) *bint ʕamma* 30
cousin (daughter of mother's brother) *bint xaaḷ* 30

cousin (daughter of mother's sister *bint xaaḷa* 30

cousin (son of father's brother) *ʔibin ʕamm* 30

cousin (son of father's sister) *ʔibin ʕamma* 30

cousin (son of mother's brother) *ʔibin xaaḷ* 30

cousin (son of mother's sister) *ʔibin xaaḷa* 30

cross-eyed *ʔaʕwal* (F *ʕoola*, P *ʕuul*, *ʕooliin*) 35

cucumber *xyaara* (*-aat*) 36

cucumbers *xyaar* (coll.) 36

curtain *parda* (*-aat*) 31

to cut *gaṣṣ* (*yguṣṣ*) 19

D

daily *yawmi* 39

date *tamra* (*-aat*) 36

dates *tamur* (coll.) 36

daughter, girl *binit* (*banaat*) 30

day *yoom* (*ʔayyaam, tiyyaam*) 13, *nahaar* 33

day after tomorrow *ʕugba* 34

day before yesterday *ʔawwal il-baarḥa* 34

daytime *nahaar* 33

deaf *ʔaṭraš* (F *ṭarša*, P *ṭuruš*, *ṭaršiin*) 35

(my) dear *ʕeeni* 27

December *kaanuun il-ʔawwal* 33

degree (of heat) *daraja* (*-aat*) 33

to be delayed *tʔaxxar* (*yitʔaxxar*) 35

to deliver (speech) *ʔalqa* (*yilqi*) 33

to depart (train) *ṭilaʕ* (*yiṭlaʕ*) 33

to depict, picture *ṣawwar* (*yṣawwur*) 33

to deserve *staḥaqq* (*yistiḥiqq*) 33

to design *handas* (*yhandis*) 40

desk *meez kitaaba* 32

to differ *xaalaf* (*yxaalif*) 40

it makes no difference *ma-yxaalif* 24

different *ġeer* (with following noun) 20

difficult *ṣaʕub* 28

dinar (Iraqi unit of currency) *diinaar* (*dnaaniir*) 17

dining-room table *meez ʔakil* 32

to direct *dalla* (*ydalli*) (*ʕala*) 40

directly *fadd raas* 35

director *mudiir* (*mudaraaʔ*) 37

dirty *waṣix* (*waṣxiin*) 28

to do *sawwa* (*ysawwi*) 17

doubt(s) *šakk* 29

to draw near *giraḅ* (*yigraḅ*) 35

to get dry *yibas* (*yeebas*) 33

dress *nafnuuf* (*nafaaniif*) 39

to drink *širab* (*yišrab*) 12

E

each *kull* 16

easy *sahil* 28

to eat *ʔakal* (*yaakul*) 33

eating; food *ʔakil* 32

an eggplant *beetinjaana* (*-aat*) 36

eggplant *beetinjaan* (coll.) 36

eight *θmaanya* 18

eighteen *θmunṭaʕaš* 19

eighth *θaamin* 33

eighty *θmaaniin* 20

(not) either *hamm* (with neg.) 34

elementary *ʔibtidaaʔi* 23

eleven *daʕaš* 19

embassy *safaara* (*-aat*) 14

employee (especially of government) *muwaḍḍaf* (*-iin*) 33

to end *ntiha* (*yintihi*) 40

engagement (for a meeting) *mawʕid* (*mawaaʕid*) 16

engagement (to be married) *xuṭba* 30

to engineer *handas* (*yhandis*) 40

engineering *handasa* 23

to enter *xašš* (*yxušš*) 21

even *ḥatta* 35

every *kull* 16

everything *kullši* 12

excellent *ʕaal* 12, *mumtaaz* (*-iin*) 36

except *ʔilla* 20

expensive *ġaali* (F *ġaalya*) 28

eye *ʕeen* (F) (*ʕyuun*) 27

F

to fall into (its) place *giʕad* (*yugʕud*) *ib-mukaana* 29

family *ʔahal* (*ʔahaali*) 35

fan *panka* (*-aat*) 17

fast *sariiʕ* 33

father *ʔab* (*ʔaabaaʔ*) 23

February *šbaaṭ* 33

feeling *keef* 16

fifteen *xṃuṣṭaʕaš* 19
fifth *xaamis* 21
fifty *xamsiin* 20
fils (Iraqi penny) *filis* (*fluus*) 17
to find *liga* (*yilgi*) 27
fine *ʕaal* 12, *mumtaaz* (*-iin*) 36
to finish *xaḷḷaṣ* (*yxaḷḷiṣ*) 21
to be finished *xiḷaṣ* (*yixḷaṣ*) 26
first *ʔawwal* (F *ʔuula*) 30
at first *bil-ʔawwal* 30
a fish *simča* (*-aat*) 36
fish *simač* (coll.) 36
five *xamsa* 16
to be folded *nṭuwa* (*yinṭuwi*) 33
food *ʔakil* 32
for *l-* 13, *maal* 19, *ʔil-* (with PS) 33
for what *b-eeš* 19
to be forced *njubar* (*yinjubur*) 33, *δ̣ṭarr* (*yiδ̣ṭarr*) 35
to forget *nisa* (*yinsa*) 27
forty *ʔarbaʕiin* 20
to be found *nliga* (*yinligi*) 33
four *ʔarbaʕa* 18
fourteen *ʔarḅaaṭaʕaš* 19
fourth *raabiʕ* 33
(one-)fourth *rubuʕ* 20
Friday (*yoom*) *il-jumʕa* 33
friend *ṣadiiq* (*ʔaṣdiqaaʔ*) 15
from *min* 20
from here *minnaa* 18
from there *minnaak* 18
furniture *ʔaθaaθ* 32

G

gentlemen *ʔixwaan* 17
to get on, ride *rikab* (*yirkab*) 18
to get straightened out *giʕad* (*yugʕud*) *ib-mukaana* 29
girl *bnayya* (*-aat*) 22, *binit* (*banaat*) 30
to give *niṭa* (*yinṭi*) 26
to give back, return *rajjaʕ* (*yrajjiʕ*) 38
glass *gḷaaṣ* (*-aat*) 13
glass (small, used for tea) *stikaan* (*-aat*) 12
to go *raaħ* (*yruuħ*) 16
to go on (doing something) *δ̣all* (*yδ̣ill*) with impf.) 26
to go out *ṭiḷaʕ* (*yiṭḷaʕ*) 33
God *ʔaḷḷa* 16
God be with you M *ʔaḷḷa wiyyaak*
(an act of) going *rooħa* 31
going to (do something) *raħ-* (with impf.) 14
good *zeen* (*-iin*) 11, *ṭayyib* 13, *xooš* (preceding a noun) 27
good-bye *fiimaanillaa* 16, *ʔaḷḷa wiyyaak, -č, -kum* 16, *maʕa s-salaama* 17
good morning *ṣabaaħ il-xeer*
to graduate *txarraj* (*yitxarraj*) 21
grant *biʕθa* 23
grape *ʕinbaaya* (*-aat*) 36
grapes *ʕinab* (coll.) 36
grateful *mamnuun* (*-iin*) 17
green *ʔaxδ̣ar* (F *xaδ̣ra,* P *xuδ̣ur*) 35
to greet *sallam* (*ysallim*) *ʕala* 15
grocer (seller of fruits and vegetables) *baggaaḷ* (*bgaagiil*)
group (of people) *jamaaʕa* (*-aat*) 16
guest(s) *xuṭṭaar* (*xṭaaṭiir*) 32

H

haircut: to have or give to (someone) a haircut or shave *zayyan* (*yzayyin*) 40
half *nuṣṣ* 20
hand *ʔiid* (F) (*ʔiideen*) 11
to happen *ṣaar* (*yṣiir*) 16
happiness *xeer* 29
happy *mirtaaħ* (*-iin*) 22, *farħaan* (*-iin*) 35
hard, difficult *ṣaʕub* 28
to have (see 12 B 2)
to have to (do something) *laazim* (with impf.) 16, *δ̣ṭarr* (*yiδ̣ṭarr*) (with impf.) 35
he *huwwa* 18
head *raas* (*ruus*) 35
to hear *simaʕ* (*yismaʕ*) 31
heavy *θigiil* (*θgaal*) 28
hello *marħaba* 11
to help *saaʕad* (*ysaaʕid*) 33
her (objective) *-ha* (suffixed to verb or prep.) 15
her (possessive) *-ha* (suffixed to noun) 15; *maalha, maalatha* (following definite noun) 32
here *hnaa* 14
hers *maalha, maalatha* 32
high-school *θaanawiyya* 23

him *-a* (or lengthened final vowel) (suffixed to verb or prep.) 15
his (possessive) *-a* (or lengthened final vowel) (suffixed to noun) 15; *maala, maalta* (following definite noun) 32
his (pron.) *maala, maalta* 32
home *beet* 12
honestly *waḷḷa* 11
honey *ʕasal* 35
(the) honeymoon *šahr il-ʕasal* 35
to hope *tmanna* (*yitmanna*) 29
hot *ḥaarr* 13
hotel *ʔuuteel* (*-aat*) 14
hour *saaʕa* (*-aat*) 16
house *beet* (*byuut*) 12
how *šloon* 11
how are you *šloonak, -ič, -kum* 11
how long *šgadd* 14
how many *čam* 17
how many (persons, things) *čam waaḥid* 17
how much *šgadd* 14, *b-eeš* 19
however (conj.) *šloon-ma* 24
however much *šgadd-ma* 24
hundred *miyya* 24
husband *zooj* (*ʔazwaaj*) 30

I

I *ʔaani* 13
idea *fikra* (*-aat, fikar*) 27
if *loo, ʔiδaa* 37
if God wills *ʔinšaḷḷa* 21
to imagine *tṣawwar* (*yitṣawwar*) 23
in *b-* 15
in a hurry *mistaʕjil* (*-iin*) 16
in order that *ḥatta* 24
in that case *laʕad* 12
inasmuch as *ma-daam* 31
to insist *ʔaṣarr* (*yṣirr*) 33
to insure *ṣoogar* (*yṣoogir*) 33
to be insured *tṣoogar* (*yitṣoogar*) 33
to interest (in) *raġġab* (*yraġġub*) (*b-*) 38
Iraq *l-ʕiraaq* 39
iron (for pressing) *ʔuuti* (*ʔuutiyyaat*) 36
it (objective) *-a* (or lengthened final vowel) (M), *-ha* (F) (suffixed to verb or prep.) 15
it (subjective) *huwwa* (M), *hiyya* (F) 18
its *-a* (or lengthened final vowel) (M), *-ha* (F) (suffixed to noun) 15; *maala, maalta* (M), *maalha, maalatha* (F) (following definite noun) 32

J

jacket *sitra* (*sitar*) 39
January *kaanuun iθ-θaani* 33
job *waḍiifa* (*waḍaayif*) 37
July *tammuuz* 33
June *ḥzeeraan* 33

K

Karrada (section of Baghdad) *l-karraada* 18
Karradat Maryam (section of Baghdad) *karradat maryam* 22
kilo(gram) *keelu* (*keeluwaat*) 36
to kiss *baas* (*ybuus*) 11
kitchen *muṭbax, maṭbax* (*maṭaabix*) 31
to knock *dagg* (*ydugg*) 39
to know *ʕiraf* (*yuʕruf*) 24

L

to be late *tʔaxxar* (*yitʔaxxar*) 35
law *ḥuquuq* (P) 23
least *ʔaqall* 31
at least *ʕal-ʔaqall* 31
to leave (something) *xalla* (*yxalli*) 22
to leave, depart *ṭilaʕ* (*yiṭlaʕ*) 33
to leave (on a trip) *saafar* (*ysaafir*) 39
lemon-tea *ḥaamuḍ* 13
to lend *daayan* (*ydaayin*) 38
less *ʔaqall* 31
let's *xal-* (with impf.) 12
library *maktaba* (*-aat*) 38
light (in weight) *xafiif* (*xfaaf*) 28
like *miθil* 23
to like *ḥabb* (*yḥibb*) 15
to listen *simaʕ* (*yismaʕ*) 31
little *ṣġayyir* (*ṣġaar*) 17
a little *šwayya* 28
long *ṭuwiil* (*ṭwaal*) 28
to look for *dawwar* (*ydawwur*) *ʕala* 37
a lot *hwaaya* 14
lower, under- *taḥtaani* 39

M

mail *poošṭa* (*-aat*) 36
to make *sawwa* (*ysawwi*) 17
manner *šikil* (*ˀaškaal*) 28
map *xariiṭa* (*xaraayiṭ*) 12
March *ˀaaδaar* 33
market *suug* (*swaag*) 14
marriage *zawaaj* 22
master *ˀuṣṭa* (*ˀuṣṭawaat*) 17
matter *mawδuuʕ* (*mawaaδiiʕ*) 26, *qaδiyya* (*qaδaaya*) 29, *masˀala* (*masaaˀil*) 31
it doesn't matter *ma-yxaalif* 24
May *ˀayyaar* 33
me *-i, -ya* (suffixed to prep.); *-ni* (suffixed to verb) 12
(piece of) meat *laḥma* (*-aat*) 36
meat *laḥam* (coll.) 36
medical *ṭibbi* 39
medical science, (study of) medicine *ṭibb, ṭibbiyya* 21
medium-sized *waṣṭaani* 36
middle *waṣaṭ* 39
milk *ḥaliib* 13
million *milyoon* (*malaayiin*) 33
mine *maali, maalti* 32
minute *daqiiqa* (*daqaayiq*) 27
misgiving(s) *šakk*
mister *sayyid* 18
Monday (*yoom*) *il-iθneen* 33
money *fluus* (F) 17
month *šahar* (*ˀašhur, tušhur*) 26
monthly *šahri* 39
more *ˀakθar* 28
morning *ṣubuḥ* 33
in the morning *ṣ-ṣubuḥ* 38
mother *ˀumm* (*ˀummahaat*) 11
to move *tḥawwal* (*yitḥawwal*) 22
movie theatre, movies *siinama* (*-aat*) 38
much *hwaaya* 14
must (do something) *laazim* (with impf.) 16
my *-i, -ya* (suffixed to noun) 12; *maali, maalti* (following definite noun) 32

N

name *ˀisim* (*ˀasaami*) 33
naturally *ṭabʕan* 27
necessary *laazim* 16
to be necessary (for) *nraad* (*yinraad*) (*l-*) 31
necessity *ḥaaja* (*-aat*) 31
to need *ḥtaaj* (*yiḥtaaj*) 33
to be needed *nraad* (*yinraad*) 31
nephew (brother's son) *ˀibin ˀax* 30
nephew (sister's son) *ˀibin ˀuxut* 30
new *jidiid* (*jiddad*) 17
news *ˀaxbaar* (P) 22
newspaper *jariida* (*jaraayid*) 15
next *jaayy* 23
next to *yamm* 12
nice *laṭiif* (*-iin*) 34
niece (brother's daughter) *bint ˀax* 30
niece (sister's daughter) *bint ˀuxut* 30
night, night-time *leel* 33
nine *tisʕa* 18
nineteen *ṭṣaaṭaʕaš* 19
ninety *tisʕiin* 20
ninth *taasiʕ* 33
no *laa* 12
to nominate *ʕayyan* (*yʕayyin*) 37
nor, and not *wala* 38
not *muu, ma-, la-* 38
November *tišriin iθ-θaani* 33
now *hassa* 21
number *raqam* (*ˀarqaam*) 18

O

o'clock (see 20 B 3)
October *tišriin il-ˀawwal* 33
of *maal* 19, *min* 20
of course *ṭabʕan* 27
office *daaˀira* (*dawaaˀir*) 14
official (of gov't.) *muwaδδaf* (*-iin*) 33
old *ʕatiig* (*ʕittag*) 17
on *ʕala* 16
one *waaḥid* (F *wiḥda*) 17
one (pron.) *l-waaḥid* 34
to open *fakk* (*yfukk*) 26
opinion *raˀi* (*ˀaaraaˀ*) 27
or *loo* 13
orange *purtaqaala* (*-aat*) 36
oranges *purtaqaal* (coll.) 36
to order from, to give (someone) an order for) *waṣṣa* (*ywaṣṣi*) *ʕala* 32
other *ġeer* 20, *θaani* 25, *laax* (F *lux*) 28, *ˀaaxar* (F *ˀuxra*) 32
our *-na* (suffixed to noun) 12; *maalna, maalatna* (following definite noun) 32

ours maalna, maalatna 32
overcoat qappuuṭ (qpaapiiṭ) 39

P

to be paid ndifaʕ (yindifiʕ) 33
(date) palm trees naxaḷ (coll.) 34
parlor (room where guests are received) ġurfat xuṭṭaar 32
to be patient ṣṭubar (yiṣṭubur) 33
to pay difaʕ (yidfaʕ) 16
peach xooxa, xooxaaya (-aat) 36
peaches xoox (coll.) 36
a pearl liiluwwa (-aat) 36
pearls liilu (coll.) 36
pencil qalam (qlaam) 12
people ʔahal (ʔahaali) 35
period of time mudda (mudad) 15
perplexed ħaayir (ħaayriin) 27
place mukaan (-aat) 29
to be placed nħaṭṭ (yinħaṭṭ) 35
pleasant ḷaṭiif (-iin) 34
please rajaaʔan 13, tfað̣ð̣al 14
position mukaan (-aat), 29 wað̣iifa (wað̣aayif) 37
post office poosṭa (-aat) 36
postman poosṭači (poosṭačiyya) 36
to pound dagdag (ydagdig) 33
praise to God lħamdilla 11
to prefer fað̣ð̣al (yfað̣ð̣il) 28
to prepare (something) ħað̣ð̣ar (yħað̣ð̣ir) 35
present ħaað̣ir (ħaað̣riin) 33
presser ʔuutači (ʔuutačiyya) 36, mukawwi (mukawwiin) 39
pretty, handsome ħilu (F ħilwa P ħilwiin) 13
problem muškila (mašaakil) 28, qað̣iyya (qað̣aaya) 29
to prove barhan (ybarhin) 33
to put ħaṭṭ (yħuṭṭ) 26
to be put nħaṭṭ (yinħaṭṭ) 35
to put on, wear libas (yilbas) 39

Q

quarter rubuʕ 20
question suʔaal (ʔasʔila) 28
to question stajwab (yistajwub) 33

R

rapid sariiʕ 33
to read qira (yiqra) 15
ready ħaað̣ir (ħaað̣riin) 33
really waḷḷa 11
red ʔaħmar (F ħamra, P ħumur) 35
to turn red ħmarr (yiħmarr) 33
to be related (to) girab̤ (yigrab̤) (l-) 37
relatives ʔahal (ʔahaali) 35
remainder baqiyya 35
to be required nraad (yinraad) 31
requirement ħaaja (-aat) 31
reservation ħajiz 33
to reserve ħijaz (yiħjiz) 33
to resign staqaal (yistiqiil) 33
rest (of) baqiyya 35
to rest staraaħ (yistiriiħ) 14
to return (something) rajjaʕ (yrajjiʕ)
to ride rikab (yirkab) 18
to ring dagg (ydugg) 39
to ripen stuwa (yistuwi) 33
river šaṭṭ (šṭuuṭ) 34
room ġurfa (ġuraf) 32
rug zuuliyya (zwaali) 32
rug merchant ʔabu zwaali 32
to be rushed nxubaṣ (yinxubuṣ) 35

S

same naf(i)s 34
Saturday (yoom) is-sabit 33
scene manð̣ar (manaað̣ir) 34
scholarship baʕθa 23
school madrasa (madaaris) 21
second θaani 25
secondary θaanawi 39
secondary school θaanawiyya 23
to see šaaf (yšuuf) 34
to seem bayyan (ybayyin) 22
self (himself, etc.) naf(i)s (with PS) 34
to send dazz (ydizz) 26
to send (something somewhere) wadda (ywaddi) 39
to be sent ndazz (yindazz) 33
September ʔayluul 33
to be settled xiḷaṣ (yixḷaṣ) 26
seven sabʕa 18
seventeen ṣbaaṭaʕaš 19
seventh saabiʕ 33
seventy sabʕiin 20
Shatt al-Arab (river in southern Iraq) šaṭṭ il-ʕarab 34

she *hiyya* 18
shirt *θoob* (*θyaab*) 39
shoe *qundara* (*qanaadir*) 36
shoemaker *qundarči* (*qundarčiyya*) 36
shopping *miswaag* 31
Shorja (section of Baghdad) *š-šoorja* 24
short *gṣayyir* (*gṣaar*) 28
to shout *ṣaaħ* (*yṣiiħ*) 27
to show *raawa* (*yraawi*) 38
to show the way (to) *dalla* (*ydalli*) (*ʕala*) 40
sight *manδ̣ar* (*manaaδ̣ir*) 34
since (prep.) *baʕad* 22
since, as (conj.) *ma-daam* 31
sir *sayyid*(*na*) 17
sister *ʔuxut* (*xawaat*) 23
to sit *giʕad* (*yugʕud*) 14
six *sitta* 18
sixteen *ṣiṭṭaʕaš* 19
sixth *saadis* 33
sixty *sittiin* 17
skirt *tannuura* (*-aat*) 39
sleep *noom* 32
to sleep *naam* (*ynaam*) 32
small *ṣġayyir* (*ṣġaar*) 17
so *hiič* 28
so (that) *ħatta* 24
(pair of) socks *jooraab* (*jwaariib*) 39
to be solved *nħall* (*yinħall*) 28
someone *ʔaħħad* 37, *fadd waaħid* 20
something *šii, fadd šii* 20
something else *šii ʔaaxar* 32
sometimes *ṃarra* 11
son *ʔibin* (*wulid*) 30
to be sorry *tnaddam* (*yitnaddam*) 38
sour *ħaamuδ̣* 13
to speak *ħiča* (*yiħča*) 27
to spend *ṣiraf* (*yuṣruf*) 38
station *maħaṭṭa* (*-aat*) 33
to stay *buqa* (*yibqa*) 25
still, yet *baʕad* 16
stopping place *mawqif* (*mawaaqif*) 20
straight, directly *fadd raas* 35
straight ahead *gubaḷ* 16
street *šaariʕ* (*šawaariʕ*) 15
study, studies *diraasa* 21
to study *diras* (*yidrus*) 23
subject *mawδ̣uuʕ* (*mawaaδ̣iiʕ*) 26
suit *qaaṭ* (*quuṭ*) 39
suitcase *junṭa* (*junaṭ*) 35
Sunday (*yoom*) *il-ʔaħħad* 33
sunset *miġrib* 33, *ġuruub* 34
sweet *ħilu* (F *ħilwa*, P *ħilwiin*) 13

T

table *meez* (*myuuza*) 32
to take *ʔaxaδ* (*yaaxuδ*) 18
to take (someone somewhere) *wadda* (*ywaddi*) 39
to take care of *daara* (*ydaari*) 33
to take out *ṭallaʕ* (*yṭalliʕ*) 36
talk *ħači* 16
to talk *ħiča* (*yiħči*) 15
tall *ṭuwiil* (*ṭwaal*) 28
tasty (of food) *ṭayyib* 28
taxi driver *ʔabu taksi* 25
tea *čaay* 12
tea vendor *čaayči* (*čaayčiyya*) 36
Teachers' College *daar il-muʕallimiin il-ʕaaliya* 23
telephone *talafoon* (*-aat*) 12
to telephone *xaabar* (*yxaabur*) 34
to tell *gaal* (*yguul*) 11
ten *ʕašra* 18
tenth *ʕaašir* 33
than *min* 28
thank you *šukran* 14
that (dem.) *hal-* 12, *δaak* (F *δiič*) 37
that (rel.) *l-*, (*ʔi*)*lli* 32
the *l-* 12
their *-hum* (suffixed to noun) 15; *maalhum, maalathum* (following definite noun) 32
theirs *maalhum, maalathum* 32
them *-hum* (suffixed to verb or prep.) 15
then *laʕad* 12, *baʕdeen* 15
there is, there are *ʔaku* 12
these *hal-* 12, *δoola* 27
they *huṃṃa* 18
thing *šii* (*ʔašyaaʔ*) 13
things *garaδ̣* (*ġaraaδ̣*) (usually P) 31
to think *tṣawwar* (*yitṣawwar*) 23, *ʕtiqad* (*yiʕtiqid*) 37
to think (about) *fakkar* (*yfakkir*) (*b-*) 26
third *θaaliθ* 33
(one-)third *θiliθ* 20
thirteen *ṭḷaṭṭaʕaš* 19
thirty *tlaaθiin* 20
this *haaδa* (F *haay*) 11, *hal-* 12

those *hal-* 12, *δoola* 27, *δoolaak* 37
thousand *ʔal(i)f* (*ʔluuf, taalaaf*) 33
three *tlaaθa* 18
Thursday (*yoom*) *il-xamiis* 33
thus *hiič* 28, *hiiči* 29
ticket *biṭaaqa* (*-aat*) 19
a time *marra* (*-aat*) 11
time *wakit* 16
tired *taʕbaan* (*-iin, tʕaaba*) 31
to *l-* 13, *ʔil-* (with PS) 33
today *l-yoom* 13, *hal-yoom* 31
together *suwa* 12
tomato *ṭamaaṭaaya* (*-aat*) 36
tomatoes *ṭamaaṭa* (coll.) 36
tomorrow *baačir* 32
tomorrow morning *baačir iṣ-ṣubuḥ* 33
too *hamm* 27
train *qiṭaar* (*qiṭaaraat*) 33
to transfer *ḥawwal* (*yḥawwil*) 33
to translate *tarjam* (*ytarjum*) 33
to travel, take a trip *saafar* (*ysaafir*) 39
trip *safra* (*-aat*) 35
trousers *panṭaruun* (*-aat, panaaṭiir*) 39
truth *ṣudug* 28
Tuesday (*yoom*) *iθ-θilaaθaa* 33
twelve *θnaʕaš* 19
twenty *ʕišriin* 20
two *θneen* (F *θinteen*) 17
two hundred *miiteen* 24

U

uncle (father's brother) *ʕamm* 17
uncle (mother's brother) *xaal* 30
uncle (husband of father's sister) *zooj ʕamma* 30
uncle (husband of mother's sister) *zooj xaala* 30
undecided *ḥaayir* (*ḥaayriin*) 27
under *jawwa* 17, *taḥat* 39
under-, lower *taḥtaani* 39
to understand *ftiham* (*yiftihim*) 33
urgent, in a hurry *mistaʕjil* (*-iin*) 16
us *-na* (suffixed to verb or prep.) 12
to use *staʕmal* (*yistaʕmil*) 33

V

very *kulliš* 22
view *manδar* (*manaaδir*) 34

W

waiter *booy* 13
to walk *miša* (*yimši*) 11
to want *raad* (*yriid*) 14
to wash *ġisal* (*yiġsil*) 39
to be washed *nġisal* (*yinġisil*) 40
watch *saaʕa* (*-aat*) 16
watch-dealer *saaʕači* (*saaʕačiyya*) 36
water *maay* 13
a watermelon *raggiyya* (*-aat*) 36
watermelon *raggi* (coll.) 36
way *šikil* (*ʔaškaal*) 28
we *ʔiḥna* 13
to wear *libas* (*yilbas*) 39
wedding *ʕiris* 35
Wednesday (*yoom*) *il-arbiʕaa* 33
week *sbuuʕ* (*ʔasaabiiʕ*) 31
to weigh *wuzan* (*yoozin*) 36
well *zeen* (*-iin*) 11
what *š-* 13, *šinu* 14
whatever *š-ma* 23
when *šwakit* 24
whenever *šwakit-ma* 24
where *ween* 12
from where *mneen* 31
wherever *ween-ma* 24
which (interrog.) *yaa* 18
which (rel.) *l-*, (*ʔi*)*lli* 32
(a) while *mudda* 15
white *ʔabyaδ* (F *beeδa*, P *biiδ*) 35
who (interrog.) *minu* 27
who(m) (rel.) *l-*, (*ʔi*)*lli* 32
whoever *minu-ma* 24
whom *-man* (suffixed to prep.) 33
whom, to whom *ʔil-man* 26
whose *-man* (suffixed to noun) 33
why *leeš* 26
wife *zawja* (*-aat*) 30
will (do something) *raḥ-* (with impf.) 14
wish *raġba* (*-aat*) 39
to wish *tmanna* (*yitmanna*) 29
with *wiyya* 15
with (in the possession of) *ʕi(n)d* 12
wonder *ʕajab* 12
work *šuġul* 11
to work *štiġal* (*yištuġul*) 33
to write *kitab* (*yiktib*) 33
writing *kitaaba* 32
writing-table *meez kitaaba* 32

Y

year *sana (sniin)* 21
yearly *sanawi* 39
yellow *ʔaṣfar* (F *ṣafra,* P *ṣufur*) 35
yes *ʔii* 12, *bali* 13, *naʕam*
yesterday *l-baarḥa* 32
yet *baʕad* 16
yoghurt *liban, šiniina* 13
you (impersonal) *l-waaḥid* 34
you (objective) *-ak, -k* (M), *-ič, -č* (F), *-kum* (P) (suffixed to verb or prep.) 11
you (subjective) *ʔinta* (M), *ʔinti* (F), *ʔintu* (P) 11
your *-ak, -k* (M), *-ič, -č* (F), *-kum* (P) (suffixed to noun) 11; *maalak, maaltak* (M), *maalič, maaltič* (F), *maalkum, maalatkum* (P) (following definite noun) 32
yours *maalak, maaltak* (M); *maalič, maaltič* (F); *maalkum, maalatkum* (P) 32

INDEX OF GRAMMATICAL FEATURES

The numbers refer to units and sections.